DAI_ EGE OF FOO_ _M & CREATI__
LLE_

DESTINATIONS

DANGEROUS DESTINATIONS

THE ESSENTIAL GUIDE TO THE WORLD'S TROUBLE SPOTS

ANDREW DUNCAN &
MICHEL OPATOWSKI

SUTTON PUBLISHING

First published in the United Kingdom in 2002 by
Sutton Publishing Limited · Phoenix Mill
Thrupp · Stroud · Gloucestershire · GL5 2BU

British Library Cataloguing in Publication Data
A catalogue record for this book is available from the British Library.

ISBN 0-7509-2978-2

Information given in this book is assumed correct at date of going to press
(Oct 2002). Situations can change rapidly however and the Publishers express
no warranty as to its continuing reliability. Travellers are strongly advised to
check with the appropriate authorities before departure.

Typeset in 8/10pt GillSans.
Typesetting and origination by
Sutton Publishing Limited.
Printed and bound in England by
J.H. Haynes & Co. Ltd, Sparkford

Contents

Foreword
By Robert Fox

The inquiry of history, wrote the great French historian Marc Bloch, may turn at will to either the individual or social, momentary convulsions or lasting developments. The momentary convulsions of our time often threaten to become lasting developments, though we hardly ever recognise the process as it happens. 'Here and now begins a new era in the history of humanity', announced Wolfgang Goethe, witnessing the rout of the Émigrés and the Prussian Army at the cannonade of Valmy in 1793. The poet and polymath was right – the victory of a citizen army over the trained forces of Prussia, professionals and military aristocrats, marked the beginning of the peoples conscripted for combat; the era of mass armies and mass war was at hand, and is still with us – at least in some parts of the world.

Much the same judgement was made, or attempted, in the wake of the attacks on the World Trade Centre and the Pentagon on 11 September 2001. 'Here and now begins a new era in asymmetric warfare and nihilistic terrorism', the sages of the print and electronic media seemed to be struggling to say. But was it really that? Hijackings, suicide bombings – crude means pitted against highly sophisticated targets – had all been attempted before. But not in quite this way. The location and the means of transmission put the attacks in a different dimension. It was a dreadful and spectacular display of terrorist action played out on television – this was the new dimension. The what, who, where, why and how? debate still contains many mysteries, not least what did Mohamed Atta and his eighteen co-conspirators in the planes really think they would achieve?

It was the spectacular terrorist crime of our era, and it sums up many of the perils that beset our world and what we conceive as its highest ideals and civilisation. The 'momentary convulsion' of '9/11' is set fair to become a stage, or important milestone, in a lasting development of profound consequence.

The implications of the 11 September events and other upheavals are a vital ingredient, perhaps the vital ingredient, in Andrew Duncan's current masterly survey, Dangerous Destinations. In many respects it is a grand tour of the momentary convulsions and lasting developments in our political and social world. In its historical and geographical crosscutting, the book demonstrates the need for a grasp of the historical coordinates of the world's troublespots and points of crisis, as well as some grasp of location. The notion, fashionable ten years ago, that history had somehow reached a culmination point with the collapse of Marxism-Leninism in Europe seems the work of academic chumps. History, even in the most European-American sense, is no more dead than is geography. The need for a better grip of the tools of history among the media is admirably pointed up by this book. In the case studies of countries and aspects and causes of conflict we see how susceptible our terminology of geography, history and politics are to fashion. The Cold War for Europe and America produced a form of geometric certainty. The US and its allies, and Soviet Russia and its allies and proxies, were held by the threat of nuclear weapons – hence the poignantly named doctrine of MAD, Mutually Assured Destruction.

With the Berlin Wall down and MAD now consigned to the historical dustbin, matters are much less certain. We have been given other terms and categories in which to think of our worst enemies and the threat to security, stability and, yes, our very notions of civilisation. Ten years ago we were warned of the perils of 'rogue states'. Today that has been converted by the 43rd President of the USA, George W. Bush, into 'The Axis of Evil', the subject of a thought-provoking essay by Andrew Duncan in the second section of the book.

The study of individual countries and nations suggests how limited public perception can be, how restricted the concentration span of the media. Countries like Algeria have been undergoing a living nightmare for ten years, yet the monthly toll of deaths and disappearances hardly rates a mention in the international news bulletins. Countries like Liberia and Somalia also tend to suffer the effects of media amnesia; while the vast tracts of the Democratic Republic of Congo – a source of riches, reward, and abject human misery – are a blank space in the world's collective memory. The most melancholy aspect of this book is the number of travel warnings that suggest a country or region is closed to all but the most privileged or highly protected traveller. As I write, officially, via the UN and its agencies, it is calculated that there are about 14 wars going on in the world. This book shows that many more people and nations are in conflict than that rather optimistic figure.

Behind the stories of nations and governments, international agencies and NGOs, there are the activities of the famous four riders of the Apocalypse, fire, famine, pestilence, and flood – their firepower and nomenclature heavily upgraded for our era. The new rules and forms of war are studied, from weaponry in space to cyber-conflict. The increase in confrontations over water from the Middle East to central and south Asia and Africa is given careful study. The notion that refugees are frequently catalysts, causes in some cases, of conflict is examined. In addition to a discussion of the events and arguments following the 11 September attacks, an essay is devoted to the 'Clash of Civilisations' thesis, promoted by Samuel P. Huntington, that conflict between the open societies of the West, and closed ones in the Islamic or Confucian traditions, is all but unavoidable.

This debate is often crude and tasteless, particularly where Islamic tradition is concerned. There has been great and productive dialogue between Islamic scholars and courts with counterparts in Occidental Christendom. Medicine, mathematics, technology and statecraft have all benefited. Yet somehow the art of dialogue has been lost, and one of the biggest issues now confronting the societies based on post-Enlightenment principles and values is how they can have a productive and beneficial dialogue with faith-based theocracies.

Two looming issues, I think, will play an increasing role in our world, and earn sections to themselves in future editions of this book: the acute swings of demography; and parallel (underground, criminal or clan) powers countervailing those of the state.

Demographically we are entering a huge convulsion, which is also a lasting development, as human society swells to more than 10 billion before this century is out. The next two decades are likely to see the greatest increase in human live births in Creation. Correspondingly, Europe and Japan are faced with acute crisis in the ageing, and shrinking, of their populations. The United States appears to escape this fate – swelling to 550 million by mid-century – while Europe west of the Urals will be about 350 million.

Parallel powers thrive on the spasms of population and the movement of people. Human trafficking, whether with large numbers of illegal migrants, humans procured for vice, and children stolen for their organs, are now one of the main lines of trade of international crime syndicates and mafias. The mafias are working increasingly close to the surface, virtually acting as trade agents in every continent. In parts of Europe itself the persistence of the nation state on familiar eighteenth and nineteenth century lines, democratically ruled and impartially administered for public good, is open to question.

This book should be an essential guide to such future debate. It is a vade mecum to the geopolitical traveller, in spirit or body. In many cases, sadly it will also be the nolle prosequere for too many peoples and places which now bear the international No Entry sign.

Robert Fox
Centre for Defence Studies
October 2002

Introduction

This Guide is a revised, expanded and updated version of *Trouble Spots: The World Atlas of Strategic Information*, published in October 2000. Thirty-four new topics have been added but only five have been dropped. The area of greatest change is under the heading Causes of Trouble, now split into two sections. One covers security concerns, and the other covers social and economic concerns, including topics such as AIDS, drugs and scarce resources. The Guide sets out the historical background to the many problems that face the world, whether they are of a global nature such as environmental issues, international conflicts like those in Kashmir and Cyprus or internal difficulties like those in Afghanistan or Macedonia. All are illustrated by maps showing not just topography and national borders but also, where appropriate, information relevant to the topic; for example, the nuclear weapon sites of India and Pakistan and the changes in borders over time in Poland and in the Balkans.

During the Cold War the world faced the threat of an all-out nuclear war that would bring catastrophic results not just to the participants but possibly to everybody; fortunately, the chance of such a war breaking out was unlikely once the reality of deterrence and mutual assured destruction (MAD) had been established. However, the possibility of global nuclear war had a limiting effect on conflict elsewhere in the world in countries where the superpowers usually supported opposing sides but themselves managed to avoid direct confrontation. In the post-Cold War world many more conflicts have broken out and without the limiting effect of superpower involvement these have become as bloody and horrific for the contestants and their civil populations as a nuclear war would have been for the US and USSR. At the same time wars *between* states have become less frequent while those *within* states have become very much more common. There has been no change to this pattern over the last few years.

Of the problems illustrated in this revised edition, some have recently been resolved but may reappear, and others have not yet erupted but may have to be faced in the future. Problems do not inevitably lead to military conflict but may also involve political confrontation, the imposition of sanctions of various kinds, and economic rivalry and competition; but if such measures and activities cannot provide a resolution, then military confrontation could eventually ensue. It is not the aim of the Guide to describe in detail the course of every war, civil conflict or economic or social problem, as such an attempt would soon be out of date. Nor is it the intention to distinguish between 'right' and 'wrong', or to prescribe policies to solve problems. The main objective is to explain why each conflict, problem and issue has arisen.

There are many reasons for confrontation and conflict, the most fundamental of which is the issue of land and its ownership. This is basically a question of natives versus immigrants – the former being the descendants of the original or earliest inhabitants and the latter being any later arrivals, however long ago they appeared, and regardless of how their settlement has been legalised since. These disputes are often made more intransigent by religious differences, whether of faith, such as Muslim and Jew in the Middle East, or factions of the same faith, as in Northern Ireland and Croatia. Ethnic differences are also cited as a reason for dispute but in many of the current trouble spots the parties come from the same ethnic base: Celts in Ireland, Semites in the Middle East and Slavs in former Yugoslavia.

Family quarrels are, of course, more vicious than those between strangers. Nevertheless there are some conflicts of a purely religious or ethnic nature, such as the Muslim–Catholic split between Indonesia and East Timor and in the Philippines. Ethnic differences, and the jealousy they can create, are the cause of the situations in Fiji, the Basque region of Spain and for the Kurds. Religion and ethnicity combine to cause the friction between the Hindu Tamils and the Buddhist Singhalese in Sri Lanka, and between the Sunni Pushtun and Shi'a northern Afghans of Tajiki and Uzbeki origin in Afghanistan.

Of course there are also other causes of conflict and confrontation, mainly associated with essential assets. Oil was the main cause of the Iraqi invasion of Kuwait and also the reason for the immediate western response to that invasion. Diamonds are fuelling the continued conflicts in Angola, Sierra Leone and the Democratic Republic of Congo. Water (or rather lack of water) is a serious concern for many, particularly for those dependent on water sources beyond their borders, such as Egypt, Iraq, Israel and Syria. Populations sometimes need fresh land to ensure their survival and, if global warming takes its predicted course, instances of this may increase.

There are knock-on effects from some problems and conflicts. Both refugees and economic migrants can cause security problems for the receiving country as the indigenous population resents their presence, however the latter may be needed to finance the old age of some undeveloped countries. In some situations there is a vicious circle as steps taken to counter an initial threat only exacerbate what they were attempting to solve. Examples include the violence, counter-violence and counter-counter-violence all too often seen in Northern Ireland and the West Bank and Gaza.

It is a sad but true fact that many nations, faced with choosing how to vote at the United Nations or deciding what to do in some other crisis, allow their decisions to be influenced by domestic public opinion and the implications on quite separate foreign policy issues, instead of focusing on taking the right action for the problem concerned. For instance, China and Russia are more likely to vote against humanitarian intervention because of their fears that Tibet and Chechnya will be raised as cases where such intervention is also valid. Likewise, US President Bush rejected the Kyoto Treaty for environmental reform because of the US's current energy shortage and its effects on the economy – and on his chance of re-election.

In its efforts to halt conflict, the world has not yet managed to reconcile quite contradictory principles. Article 1 (section 2) of the United Nations Charter states that the purpose of the UN is to ensure 'friendly relations among nations based on respect for the principle of equal rights and self-determination'. On the other hand, Article 2 (section 7) declares that 'nothing contained in the present charter shall authorise the United Nations to intervene in matters which are essentially within the domestic jurisdiction of any state'. Most intra-state conflicts are caused by the lack of human rights and the desire for self-determination. NATO's intervention over Kosovo would appear to be in violation of Article 2, however justified the intervention was under Article 1 or as an attempt to halt genocide. Nor can the right to self-determination, also set out in the 1966 International Convention on Civil and Political Rights, co-exist with the principle of the inviolability of modern international borders as set out in Basket 1 of the Helsinki Final Act of 1975. This contradiction is at the heart of the disputes in, for example, Cyprus, Kashmir and, once again, former Yugoslavia. In most cases the inviolability of borders is given priority as other states foresee that the granting of self-determination to minorities may have unwanted repercussions for themselves. There is no international law governing secession and many of today's international crises are concerned with the secessionist aims of the dissident party. Drafting such a law will be difficult but perhaps it has now become necessary. Separatism remains a likely cause for instability and conflict even in the most civilised parts of the world, obvious examples being the IRA and Basque ETA campaigns.

The first half of the book is devoted to 'trouble spots' and is divided into regions, such as Europe, the Balkans, the Middle East and so on. Deciding where to place topics relating to the United States was problematical, as it faces both social and security difficulties, although this does not imply that the US is a dangerous destination. A short separate section therefore covers the US. In addition to examining a number of problems that involve only one or a few countries, the Guide also looks, in the second half, at several much wider potential security problems such as piracy, the effects of terrorism, the legacy of anti-personnel mines and perennial topics such as nuclear disarmament and the proliferation of chemical and biological weapons. A new topic is 'Cyberwarfare'. This part of the book also examines topics of an economic or social nature that nevertheless have implications for security and stability. Economic topics include oil, diamonds and the shortage of resources like water. Social matters include the impact of drugs, Aids and refugees.

To aid further study, each problem is accompanied by a bibliography and a list of websites where up-to-date information can quickly be obtained. In addition, each topic ends with a current assessment of the risk in travelling to the region, advice which was correct at the end of September 2002. *FCO* refers to the Foreign and Commonwealth Office Great Britain and *State* to the US State Department. There is also a general bibliography and a list of websites covering many of the topics discussed here.

General Key

────────	International border
- - - - -	Regional boundary
□	Capital
●	City
────────	Main road
────────	River
⟩-	Pass
✕	Battle
☢	Nuclear facility
⋏	Oil field
├────	Oil pipeline
◆	Diamond mine

List of Maps and Diagrams

Trouble Spots

Europe

This section covers all of Europe except for the Balkans and Russia and former Soviet Union countries. Two topics – relating to Europe's security arrangements and its border changes over history – cover the whole of Europe. The main security issues – Northern Ireland, Cyprus, the Basque Separatists, Greek and Turkish problems and the future of Gibraltar – receive individual treatment. But these are not Europe's only problems and a number of others are discussed below.

The French island of Corsica has, since 1975, suffered from a militant independence movement – the National Liberation Front of Corsica-Canal Historique (FLNC). The movement split into factions in 1990, with some giving up their demand for independence and others turning to guerrilla war and organised crime, and this led to fighting between factions as well as against the authorities. The Corsican situation has caused splits in mainland France, notably between President Chirac and Prime Minister Jospin over the latter's bill to give Corsica limited law-making powers, and within the Green party over a call to offer an amnesty to Corsican terrorists. In December 2001 the French Parliament voted to give the island some powers and to extend Corsican language training; the opposition now plans to refer the bill to the national Constitutional Court. During 2001 there were 135 bomb attacks and 28 separatist-linked murders in Corsica.

France also has a Breton problem. The people of Brittany are ethnically Celts – brothers of the Irish, Scots and Devonians – and some have formed a small terrorist group, the Breton Revolutionary Army (ARB). This has been responsible for planting a number of bombs since 1998. The ARB is a follow-on group from the Brittany Freedom Front that carried out some 250 attacks in the 1960s and 1970s. The Bretons formed an alliance with French Basques (see pp. 11–14) and the overseas possessions in the Caribbean and Pacific. Less serious is the movement for independence in Savoie.

Belgium has its Fleming–Walloon split between the Dutch- and French-speaking populations, with Brussels considering itself above and separate from the controversy. The change of name on motorway signs is perhaps confusing for visitors but more serious is the number of Flemish communities that will only conduct business in Dutch.

In Italy the Lombard League seeks independence for the economically better-off provinces of Lombardy, Piedmont and Venice as Padania.

European Security

For the last fifty years western Europe has relied on the North Atlantic Treaty Organisation (NATO) for its security and defence. At the same time there have always been voices, led by France, calling for a European Defence Identity. Today the voices are louder, despite the end of the Cold War over ten years ago. There is, in fact, a plethora of European fora in which defence issues are debated but as yet none can match the military capability built up by NATO over the years. NATO's capability relies on the US to provide several essential elements, such as satellite-derived intelligence and strategic air transport lift. Is a separate European Security and Defence Policy (ESDP), as envisaged by European Union members, necessary or even achievable? Should Europe develop its own independent armed forces to support ESDP or should it continue to promote a second pillar within NATO, a European Security and Defence Identity (ESDI)?

The main contender for the ESDI was the Western European Union (WEU), an organisation established initially as the Western Union by the Brussels Treaty in March 1948 with Belgium, France, Luxembourg, the Netherlands and the UK as members. The Union was designed to provide security guarantees to its members. However, it was quickly superseded when NATO was formed by the Washington Treaty in 1949. The Brussels Treaty never lapsed. In 1954, after the failure to form a European Defence Community, Germany and Italy joined the Union, which then became the WEU. The first military activity coordinated by the WEU was the minesweeping operation in the Persian Gulf towards the end of the Iran–Iraq war. Since then it has coordinated other naval operations, during the Gulf War and in the Adriatic to enforce sanctions imposed on former Yugoslavia. It has not yet commanded any ground or air operations.

At the European Union summit on 3 June 1999 it was agreed that there should be a common policy on security and defence (CFSP) and that there should be a 'capacity for autonomous action, backed up by credible military forces'. The EU absorbed the WEU (the WEU Satellite Centre and the WEU Institute for Security Studies became EU agencies on 1 January 2002) and has appointed a High Representative for Security and Foreign Affairs, the first incumbent being the last NATO Secretary General, Javier Solano. How easy it will be for him to obtain agreement from the very diverse countries of the Union, each with different foreign policy priorities and domestic concerns, remains to be seen. The EU and NATO cooperated closely over the situation in Macedonia, with Solana and George Robertson, the NATO Secretary General, making a number of joint visits there. However, troops deployed there have been under NATO command despite the EU's requests to lead the force.

France is in a special position: although it is a political member of NATO, its military forces do not form part of the NATO command structure. France has, though, taken part in a number of NATO-led operations, such as those in Bosnia and Kosovo. There are those who think that France's support for European defence structures is aimed at reducing American influence in Europe, but the French attitude to US policies has changed since 11 September. For its part, the US has no objection to Europe pursuing the aim of making its forces more readily deployable but insists that Europe cannot have a separate planning authority and that planning must remain the preserve of NATO.

On 15 November the European Union held its first joint meeting of Foreign and Defence Ministers to discuss the essential increase in military capability needed in order to be able to conduct operations such as that in Kosovo without US assistance. European forces lack strategic airlift, satellite-derived intelligence and precision-guided weapons – all expensive items. British Prime Minister Blair proposed the establishment of a European Army wearing a common cap-badge by 2003; it should be capable of putting 30,000 men into the field in 60 days, though smaller elements should deploy much more quickly. Next, at the Anglo-French summit in London, also in November 1999, it was decided that in order to improve Europe's ability to react to crisis they would pool their logistic and transport assets when necessary. At the European summit at Helsinki it was agreed to form an EU rapid reaction force – 60,000 men strong, organised into 15 brigades – by 2003. It is doubted that the force would be capable of combat operations before 2012. Members will have to commit troops to the force but they will be based in their national locations and will not change their badges. The force will have air and naval components and will develop its own satellite reconnaissance system, and its aim is to be capable of operating independently of NATO should that become politically necessary. In March 2002 it was

| NATO | NATO Applicants | Partnership for Peace | OSCE |

NATO	NATO applicants	PfP/EAPC	OSCE
BELGIUM	ALBANIA	ARMENIA	ANDORRA
CANADA	BULGARIA	AUSTRIA	BOSNIA & HERZEGOVINA
CZECH REPUBLIC	CROATIA	AZERBAIJAN	CYPRUS
DENMARK	ESTONIA	BELARUS	HOLY SEE
FRANCE	LATVIA	FINLAND	LIECHTENSTEIN
GERMANY	LITHUANIA	GEORGIA	MALTA
GREECE	FORMER YUGO. REP.	IRELAND	MONACO
HUNGARY	OF MACEDONIA	KAZAKHSTAN	SAN MARINO
ICELAND	ROMANIA	KYRGHYZSTAN	SERBIA & MONTENEGRO
ITALY	SLOVAKIA	MOLDOVA	
LUXEMBOURG	SLOVENIA	RUSSIAN FEDERATION	
THE NETHERLANDS		SWEDEN	
NORWAY		SWITZERLAND	
POLAND		TAJIKISTAN	
PORTUGAL		TURKMENISTAN	
SPAIN		UKRAINE	
TURKEY		UZBEKISTAN	
UNITED KINGDOM			
UNITED STATES			

European
Security
Organisation

3

leaked that the British Prime Minister was proposing that the US should be able to veto any European military action. In the event there will, of course, be no new troops, only existing forces that will now be 'double, or even treble, hatted'. A European Military Staff has been established. Lady Thatcher warned against a European Army in 1996 on the grounds that it would be a step towards a federal Europe.

A complicating factor for EU and NATO cooperation is that some members of the EU are not members of NATO (neutralist Sweden, Austria and Ireland), and rather more members of NATO are not yet members of the EU (Norway and the three new NATO members, the Czech Republic, Hungary and Poland). More importantly, Turkey is not an EU member and is using the problems regarding its future membership and the Cyprus question to obstruct plans for the use of NATO assets in EU operations.

Meanwhile NATO is considering a second wave of new members with Albania, Bulgaria, the Former Yugoslav Republic of Macedonia, Slovakia, Slovenia and the three Baltic States as candidates for membership. All these countries are already members of NATO's Partnership for Peace (PfP) programme, which involves a partnership between NATO and individual states, which can decide their own level of involvement. Members are committed to the following: transparency in defence planning and budgeting; ensuring the democratic control of forces; maintaining a capability to contribute to UN or Organisation of Security and Cooperation in Europe (OSCE) operations; and developing in the longer term forces able to operate with NATO. Russia and all the former republics of the Soviet Union are members of PfP, as are Austria, Finland, Ireland, Sweden and Switzerland. PfP was introduced in 1991 when the North Atlantic Cooperation Council was formed; in 1997 it was superseded by the Euro-Atlantic Partnership Council, which had the same membership but allowed neutral states to be full members and had an expanded remit.

All European states plus the US and Canada are members of OSCE, which was set up at a conference in Helsinki in 1975. Its final act includes three baskets dealing with political/military, economic and cultural/humanitarian issues. Agreement was reached on a package of Confidence and Security Building Measures (CSBM) including: exchange of military information; invitation to observe military exercises; and notification of future large-scale military exercises. The OSCE has mounted a number of missions, usually with the aim of promoting negotiations. For example, it sent an unarmed force of observers, known as the Verification Mission, to Kosovo in 1998. It was withdrawn when the bombing campaign began. The OSCE now has a much larger role in the UN efforts to rebuild Kosovo as a democratic entity. The OSCE is active in twenty countries in south-east Europe, the Baltics and eastern Europe, the Caucasus and Central Asia.

A number of other, less all-embracing, security organisations have been formed in Europe. The first was the Franco-German brigade, formed in 1989, which has participated in NATO's force in Bosnia. In 1992 a Franco-German Corps was established with the role of 'contributing to the Allies' joint defence, peacekeeping and peacemaking tasks, and humanitarian assignments'. The Corps now includes formations from Spain and Belgium. Two southern European forces have been formed: Euro Force (EUROFOR) and the European Maritime Force (EUROMARFOR). EUROFOR became operational in November 1997. It comprises a permanent international HQ in Florence and has units provided by the member nations, France, Italy, Portugal and Spain. The same countries have earmarked naval ships for EUROMARFOR. Neither force has yet been committed to operations. To some extent they were formed as a reaction to the fears of mass immigration from North Africa. In January 1999 Albania, Bulgaria, Greece, Italy, Macedonia, Romania and Turkey agreed to form a brigade-sized peacekeeping force to be known as the South-Eastern Europe Multi-National Force.

There is, therefore, no shortage of defence-oriented organisations in Europe but security is being challenged by the more-difficult-to-deal-with threats of refugees, drugs, terrorism and, further afield, the spread of weapons of mass destruction and their means of delivery.

The European Union

European efforts to establish a parallel organisation may well reduce the US's willingness to lead NATO; indeed, it has already expressed its concern over European plans that it fears may undermine NATO. Former British Foreign Secretary David Owen believes that a United States of Europe will never achieve the cohesion, purpose or resolve to act as decisively as NATO did over Kosovo, because of the US's binding power. For the present, NATO still remains Europe's premier defence organisation, and European forces have not yet improved their capability, however they are to be led.

BIBLIOGRAPHY AND WEBSITES

Aggestam, Lisbeth and Hyde-Price, Adrian, *Security and Identity in Europe: Exploring the New Agenda*

Rutten, Maarrtje, *From St Malo to Nice. European Defence: Core Documents*, Institut d'Etudes de Sécurité Union de l'Europe Occidentale, 2001

Ryter, Marc-André, *EU Capabilities for Autonomous Military Crisis Management: Possibilities and Limits*, National Defence College, Helsinki

Sperling, James, *Two Tiers or Two Speeds? The European Security Order and the Enlargement of the European Union and NATO*, Manchester University Press, 1999

Weaver, Robert, *Building Security Through Partnership*, NATO Review, Autumn 2001

Centre for European Policy Studies: www.ceps.be
European Union: www.europa.eu.int
North Atlantic Treaty Organisation: www.nato.int
Organisation for Security and Cooperation in Europe: www.osce.org
Programme for the Northern Dimension of CFSP: www.northerndimension.org
Western European Union Institute for Security Studies: www.weu.int/institute

Northern Ireland

Population: 1,640,000
Protestant: 58%, Catholic: 42%
Armed Forces: 11,000

The Irish are a Celtic race and are of the same ethnic extraction as the Scots, Devonians and Bretons. Until the late twelfth century Ireland was divided into a number of chiefdoms whose rulers were constantly squabbling and attempting to acquire one another's land. The earliest invaders were Vikings. The English first became involved in 1152 after an Irish chief abducted another's wife and lost his chiefdom; he appealed to the Normans in England for help in recovering it. The Normans landed in May 1169 and captured the town of Wexford. Other Norman barons landed in 1170 and by 1171 had captured Dublin. King Henry II then stepped in to curb the power of the barons and to subdue the Irish chiefs. After a six-month campaign Henry had marked out in south-east Ireland an English-ruled province known as the Pale, and had received submissions from most of the important Irish chiefs. English colonists became major landowners and were known as the Anglo-Irish.

Scotland's involvement in Ireland began after Bannockburn in 1314, when it invaded and occupied Ulster for three years. Ireland had had no strategic value until the defeat and eviction of the English from France, but with the growing utility of sea transport Ireland represented another point from which England could be attacked. The first example of this was the invasion led by Lambert Simnel, which was defeated by Henry VII at Newark in 1487. The English conquest of Ireland was a pre-emptive move to forestall attacks on England from Ireland by other enemies.

Henry VIII's predecessors had received their lordship of Ireland by a papal grant given in 1155 and approved by the Irish Church. Henry, the Irish Church argued, had forfeited this lordship by his break with Rome and the papal bull Rex Hibernia gave Ireland to Mary and her husband Philip. Irish opposition to the English now became both nationalistic and religious. English hatred of Catholicism was based on a combination of Queen Elizabeth's excommunication, the Spanish threat and Irish rebellion.

The Spanish Armada, which was defeated in 1588, had Ireland as a secondary objective, and on the return journey some twenty-four ships were wrecked off the Irish coast. The Spanish armed and encouraged Irish rebellions but two other armadas en route for Ireland in 1596 and 1597 were both broken up by stormy weather. However, the Irish rebellion spread and Elizabeth dispatched an army of 20,000 men with instructions to subdue the country systematically. The Spanish sent another expeditionary force which successfully landed and captured Kinsale; there the English army beat both the rebels and the Spanish, who surrendered in January 1602. There followed a protracted campaign to defeat the Irish rebels and this was achieved with the surrender of the Earl of Tyrone on 30 March 1603.

Queen Elizabeth was succeeded by the Scottish James I. He established a colony in Ulster and the 'plantation' of Ulster with Lowland Scots began. The settlers found that they became responsible for order and property rights and so began the history of Protestant domination of the Catholic population. The settlement also led to the rebellion of 1641 in which 2,000 settlers were killed. Not unnaturally, during the English Civil Wars Irish Catholics sided with the Royalists. After the execution of Charles I in 1649, Cromwell embarked on a bloody conquest of Ireland. Some 500,000 native Irish and 112,000 colonists out of a total population of 1,448,000 are thought to have perished between 1649 and 1652; another 100,000 Irish people were transported to the American colonies. Ethnic cleansing began but was halted once the new colonists realised that they needed the Irish workforce.

The restoration of Charles II in 1660 made little difference to the situation of the Irish. After succeeding to the throne in 1685 James II began to change matters with a parliamentary Act that overturned the land settlement. However, its implementation was halted by the crowning in 1688 of the Dutch Prince William of Orange, who was married to James's daughter. The Catholic Irish remained loyal to the defeated James and captured most of Ulster. But in 1689 they failed to win the siege of Derry and the next year were defeated by William at the battle of the Boyne (two notable landmarks in Northern Irish mythology). Although the Irish were treated as second-class citizens, denied the right to own property or to have a Catholic education or burial, they did not take advantage of the Jacobite uprisings in favour of James II's descendants in 1715 and 1745.

From the end of the seventeenth century until the beginning of the nineteenth, Ireland was owned and ruled by Anglo-Irish Protestants although the Dublin Parliament was subordinate to that at Westminster. Scotland, on the other hand, after the Union of 1707 became part of Great Britain. Both the French and American revolutions had a beneficial effect on Ireland in terms of land reform, religious toleration and the repeal of some oppressive laws. Ireland became part of the United Kingdom of Great Britain and Ireland and not part of Great Britain itself. However, it remained to all intents and purposes a colony with a separate parliament.

There were small-scale Irish rebellions in 1803, 1848 and 1867, and while these established a tradition of revolution they failed to have any effect on the British government and the Protestant colonists blocked the political movements they represented. Ireland remained primarily an agricultural economy and only in Ulster was there any

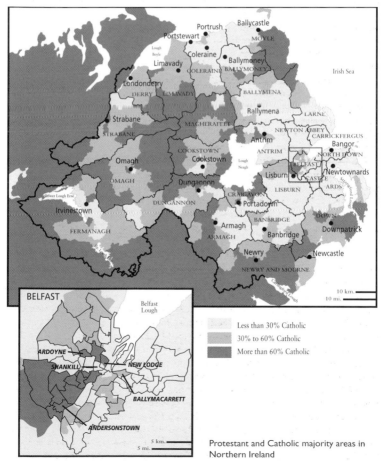

Protestant and Catholic majority areas in Northern Ireland

industrialisation; where it did occur, industrialisation bred discrimination in employment, further alienating the Catholics. While the British did not deliberately cause the Great Famine of 1846 in the same way that hunger had been forced on Ireland by Cromwell and others before him, the British government did too little to counter the results of the disaster. In ten years the population was reduced by a quarter, with a million people dying and another million emigrating.

In another difference from the rest of the United Kingdom, the Irish police force, established in 1814 by Robert Peel, the then under-secretary for Ireland, was a centralised, armed, para-military force from the start. By the mid-nineteenth century the churches had secured control of education and hatred of the other community became part of the curriculum, just as it is today.

The first instances of Irish terrorism in mainland Britain took place in 1867; though poorly carried out, they had the effect of persuading the Prime Minister, Gladstone, that reform in Ireland was necessary. In 1886 and 1893 Gladstone introduced Home Rule bills: the first was defeated in the Commons and the House of Lords threw out the second. On both occasions the government fell. On both occasions the Irish Party MPs at Westminster had supported Gladstone but Home Rule was violently opposed by the Ulster Protestants. A third bill did make progress through Parliament. Passed twice in the Commons and rejected twice by the Lords in 1913, it was then amended to allow Ulster counties to opt out of Home Rule. Both the Ulster Volunteer Force and the Irish Volunteers began to stockpile arms and ammunition purchased from Germany and the Lords amended the bill to exclude all of Ulster. The outbreak of the First World War postponed further consideration of Irish Home Rule; both Nationalists and Unionists supported the war effort and many served – and died – in the armed forces.

In 1916 the Irish Republican Brotherhood organised the Easter uprising, which was swiftly crushed and its ringleaders executed. The Brotherhood then merged with Sinn Fein, which began to make electoral progress at the expense of the Irish Party; in the 1918 election its candidates won seventy-three seats but they refused to take their places at Westminster. An Irish Parliament, the Dail, was set up, guerrilla warfare broke out and the Irish Republican Army was formed. In 1920 the Government of Ireland Act established two Home Rule parliaments, one in Dublin and one in Belfast, which became the capital of a six-county Ulster. The Anglo-Irish Treaty of 1921 gave Ireland Dominion status – a status that was quietly dropped in 1937 when the twenty-six counties became the Irish Free State.

The Protestants of Northern Ireland enjoyed an electoral majority and ensured that their community was favoured at the expense of the Catholics. The latter suffered discrimination in many fields, particularly in employment and housing, while gerrymandering ensured they had little political influence. The minority community regarded the police – the Royal Ulster Constabulary, which had few Catholic officers, and the B Specials, which had none – as fundamentally hostile. A series of Catholic civil rights demonstrations were held in 1968 when the RUC over-reacted to provocation. Initially British Army reinforcements were welcomed by the Catholics they had come to protect but the mood soon changed to one of confrontation. The IRA took advantage of the situation, assumed the role of protector of the Catholic community and attacked both the army and police. Initially the IRA concentrated their activities in Belfast and Londonderry so that it could obtain the maximum publicity. By the beginning of 1972 the Army appeared to be getting the upper hand, certainly in Belfast. In March the Northern Ireland Parliament, Stormont, was prorogued and William Whitelaw was appointed Secretary of State. He instituted a policy determined to find a political rather than a military solution to the troubles. It was a brave decision but one which ensured that the violence continued for thirty years.

Considerable progress towards achieving peace was made in the mid- and late 1990s. The taboo of involving the Irish government was dropped, and in December 1993 the British Prime Minister and the Irish Taoiseach drafted the Downing Street Declaration. For their part the British stated that they 'had no selfish strategic or economic interest in

Northern Ireland' while the Irish affirmed that the principle of self-determination should be respected and that the Irish constitution would be changed. The IRA declared a ceasefire in August 1994 and this was followed by one declared by the Combined Loyalist Military Command in October. Throughout 1995 the British linked political talks to terrorist disarmament. In January 1996 former US Senator George Mitchell, brought in to chair an international commission, recommended that disarmament and talks should take place simultaneously. In July 1997 a second ceasefire came into effect and after six weeks Sinn Fein – the nationalist party seen by many, though denied by its members, as the political wing of the IRA – were admitted to the peace talks. Sinn Fein also signed up to the 'Mitchell Principles' that required participants to the talks to agree to the verifiable disarmament of all para-military organisations during the course of the talks. At the same time the IRA declared it had no intention of disarming; the term disarmament was abandoned in favour of the word 'decommissioning'.

Despite some terrorist incidents and the continuance of punishment beatings, the talks carried on. A peace resolution known as the Good Friday Agreement was signed on 18 April 1998. Its main provision was the establishment of an assembly elected by proportional representation and a power-sharing executive to take over the responsibilities of the Northern Ireland government departments. Cross-border institutions were to be established, and the police force and the judicial process reviewed. Disarmament was not mentioned. Not unnaturally the Unionists insisted that decommissioning must start before Sinn Fein could be admitted to the executive, while Sinn Fein maintained that decommissioning was not a 'Good Friday' commitment. Meanwhile the release of convicted terrorists, both Republican and Unionist, had begun. Eventually the Unionist leader, David Trimble, became convinced that risks had to be taken if peaceful progress was to be made and he persuaded his party to agree to let Sinn Fein participate in government in return for a pledge that decommissioning would take place. However, he stated that the Unionists would withdraw from the executive if they were unsatisfied by the progress made in decommissioning by February 2000.

The IRA has said several times that it will not give up its arms but in March 2000 it announced a compromise over weapons, which it claims have not been used since the Good Friday Agreement was reached. These arms, it said, 'will be put completely and verifiably beyond use', but this did not mean they would be destroyed, as demanded by the Unionists, nor was it clear that all the weapons had been put beyond use. A number of sealed dumps have been inspected by Cyril Ramaphosa, former Secretary General of the African National Congress, and Marti Ahtisaari, a former Swedish President. In June that year they issued their first report; having inspected a number of dumps they reported: 'We observed that the weapons and explosives were safely and adequately stored. We have ensured that the weapons and explosives cannot be used without our detection.' The IRA agreed in October to a second round of arms inspections and a third inspection was made in May 2001 which 'confirmed that the arms dumps had not been tampered with'. There is also an international commission on decommissioning led by Canadian General John de Chastelain. This has held lengthy talks with IRA representatives but reported in July 2001 that it had made no progress on achieving decommissioning and the general even hinted that he might leave the body. The government set two deadlines for the start of the decommissioning process, May 2000 and 1 July 2001, but both passed without any movement by the IRA.

The passing of the second deadline caused David Trimble to carry out his threat to resign as First Minister of the Assembly; within six weeks, by 12 August, the assembly must either be suspended or elections held for a new assembly. In an attempt to curb the crisis the British and Irish Prime Ministers handed the political parties a revised package of measures to ensure the full implementation of the Good Friday Agreement. The package had to be accepted in its entirety. It included a promise to publish a revised implementation plan of the Patten Report, and listed a number of army border observation posts that were to be dismantled. It also intimated that those people still sought for terrorist offences would not be prosecuted. With regard to decommissioning it simply stated that both governments considered it an indispensable part of implementing the Good Friday Agreement. The Secretary of State suspended the Assembly but only for twenty-four hours, a move which gave a further six weeks to obtain agreement.

In October 2001 General de Chastelain was invited to see arms being 'put beyond use'; he confirmed that this had happened but was unwilling to say how many arms or how many dumps were involved. David Trimble accepted that decommissioning had begun and returned his party's ministers to the Belfast executive which they had left earlier in October. The British and Irish governments announced a package of measures which included an amnesty for paramilitaries (terrorists) still at large and a progressive rolling programme of reducing levels of troops and installations as security improves. A number of border watch-towers have been dismantled. The Royal Ulster Constabulary has been renamed the Police Service of Northern Ireland.

Despite all this, violence and confrontation have not ended. An IRA splinter group, the Real IRA, emerged in 1998 and claimed responsibility for the Omagh bomb in August 1998; since then it has exploded several bombs in London, the most recent in Ealing on 3 August 2001. The US has designated the Real IRA, the Continuity IRA, the Loyalist Volunteer Force, the Orange Volunteers, the Red Hand Defenders and the Ulster Defence Association/Ulster Freedom Fighters as terrorist organisations under Executive Order 13224. By early 2002 the worst offenders were the Loyalist paramilitaries who have continued to harass the Catholic community. The Loyalist community feels betrayed by the British government and that they and their government have given much and received little in return. They point to broken political promises and to many missed deadlines.

In April 2002 General de Chastelain announced that he had witnessed the placing of a further substantial quantity of arms permanently beyond use, but as before no other details were given. The Secretary of State called on Loyalist groups to follow the IRA's example. Sinn Fein continues its political campaign to achieve a united Ireland; on 31 March Martin McGuiness, on the 86th anniversary of the 1916 Easter uprising, stated that 'the count-down to a united Ireland had begun'. In April the US government released its opinion that the IRA is part of an international terror network, citing its involvement in Colombia (more than two dozen IRA members have been to Colombia in recent years). Recent US intelligence links the IRA with ETA in Spain, the El Salvador National Army of Liberation, as well as the Colombian FARC. The Colombian authorities claim that IRA members had trained with the FARC at the same time as Iranians, thus linking them to the Axis of Evil. Gerry Adams has declined an invitation to appear before the US House of Representatives international relations committee.

A worrying development is the drop in police numbers, said to be caused by the effects of the Patten reforms and the failure to recruit the full quota of Catholics. The force is now 2000 understrength and is having to rely more and more on army back-up.

BIBLIOGRAPHY AND WEBSITES

Bardon, Johnathan, *A History of Ulster*, Blackstaff Press, 1992

Bew, Paul and Gillespie, Gordon, *A Chronology of the Troubles 1968–99*, Gill & Macmillan, 1999

Cox, Michael A., *A Farewell to Arms? From 'Long War' to Long Peace in Northern Ireland*, Manchester University Press, 2000

Falls, Cyril, *Elizabeth's Irish Wars*, Constable, 1950

Hawsedell, Corinne and Kris Brown, 'Burying the Hatchet: The Decommissioning of Paramilitary Arms in Northern Ireland', Initiative on Conflict Resolution and Ethnicity, Brief 22

Mally, Eamonn and Mckittrick, David, *Endgame in Ireland*, Hodder & Stoughton, 2001

O'Leary, Brendan, and McGarry, John, *The Politics of Antagonism: Understanding Northern Ireland*, Athlone Press, 1996

Sloan, G.R., *The Geopolitics of Anglo-Irish Relations in the 20th Century*, Leicester University Press, 1997.

Democratic Unionist Party: www.dup.org.uk
Independent Commission on Policing for Northern Ireland: www.belfast.org.uk/report
Irish Department of the Taoiseach: www.irlgov.ie/taoiseach
Northern Ireland Assembly: www.niassembly.gov.uk
Northern Ireland Office: www.nio.gov.uk
Sinn Fein: www.sinnfein.org.ie
Socialist Democratic Party: www.sdlp.ie
Unionist Democratic Party: www.udp.org
Ulster Unionist Party: www.uup.org

Spain and Basque Separatism

The Basques are known to have lived in an area crossing the Spanish-French border for at least two thousand years; there are claims, based on the remnants of 10,000-year-old skulls, that they preceded other Iberian people and so can claim a right to nationhood. At one time Basque territory ran from Bilbao to Bayonne along the coast and to Tudela in Spain, up to Pic d'Anie in the Pyrenees and then to Mauleon in France: in all, an area of about 20,000 square kilometres. There are seven provinces that bear Basque names: in France, Benafarrao, Lapurdi and Zuberoa (Basse Navarre, Labourd and Soule in French); and in Spain, Araba, Bizkaia, Gipuzkoa and Nafarroa (Álava, Vizcaya, Guipúzcoa and Navarra in Spanish).

The Basque tradition of independence goes back a long way: they were never conquered by the Romans, Moors, Visigoths or Franks. The Basques were never united in one separate country but in the early eleventh century Sancho the Great ruled over the Basque region in southern France and north-western Spain. They joined with other Spaniards in defeating the Moors and in crossing the Atlantic to the New World, but they also enjoyed elements of separateness, known as *fueros*, in the fields of taxation, customs dues and exemption from military service. The Basques were brought into the Spanish state by the Carlist wars in 1833 and 1872. The wars actually accentuated the split between the Basque countryside and cities (caused by disagreement over the customs *fuero*), the former backing Don Carlos and the latter the more liberal Isabella in their battle for the throne. Don Carlos's defeat led to a major expansion of industry based on the cities, a process which required more workers. Many people immigrated from Andalusia and Galicia, much reducing Basque separateness in terms of language and ethnicity. The *fueros* were abolished.

The Basque Nationalist Party (Partido Nacionalista Vasco or PNV) was founded by Sabino Arana in 1895. For him racial characteristics were the most important element of Basque nationality rather than language. He also argued against the abolition of the *fueros*, and for the distinctive elements of Basque culture. Between 1900 and 1920 the PNV grew to become the nationalist party in the whole of the Basque region except for Navarre (which remains out of the Basque Autonomous Community today). The PNV formed its own trades union and friction between it and the other unions led to violence, including shooting.

The PNV was reluctant to support the Second Republic, established in 1931, and so the Basques were not rewarded as the Catalans were with a degree of self-government. The Republicans were, however, willing to negotiate on autonomy but progress was slow and was halted altogether in 1934 by the election victory of the Right, followed by the example made of the Asturian miners who staged an uprising. In 1936 the Left regained power leading to the Fascist military uprising led by Franco. This was supported by Navarre but the PNV remained loyal to the Republic and the Basque region gained autonomy by being cut off from the rest of Spain. In 1937 the Basques were defeated by Italian troops and the Fascists executed many nationalists and imprisoned many more.

ETA, in full Euskadi Ta Askatasuna (Basque Homeland and Unity), began in the 1950s as a small secret study group in Bilbao, known then as EKIN (meaning to act). They tried to

The Basque regions of France and Spain

come to terms with the fact that, while Basque nationalism remained, the PNV did nothing to create an effective opposition to Franco's government, which had instituted a repressive regime in Vizcaya and Guipúzcoa where the use of the Basque language was prohibited. Many young militants in the PNV joined EKIN and it merged with the party's youth wing until they split in 1958, renaming themselves ETA a year later.

ETA's insurrection started with painting graffiti; its first military action was the failed attempt to derail a train in 1961 which provoked the immediate arrest of a hundred activists. ETA gained some credibility throughout the anti-Franco community. Next it turned to blowing up Francoist monuments and to robbing banks. A young leader of ETA, Juan Extebarrieta, was shot dead by police in June 1968 after he had shot several *guardia civil*; his funeral masses were attended by large crowds. In August the head of police in Guipúzcoa was shot by ETA and the government declared a state of emergency. Most ETA leaders had fled to France but the remainder were arrested and a show-trial of sixteen of them took place at Burgos. Nine were sentenced to death but international appeals had the sentences commuted to imprisonment. ETA turned this into a propaganda victory.

In December 1973 ETA managed to assassinate the newly appointed Prime Minister, Carrero Blanco, by exploding a bomb in a tunnel under the road as his car passed by. The Basques suffered from two 'dirty' wars. The first, from 1975 to 1981, was organised by the Spanish intelligence services. In addition to militant policemen and soldiers, they also employed, unofficially, a number of right-wing foreigners who had taken refuge in Spain. The war was not one-sided and far more deaths were caused by ETA than by their opponents. In 1978 the Spanish constitution gave the Basques, along with other regions, a degree of autonomy, including recognition of their nationality, when the Basque Autonomous Community was established; Navarre was not a member of the community. The community has its own parliament, administration, courts, police and tax-raising powers, and there are Basque language schools. However, it was rejected by ETA as they were not given the option of remaining in or leaving the state. Their campaign of terror continued, escalating in 1980.

There was a pause in the 'dirty war' in 1981–2, during the short premiership of Calvo Sotelo, and ETA's attacks declined by some two-thirds. The second 'dirty' war did not begin immediately after the re-election of a socialist government in 1982 and the resumption by ETA of full-scale terrorism. It was not until an army medical officer was kidnapped in October 1983 that the security forces were allowed to renew their operations in ETA's haven in the French Basque region. The Grupos Antiterroristas de Liberación (GAL) was more directly controlled by the state than the activists of the first 'dirty' war, but it is still not clear from how high in the Spanish government their authorisation came. The majority of GAL's operations took place in France, where ETA had long taken refuge. The French originally turned a blind eye to what was going on but would not extradite ETA members to Spain. At the end of 1983 French policy changed as it came to realise that ETA was a terrorist organisation. A major police operation took place in January 1984 resulting in forty arrests. GAL's operations were also having an effect on the French Basque economy, especially on tourism. Other causes of the French policy change were the emergence of a French Basque separatist group known as Iparretarrak (ETA of the north), which carried out several terrorist attacks, including a failed attempt to bomb the Paris–Madrid train, and the large increase in Arab terrorist activity which had killed 21 people and injured 191 others in Paris during 1982.

The war between GAL and ETA escalated during 1984. Although GAL's attacks often caused innocent casualties, ETA killed and maimed far more in their attacks. The turning point came in February 1986 when a GAL ambush in Bidarray killed an innocent passing motorist, a sixty-year-old man and a sixteen-year-old girl. With one isolated exception in July 1987 this was the last GAL 'dirty war' attack. In March 1986 the French government classified ETA as an illegal organisation, which allowed its members to be tried in France purely for membership. During the last six months of 1986 twenty-six ETA members were handed over to the Spanish. From 1987 the French regularly jailed, expelled or extradited ETA members.

The repercussions of the 'dirty war' continue today as some of those who carried out the killings and some of those thought responsible are brought to trial. Those who consider the GAL campaign a success point to the closure of France as a safe haven for ETA. The majority who think it a failure point to the public relations value to ETA, to the increased number of ETA killings it provoked and to the immoral aspect of the whole affair that brought the Spanish government into disrepute.

ETA called a cease fire in September 1998 but this only lasted for fourteen months as ETA announced in December 1999 that it was resuming its campaign for independence. Bombing and assassination began straight away. The Spanish election in March 2000 saw a reduction in the pro-independence vote in the Basque region, mainly caused by the boycotting of the election by Herri Batasuna, the party which supports ETA and which won 12 per cent of the vote in 1996. By the end of August ETA had been blamed for murdering twelve people and wounding many others. In September the authorities struck back; the French arrested ETA's leader, Ignacio Gracia Arregui, and eleven others, while in Spain eighteen arrests were made.

However, ETA's campaign continues and its targets include journalists, members of the police, army and judiciary, and in May 2001 a senator. Most but not all attacks have taken place in the Basque region; bombs have been detonated in the Bravas, at Madrid airport and in France. On 6 November 2001 ninety people were injured by a car bomb that exploded in the centre of Madrid. ETA was designated a foreign terrorist organisation by the US State Department on 5 October 2001 and bank accounts of a number of those suspected of links with ETA have been blocked in the US. ETA violence continues in 2002.

The Spanish government introduced a law in July 2002 that will allow them to ban any political party that does not condemn terrorism in the name of independence; the law is aimed mainly at Batasuna, the political wing of ETA. There is considerable opposition to the law from moderate Basques and many thousands held a peaceful march and demonstration in Bibao in June 2002. Batasuna was banned for three years on 26 August

2002; already some of its offices have been closed. Its funds will be frozen and it is forbidden to hold meetings.

TRAVEL ADVICE
FCO and State: Most visitors will be safe but ETA has carried out attacks in tourist areas to harm the Spanish economy. Warnings have been given before bomb attacks.

BIBLIOGRAPHY AND WEBSITE
Heiberg, Marianne, *The Making of the Basque Nation*, Cambridge University Press, 1989
Hooper, John, *The New Spaniards*, Penguin, 1995
Sullivan, John, *ETA and Basque Nationalism*, Routledge, 1988
Woodworth, Paddy, *Dirty War, Clean Hands: ETA, the GAL and Spanish Democracy*, Cork University Press, 2001

Presidencia del Goberno: www.la-moncloa.es

Cyprus

Population: 665,000
Armed Forces: National Guard 10,000
Foreign Forces: Greece 1,250; UK 3,200; UNFICYP 1,200
Per Capita GDP: $US 13,000
Currency: Cypriot pound

Turkish Republic of Northern Cyprus
Population: 215,000, roughly half being mainland Turks
Armed Forces: 5,000
Foreign Forces: Turkey 36,000

The earliest inhabitants of Cyprus are thought to have been Ionians who colonised the island around 1400 BC and so there has always been a Greek influence in terms of language, culture and religion. Despite the Greek presence, its early history was dominated by the Assyrians, the Egyptians and the Persians. In 330 BC the island's city states welcomed Alexander the Great and supported his campaigns; after his death Cyprus became part of the Ptolemaic Empire. Rule by Rome until AD 330 was followed by Byzantine control until the Arab invasions between 649 and 965, after which Byzantium recovered the island. Captured by Richard I of England for the Crusaders in 1191, it was occupied by them and their descendants for nearly three hundred years. The Venetians lost the island to the Ottomans in 1571, and the latter, as was their custom, brought in colonists who settled in the same villages as the native inhabitants but always remained quite separate. Until this point the language and culture of the indigenous population had been Greek.

The British came to Cyprus in 1878 after leasing the island from Turkey as a base for their support of the Turks in their war against the Russians. Britain annexed Cyprus during the First World War and British rule was recognised in 1923 by the Treaty of Lausanne; two years later the island became a Crown Colony. The fact that the British had offered Greece the island in return for a Greek attack on Bulgaria during the First World War – an offer that was refused – later led to Greek Cypriots renewing their demands for *enosis* (union with Greece), a demand encouraged by the schoolteachers brought in from Greece. An uprising in 1931 was suppressed but both Greek and Turkish communities were then given a small role in the government.

The movement for enosis became more militant after the Second World War and was encouraged by Greece, which requested that the UK transfer the colony to it; the request was declined. In 1950 Makarios was appointed Archbishop and took over the leadership of the campaign for enosis. He organised a plebiscite which showed that 95 per cent of Greek Cypriots supported union with Greece. As British influence in Egypt was reduced, Cyprus was seen as an essential base in the region should the British have to leave the Suez Canal Zone. In December 1954 Greece took its case for control of Cyprus to the UN General Assembly. Colonel Grivas, a Greek-Cypriot officer in the Greek Army, led the EOKA (National Organisation of Cypriot Fighters) campaign begun in 1955 to induce the British to withdraw.

In August 1955 the British held a conference in London with Greece and Turkey but without Cypriot representation. The Greeks repeated their call for self-determination while the Turks recalled their four hundred years of sovereignty and claimed that Britain had no right to turn the island over to anyone but Turkey. The British then offered a scheme for self-government; it fell far short of self-determination and Archbishop Makarios rejected it. The Turks called for equality with the Greek-Cypriot community should self-government be granted and insisted that enosis should be permanently excluded as a possibility. In 1956 Archbishop Makarios, who was known to be actively involved in terrorism, was banished to the Seychelles and British security forces waged a successful campaign against the EOKA guerrillas. Late in 1956 a new British scheme was proposed, but this was rejected by the Greek Cypriots because it did not meet their demand for self-determination. However, the Turks, despite the unequal representation which the Turkish Cypriots would receive, accepted it. The Turks were much reassured by the Colonial Secretary's statement that 'any exercise of self-determination ... must include partition'.

In 1957 Greece again appealed to the UN for self-determination for Cyprus but agreed that this could not lead to joining another state. Makarios was released, just when the security forces were close to defeating EOKA, on the understanding that terrorism would end. By 1957 the UK had changed its position to one of requiring only bases in Cyprus rather than the whole island.

The next proposal, known as the Macmillan plan, was put forward as the antagonism between the two communities increased; the scheme gave each community self-government but with a joint council, chaired by the British governor, on which representatives of Greece and Turkey would sit. The council would be responsible for foreign affairs, defence and security. Turkey accepted the plan but Greece did not, and Makarios countered with a proposal for independence under UN supervision with

Cyprus since 1974

guarantees for Turkish Cypriots as a minority but not as equals. Makarios's plan was not acceptable to either the UK or Turkey; Greece threatened to leave NATO if the Macmillan plan was implemented and returned to lobby the UN again but without success.

Greece and Turkey now worked to produce a formula, agreed at conferences at Zurich in 1959 and London in 1960, for independence; Turkey dropped its demand for partition and Greece its demand for enosis. The new republic, which became independent on 16 August 1960, was a bi-communal federal state guaranteed by Greece, Turkey and the UK. A House of Representatives had most legislative powers, with two communal assemblies having responsibility for religion, education and culture. Checks and balances were built into the constitution. The British retained a number of military assets located on Sovereign Base Areas. At the end of 1963 Makarios proposed a long list of changes to the constitution, many reducing Turkish-Cypriot rights; this was rejected by the Turkish side and inter-communal fighting broke out. Both sides committed atrocities and some five hundred people were killed in the first few days. British troops managed to halt some of the violence but were unable to prevent the flight of 25,000 Turks to areas with a Turkish majority (and therefore safe). In March 1964 the United Nations Peacekeeping Force in Cyprus (UNFICYP) was established but the mandating UNSC resolution referred to the by-now wholly Greek-Cypriot government as the legal government of all Cyprus. UNFICYP established itself between the two sides in Nicosia, Kyrenia and Lefka. Elsewhere, UN troops were located across the island so that they could react quickly should a confrontation arise. The Greeks refused to allow the Turkish members to retake their seats in the House of Representatives. The Turks appealed to the British to call a meeting under the Treaty of Guarantee but they refused, thus losing Turkish respect.

In August 1964, after a further proposal had been rejected, the enclave at Kokkina was attacked and the Turks responded with air strikes from the mainland. Makarios threatened an all-out attack on Turkish Cypriots unless the air attacks stopped. The Greek Cypriots formed a National Guard from para-military groups, conscripts and mainland Greek officers; Greece covertly sent 10,000 men to join Grivas's command. The Turks also formed a defence force, Mücahit (or fighters), under Turkish Army officers. A UN report and a further proposal came to nothing as the Greek 'colonels' junta came into power in Greece; it was even more determined to achieve enosis. The Turks dismissed their proposals. In October 1967, after twenty Turkish Cypriots were killed by the National Guard in two southern villages, the Turks mobilised but were unable to invade the island because of foul weather; they only demobilised when Greek troops were withdrawn. An autonomous Provisional Cyprus Turkish Administration was then declared. Inter-communal talks began in June 1968 and continued until they reached deadlock in the spring of 1971; the opportunity was taken to renew Greek-Turkish talks but the Turks' proposals were unacceptable to Makarios who saw that autonomy for the Turkish Cypriots would lead to partition. Grivas, who had been under house arrest in Athens since 1967, escaped to Cyprus where he formed a new terrorist group, EOKA B, and started a campaign against the supporters of independence.

In November 1973 the leader of the Greek junta was overthrown and plans were made for a coup to overthrow Makarios and achieve enosis. The coup took place on 15 July 1974 but Makarios escaped to a British base while heavy fighting took place; the coup succeeded and a former EOKA terrorist, Nikos Sampson, became president. Although the Turkish Cypriots were not attacked they feared that they soon would be and, after failing to get the British to join them, the Turks invaded on the 20th, took Kyrenia and secured a corridor to Nicosia. Greek resistance was stronger than had been expected and the Turks agreed to a cease fire but continued to build up their forces while talks on establishing a bi-zonal federation took place; meanwhile a number of Turkish-Cypriot villages were surrounded by Greek and Greek-Cypriot forces. In August a number of massacres took place at Turkish villages. At Athlar and Murataga mass graves were later discovered, and at four other villages the able-bodied men were taken away and shot. On the 14th the Turks broke out of the Kyrenia salient and established a line across the island from the north coast east of

Kokkina to Varosha on the east coast south of Famagusta. About 150,000 Greek Cypriots living north of this line fled to the south and were replaced by colonists from the Turkish mainland. A cease fire was finally agreed and UNFICYP troops were deployed in a buffer zone along the cease fire line. They are still there.

Since 1975 negotiations sponsored by the UN have taken place. In the earliest meeting Makarios and Rauf Denktash, the Turkish-Cypriot leader, agreed guidelines for a solution that included provision for an independent, non-aligned, bi-communal federal republic with a central government to safeguard both the unity of the country and its bi-communal nature.

The basic difference between the two sides is that the Greeks stress the unity of Cyprus as an indivisible territory with a single citizenship. The Turks argue for two zones and two communities joined by a federal government responsible only for foreign affairs, tourism and some health matters; in the federal legislature and the Council of Ministers there would be equal representation. There have been numerous initiatives and the appointment of several special representatives, but a solution is not much nearer.

The Cypriot situation has now become entangled with the question of membership of the European Union. In July 1990 Cyprus applied for EU membership and is expected to join in 2004. Greece has made it clear that unless Cyprus *as a whole* is included in the 2004 wave of expansion it will block the accession of the other applicants. Turkey has threatened to annex northern Cyprus if Cyprus as a whole is admitted to the EU before agreement has been reached on a confederal solution in which the north would be recognised as a sovereign state; Turkish Cypriots support the threat. EU members are divided on the subject; some believe that membership would have both economic and political advantages for achieving a solution but France, the Netherlands and the EU Commissioner for Enlargement think the accession of a divided Cyprus could be risky. As usual, other considerations will affect the outcome. Turkey is unlikely to abandon the Turkish-Cypriot cause so as to avoid appearing weak to the Turkish Kurds.

In January 2002 the situation improved when the two leaders, Rauf Denktash and President Glafcos Clerides, began a series of face-to-face meetings to resolve the issue, the first for four years. Denktash's change of heart was most probably influenced by Turkish worries over their entry to the EU. Both men are old – Denktash is seventy-seven and Clerides eighty-two – and they know this is their last chance to reach an agreement before the EU decides on its next round of members. The four outstanding issues to be resolved are: the boundary between the two zones; the recognition of each's autonomy; the return of refugees; and compensation for the loss of property.

BIBLIOGRAPHY AND WEBSITES

Dodd, Clement H., *The Cyprus Imbroglio*, Eothen Press, 1998
——, *Cyprus: The Need for New Perspectives*, Eothen Press, 1999
——, *Storm Clouds Over Cyprus*, Eothen Press, 2002
McDonald, Robert, *The Problem of Cyprus*, IISS Adelphi Paper 234, Winter 1988/9
Stephen, Michael, *The Cyprus Question*, Northgate Publications, 2001

Cypriot Press and Information Office: www.pio.gov.cy
Turkish Republic of Northern Cyprus: www.trnc.washdc.org

Greece and Turkey

	Greece	Turkey
Population:	10,863,000 (Muslims 1%)	67,652,000 (Kurds 20%)
Armed Forces:	159,000	515,000
Per Capita GDP:	$US 14,624	$US 6,101
Currency:	drachma	lira

Greece's involvement with Asia Minor began long before the creation of the modern Turkish state. History is responsible for much of the controversy that exists today, when the main differences between these two NATO allies are over Cyprus (see pp. 14–17) and the whole question of sea and air-space control off the Turkish coast and around the Greek islands in the Aegean.

The first Greek settlers arrived in the region after the collapse of the Mycenean Empire in 1200 BC and some two thousand years before the Seldjuk Turks. They established Ionia along the western coast of Asia Minor and other settlements also took place, such as those by the Aeolians and the Dorians. Greek centres of population stretched around the Black Sea coast but further Greek expansion was halted by the Phrygians who inhabited the Anatolian plateau.

In the sixth century BC Asia Minor was part of the Persian Empire, which stretched into Thrace where its advance was halted by the Scythians. In 496 BC the Ionians revolted against the Persians but were defeated, despite help from Greece. This led to the wars in which the Persians were defeated by the Greeks in naval battles at Marathon and Salamis. In 334 BC Alexander the Great began a campaign during which he conquered most of Asia Minor, Syria, Mesopotamia, Lower Egypt and Persia, even reaching the Indus and Samarkand. After his death in 323 BC the division of Alexander's empire put Cyprus and the settlements on the eastern and southern coasts under Ptolemy, while the remainder of the southern half of Asia Minor fell to the Seleucids. Next followed the Roman conquest and the establishment of Byzantium, now Istanbul; after the split from Rome, the Eastern Empire adopted the Orthodox faith. The Ummayids, representing the first Arab Islamic empire, twice failed to capture Byzantium, nor did Asia Minor form part of the empire of the Abbasids, their successors. On the break-up of the Abbasid Empire there was a Byzantine revival which recovered Cyprus from the Arabs and for a short time regained part of the Levant. The Seldjuk family were the leaders of a Turkmen tribe called the Ghuzz, who migrated to Bokhara at the end of the tenth century and embraced Islam. In 1071, under Alp Aslan, they broke through the Byzantine defences and after a fierce battle at Manzikert occupied over half of Asia Minor.

In the second half of the fourteenth century the Ottomans crossed the Dardanelles and first took Gallipoli and then Salonika, Sofia and the Black Sea. In 1389 the Turks defeated the Serbs at Kosovo Polje. It was not until 1453 that the Ottomans, after a long siege, finally took Constantinople. Before then they had occupied Bulgaria and the eastern half of Greece, completing their conquest of the latter by 1460. The Turks ruled Greece until the War of Independence, which ended in 1829 after the British, French and Russian defeat of the Turkish navy at the battle of Navarino (Pylos Bay) in 1827. However, at that stage the Greeks had not recovered Macedonia or Crete. The Congress of Berlin, which met to revise the Balkan borders instituted by the Treaty of St Stephano after the Russian defeat of Turkey in 1878, also left Salonika, Crete and the Eastern Aegean islands under Turkish rule. Then a major revolt broke out in Crete in 1897 and a Greek force landed on the island. This resulted in the island being given autonomous status and both Turkish and Greek troops withdrew.

The Italian–Turkish war of 1911–12 was mainly caused by Italy's acquisition of Tripolitania and Cyrenaica. The 1915 Treaty of London, in a secret clause, gave Italy temporary control of the Dodecanese Islands that it had occupied in the 1912 war. They were to be handed back to Turkey when 'the conditions of peace had been fulfilled' (Turkish troops withdrawn from Libya). They never were and Turkey gave up all claims to the islands under the Treaty of Sèvres, which also granted Greece the islands of Imbros and Tenedos. Crete united with Greece in 1913 after most of the Muslim population had emigrated.

After the First World War Greece was given a mandate to administer Smyrna for five years, after which a plebiscite would be held to decide whether it would remain Greek or not. Greece landed troops at Izmir to support its administration and in 1921 the Greeks decided to launch an attack against Kemal Ataturk, who opposed the Greek occupation. The Greek army advanced towards Ankara but was defeated by a combination of an unusually severe winter, over-extended lines of communication and a much-improved Turkish army. The Greeks were forced out of Asia Minor leaving 30,000 dead and taking 1,350,000 refugees back to Greece. The Treaty of Lausanne (1923) created new borders. The European land frontier was adjusted to give more territory to Greece. After a long siege Greek sovereignty over the islands of Límnos, Lésvos, Khíos, Sámos and Ikaria was recognised. Turkey gained sovereignty over the whole of Anatolia, the islands of Gokcead (Imbros) and Bozcaada (Tenedos), and a maritime belt extending 3 miles from the coast. There was an exchange of populations. After the Second World War the Paris Treaty of 1947 transferred the Dodecanese Islands from Italy to Greece.

There are several elements to the Greek–Turkish dispute: the continental shelf; territorial waters, with the possibility of Greece extending its to a 12-mile limit; and airspace and air traffic control. The continental shelf issue revolves around the status of islands: Turkey does not recognise that they have a right to a continental shelf and so claims that its continental shelf stretches to the west of the Greek islands. There is also disagreement on how the issue should be resolved, with Turkey arguing for a political settlement to partition the Aegean continental shelf, while Greece wants the issue settled on legal interpretations of the Law of the Sea by the International Court of Justice. The Law of the Sea recognises that coastal states have the right of territorial waters up to 12 miles off their shores including islands. At present Greece only claims a 6-mile territorial water but has stated that it will extend it to 12 miles when it sees fit to do so. Turkey sees access to the high seas as vital and an extension of the Greek territorial waters would be a *casus belli*. In June 1995 the Turkish National Assembly resolved that the government should take military measures to protect Turkish interests should the Greek limit be extended; Greece considers this resolution a violation of the UN Charter. The internationally agreed Athens Flight Information Region (FIR) extends from the Greek mainland as far east as the edge of Greece's 10-mile national air space; however, Turkey only recognises a 6-mile Greek air space as this should equate to territorial waters. In 1974 Turkey issued a notice to airmen (NOTAM) requiring aircraft flying over the eastern half of the Aegean, in which a number of Greek Aegean and Dodecanese Islands lie, to report to the Istanbul FIR. The NOTAM was withdrawn in 1980 but since then Turkish military aircraft regularly fly in the outer 4 miles of Greek-claimed air space. A further element in the Greek–Turkish dispute is the question of the demilitarisation of certain Aegean islands as demanded by the Treaty of Lausanne, and the Dodecanese Islands as demanded by the Treaty of Paris. The Turks accuse the Greeks of fortifying the Aegean islands, while the Greeks maintain that only partial demilitarisation was required and that the Montreux Convention of 1923 ended the demilitarised status of Lemnos and Samothraki. In response to the militarisation of the islands the Turks formed their Army of the Aegean; the Greeks demand it be disbanded.

The most recent and dangerous incident in the Dodecanese concerned the uninhabited islets of Imia that lie halfway between the Greek island of Nisidha Kalolimnos and the Turkish Cavus Ada. In December 1995, after a Turkish freighter suffered engine trouble and was stranded on one of the islets, Turkey issued a statement claiming the islets belonged to it. Greece rejected the claim and the mayor of Kalimnos visited Imia and planted a Greek flag; a week later a group of Turkish journalists was filmed replacing it with a Turkish flag. At the end of January Turkish commandos landed on the islets but were soon withdrawn and the incident was settled peacefully after both sides had deployed naval forces.

Greek-Turkish Maritime Boundaries

Relations between Greece and Turkey continue to be tense and are not aided by the experiences of their joint history. However, Greece came quickly to Turkey's aid after the major earthquake of August 1999 and Turkey as rapidly helped Greece after the earthquake that hit on 7 September 1999. There has been a definite improvement in their relations, with Greece withdrawing its objections to Turkish membership of the European Union. It did, however, impose several tough conditions at the Brussels meeting in December 1999: the Aegean dispute must be referred to the International Court of Justice; the Greek half of Cyprus should be admitted to the European Union even if a settlement over the island's future has not been reached; and Turkey must improve both its democracy and economy. However, the following month Turkey and Cyprus signed a number of accords in respect of: commerce, protecting investment and abolishing double-taxation; fighting crime; illegal immigration; promoting tourism and environmental protection.

What was hailed as a breakthrough occasion, when elements of all three armed services of Greece were to use Turkish facilities during a NATO exercise in October 2000, turned sour when Greece pulled out of the exercise. The Turks had said that Greek warplanes should not fly over the islands of Lémnos and Ikaria because of their demilitarisation. When they did, the Greek aircraft were tailed by Turkish fighters and Greece consequently withdrew from the exercise. Turkish planes flying close to Cyprus were illuminated by Russian-supplied air defence radar there. In 2001 a more successful exercise was held with troops and aircraft of both countries visiting each other. Greece and Turkey are holding 'talks about talks' but have not, as yet, addressed the key divisive issues of the Aegean and Cyprus, although a number of confidence-building agreements have been reached including expanding trade and tourism and cooperating on security matters. Both countries were committed to clear the landmines laid on their common border but this has not happened yet. The ministers said they would also conduct joint seismic research, and cooperate in the event of floods, landslides and forest fires.

BIBLIOGRAPHY AND WEBSITES
Alford, Jonathan (ed.), *Greece and Turkey: Adversity in Alliance*, IISS Adelphi Library 12, 1984
Howard, Harry, *The Partition of Turkey: A Diplomatic History 1913–1923*, Harry Howard/University of Oklahoma Press, 1966
The International Status of the Aegean, Ministry of Press and Mass Media, Athens, 1998

Greece: www.mfa.gr/foreign/bilateral
Turkey: www.mfa.gov.tr/grupa/ad/ade/default

Gibraltar

Population: 30,000
Armed Forces: 565
Per Capita GDP: £11,680
Currency: Gibraltar pound

Gibraltar's original name was Calpe, thought to be derived from the Phoenician word 'kalph' (to hollow out), possibly on account of what is now known as St Michael's Cave. It was first described by a Roman geographer, as the Roman city of Carteia was just north of the colony. The Muslims first landed in Spain close to Gibraltar and the mountain was named Jebel Tarik after the Berber chief who led the landing. The Muslims fortified Gibraltar and occupied it until 1309 when it was besieged and captured by King Fernando IV of Spain. He ordered the walls to be repaired and a dockyard constructed; other fortifications were also built. In 1333 Gibraltar was recaptured by the Moors after a siege lasting four-and-a-half months; the Spanish failed to regain it and the Moors improved the defences. The Spanish were unable to take Gibraltar until 1462, after four more sieges had failed.

The English first became interested in Gibraltar during the maritime war with Spain in 1625 as its occupation would help the navy control maritime communications. However, the plan was dropped and Cadiz was raided instead. After a visit by Philip IV Gibraltar's defences were substantially improved. During Cromwell's rule it was again suggested that the English fleet, which had been sent to stop any Spanish naval force from sailing to the Caribbean and to hijack any treasure-ships, should take Gibraltar but again the plan was dropped as the necessary landing force could not be spared from Ireland. In the years leading up to the War of the Spanish Succession (which began in 1701) there were lengthy negotiations between the English and the French over concessions the English might win if they supported France's candidate for the Spanish throne. The English suggested they should be rewarded with Oran, Ceuta, Mahon (in Minorca) and Gibraltar; this last the French were reluctant to see in English hands.

Admiral Rooke was dispatched in June 1702 with a fleet of 160 warships and transports carrying some 14,000 troops to take Cadiz. The secondary objective was Gibraltar. The troops landed at Cadiz but became a disorderly rabble after plundering the wine stores and were re-embarked three weeks later. In 1704 Rooke's fleet was sent to Toulon to draw off French troops opposing Marlborough in central Europe. After a council of war the fleet sailed back to the Straits of Gibraltar to meet up with reinforcements. On 1 August twenty ships entered the Bay and the Prince of Hesse was landed with some 2,000 Dutch and English marines to cut off Gibraltar from the mainland. An adverse wind prevented the bombardment of the fortifications, which lasted five or six hours, until 3 August. Two other landings were made and on 5 August the articles of surrender were signed; Gibraltar had been taken in the name of Charles III of Spain. By the end of August Gibraltar was under siege again; this time it lasted until May 1705.

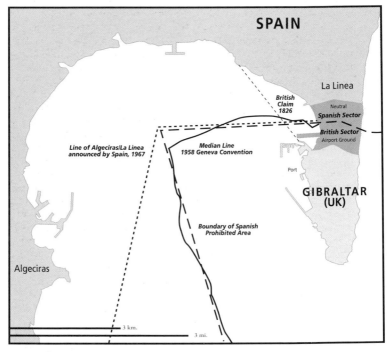

Gibraltar

In the negotiations leading up to the drafting of the Treaty of Utrecht in 1713, the French betrayed their Spanish allies and England the Dutch when it was agreed that Gibraltar should become wholly English and not be shared with the Dutch as the latter expected. In the treaty, therefore, Spain ceded Gibraltar to England in perpetuity. However, Spain had to be offered the territory if Britain decided to surrender its sovereignty. Article X of the treaty read that 'no leave shall be given under any pretence whatsoever, either to Jews or Moors, to reside or have their dwellings in the said town of Gibraltar'. As both Jews and Moors were allowed to live there the Spanish claimed that the English were in breach of the treaty and should hand Gibraltar back. Spain made a number of attempts to recapture the Rock in the eighteenth century, notably in 1727 and then in the great siege which lasted from 1779 to 1783. Gibraltar became a Crown Colony in 1830. It was obviously a strategic asset and remained so until the end of the Cold War.

Under General Franco Spain renewed its claim to Gibraltar and in 1963 the Spanish challenged British sovereignty at the United Nations General Assembly. A UN vote called on Britain to hand over Gibraltar within two years. However, Britain has always maintained that UN Resolution 2429 violated the UN Charter, which takes precedence over any other treaty or resolution. The Gibraltarian population is composed mainly of descendants of British, Genoese and Maltese, and has always maintained its desire to be considered British. In 1967 a referendum was held. Only 44 people voted to join Spain compared with the 12,138 who opted to remain British. Gibraltar received a new constitution in 1969 which gave it a large degree of self-government, with Britain only retaining responsibility for defence, foreign policy and internal security. The constitution included the pledge: 'Her Majesty's Government will never enter into arrangements under which the people of Gibraltar would pass under the sovereignty of another state against their freely and democratically expressed wishes.' All succeeding British governments, including the present one, have confirmed that pledge.

While Spain will not use force to gain control it has severely harassed Gibraltarians and visitors to the Rock over the years. Before 1969 there were regular air and sea links between Gibraltar and Spain. All sea links were suspended in 1969 and have still not been renewed, despite an agreement to resume them in 1984. Direct air flights were ended in 1978. The border with Spain was closed in 1969 (it had been closed to vehicles since 1966) and not reopened until 1985 but even then Spanish controls severely restricted road access to Gibraltar with travellers waiting to cross the border experiencing long delays. The Spanish have admitted (in the *ABC* newspaper on 27 June 1969) that the restrictions were intended 'to make life on the Rock very unpleasant' but it has backfired as they have only served to strengthen the Gibraltarians' resolve to remain British. While Gibraltarians are adamant about the retention of British sovereignty, they frequently visit Spain to go shopping and to eat at restaurants. Those who can afford it have second homes in Spain.

In addition to difficulties over access and sovereignty, there has been confrontation over smuggling and fishing. In 1994 Gibraltar imported some 1,500,000 cigarettes (the equivalent of 50,000 for each inhabitant), the majority of which were smuggled by fast launches into Spain. Gibraltar was used as the base for large numbers of Spanish smugglers' boats engaged on smuggling drugs from Morocco to Spain. There has been a crack-down on the trade and in 1995 the type of boat favoured by the smugglers was banned. The smugglers are now based in Morocco but still prefer to approach the Spanish coast through Gibraltar's waters.

While Spain considers Gibraltar has no right to be British, it takes quite a different view of its two enclaves of Ceuta and Mellila on the Moroccan coast. These were taken from the Moors by Portugal and ceded to Spain in 1580. Morocco claims the enclaves, but has been ignored by Spain. The Spanish government maintains the two enclaves are quite different from Gibraltar, their populations being entirely of Spanish descent and not the descendants of a variety of settlers. Morocco has said it will intensify its efforts to recover the enclaves should Gibraltar revert to Spanish sovereignty.

In July 2002 a small group of Moroccan soldiers occupied the uninhabited island of Perejil (parsley) claimed by Spain, that lies only 200 metres from the Moroccan coast opposite Bei Youneeh. Spanish troops evicted them six days later after a show of naval strength. There are three other Spanish-claimed islands lying close to the north Moroccan shore. At the end of July the Moroccan King, Mohamed VI, demanded that Spain leave North Africa.

At present, the British and Spanish governments are negotiating a set of principles regarding Gibraltar's future status. These principles are: respect for Gibraltar's way of life; respect for Gibraltar's European Union rights; maximum degree of self-government; and a yet-to-be-agreed principle on joint or shared sovereignty. After agreement on these principles work will start on the implementation policy; implementation matters can be rejected by the Gibraltarians in a referendum but the principles cannot be rejected and will remain in force even if not implemented. Differences between the British and Spanish positions include the British requirement that agreement on principles must be final and unalterable, while Spain sees them as the first step in recovering full sovereignty over Gibraltar. Spain states that it will never give up its claim. The British Ministry of Defence wants to retain exclusive use of military assets on the Rock, but Spain wishes to share them. The Chief Minister, Peter Caruana, claims that no British military operation in recent years could have been mounted without using Gibraltar's facilities. He also compares Britain's actions and statements over the non-negotiability of the sovereignty of the Falklands with the effort being put in to giving Gibraltar's away.

BIBLIOGRAPHY AND WEBSITE

Hills, George, *Rock of Contention: A History of Gibraltar*, Robert Hale, 1974

Gibraltar Government Office London: www.gibraltar.gov.uk

Europe's Changing Borders

As this book demonstrates, border disputes are one of the commonest causes of war, particularly when the changes to territorial limits have been enforced. Probably no other region of the world has experienced more redrawing of its borders over the centuries than Europe. The analysis that follows concentrates on changes made in the twentieth century after the First World War but, of course, there were many more in the preceding centuries. The implications of some, particularly in the Balkans, are still being suffered today. The various border movements in the Balkans laid down by the 1878 Treaty of Stefano, the Congress of Berlin and the 1913 Treaty of Bucharest are shown in the maps in the section on the Balkans on pp. 28–50.

Europe's borders were probably first drawn with the arrival of the Germanic tribes in the fifth century AD but they were soon altered, for instance by the Treaty of Verdun in 843 and the Partition of Meersen in 870. In medieval times land was often given as a dowry when royal marriages took place. In the next thousand years there were numerous border changes mainly brought about by war. The Holy Roman Empire, the Hapsburgs, the Napoleonic era and the Austro-Hungarian Empire all rose and fell. In the nineteenth century territorial divisions were redrawn by diktats issued after meetings of the Great Powers: Britain, France, Germany and Russia. The century also witnessed the unification of Germany (1815–71) and Italy (1859–70), and Belgian independence (1830–9). The Congress of Paris in 1856, after the Crimean War, decreed reform in Turkey (which did not take place), the neutralisation of the Black Sea (which lasted until 1871) and the freeing of the Danubian Principalities (which led to an independent Romania). The Franco–Prussian War in 1870 ended with the French losing Alsace and Lorraine.

The early years of the twentieth century saw Italy at war with Turkey, in which the Italians took Libya and the Dodecanese Islands, and the two Balkan Wars followed by the Treaty of Bucharest, which broke up Macedonia between its neighbours.

The First World War witnessed the end of two European empires: the Austro-Hungarian and the Ottoman. The collapse of the latter led to border changes far beyond Europe. The Austro-Hungarian Empire broke up into Austria, Czechoslovakia and Hungary, while Romania, the Ukraine and the new kingdom of Serbs, Croats and Slovenes gained territory. Austria also lost land – and its access to the Adriatic at Trieste – to Italy, and the same area was contested at the end of the Second World War and was eventually divided between Italy and Yugoslavia. Also included in the Yugoslav kingdom was a Hungarian minority population in Voyvodina. Czechoslovakia also included the Sudetenland, which had a German population – one reason for the German invasion in 1938.

The end of the First World War also witnessed the Russian Revolution and the founding of the Soviet Union. This also caused border changes. The growth of the Russian Empire

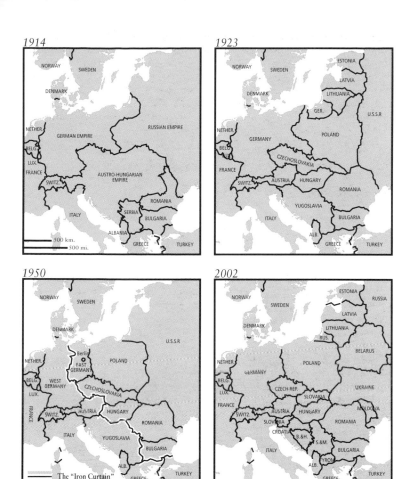

Europe's changing borders

into the Soviet Union and its subsequent break up are illustrated on [p. 26]. Russia's collapse at the end of the First World War allowed Estonia, Latvia and Lithuania to gain their independence. This they lost again, first to the Soviet Union in 1939 and then to Germany. The Soviet Union recaptured the three Baltic States in 1944 and held them until its break-up in the late twentieth century. Over the years since 1919 the Baltic States have lost and gained territory that could possibly lead to future disputes. France regained Alsace and Lorraine in 1919.

Poland has probably suffered more border changes and exchanges of territory than any other European country and these are illustrated in the maps on [pp. 00 and 00]. While there have always been Polish people there has not always been a Polish state. At various times the Germans, Prussians, Russians and Lithuanians have absorbed its territory. Towards the end of the tenth and in the early eleventh centuries Poland was at its most powerful after its occupation of Pomerania, Bohemia and Moravia and its progress as far east as the River Bug. By the start of the First World War it was part of the Russian Empire and had no access to the Baltic Sea. It became independent in 1918 and was awarded more territory by the Treaty of Versailles in 1921, including the Danzig corridor and a broad strip to the east

1772

Riga · RUSSIA · Vilna · Minsk · GERMANY · Berlin · Warsaw · POLAND · Kiev · GERMANY · Prague · Vienna · HUNGARY · Budapest · MOLDAVIA

500 km.
500 mi.

1795

Riga · RUSSIA · Vilna · Minsk · GERMANY · Berlin · Warsaw · Kiev · Prague · Vienna · HUNGARY · Budapest · MOLDAVIA

1815

Riga · RUSSIA · Vilna · Minsk · PRUSSIA · Berlin · Warsaw · Kiev · Prague · AUSTRIA · Vienna · Budapest · MOLDAVIA

Duchy of Poland, 1807-1815

1921

Riga · LATVIA · LITHUANIA · Vilnius · RUSSIA · GERMANY · Minsk · Berlin · Warsaw · POLAND · Kiev · Prague · CZECHOSLOVAKIA · Vienna · AUSTRIA · HUNGARY · ROMANIA

☐ Polish Republic, 1918
▪▪▪▪ Curzon Line, 1919

1942

Riga · Vilna · RUSSIA · Minsk · GERMANY · Berlin · Warsaw · Kiev · Prague · SLOVAKIA · Vienna · HUNGARY · Budapest · ROMANIA

▪▪▪▪ Ribbentrop-Molotov Line, 1939
  General Government Poland (Great Germany)

Poland's changing borders

1999

Riga · LATVIA · RUSSIA · LITHUANIA · Vilnius · RUSSIA · Minsk · POLAND · BELARUS · Berlin · Warsaw · CZECH. REP. · Kiev · SLOVAKIA · UKRAINE · AUSTRIA · HUNGARY · MOLDAVIA · ROMANIA

 Polish borders since 1945

26

of the Curzon Line (a Polish–Soviet border suggested at the Versailles Conference, and to the west of which Lord Curzon suggested the Poles should withdraw in 1920). During the Second World War Poland was divided initially between the Germans and Russians, until the Germans occupied it all after their attack on Russia. The most recent border changes came at the end of the Second World War and gave Poland territory that had been German before 1939. However, it had to surrender land in the east to the Soviet Union; this land is now part of Belarus. In 1946 some twelve million Germans were displaced from Silesia and Pomerania and had to find new homes in East and West Germany. The refugees included nearly two million from East Prussia, which was divided between Poland and the Soviet Union, whose portion is now the *oblast* of Kaliningrad. Not surprisingly, some of the descendants of those displaced still consider their homeland to be in Poland. A growing number of German tourists have visited the former East Prussia and there are some who believe Russia will give up Kaliningrad as being economically unaffordable. In the 'Four + Two' Treaty that reunified Germany, the Germans recognised the Oder–Neisse line as the permanent border between Germany and Poland, but, again, there are some who still want to recover their historic lands.

The 2.5–3 million Germans who had lived in the Sudetenland were expelled in 1946 and their representatives still meet each year in Bavaria, demanding that their expulsion be recognised as a crime. Some hope to regain their property or receive compensation. In 1938, when 90 per cent of Sudetans voted for the local party, the Nazis there expelled most Czechs. The Sudetan question is now threatening the Czech Republic's bid to join the EU. There has been a public row between the Bavarian and Czech prime ministers, Edmund Stoiber and Milos Zeman, the latter accusing the Sudetan Germans of being traitors in 1938. Zeman's right-wing challenger, Vaclav Klaus, then proposed that the Benes Decrees, which legitimised the confiscation of German-owned property, should be reconfirmed in the Czech accession contract. Before the Second World War Czechoslovakia also contained Ruthenia which, when the Germans broke up the country in 1939, gained its autonomy as Carpatho-Ukraine. After it declared its independence it was annexed by Hungary. At the end of the war, when Czechoslovakia was reformed, it did not get the region back and Carpatho-Ukraine was incorporated into the Ukraine and the Soviet Union.

There are Hungarian minorities in Romania (1.6 million, mainly in Transylvania), in the Voyvodina province of Serbia (400,000) and in Slovakia (560,000). Hungary signed a Treaty of Good Neighbourly Relations and Friendship with Slovakia in 1995 but has been unable to reach a similar agreement with Romania. The Romanian-populated Republic of Moldova has changed hands and names over history. Russia gained Bessarabia, the land between the Prut and Dniester, from the Ottomans in 1812. They occupied Moldavia and Wallachia in 1853 – providing one of the causes of the Crimean War. Bessarabia remained in Russian hands when Romania became independent, while Romania annexed the province of Dobruja in 1878. Bessarabia declared its independence as the Democratic Republic of Moldavia in 1917 and in 1918 joined Romania; Russia did not regain it until 1939. Russia altered the borders by transferring Northern Bukovina and Southern Bessarabia to Ukraine. At the same time it added a strip of land to the east of the Dniester to Bessarabia. The country became independent as Moldova in 1991 when the USSR ceased to exist, but the left bank territory of Transdniestria, backed by its Russian garrison, attempted to break away. A complicating factor for Moldova is the minority Gauguz population in the south-west.

WEBSITE
International Boundaries Research Unit: www.ibru.dur.ac.uk

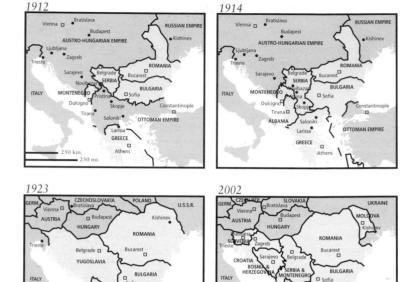

The Balkans 1912–2002

The Balkans

Europe and the US have been concerned by and involved in events in the Balkans for the last ten years, as the collapse of communism was replaced by nationalism and to a lesser extent by a return to religion. The Balkans have been an unstable area for many years, being the interface of a number of conflicts – most notably the split between Rome and Byzantium and between the Austro-Hungarian and Ottoman Empires. The region had divided loyalties in both the First and Second World Wars. Its borders have been altered by wars and by international decree. The success rate in solving modern problems has been mixed. Even preventive diplomacy and the deployment of peacekeepers in Macedonia stabilised it only until ethnic fighting broke out after the intervention in Kosovo. In Albania the Italian-led intervention contributed to stabilising that country when it was in danger of imploding. Elsewhere it was either a case of doing too little too late or going to the other extreme and, for example, using massive air power to force the Serbs into halting their ethnic cleansing in Kosovo – but only at the risk of sending the wrong message to the watching world.

Seventy-eight war criminals have been handed over to the International Criminal Tribunal at The Hague; so far 15 have been convicted and five found not guilty. However, neither Radovan Karadzic, the Bosnian Serb president, nor Ratko Mladic, the Army commander, has yet been apprehended.

BIBLIOGRAPHY AND WEBSITE
Allan, Dana H., 'NATO's Balkan Interventions', IISS Adelphi Paper No. 347, 2002
Balkan Information Exchange: www.balkan-info.com
Balkan Stability Pact: www.stability.org

Serbia and Montenegro

	Serbia	Montenegro
Population:	9,900,000	700,000
	Serb 66%, Albanian 17%	Montenegrin 62%
	Hungarian 4%	Serb 9%, Albanian 7%
Armed Forces:	105,000	nil
Paramilitary:	87,000	6,000
Per Capita GDP:	US$ 4,930	US$ 4,930
Currency	new dinar	Euro

The Federation called Yugoslavia that started to disintegrate in 1991 was established in 1918 after the end of the First World War in an attempt to stabilise the Balkans. Initially known as the Kingdom of the Serbs, Croats and Slovenes, it was created by merging the previously independent states of Serbia and Montenegro and parts of the Austro-Hungarian and Ottoman Empires, both of which had been destroyed by the war. In 1920 the province of Voyvodina was added. In the 1920s the bitter ethnic divisions within the federation encouraged the king to establish a strong dictatorial government in Belgrade, supported by a system of *banovina* or governorships, which deliberately took account of neither historical boundaries nor the ethnicity of the population.

The German occupation of the kingdom in the Second World War gave an added dimension to the centuries-old divisions as Yugoslavia was broken up by the Axis. The southern half of Slovenia became part of Italy, along with the Dalmatian coastal strip; Italy also took control of Montenegro, parts of Macedonia and Albania. (By this time Albania had been expanded into Kosovo, which was mainly inhabited by ethnic Albanians.) Hungary took the two northern districts of Croatia and the larger part of Voyvodina, while the ethnic German population there took over the administration of Banat District. Bulgaria took eastern Macedonia and parts of southern Serbia. All that was left was a truncated Serbia directly governed by the Germans and an 'independent' state of Croatia, which included Bosnia-Herzegovina under the rule of Croat Ustashe, a Nazi puppet state. The Ustashe were violently anti-Serb. They forcibly converted many to Catholicism and are said to have massacred as many as 400,000.

Opposition to the German occupation was divided. The Serbian guerrillas, the Chetniks, were only nominally under the control of Draza Mihailovic´[c], whose loyalty lay with the government in exile; some collaborated with the Italians. The other main guerrilla group was the 'Partisans' organised by Tito. They drew their support not just from Croats but also from Serbs and others. Like the Chetniks they spent as much time fighting rival Yugoslav groups as they did the occupation forces, which relied heavily on non-German units and which included a Muslim SS Division. The Partisans are believed to have killed as many as a million fellow Yugoslavs during and immediately after the war including 18,000 prisoners of war returned from Austria.

After 1945 Tito held Yugoslavia together by a combination of centralised bureaucracy, a high degree of ruthlessness and an emphasis on communism as an alternative to nationalism. The country was redivided into six republics and two autonomous provinces, Voyvodina and Kosovo, both of which were within Serbia. Unfortunately the post-war borders left many communities, particularly Serbian, on the 'wrong' side of the boundary lines. The only difference between the provinces and the republics was that constitutionally the former could not secede while the latter could. Slowly centralisation withered and a new constitution established in 1974 left the Federal government responsible only for defence, foreign affairs and some economic matters.

Tito died in 1980 leaving a rotating leadership for the Federation as his legacy. As decentralisation developed so did nationalism, which was given a new purpose with the

Serbia and Montenegro

collapse of communism throughout eastern Europe. In 1987 Slobodan Milosevic gained the leadership of Serbia and with a new constitution in 1990 he abolished the autonomous status of Voyvodina and Kosovo, much to the dismay of the Hungarian and Albanian populations there. His actions also alarmed the republics of Slovenia and Croatia who foresaw an unacceptable rise in Serbian nationalism and power.

Milosevic and Serbia are regarded as the direct cause of the break-up of the Federation and of the fighting which has taken place since. Serbia has had to absorb a large number of refugees, mainly from the Serbian enclaves in Croatia, and a number of these were housed in Kosovo. (The conflict in Kosovo is dealt with on [pp. 42–7].) While the Serbs considered the fighting throughout former Yugoslavia as civil wars *within* the independent republics, many believe that the level of military support given to the Serb communities in Croatia and Bosnia-Herzegovina more than justifies their description as 'inter-state wars'. For this Rump Yugoslavia had sanctions imposed on it by the United Nations.

His policy of ethnic cleansing provoked international intervention and led to Milosevic's downfall. Elections for the Yugoslav Federation's president and government were held in September 2000 and resulted in the election of Vojislav Kostunica. The US and the European Union lifted the sanctions they had imposed on Yugoslavia and the UN lifted its arms embargo. Yugoslavia was admitted to the Stability Pact for South-Eastern Europe. In March 2001 Milosevic was arrested and is now on trial before the International Criminal Tribunal for Former Yugoslavia at the Hague.

With a new regime in Serbia and Milosevic no longer the president of Yugoslavia it was much less likely that Montenegro would secede from Federal Yugoslavia; probably about half the population wanted independence. In

Greater Serbian State of Tsar Dusan, 1355

many ways Montenegro is virtually independent already. It has its own currency (the Euro), but it does not have its own army. In March Serbia and Montenegro agreed to remain in a federation but to be called Serbia and Montenegro and not Yugoslavia. They will retain their separate currencies and customs services but will share foreign and defence policies and a supreme court.

The Federal Yugoslav Parliament voted to abolish the Federation in June 2002.

TRAVEL ADVICE
No warnings.

BIBLIOGRAPHY AND WEBSITES

Carter, F.W. and Norris, H.T. (eds), The Changing Shape of the Balkans, SOAS/GRC Geopolitical Series, UCL Press, 1996

Glennie, Misha, The Balkans 1804–1999: Nationalism, War and the Great Powers, Granta Books, 1999

Judah, Tim, The Serbs: History, Myth, and the Destruction of Yugoslavia, Yale University Press, 1997

Silber, Laura, and Little, Alan, The Death of Yugoslavia, Harmondsworth, 1995

Balkan Stability Pact: www.balkanstabilitypact.org

Helsinki Committee for Human Rights in Serbia: www.helsinki.org.yu and www.ihf-hr.org.serbia

International Criminal Tribunal for the Former Yugoslavia: www.un.org/icty

Serbian Ministry of Information: www.serbia-info.com

Slovenia

Population: 1,981,000
Slovene 96%, Croat 3%, Serb 2%, Muslim 1%
Armed Forces: 7,600
Per capita GDP: US$ 12,518
Currency: tolar

Slovenia was the least Balkan-orientated element of Yugoslavia. It had had a long experience of association with its Italian and Austrian neighbours but had maintained its language and Slavonic identity. During the Hapsburg era Slovenia was in the Austrian part while the rest of the Balkans north of the Ottoman Empire were in the Hungarian part. For many years the Adriatic eastern coast had been settled and developed by Romans and Venetians. After the First World War the Istrian peninsula was annexed by Italy. During the Second World War Slovenia was split between Italy and Austria, but after 1945 it was expanded by being given most of the Slovene-populated areas of north-east Italy. Some 350,000 Italians left Slovene and Croat Istria after 1945.

Slovenia was the only republic of the Yugoslav Federation to have a homogeneous population with a common religion, Roman Catholicism. It was eager to join Yugoslavia in 1918 to escape the influence of its much larger neighbours. Throughout the inter-war years it had been a moderating influence in Yugoslav politics and its people had no desire, unlike the Croats, for separatism. Until the collapse of communism Slovene nationalism was hardly

Slovenia and Croatia post independence, showing former UN protected area

an issue but in the late 1980s it became the most critical part of the Yugoslav situation. In the first multi-party elections of 1990 the centre-right coalition, DEMOS, campaigned for independence and won. In July the National Assembly voted for a declaration of sovereignty giving precedence to Slovene over Federal law and powers to develop its own foreign and defence policy. Next it took control of the Territorial Defence Force, the Yugoslav-wide system for mobilising and arming the country in the event of war. In a referendum in December 1990 the country voted overwhelmingly for independence and in March 1991 it stopped sending conscripts to the Federal Army.

The Serbs were not concerned by Slovene independence other than its potential impact on Serbian efforts to stop Croatia leaving the Federation. Slovenia declared its independence on 25 June 1991 and the Federal Army immediately sent in armoured forces but without infantry support which was essential for operations in the heavily forested mountainous area. The Serbian aim was to reach and seal off the external borders of the Federation. However, few of the columns got through, being held up on narrow roads which appeared to run either through gullies or along embankments with the result that the tanks could not deploy off the roads. The European Community (EC) managed to broker a peace agreement but the Slovenes failed to meet their commitment to lift the blockade of army barracks. On 18 July the Federal Army was ordered to pull out of Slovenia. Casualties in the fighting had been light: nineteen Slovene men and forty-five Federal soldiers were killed. In January 1992 the EC, at German insistence, recognised Slovenia as an independent state. Slovenia is now a candidate for membership of both NATO and the European Union.

WEBSITE
Slovene Ministry of Foreign Affairs: www.gov.si/mzz/ang

Croatia

Population: 4,410,000 (Croat 96%, Serb 3%, Slovene 1%)
Armed Forces: 58,000
UN: UNMOP 27 Observers
Per Capita GDP: US$ 7,192
Currency: kuna

The national divisions and border changes throughout history have seriously affected Croatia, as they have Bosnia and Herzegovina (see pp. 35–8). After the split of the Roman Empire, the Croats became Catholics and used Roman script, while the Serbians adopted Orthodox Christianity and the Cyrillic alphabet. Large numbers of Serbs fled the Ottoman Empire and came to inhabit the Croatian/Bosnian and Croatian/Voyvodina border areas.

Croatia formed the main part of the Austro-Hungarian Empire's military frontier region with the Ottoman Empire, which stretched from northern Dalmatia to Transylvania. During the Second World War Croatia was greatly enlarged, incorporating the whole of Bosnia-Herzegovina, and was ruled as a Nazi puppet state by the violently anti-Serb Ustashe. After the war Croatia was also given parts of Italy including the Istrian peninsula and Italian Dalmatia; the post-war border changes also left many Serbs within Croatia.

The multi-party elections in Croatia in April 1990 brought Franjo Tudjman, a former communist, partisan and army general, to power as leader of the right-wing Croatian Democratic Union (HDZ). Tudjman reintroduced the old Croatian flag and the new constitution made no mention of the Serbs, who for their part organised the Serbian Democratic Party (SDS) and boycotted the National Assembly. By October they had declared regional autonomy in those regions (Krajina, Eastern and Western Slavonia) in which the Serbs predominated. After a referendum in May 1991 in which Croats voted overwhelmingly in favour, Croatia declared its independence on 25 June 1991. Even before that there had been frequent violent clashes between Serbs and Croats. Now there was open war as the Serbs began to expand their enclaves and to force out the Croatian minorities there in a process now known as ethnic cleansing. Unlike the Slovenes, the Croats had been unable to take over the Territorial Defence Force armouries and so were poorly armed, while the Federal Army gave support to the Serbs. Vukovar in Eastern Slavonia was taken and destroyed, the ancient port of Dubrovnik was shelled and many other towns and villages were badly damaged as their Croat populations were driven out by the Serbs.

In mid-January 1992 the EC recognised Croatia's independence. The UN envoy Cyrus Vance arranged a cease fire and obtained agreement for the deployment of a UN peacekeeping force, the United Nations Protection Force (UNPROFOR). The peacekeeping plan required the withdrawal of the Yugoslav Peoples Army (PLA), the demilitarisation of the UN Protected Areas, the return of refugees and the establishment of a Croatian police force. The UN authorised a force of nearly 14,000 men including police, but only 9,700 were initially deployed; the UN so misjudged future events that its original plan nominated Sarajevo as the UNPROFOR HQ and logistic base. Fighting around the airport required the move of a battalion from Croatia to Sarajevo.

No progress was made in returning the Serb-held areas – Eastern and Western Slavonia and Krajina – to Croat control during 1993 and 1994. By mid-1994 some 250,000 Croats had been displaced from Krajina and there were as many as 420,000 Croat refugees from Bosnia in Croatia. During this time the Croatian Army was being established; armed with smuggled weapons, its troops were trained and advised by an American commercial company employing retired US Army officers. Then in May and August 1994, in two swift and well-planned operations, the Croats recovered first Western Slavonia and then Krajina. This resulted in some 200,000 Serbs fleeing as refugees to Bosnia and Serbia. Few of these refugees have returned to their homes.

In a move to prevent a Croatian assault on Eastern Slavonia which could escalate into a war with Serbia, the Contact Group (a team of representatives from France, Germany, Russia, the UK and the US) negotiated an agreement in November 1995 that would allow the UN to implement the peaceful return of the region to Croatian rule. The UN Transition Authority in Eastern Slavonia (UNTAES) was established and the UN troops already deployed there increased in strength from 1,600 to about 5,000 and were reinforced with tanks, artillery and attack helicopters. These heavy weapons had on occasion to be deployed in a show of force to induce Serb elements to withdraw. Demilitarisation of Eastern Slavonia began in May 1996; Serb heavy weapons were taken to Serbia and the soldiers disbanded. A programme to 'buy back' the many small arms and ammunition held by most adults was instituted, funded by the Croat government; it resulted in nearly 10,000 weapons being handed in. UNTAES's civilian component supervised the establishment of local government and a Serbo-Croat police force. In April 1997 the region took part in the Croat national and local elections. On 15 January 1998 the UN handed full control of Eastern Slavonia back to the Croatian authorities. Both before and since then there has been a movement of Serbs, mainly those who had fled from the other two Serb enclaves, out of Eastern Slavonia; Serbs still complain of discrimination in the area.

A small UN operation, the UN Mission of Observers in Prevlaka (UNMOP), still continues to monitor the demilitarised zone and heavy weapons exclusion zone on the Prevlaka peninsula which controls access to the Bay of Kutor. In 1995 the Croats agreed to demilitarisation in return for the withdrawal of Yugoslav artillery from around Dubrovnik. In October 1998 the UN Police Support Group was replaced by the OSCE Police Monitoring Group, which was withdrawn from the Croatian Danube region, having successfully completed its mission, in December 2000.

Following the death of President Franjo Tudjman in December 1999, his Croatian Democratic Union (HDZ) was voted out of power and replaced by a centre-left coalition with Ivica Racan as prime minister. In the presidential elections Stepe Mesic, a democrat opposed to centralisation, was elected. The Croat government has voted to cooperate with the war crimes tribunal at the Hague and to hand over two indicted former Croat generals, but the decision to do so resulted in the resignation of four government ministers.

TRAVEL ADVICE
Neither the Foreign and Commonwealth Office nor the US State Department warn against travelling to Croatia but they do warn that there are still uncleared and unmarked mines.

BIBLIOGRAPHY AND WEBSITE
Tanner, Marcus, *Croatia: A Nation Forged in War*, Yale University Press, 1997

Croatian government: www.vlada.hr/english

Bosnia and Herzegovina

Population: 3,889,000 (Bosnian Muslim 44%, Serb 33%, Croat 17%)
Armed Forces: Forces of the Federation 24,000 – VF-B (Muslim) 16,800; VF-H (Croat) 7,200
    Republika Srpska Army: 14,000
    NATO SFOR: 20,000
Per Capita GDP: US$ 8,550
Currency: convertible mark

The origins of the Bosnian people are buried in ancient history but they are probably the descendants of the Illyrian tribes that lived in the mountainous and forested area between the two main north–south routes, one along the Dalmatian coast and the other running from Belgrade down the Morava valley. The Romans conquered these tribes in AD 9 and since then the purity of Bosnian blood has been diluted by the various invaders of the region: settlers from other parts of the Roman Empire, Goths (who drove out the Romans) in the fourth century, Mongol-Turkic Huns and Iranian Alans in the fourth and fifth centuries, and Slavs and Avars in the sixth century. In the 620s the Slavic Serb and Croat tribes arrived, the latter said to have been invited in by the Byzantine Emperor to evict the Avars.

Bosnia was situated on the western side of the boundary between the eastern and western parts of the Roman Empire when it was divided in 284. Then, after the expulsion of the Goths, it came under Byzantium, which was only able to exercise direct control infrequently. The Emperor Constantine made the first known reference to Bosnia, as the territory of Bosona, in 958. Byzantine control was re-established by Basil II in 1018 and Bosnia was then ruled alternately by Serb and Croat governors. Hungary, after taking Croatia, extended its rule into Bosnia in 1102 and periods of both Hungarian and Byzantine rule followed until 1180 when Bosnia achieved a form of independence. This it maintained, thanks to its difficult terrain, until it was conquered by the Ottomans in 1463. It then became the border region between the Ottoman and Austrian-Hungarian Empires.

During the Ottoman period conversion to Islam took place slowly over more than a hundred years, with some 40 per cent of the population being Muslim in 1548. There was no forced conversion, other than of boys who were conscripted into the Janissaries, though it was obviously advantageous in many ways to be Muslim. Both the Ottomans and the Hapsburgs brought in martial peoples such as Serbs and Vlachs to settle their border areas, further muddling the population of Bosnia. The Ottomans also settled *spahi* or cavalrymen with estates in return for their guaranteed availability for military duty. Such duty, depending on the size of the estate, might include the provision of additional manpower. Naturally *spahi* were Muslims. After a series of wars between the Ottomans and the Austrians and Venetians, Bosnia was occupied by Austria in 1878 and annexed in 1908. It remained so until the First World War. By then three distinct religious groups peopled Bosnia: Orthodox and Catholic Christians and Muslims. Only since the late nineteenth century have the

Orthodox Christians begun describing themselves as Serbs and the Catholics as Croats, regardless of their actual descent.

After the war Bosnia became part of the new Yugoslav kingdom. When that country was reorganised in 1921 into thirty-three *oblasts* or provinces six were Bosnian and together they conformed to Bosnia's previous borders. In 1929 ethnic divisions led the king to redivide the country into *banovina* or governorships which deliberately took no account of historical boundaries; Bosnian territory was divided between four *banovina*. The German occupation of the kingdom during the Second World War gave an added dimension to the centuries-old divisions as Yugoslavia was broken up; Bosnia and Herzegovina were included in a Nazi puppet state ruled by the Croat Ustashe. The Ustashe directed most of their efforts against the Serbian population and to a lesser extent against the Muslims who formed a Muslim Volunteer Legion for their defence. In late 1942 the Muslims appealed to the Germans to halt Ustashe action against them and offered to expand the Legion under German control. The Germans would not agree to Bosnian autonomy but took the opportunity to raise a Muslim SS division that later carried out reprisals against Serbs. By the end of the war many Muslims had also joined Tito's Partisans.

In post-war Yugoslavia Bosnia-Herzegovina was one of the six Federal republics. Its borders now enclosed an area in the north that included the Muslim-populated enclave around Bihac and a Serbian-dominated strip along the border with Croatia. The first step towards the recognition of Muslim national status came in May 1968 when the conference of the Central Committee of the League of Communists of Bosnia and Herzegovina concluded that 'the Muslims are a distinct nation'. The new Yugoslav constitution of 1974 passed a great deal of power to the individual republics and also recognised the Bosnian Muslims as a nationality; by then the Muslim proportion of the population had risen from 30.7 per cent in 1948 to nearly 40 per cent.

When the Communist Party collapsed in early 1990 various nationalist parties, all with different agendas, replaced it. Both Serbia and Croatia were seen as a threat to Bosnia and Herzegovina, though the Croatian president Franjo Tudjman opposed border changes mainly on account of the Serbian enclaves in Croatia. The Bosnian president Alija Izetbegovic, a Muslim, opposed Croatian and Slovenian independence as this would leave Bosnia at the mercy of Serbia. In May 1991 three Serbian-dominated areas of Bosnia declared themselves to be 'Serb Autonomous Regions' and Serbia began secretly supplying the Bosnian Serbs with arms. In September the Bosnian Serbs called on the Federal Army for protection and the army duly assisted in establishing the borders of the Serb Autonomous Region of Herzegovina. The European Community's Badinter Arbitration Commission recommended that a referendum be held in Bosnia before the EC considered its recognition. In the referendum, which most Serbs boycotted, 64 per cent of the country voted almost unanimously for independence and the EC recognised this in April 1992.

Almost immediately the Serbs began the process known as ethnic cleansing, evicting the Muslim populations from a number of towns. Their main aim was to link together the Serbian enclaves by controlling the area between the army base at Banja Luka in Bosnia and the Serb-occupied areas of Croatia to the west and Serbia to the east, as well as a strip of territory running down the eastern border to the Serb enclave in eastern Herzegovina. In April 1992, when Milosevic declared a new federal state of Yugoslavia comprising only Serbia and Montenegro, he also transferred the Bosnian-Serb members of the Federal Army with their weapons to the Bosnian-Serb Army (BSA).

A great many lessons can be learnt from the way the Bosnian crisis was handled. Many countries based their policy not on what was best for Bosnia but on either domestic political concerns or the implications for other foreign policy matters. For example, the EC initially opposed the break-up of Yugoslavia because of the effect this might have on the disintegrating Soviet Union. The US called for a policy of lifting the arms embargo on the Bosnian Muslims and carrying out air strikes against the Serbs but was not willing to

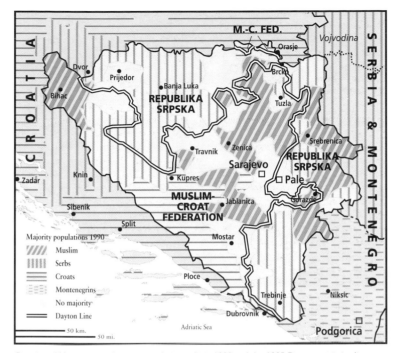

Bosnia and Herzegovina showing population split in 1990 and the 1995 Dayton armistice line

commit ground troops; the Europeans, with troops already on the ground in Bosnia, strongly opposed this policy. The Contact Group worked out its political settlement plan without consulting UNPROFOR and then presented it on a 'take it or leave it' basis. The UN gave UNPROFOR unrealistic mandates and then failed to provide the resources, usually sufficient troops, to enable them to be carried out successfully – for example, as in the case of the 'safe' areas. Once bombing was accepted as necessary there was disagreement between NATO and the US, both of which wanted to carry out strategic bombing, and UNPROFOR, which required tactical bombing on a scale sufficient to be counted as the minimum use of force.

The Croat success in recovering territory from the Serbs, both in Croatia and in Bosnia, combined with British and French artillery immediately engaging anyone firing on Sarajevo; NATO bombing, and NATO bombing and the effects of sanctions on Serbia, brought about the Dayton conference in November 1995. The military tasks set by Dayton were quickly achieved: NATO deployed a strong presence known as the Implementation Force (IFOR) and renamed the Stabilisation Force (SFOR) a year later, the two sides were separated and heavy weapons returned to barracks. Although the state presidency consists of three members – one Bosnian Muslim, one Croat and one Serb – the country is virtually partitioned between the Muslim-Croat Federation and the Republika Srpska.

Since Dayton a large number of refugees and displaced persons have managed to return home. Some 70,000 Bosnian Muslims have returned to Srpska but only 118 went to Srbrenica and 144 to Goradze; 80,000 Serbs have returned to Serbia and Montenegro, but by no means all. Over 227,000 refugees have returned from other countries but 48,000 still remain to be repatriated. There are also 133,000 displaced persons still in Serbia, 19,000 in Croatia and 10,000 in Montenegro..

TRAVEL ADVICE
FCO: Warns of the danger of landmines.
State: Avoid crowds and keep a low profile.

BIBLIOGRAPHY AND WEBSITES

Bildt, Carl, *Peace Journey: The Struggle for Peace in Bosnia*, Weidenfeld & Nicholson, 1998
Carter, F.W. and Norris, H.T. (eds), *The Changing Shape of the Balkans*, SOAS/GRC Geopolitics Series, UCL Press, 1996
Holbrooke, Richard, *To End a War*, Random House, 1998
Malcolm, Noel, *Bosnia: A Short History*, Macmillan, 1994
O'Shea, Brendan, *Crisis at Bihac: Bosnia's Bloody Battlefield*, Sutton, 1998
Rose, Michael, *Fighting for Peace*, Harvill Peace, 1998
Sims, Brendan, *Unfinest Hour: Britain and the Destruction of Bosnia*, Allan Lane, 2001

Bosnia Report: www.bosnia.org.uk
Bosnia Link: www.dtic.dla.mil/bosnia
Bosnian Ministry of Foreign Affairs: www.mvp.gov.ba
International Criminal Tribunal for the Former Yugoslavia: www.un.org/icty
NATO Stabilisation Force: www.nato.int.sfor
OSCE Mission to Bosnia: www.oscebih.org
UNHCR: www.unhcr.ba

Macedonia

Author's Note: The Former Yugoslav Republic of Macedonia (FYROM) is referred to as Macedonia here.

Population: 2,322,000 (Macedonian 61%, Albanian 22% (they claim more), Turkish 4%, Romany 3%, Serb 2%)
Armed Forces: 16,000, Paramilitary Police 7,500
Paramilitary: Non-Government Paramilitary Lions of Macedonia 2,000
Opposition: National Liberation Army (NLA) (Armata Kombetare Shqiptare) 4,000+
Foreign Forces: NATO Operation Amber Fox 700, KFOR logistics 2,500
Per Capita GDP: US$ 3,900
Currency: dinar

The history of Macedonia is inextricably linked to that of Greece. However, while the Macedonians never considered themselves to be Greeks, the latter now claim that the former *were* a Greek tribe, despite the ancient Greek view that they were barbarians. It was Philip II, father of Alexander the Great, who formed Macedonia into a strong state during the fourth century BC. He extended the state but not at the expense of the Greeks with whom he forged agreements so that among his titles was Hegemon of the Greek League. Alexander conquered a vast empire that broke up on his death. The various generals, who had inherited parts of the empire, were constantly at war, from which Macedonia (including Greece) kept apart. The origins of the people now living in Macedonia and calling themselves Macedonians are hard to define. For some thousands of years the population of Macedonia and Thrace had a different culture from those people living to the south, in the area occupied by the Greek-speaking tribes in the third century BC.

'Geographic' Macedonia refers to the area between the Sar Mountains and Mount Skopska Crna Gora to the north, the Rila and Rhodope mountains to the east, the Aegean coast as far west as Mount Olympus in the south, and the Pindus Mountains and Lakes

Ohrid and Prespa in the west. The Bulgarian portion is known as Pirin Macedonia and the Greek as Greek Macedonia.

Geographic Macedonia fell to the Romans and after the split between Rome and Byzantium it became part of the Byzantine Empire. It was conquered by the Bulgars in the seventh century but was recovered and ruled by Byzantium from 1014 until 1230. The next hundred years witnessed several changes of rule and splits in the region, with the Serbs taking Skopje in 1282. By 1346 the Serb Empire stretched from the Danube in the north to central Greece in the south, and from the Drina in the west to Thrace in the east. The Ottomans gained control over Macedonia and the Balkans following their defeat of the Serbs at Kosovo Polje in 1389, and Macedonia remained part of the Ottoman Empire until the Balkan Wars of 1912–13.

After the Turkish-Russian War the 1878 Treaty of Stefano created a 'Greater Bulgaria' which included Macedonia and part of Greece. A few months later the treaty was overturned; the Congress of Berlin redrew the borders and created Greater Macedonia. This new border arrangement pleased none of Macedonia's neighbours and was a constant source of friction and conflict. After the Balkan War of 1912–13 the Treaty of Bucharest divided Macedonia between its neighbours Bulgaria, Greece and Serbia. After the First World War Serbian Macedonia became part of the newly formed Kingdom of the Serbs, Croats and Slovenes, renamed Yugoslavia in 1921. Macedonia plus part of Serbia was one of the *banovina* created by the king in 1929 in an effort to override historical boundaries and ethnicities. During the Second World War Macedonia was split between Italian-controlled Albania and Bulgaria. After the Second World War it became one of the republics of the Yugoslav Federation.

With such a history of changing borders and population movements it is not surprising that Macedonia has a very mixed population. According to a census in 1994 it comprised a majority of Macedonians (70 per cent, including about 40,000 Macedonian-speaking Muslims), and minorities of Albanians (22.5 per cent; they complain their numbers were under-represented in the 1991 census), Turks (4 per cent), Roma or Gypsies (2 per cent) and Serbs (2 per cent). There is also a small number of Bulgarians. People of Macedonian origin still live in Bulgaria but the numbers registered at censuses there have dropped considerably since 1946, probably on account of the fact that Bulgaria no longer recognises a separate Macedonian nationality. Macedonians also live in Greece where there is controversy over the number of Slav Macedonians. It is also not surprising that there is debate about who exactly the Macedonians are. Certainly the Macedonians of FYROM are Slavs, more probably of the Bulgar line than the Serb.

When the Yugoslav Federation broke up, Greek opposition to the use of the name Macedonia delayed its international recognition until the compromise name of the Former Yugoslav Republic of Macedonia (FYROM) was agreed upon. Greek opposition to the name may appear petty but there are valid reasons for it. There is bitterness stemming from the Greek civil war of 1948 in which many Slav-speaking Greeks joined the communist guerrilla army ELAS; many went into exile and gained positions of importance in Macedonia. Nor did FYROM help matters by printing banknotes showing a historic building in Thessalonika and by using Alexander the Great's symbol, the star of Vergina, on the national flag. The Greeks also fear that allowing the country to be called Macedonia might kindle expansionist flames for other parts of historic Macedonia.

In a worst-case scenario, civil war in FYROM could well involve Albania, Bulgaria and Serbia and might even drag in Greece and Turkey. In November 1992 FYROM's President Kiro Gligorov requested the UN to deploy observers to the country. After reconnaissance it was decided to deploy a battalion of 700 men plus 35 military observers and 26 civil police monitors; in July 1993 the UN Nordic battalion was reinforced by 300 US troops. The UN force was known as the UN Preventive Deployment Force (UNPREDEP). There have been a number of border incidents but the UN presence prevented any escalation. At the UNSC the Chinese vetoed the further extension of UNPREDEP's mandate following Macedonia's establishment of diplomatic relations with Taiwan in January 1999.

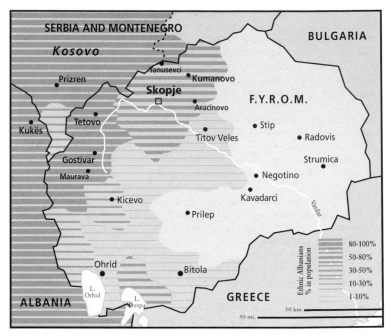

Former Yugoslav Republic of Macedonia

UNPREDEP's role was then assumed, unofficially, by the troops assembled in Macedonia as an extrication force for the unarmed Organisation for Security and Cooperation in Europe (OSCE) 'verifiers' in Kosovo.

A flood of some 300,000 refugees from Kosovo began to stream into Macedonia shortly after NATO's bombing campaign began in March 1999. There were some ugly scenes at the border as the Macedonian authorities tried to regulate the flow into the country and thousands had to spend days in the open waiting to be admitted. Humanitarian agencies helped by NATO troops erected a number of large camps for the refugees and organised measures to meet their feeding and medical needs. There were fears that the alteration to the ethnic balance in Macedonia, even for a short period, would destabilise the country. When Milosevic finally gave in and the bombing stopped on 10 June some refugees began to return to Kosovo immediately, far sooner than was expected or planned. Within weeks virtually all the refugees had gone home.

Although there were some NATO troops in Macedonia, they were mainly logistic units to support NATO's Kosovo Force (KFOR) and did not patrol the border as UNPREDEP had done. The Kosovan Albanians soon became aggressive, initially in Albanian-populated areas of Serbia, and then began supplying and encouraging Albanians in Macedonia to rebel against the government. A militant group called Armata Kombetare Shqiptare (AKSh) or the Albanian National Army was first noted in January 2000 when its members killed four policemen in the village of Aracinovo. The aim of the AKSh is to free Albanians from Slav domination either in a state comprising all Yugoslav Albanians or even in a greater Albanian state. More moderate Albanian political parties, such as the Democratic Party of Albanians which forms part of Macedonia's governing coalition, are calling for a greater role for Albanians in the country's bureaucracy and police.

AKSh activity increased dramatically in early 2001, particularly but not exclusively in the mountain villages around Tanusevci, close to the border with Kosovo. Mines have been laid, a helicopter shot at and police attacked. In March that year US troops of KFOR cooperated with the Macedonian army in an assault on the rebels. A day later the rebels attacked a police convoy. The Macedonian army is mainly made up of poorly trained conscripts and so the main tactic for engaging the rebels has been to attack their villages with artillery and helicopter strikes. This has caused another flood of refugees as the local population seeks safety. NATO has stepped up its patrolling and surveillance of the border in an attempt to stop resupply and reinforcement of the AKSh from Kosovo.

Great efforts have been made to establish a cease fire and peace talks; NATO's Secretary General, Lord Robertson, and the EU's High Representative for Common Foreign and Security Policy, Javier Solana, have visited the region on several occasions, while the EU and the US have also appointed special envoys. It is difficult to keep track of the many cease fire offers, unilateral cease fires and agreed cease fires, all of which have been violated soon after they came into effect. Nor can blame for such violations be apportioned easily as both government forces and Albanian militias seem equally guilty; whoever fires the first round, the other responds with speed. Although the fighting continued virtually uninterrupted, however, there was some political progress and a coalition government including the two main Albanian parties was formed.

An agreement with NATO and the European Union was reached in which NATO force would supervise AKSh disarmament and the government would alter the constitution to give Albanians the right to be considered a constituent nationality and to make their language official. Such changes could lead to a division in the country between those parts dominated by an Albanian population and those where the Slavs are in the majority. NATO duly collected some weapons and rounds of ammunition and after some delay the government amended the constitution, although not initially to the full extent agreed to. The collection of weapons, codenamed Operation Essential Harvest, took place between 22 August and 26 September 2001. Some 3,500 troops were provided by 11 NATO countries and they gathered 3,875 weapons (including four tanks and APCs and 160 support weapons such as mortars and anti-tank weapons) together with 400,000 rounds of ammunition. In addition, NATO had seized 3,300 weapons and 73,000 rounds of ammunition as these were being smuggled out of Kosovo.

The Macedonian parliament adopted the constitutional changes giving the Albanian population a greater role in the police, education and parliament on 16 November 2001. The president announced an amnesty for all former guerrillas. On 21 November the moderate Social Democratic Alliance of Macedonia left the national unity government. A small (700-strong) NATO force, Task Force Fox, has remained in Macedonia to protect the group of peacekeeping monitors being provided by the EU and OSCE. It is said that the AKSh are rearming, notably with shoulder-fired surface-to-air missiles, paid for by money gained by drug-trafficking.

Despite all international efforts the situation in Macedonia remains fragile and following the kidnapping of five Macedonians by ethnic Albanians a fresh round of violence is feared.

TRAVEL ADVICE
FCO: Exercise caution in northern and western border regions, particularly in Gostivar and Tetovo.
State: Defer all travel.

BIBLIOGRAPHY AND WEBSITES
Ackermann, Alice, *Making Peace Prevail: Preventing Violent Conflict in Macedonia*, Syracuse University Press, 2000
Danforth, Loring, *The Macedonian Conflict*, Princetown University Press, 1995
Pettifer, James (ed.), *The New Macedonian Question*, Macmillan, 1999
Poulton, Hugh, *Who Are the Macedonians?*, Hurst, 1995

Tziampris, Aristotle, *Greece, Europe's Political Cooperation and the Macedonian Question*, Ashgate, 2000

Balkan Stability Pact: www.stabilitypact.org
International Crisis Group: www.crisisweb.org
Macedonian Information Agency: www.mia.com.mk/webang.asp
Macedonian Ministry of Information: www.sinf.gov.mk
NATO Allied Forces Southern Europe: www.afsouth.nato.int

Kosovo

Population: 1,700,000 (Albanians 1,615,000, Serbs 90,000)
Armed Forces: Kosovo Protection Corps 5,000
Opposition: Kosovo Liberation Army – officially disbanded
Foreign Forces: Kosovo Force (KFOR) NATO-led 42,500, plus 7,500 logistic troops in Macedonia, Albania and Greece

The region known today as Kosovo is the southernmost part of Serbia. Albania lies to the south-west and Macedonia to the south and south-east. It is surrounded by mountains that gave it valuable strategic importance in that whoever held Kosovo could threaten movement both to its south and its north. The region's name derives from Kosovo Polje, or plain, which lies to the south-west of Pristina. A tremendous battle was fought there in 1389 between the Serbs under Prince Lazar and the Ottomans of Murat. Little is known of the course of the battle other than that it was intense and both sides suffered heavy casualties. Both Murat and Lazar were killed. Although the Ottomans were left in command of the field they soon withdrew and so it is uncertain whether the outcome was an Ottoman victory, a draw or even, as in some accounts, a Serbian victory. Ever since it was fought the battle has held an emotional place in Serbian history – not quite a myth but certainly an epic occurrence never to be forgotten and now the source of Serbian determination to keep control of the region.

It is not possible to say with any certainty who the original inhabitants of Kosovo were but they must have been assimilated by both Serbian Slavs and by Albanians who crossed into the region from neighbouring areas. Nor is there any certainty over the origins of the Albanians; one theory is that they could be the descendants of the Albanoi tribe referred to by Ptolemy, Alexander's general, in the second century. It has also been argued that they could be descended from either the Illyrians or Thracians, two of the earliest inhabitants of the Balkans. Counter-arguments refute both these possibilities. But whoever inhabited Kosovo first, it was not the Serbs, whose control stopped at the Kopaonik Mountains. They did not take control of Kosovo until the late twelfth century. Before then the area was under Bulgarian or Macedonian rule from the 850s to 1014 when Byzantine rule was re-established by Emperor Basil. The Serbs ruled Kosovo only from the 1180s – when it was taken by the Grand Zupan, Stefan Nemanja – to the 1450s when the Ottomans conquered the region.

In 1689 the Austrians conquered and occupied Kosovo but were forced out the following year by the Ottomans who went on to take Belgrade. It is claimed that as many as 500,000 Serbs may have fled with the retreating Austrians, further adding to the Kosovo Serbian myth. In 1876 the Serbs, in alliance with the Russians, who had declared war on the Ottomans, managed to advance into Kosovo and were only halted by the Ottoman–Russian armistice of January 1878. The Treaty of San Stefano completed by Russia and the Ottoman Empire in March 1878 created a Greater Bulgarian state and gave northern Kosovo to the Serbs. The treaty was unacceptable to the other European powers who replaced it with the Congress of Berlin that cut Bulgaria down in size, restoring Macedonia and the *vilayet* of Kosovo to the Ottomans.

At a meeting of the Albanian clan chiefs in 1878 a 'League' was formed but initially it was totally loyal to the Ottoman sultan. In September that year, Mehmet Ali, an official sent to demarcate the new border between Montenegro and Kosovo, was killed when fighting broke out; this brought to an end cooperation between the Ottoman government and the League which called for a single Albanian *vilayet* to be formed. During this time the Serbs had introduced ethnic cleansing and expelled some 60,000 Muslim families to Macedonia and 70,000 Albanians to Kosovo. As the Muslim population grew so Serbs emigrated to Serbia.

Many of the important events leading to the Albanian declaration of independence from the Ottoman Empire in November 1912 took place in Kosovo. A revolt broke out aimed at overturning the 'Young Turk' regime; by late June 1912 the revolt had spread to many parts of Kosovo and to Tirana and Shkodra. By the end of July most of Kosovo had been taken and some 45,000 men assembled; a list of demands was submitted and when no reply was received the force marched on Skopje. In August the majority of the demands were agreed to and an Albanian state was to be formed within the Ottoman Empire. The Albanian success encouraged other Balkan states to rebel against the Ottomans. The Serbs and Bulgarians secretly agreed the division of the territory they proposed to capture; the Greeks and Montenegrins joined the alliance. The Serbs delivered arms to Kosovan Serbs, border incidents were manufactured and reports of Albanian atrocities spread. The Serbian attack began on 16 October. The Albanians resisted strongly but they and the Ottomans were heavily outnumbered and the Serbs and Montenegrins completed the conquest of Kosovo by early November. The Serbs pressed on until they reached the Adriatic. They had massacred thousands of people on their way. The European powers then deliberated the future of the territorial changes; eventually Albania became independent, but crucially Serbia held Kosovo.

During the First World War the Albanians supported the Austro-Hungarians. Afterwards the Serbs took revenge for Albanian hostility during their withdrawal of 1915 and some 6,000 Albanians were killed in the first two months of 1919. The Serbs did not allow Kosovan schools to teach in Albanian and refused to recognise Albanians as a national minority; at the same time Kosovo suffered a campaign of colonisation by Serbs from other parts of Yugoslavia and land was confiscated. A number of revolts took place in the early 1920s but all were ruthlessly suppressed. In the 1929 redivision of Yugoslavia into *banovina* Kosovo was split between three: one which included Montenegro; one with eastern Serbia; and one with Macedonia. The *banovina* were governed by hard-line Serbs.

There is a legal argument against Kosovo being part of Serbia as the 1913 Treaty of London which recognised this move was never ratified by Serbia, nor was a Grand National Assembly called to agree the new borders of Serbia, as required by the Serbian constitution of 1903. It is claimed that the Treaty of Bucharest, also of 1913, cannot legalise the transfer of former Ottoman territory as the Ottoman government was not a party to the Treaty. It is also argued that the 1925 Treaty of Ankara signed by Turkey and the newly formed Yugoslavia can be used as a basis for claiming that Kosovo is Yugoslavian rather than Serb. In fact the Kosovans have been treated as Yugoslav citizens since 1918, but as Albanian-speaking Serbs rather than as Albanians.

During the Second World War most of Kosovo was incorporated into Albania, which had been captured by the Italians. The Kosovans took the opportunity to drive out a number of Serbian and Montenegrin colonists. When Italy capitulated in September 1943 the Germans quickly took over in the enlarged Albania, which they recognised as an independent state; the Kosovans again took advantage of the situation to expel more colonists. Kosovans played little part in the Yugoslav resistance movements. At the end of the war the German withdrawal route from Greece and Albania was through Kosovo and some 5,000 Albanians fought with the German rearguard against the advancing Bulgarian and Soviet forces.

Constitutional events immediately after the war also provided ground for legal argument over Kosovo's status. It was established as the Autonomous Region of Kosovo-Metohija by the People's Assembly of Serbia in September 1945, two months before the communist Popular Front won the Yugoslav-wide elections and then passed a new constitution confirming the six-republic federation with two autonomous provinces in Serbia. In the 1950s and early 1960s Kosovo saw the Serb minority population (27 per cent) given preference in many fields: communist party membership, official positions and industrial employment. At the same time Kosovo received far less development investment than other areas. After Tito's first visit to Kosovo in March 1967 improvements were made and changes to the 1963 constitution established the territory as a federal legal entity. The constitution of 1974 awarded both Kosovo and Voyvodina equivalent status to the republics and direct representation on federal bodies, including one representative on the collective Presidency of Yugoslavia (the republics had two representatives).

The death of Tito in 1980 was followed by an Albanian revolt in Kosovo in 1981 which was brutally suppressed. Slobodan Milosevic used the situation of the Serb minority in Kosovo in his campaign for election as President of Serbia in 1987. Kosovo experienced a tightening of Serb control with the press being brought into line, the police presence increased, many professionals dismissed and politicians either silenced or imprisoned. Milosevic pressed for a new Serbian constitution, which abolished the autonomous status of Kosovo and Voyvodina, and in July 1990 the Serbs dissolved the Kosovan Assembly and government. The local law court was abolished and the judges removed. In 1992 the Kosovans held their own elections, not recognised by the Serbs, and chose Ibrahim Rugova as the president of the 'Republic of Kosovo', which set up a parallel apparatus to the Serbian administration.

KFOR Contributing Countries

NATO	Non NATO
Belgium	Argentina
Canada	Austria
Czech Rep.	Azerbaijan
Denmark	Bulgaria
France	Finland
Germany	Georgia
Greece	Ireland
Italy	Lithuania
Netherlands	Morocco
Norway	Russia
Poland	Slovakia
Portugal	Slovenia
Spain	Sweden
Turkey	Switzerland
United Kingdom	Ukraine
United States	United Arab Republics

For the next five years Rugova campaigned for the return of the pre-1990 autonomy but was resolute in pursuing this without resort to violence, despite the growing militancy of the Serb police and the resettling of 19,000 Serbian refugees in early 1996. While there had been instances previously of Albanian attacks on Serbian police, the Kosovo Liberation Army first made its presence known in February 1996 when it organised a number of bomb attacks at five camps for Serb refugees from the Krajina region of Croatia. Until December 1997 KLA operations were confined to isolated attacks on the police and their stations, but after the rebellion in Albania in March 1997 the KLA received many weapons from the hundreds of thousands looted from the arsenals there. KLA attacks became more daring and by early 1998 included the over-running of police stations and attacks on police patrols and road checkpoints. Over fifty policemen and officials were killed. By March 1998 Serbia had had enough and considered that the attacks it had suffered justified the taking of tough measures to suppress the KLA, for whom complete independence had become the goal.

Strong contingents of the Yugoslav Army and the paramilitary police moved into Kosovo. Wherever there was an excuse villages were shelled, cleared of their remaining population, looted and set alight. While the KLA fought back as best they could, thousands of refugees fled into the hills and forests. The western world was appalled but decided there was little they could do. Plans for deploying a NATO force along the Albanian side of the border were abandoned as being both difficult to implement and probably aiding the Serbs more than the Albanians. On 15 June 1998, in a show of strength, a NATO force of over eighty aircraft from thirteen countries carried out air manoeuvres over Albania close to the border with Kosovo. It was thought likely that launching air strikes against Serb forces in order to stop the fighting would be seen as taking sides in the dispute.

In October US negotiator Richard Holbrooke, backed by the threat of NATO air strikes, persuaded both sides to accept and maintain a cease fire. The Serbs were to withdraw their special police forces and army units, other than those normally based in Kosovo which were to return to their barracks. The OSCE was to establish an unarmed team of 2,000 observers (to be called 'verifiers'). At the same time NATO agreed to deploy a force to Macedonia which would be on standby to rescue the verifiers should they become the targets of either side. The Holbrooke agreement also included provisions for early elections. By December

Kosovo, showing its borders in 1919, 1939 and today

the cease fire was in danger of breaking down completely as the Serbs set ambushes along the Albanian border and Serb officials were murdered in isolated incidents.

The discovery, on 15 January 1999, of the massacre of forty-five Albanian Kosovan men, all unarmed and in plain clothes, outraged the US and European states. Two senior NATO generals were sent to Belgrade to warn President Milosevic that such behaviour by the Serbs was unacceptable. At about the same time the Serbs ordered the expulsion of the head of the OSCE verifiers and denied the Chief Prosecutor of the UN War Crimes Tribunal entry into Kosovo. An ultimatum was issued to both the Serbs and the Albanian Kosovans that they must agree to a Contact Group peace plan or suffer NATO air attacks. The meeting began at Rambouillet on 14 February and the talks had to be extended twice, first to the 20th and then to the 23rd. Meanwhile NATO air forces began to concentrate for the operations that would be carried out if agreement could not be reached and advance units of a NATO peacekeeping force, to be deployed if agreement *was* reached, started to arrive in Macedonia. On the 23rd the Serbs were still refusing to allow NATO troops into Kosovo and the Kosovans were still unhappy about there being no commitment to a referendum on independence in three years' time. As the Kosovans had not signed the agreement (and as bombing them was impractical) the talks ended without a settlement but the Kosovans agreed to the plan in principle and were to return in two weeks' time after it had been discussed in Kosovo.

The Kosovans duly signed the peace agreement on 18 March but the Serbs showed no signs of agreeing to the deployment of NATO peacekeepers and the meeting was terminated. NATO, without a specific UN mandate as this would certainly have been vetoed by Russia, then embarked on a bombing campaign to force Milosevic to agree to its terms. No doubt Milosevic expected the Alliance to crack before he did, while some optimists believed the bombing would give Milosevic an excuse for caving in without losing face. In the event, despite the adverse publicity, NATO continued bombing for seventy-eight days. Milosevic eventually agreed to new terms not as intrusive for Serbia as those proposed at Rambouillet; by then some 840,000 refugees had been forced out of Kosovo into Albania and Macedonia and their homes had been destroyed. NATO troops (Kosovo Force or KFOR) and others, including Russians, entered Kosovo on 12 June 1999 and began the task of rebuilding the province. A fresh round of ethnic cleansing ensued as vengeful Albanians forced out most of the Serb population.

A number of international organisations now assumed responsibility for Kosovo's rehabilitation. The UN established the UN Interim Administration Mission in Kosovo (UNMIK) which had authority over the people and territory of Kosovo, including all legislative and executive powers. Its main tasks were to promote the establishment of autonomy and self-government, to perform basic civil administrative functions and to support reconstruction and disaster relief (this last was to be the responsibility of UNHCR). Reconstruction and development was to be managed by the European Union, and responsibility for democratisation and institution-building was given to OSCE. The long-term status of Kosovo was not addressed but it was assumed that the territory would remain part of Serbia.

Although the KLA was officially disbanded in September 1999, as required by UNSC Resolution 1244, armed violence by Albanian Kosovans against Kosovan Serbs, mainly in the north-eastern town of Mitrovica, and across the border into Serbia where there is an Albanian population, has continued despite NATO's efforts. The Military Technical agreement signed on 9 June 1999 required Serb military withdrawal not just from Kosovo but also from a 5km-wide belt on the Serbian side of the border. The purpose of this belt was to avoid clashes between NATO and Serbian forces, but Kosovan Albanians took advantage of the demilitarised zone by training former KLA elements there, now known as the Liberation Army of Presevo, Medvedja and Bujanovac (UCPMB). NATO was unable to stop them as its forces could not cross the frontier, but greater efforts were made to seal the border – a difficult task. Serbian efforts to restore order in the strip led to disagreement with NATO. Eventually, in March 2001, and only after the fall of Milosevic, NATO agreed that Serbian forces should re-enter the border strip and take control there, and this took place in May that year without conflict. As well as attempting to prevent KLA men crossing into the Serbia border area, KFOR has also had to take similar action along the border with Macedonia where Albanian rebels, with support from Kosovo, have been fighting the Macedonian government. NATO troops are often unfairly criticised but they undoubtedly operate under different principles. The British and French are seen as the most professional and the least averse to taking risks. In contrast US units take every possible precaution against suffering casualties, which makes them much less effective in the difficult terrain.

In May 2001 the UN authorised 'The Constitutional Framework for Provisional Self-Government in Kosovo'. It satisfies neither the Albanians – because it does not provide for a referendum on Kosovo's future status, the independence they expect – nor the Serbs – because it does not protect their interests. The Serbs are convinced that only the return of Serbian rule or the partition of the region can ensure that. The Framework provided for an Assembly, to be elected in November 2001, with 120 members with ten seats reserved for Serbian Kosovans and ten more for the other minorities in Kosovo. The Assembly will elect the president, who will appoint the prime minister. In January 2002, the moderate leader Ibrahim Rugova's party won the Assembly elections but with an insufficient majority to govern without forming a coalition. In the presidential election a number of assembly members boycotted the vote and although Rugova gained a majority it was ten short of the number needed for him to become president. In March he was elected with a large majority.

The long-term future of Kosovo is not yet decided. The agreement made with the UN and NATO confirms that Kosovo is a constituent part of Yugoslavia, and any UN resolution to alter its status is likely to be vetoed by Russia and China. However, sooner or later the Albanian Kosovans will press for independence and should it be granted then calls for a greater Albania are inevitable and that could destabilise the region again.

TRAVEL ADVICE

FCO: Advise against any travel for holidays and non-essential reasons. Avoid border areas and military areas. Avoid driving at night. State: Situation potentially dangerous; some danger from landmines; road conditions hazardous; incidents of violence continue to be reported.

BIBLIOGRAPHY AND WEBSITES

Judah, Tim, *Kosovo: War and Revenge*, Yale University Press, 2000
Malcom, Noel, *Kosovo: A Short History*, Macmillan, 1998
Veremis, Thanos (ed.), *Kosovo: Avoiding Another Balkan War*, University of Athens, 1998
Vickers, Miranda, *Between Serb and Albanian: A History of Kosovo*, Hurst, 1998
Weller, Marc, *The Crisis in Kosovo 1989–1999, from the dissolution of Yugoslavia to Rambouillet and the Outbreak of Hostilities*, Documents and Analysis Publishing, 1999

American Muslim Assistance, Kosovo Crisis Centre: http://amahelp.com/kosova
Balkan Peace, (University of Ottawa): www.uottawa.ca/associatio.balkanpeace
Kosovo Crisis Centre: www.alb-net.com
Independent International Commission on Kosovo: http://kosovocommission.org
NATO Kosovo Force: www.kforonline and www.nato.int/kosovo
UN Mission in Kosovo: www.un.org/peace/kosovo

Albania

Population: 3,028,000 (Muslim 70%, Albanian Orthodox 20%, Roman Catholic 10%, Greek 3%+)
Armed Forces: 27,000
Foreign Forces: NATO Logistics for Kosovo 2,400
Per Capita GDP: $US 5,539
Currency: leke

In ancient history this region was inhabited by Illyrians, but the identity of the original Albanians is disputed. They may have been descendants of the Albanoi tribe mentioned by Ptolemy, Alexander the Great's general, in the fourth century BC, or perhaps the descendants of the original Illyrians and Thracians. Alexander never conquered the independent Greek state of Epirus that stretched over today's north-west Greece and south-west Albania. Epirus remained neutral during the Persian and Peloponnesian Wars; its king, Pyrrhus, twice defeated the Romans but with very heavy losses (giving us the term 'Pyrrhic victory'). The region became part of the Roman province of Illyricum in AD 169 and then the Byzantine despotate of Epirus until 1347. For the next hundred years the whole region suffered a series of invasions by Bulgarians, Serbs, Venetians and finally the Ottomans who made Albania part of their Empire after the battle of Scutari in 1478. The hatred between the Serbs and Albanians started when Orthodox Serbs began persecuting Catholic Albanians.

The Albanians converted to Islam during the Ottoman occupation but always retained their Albanian nationality. Christians and Muslims both preserved their language, customs and laws. After the Russian–Ottoman war of 1876–8 the Albanians beseeched the Congress of Berlin to give them independence but they were to remain under Ottoman rule. The clan chiefs formed the League of Prizren in 1878; initially loyal to the Ottoman sultan, it ended cooperation with the government after fighting broke out in Kosovo. The League called for a single Albanian *vilayet* to be formed but only Britain supported the claim and the leaders of the League were arrested and either executed or exiled.

The Turkish control of education, with Turkish schools for Muslims and Greek for Christians, ended with the 'Young Turks' revolution. An Albanian uprising began in 1910 and fighting continued for three years until the Turks agreed to autonomy for Albania, which then included Kosovo. Albanian success encouraged other Balkan states to rise up against the Turks. The Serbs and Bulgarians secretly agreed a division of the territory they intended to capture, and Greece and Montenegro joined their alliance. The Serb attack on the Turks and Albanians began in October 1912 and carried on until they had reached the Adriatic. The first Balkan War would have ended in December 1912 but for the overthrow of the government by the 'Young Turks'; in fact it was concluded in April 1913. The settlement agreed by the Treaty of London gave Albania its independence as Austria was determined that Serbia should not have access to the sea. Albania was not affected by the second Balkan War or the Treaty of Bucharest, also in 1913.

In the First World War the Albanians sided with the Austro-Hungarians, who drove the Serbian army south until it had withdrawn through Albania and was taken off by Allied shipping to Corfu. When the Serbs returned they killed over 6,000 Albanians in early 1919. The Italians invaded and annexed Albania in April 1939 and most of Kosovo was incorporated into Albania. After the Italian capitulation in 1943 the Germans occupied Albania and treated it as an independent state. The communists under Enver Hoxha formed a guerrilla resistance force and took over the country in 1946. Rural collectivisation, nationalisation of industry, the closure of mosques and churches, and one-party control were effected. Hoxha chose isolation and Albania became a closed country. It broke off relations with the Soviet Union and left the Warsaw Pact in 1961; similarly it broke with China in 1978. The Albanian population became impoverished. In 1967 it was declared the world's first atheist state.

There was some improvement in trade relations after Hoxha's death in 1985 but internal opposition to the regime did not develop until 1990 when plans were agreed to hold elections. The communists were returned to power in March 1991 and set about introducing reforms but not much was achieved. The state was very much dependent on

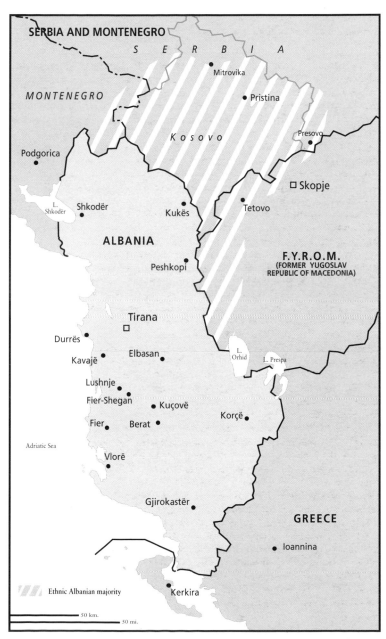

Albania

Italian aid. In 1991 Italian aid totalled $120 million, including food valued at $98 million. Emigration numbers soared after permission to leave was granted in May 1990 and soon got out of hand. There were violent scenes both at the departure ports and at the countries of arrival, mainly Greece and Italy, which did not welcome the influx. During 1991 an estimated 100,000 Greek Albanians crossed into Greece and some 40,000 other Albanians managed to reach Italy.

Elections in March 1992 saw the Democratic Party win a two-thirds majority and Dr Sali Berisha became president. One of the few people who had been allowed to travel outside Albania, he had enjoyed postgraduate studies in Paris and so had some experience of western democracy. By the summer of 1993 some improvements had been achieved and the majority of the people felt they were better off. At the same time there had been widespread fraud and corruption, the main manifestation of this being the 'pyramid' sales that lost many thousands their life savings and which helped to precipitate the violent upheaval in 1997 when army barracks and ammunition dumps were looted. Over 750,000 weapons and 1.5 billion rounds of ammunition are believed to have been stolen. Huge explosions at some arsenals scattered a large amount of unexploded ordnance over the country, subsequently causing civilian casualties. NATO sent a team of ammunition experts to survey the problem and to train the Albanian army in bomb-disposal techniques. In April 1997 Italy led an international force, 7,000-strong, from eight European countries to restore law and order. Operation Alba lasted until August 1997.

Currently three million people live in Albania and there are approximately another three million Albanians elsewhere in the Balkans – two million in Kosovo, 50,000 in Montenegro and 500,000 (maybe more) in Macedonia. Some 50,000 more live close to the border in Greece in an area known to Albanians as Cameria; there are also a large number, perhaps as many as 300,000, Albanian illegal immigrants elsewhere in Greece. There is a Greek minority living in southern Albania in the area they call Northern Epirus – a region that Greek nationalists consider should be theirs.

During the NATO operation in Kosovo Albania became one of the deployment areas for both ground troops and logistic support. (The latter still operate from Albania.) However, US Apache attack helicopters based in Albania were not used in the air campaign as they experienced difficulties in crossing the mountain range on the border. A large number of Kosovan Albanians crossed into Albania as refugees.

TRAVEL ADVICE

FCO: Advises against visiting the north-east border with Kosovo. Warns of crime on main roads leading to Greece. State: Warns of potential dangers of travel. High crime rate throughout country but particularly bad in Shkoder and the north and north-west.

WEBSITES

Albanian Ministry of Information: hhtp://mininf.gov.al/english

Russia and its Neighbours

This section examines the problems of Russia and its immediate neighbours in the Baltic and Transcaucasus, all countries that were once part of the Soviet Union. The problems of the North Caucasus are addressed separately. The question of the Japanese claims to recover the Kuril or Northern Islands is also discussed.

Russia

Population: 146,720,000 (Russian 81%, Tatar 4%, Ukrainian 3%, Chuvash 1%, Bashkir 1%, Belarussian 1%, Moldovan 1%)
Armed Forces: 977,000; Paramilitary: 409,000
Per Capita GDP: US$ 7,600
Currency: rouble

It took Russia some nine hundred years to acquire its empire, and it was further expanded by the Soviet Union immediately after the Second World War – but the Soviet Union broke up in 1991 in only a matter of weeks. While the west European states built up their overseas colonial empires, Russia concentrated on acquiring continental territory.

Although many different races had lived in the region in earlier times, the Russian nation seems to have been born when the East Slavs, who had settled in the river valleys of today's western Russia, Ukraine and Belarus, developed into a series of tribes in the fifth and sixth centuries. The Mongol Tatars first appeared in the region in 1223 and by 1240 they had seized the southern cities of Kiev and Chernigov. They ruled the region until 1480 when they agreed not to fight Ivan III; all the Tatar kingdoms had been conquered by 1554. Ivan III also created Muscovy, with Moscow as its capital. The Russians crossed the Urals and reached the Bering Sea in 1648, but their westward expansion met greater opposition. In 1721 they gained Estonia, Livonia (Latvia) and part of Karelia. Catherine II gained control of the northern Black Sea coast and the Crimea in the 1790s. (Russia's conquests of the North Caucasus and the Transcaucasus are described on pp. 60–4 and 64–9. The acquisition of Central Asia that took place between 1865 and 1900 is described on pp. 155–9.) The Russian revolution in 1918 led to the creation of the Union of Socialist Soviet Republics (USSR). Poland, Finland and the Baltic States gained their independence, the latter being brought back under Russian rule during the Second World War.

When the Soviet Union broke up into fifteen independent states in 1991 there were those who forecast the disintegration of the Russian Federation, which could result in civil war between Russians and ethnic minorities. So far, with the exception of the revolt in Chechnya, this has not occurred. The main problems facing Russia are corruption and the economy; neither should lead to disintegration. If anything, they should unite the country in its efforts to put things right. The division of Russia into regions and sub-regions is complicated and needs some explanation.

In the Soviet Union at the top level were the Union Republics, and these were the entities that became independent countries in 1991. Within the Russian Federation there

49 REGIONS

1. *Amur*	18. *Leningrad*	35. *Samara*	
2. *Arkhangelsk*	19. *Lipetsk*	36. *Saratov*	
3. *Astrakhan*	20. *Magadan*	37. *Smolensk*	
4. *Belgorod*	21. *Moscow*	38. *Sverdlovsk*	
5. *Bryansk*	22. *Murmansk*	39. *Tambov*	
6. *Chelyabinsk*	23. *Nizhni Novgorod*	40. *Tomsk*	
7. *Chita*	24. *Novgorod*	41. *Tula*	
8. *Irkutsk*	25. *Novosibirsk*	42. *Tver*	
9. *Ivanovo*	26. *Omsk*	43. *Tyumen*	
10. *Kaliningrad*	27. *Orel*	44. *Ulyanovsk*	
11. *Kaluga*	28. *Orenburg*	45. *Vladimir*	
12. *Kamchatka*	29. *Penza*	46. *Volgograd*	
13. *Kemerovo*	30. *Perm*	47. *Vologda*	
14. *Kirov*	31. *Pskov*	48. *Voronezh*	
15. *Kostroma*	32. *Rostov*	49. *Yaroslavl*	
16. *Kurgan*	33. *Ryazan*		
17. *Kursk*	34. *Sakhalin*		

21 REPUBLICS

50. *Adygeia*	66. *North Ossetia*
51. *Altai*	67. *Tatarstan*
52. *Bashkortostan*	68. *Tyva*
53. *Buryatia*	69. *Udmurt*
54. *Chechenya*	70. *Yakutia*
55. *Chuvash*	
56. *Daghestan*	
57. *Ingushetia*	
58. *Kabardino-Balkaria*	
59. *Kalmykia - Khalm Tangch*	
60. *Karachai-Cherkess*	
61. *Karelia*	
62. *Khakasia*	
63. *Komi*	
64. *Marii El*	
65. *Mordovia*	

The Regional Divisions of Russia

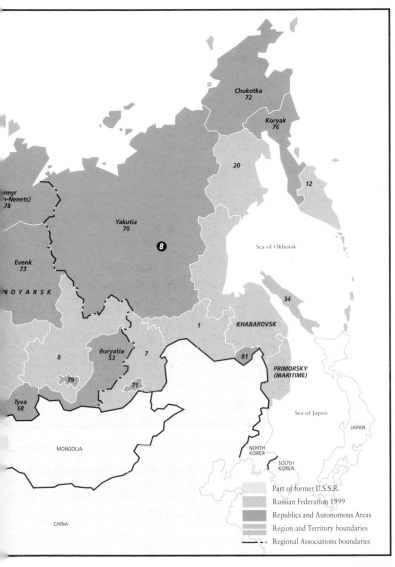

Chukotka
72

Koryak
76

20

12

Taimyr
(Dolgan-Nenets)
78

Yakutia
70

⑧

Evenk
73

Sea of Okhotsk

KRASNOYARSK

34

1   KHABAROVSK

Buryatia
53   7

8   81

PRIMORSKY
(MARITIME)

79

71

Tyva
68

Sea of Japan

JAPAN

MONGOLIA

NORTH
KOREA

SOUTH
KOREA

Part of former U.S.S.R.

Russian Federation 1999

Republics and Autonomous Areas

CHINA

Region and Territory boundaries

Regional Associations boundaries

11 AUTONOMOUS AREAS

71. Aga Buryat
72. Chukotka
73. Evenk
74. Khanty-Mansi
75. Komi-Permyak
76. Koryak
77. Nenets
78. Taimyr (Dolgan-Nenets)
79. Ust-Ordyn Buryat
80. Yamal-Nenets
81. Jewish Autonomous Region

6 TERRITORIES

82. Altai
83. Khabarovsk
84. Krasnodar
85. Krasnoyarsk
86. Primorsky (Maritime)
87. Stavropol

2 CITIES

88. Moscow
89. St. Petersburg

8 REGIONAL ASSOCIATIONS

❶ Central Russia
❷ Black Earth
❸ Greater Volga
❹ North West
❺ Urals
❻ North Caucasus
❼ Siberia
❽ Far East

were initially four differently named sub-divisions. The six largest regions of these are called *krais* or territory; the next group are the forty-nine *oblasts* or regions. There are also twenty-one autonomous republics and *oblasts*, mostly linked to an ethnic group although in only four is there a non-Russian ethnic majority, and the two major cities of Moscow and St Petersburg. Eight of the Republics are in the Caucasus. Each entity sends two representatives to the Federal Council or upper house of the Federal Assembly or parliament. Election to the Duma, the Lower House, is partly through regional constituencies and partly from party lists. Below this level come ten autonomous *okrugs* and the Jewish Autonomous *Oblast* in the far east; also having non-Russian ethnic populations, these are administratively subordinate to the region of which they form a part but constitutionally are equal and also send two representatives to the Council. In 1992 all these entities bar Chechnya and Tartarstan signed the Federation Treaty. The *krais* and *oblasts* believed themselves to be disadvantaged by the treaty, which gave the republics greater economic autonomy, and so some declared themselves republics in the hope of gaining the benefits of that status. Many of the entities have signed bilateral treaties with Moscow. Some are power-sharing agreements, others are concerned with fiscal matters; all give different advantages to the regional partner but virtually all give them a share of Federal funding.

When the Soviet Union delineated its internal borders it often deliberately excluded a part of the local ethnic nationality from its natural region, for example the split of the Ossetians between the Republic of North Ossetia in Russia and South Ossetia in Georgia. Boundaries were altered repeatedly throughout the history of the USSR for a variety of reasons. By the end of 1991 some 164 territorial and boundary disputes had been identified in the territory of the former Soviet Union. Many of these had an ethnic or nationality aspect. Of the new independent states only Belarus and Russia, and Latvia and Lithuania, did not have disputes with each other – all the others had claims against their neighbours.

In 1993 Boris Yeltsin abolished the regional Soviets and appointed governors to be the head of their regional administration. His aim was to exercise control by his ability to appoint and dismiss governors. However, a number of governors were regionally elected and by 1995 Yeltsin had had to agree to the election of both governors and leaders of legislatures. Governors became more concerned with their own power and the economy of their region than with following Moscow's policies. A larger threat to centralised rule came from the so-called 'elites' of oligarchs formed in each region by leading politicians, industrialists and financiers who were joined, and to some extent taken control of, by privatised business enterprises and criminal factions. They have managed to acquire major denationalised assets in their regions and have formed corporations that ensure they receive the profits. In the autonomous republics the 'elites' are usually members of the ethnic nationality. Governors and 'elites' are usually in alliance. The federal authorities still collect taxes and control the major utilities such as the gas and electrical power industries and the railways and so can influence regional economies to a degree by the level of subsidy each receives.

Some see the resurgence of the Cossacks as a potential source of trouble. The Cossacks are most probably descended from the Mongol or Tatar horsemen who invaded the southern valleys of the Dnieper, Don and Volga rivers in the mid-thirteenth century. Over the years they were employed on internal security and soon gained a reputation for ruthlessness and brutality. They enjoyed certain privileges, owning land and carrying arms for example, that were not allowed to the peasants. The Tatar character of the Cossacks changed over the years as those fleeing from authority joined their ranks; the Cossacks therefore became more Russian but of a particularly independent nature. Two Cossack groups were established in 1990 – the Union of Cossack Russians and the Union of Cossack Hosts in Russia and Abroad – and they set about re-establishing Cossack traditions and way of life. Though Cossacks have been eager to volunteer for service in war zones such as Chechnya, Ossetia and Tajikistan, they have not been as successful as in the past. They were often employed to do the government's 'dirty work', so allowing it to avoid responsibility. They have been employed as official vigilantes in Krasnodar and St Petersburg.

Russian populations living in the newly independent former Soviet Union republics were another possible source of confrontation. At one time it looked as if there would be a serious confrontation between Ukraine and Russia over the Crimea, which had been handed to Ukraine by President Khrushchev in 1954, together with a sizeable Russian population, to mark the 300th anniversary of the Russian–Ukrainian union. When those people deported by Stalin during the Second World War were restored to their original land by Khrushchev, the Crimean Tatars were not included. However, a large number are now returning; they are more separatist-minded than the Russian population there and would be the most likely cause of trouble within Ukraine. As the base for the Soviet Black Sea Fleet had to be shared between Russia and Ukraine, settlement of the issue had some urgency as the Russians demanded (and have been allowed) to retain control of major docks and naval facilities in Sebastopol.

The expected problems of the Russian population in Kazakhstan have not materialised, nor have those concerning the Russians in eastern Ukraine. Though many Russians might prefer to return to Russia this is not easy owing to the cost and shortage of housing. Only in the Transdniestr region of Moldova has the Russian, or rather the Soviet, population openly declared its wish – and indeed fought for its right – to remain Russian but this area had never been part of Romania, had had a Slav population for over a thousand years and had been taken by the Russians from the Ottomans. There is still a small Russian garrison and Dniestr has formed its own armed forces of between 5,000 and 10,000 men. A hot-bed of smuggling and a centre for money-laundering, it is also responsible for exporting small arms to trouble spots.

It had been forecast that Tartarstan (48.5% Tatar, 43.5% Russian) and Bashkyria (22% Bashkiri, 39% Russian, 28% Tatar) would be the most independence-minded areas. Both have Muslim majority populations and Tartarstan is the richest republic because of its oil which Bashkyria refines. Tartarstan replaced Cyrillic script with Latin, but later abandoned plans to issue its own passports. Bashkyria has said 'it was part and parcel of Russia'. It is suggested that the far east and north-west of Russia are the areas most likely to benefit from arrangements made directly with foreign powers, bypassing Moscow. A number of inter-regional economic zones have been established. However, even these more prosperous regions will still rely on the central government for subsidy. Nationalism is fuelled as much by economic prospects as by ethnic considerations. There have been some instances of ethnic violence in Tyva, Buratiya and Yakutia. Demands for ethnic separatism are not strong as there has been a good deal of inter-marriage and it is becoming harder to differentiate between Russians and the original ethnic nationals.

Vladimir Putin was elected president in March 2000. His first task was to attempt to restrict the power of the self-appointed 'elites' and to restore a stronger degree of centralisation. This he did by appointing seven governor-generals to oversee the seven new regional associations into which he has divided Russia; this scheme has had little success so far. A small number of rich men have fallen foul of the authorities; three are facing trial for corruption, and two leading oligarchs, Boris Berezovsky, who has oil and media interests, and Vladimir Gusinsky, a media potentate, have decided to live abroad. Putin won the support of the Duma for his other reforms: the Federation Council membership, for example, was to be reformed so that members are elected by the regional legislatures rather than regional governors and legislature leaders gaining automatic membership. The Kremlin has the power to dismiss regional governors, and they in turn will have the power to dismiss local leaders. As expected, the Federal Council initially voted against the reforms but two months later it voted for them. In return Putin set up the State Council comprising the eighty-nine regional governors, but it was never expected to have much real power. So far one regional governor, Yevgeni Nazdratenko of Primoriye, has been dismissed (for mismanaging his province's energy supply). There has been tax reform, too: income tax which had a top rate of 35 per cent now has a flat rate of 13 per cent, and the unpopular cash-flow tax has been reduced from 4 to 1 per cent. The economy has benefited from increased oil prices.

In the Soviet era the armed forces had enormous influence, not just in the USSR but across the world, on account of their size and weaponry. The break-up of the Soviet Union coupled with the force reductions required by the Conventional Armed Forces in Europe Treaty (CFE) resulted in a dramatic reduction in Moscow's armed strength. The task of meeting CFE's commitments fell more heavily on the Russians than on any other country as the demise of the Warsaw Pact and the unification of Germany required the withdrawal of all Soviet forces from eastern Europe. These comprised nineteen divisions in the former East Germany, two in Poland, four in Czechoslovakia and four in Hungary. When the Soviet Union broke up further withdrawals became necessary: five divisions from the Baltic States, two from Moldova and twelve from the Transcaucasian republics. The divisions in Belarus (ten) and Ukraine (twenty-two) remained where they were and became the armies of those countries. In 1990 the Soviet Union had 20,700 tanks, 14,000 artillery pieces and 6,600 combat aircraft west of the Urals: today the figures are 5,300, 6,100 and 2,600 respectively. Manpower and weapons have been greatly reduced, as has the generals' influence. President Putin has been able to take decisions that probably would not have been allowed before. The events of 11 September may have helped, but there have been no real Russian objections to the US withdrawal from the ABM Treaty or to its plans to keep troops in Central Asia.

In return, Russia has been given a special partnership arrangement with NATO. Russia will now be able to join NATO discussions but will not have the power to veto any decisions.

TRAVEL ADVICE

See section on North Caucasus.

BIBLIOGRAPHY AND WEBSITES

Alexseev, Mikhail (ed.), *Center-Periphery Conflict in Post-Soviet Russia: A Federation Imperilled*, Macmillan, 1999

Kolossov, Vladimir, *Ethno-Territorial Conflicts and Boundaries in the Former Soviet Union*, International Boundaries Research Unit, 1992

Nicholson, Martin, *Towards a Russia of the Regions*, International Institute for Strategic Studies, Adelphi Paper 330, 1999

Ure, John, *The Cossacks*, Constable, 1999

Russian Federation Government: www.government.gov.ru

Russian Information Agency: www.rian.ru/ria

Russian Military News Agency: www.militarynews.ru

Russian Ministry of Foreign Affairs. www.diplomat.ru

The Baltic States

	Estonia	Latvia	Lithuania
Population:	1,375,000	2,308,000	3,655,000
	Estonian 67%	Latvian 56%	Lithuanian 83%
	Russian 28%,	Russian 34%	Russian 8%
	Ukrainian 3%	Belarussian 5%	Polish 7%
	Beloruusian 2%	Ukrainian 3%, Polish 2%	Belarussian 2%
Armed Forces:	4,500	6,500	12,200
Per Capita GDP:	US$ 9,753	US$ 7,219	US$ 6,000
Currency:	kroon	lats	litas

The three Baltic States – Estonia, Latvia and Lithuania – only gained their independence at the end of the First World War. The territory had been fought over since the twelfth century and had been the objective of early Crusades. The Teutonic Order, the Swedes and the Poles have all ruled the region, as have the Lithuanians, who created their own empire in 1316, extending it further with the marriage of the Grand Duke to a Polish princess in 1386. After the partition of Poland in 1795 the three Baltic States became part of Russia, except for the southern part of Lithuania which became Prussian. Estonians differ ethnically from Latvians and Lithuanians in that they are of Finno-Ugric origin. Their ancestors arrived on the east Baltic coast around 2500 BC, while the Latvians and Lithuanians are descended from Balts who arrived in 600 BC and later inter-bred with East Slavs.

During the First World War the Baltic States were over-run by the Germans, Lithuania in 1915 and Latvia and Estonia in 1918. Only Estonia had suffered from Bolshevik administration since the 1917 revolution. Immediately after the end of the war Estonia supported the White Russians and advanced into Russia, seizing territory which was incorporated into an independent Estonia by the 1920 Treaty of Tartu. The land was recovered by the USSR in 1945, although Estonia still claims it. In 1918 Latvia was over-run by the Bolsheviks who were opposed by Germans and Latvians separately; eventually, with Estonian assistance, Latvia defeated both the Bolsheviks and the Germans. Lithuania was the scene of fighting between the Poles and the Bolsheviks, which finally resulted in Vilnius being left in Polish hands. It was not returned to Lithuanian control until 1940. In 1923 Lithuania occupied the Klaipeda district of East Prussia which remains part of its territory. Peace treaties were signed with the USSR and the three states were admitted to the League of Nations in 1922.

Baltic independence came to an end in 1940 following the Molotov–Ribbentrop Pact of 1939 which placed them in the Soviet sphere of influence. They were forced to sign military agreements and the Soviet Army moved in. Elections were held and the new parliaments each requested their state's inclusion in the USSR.

In June 1941 the Germans attacked the USSR and soon over-ran the Baltic States, helped to some extent by the Balts who hoped to regain their independence by revolting against the Soviets, they were to be disappointed. When the Soviet Union reoccupied the region Balt partisans waged a campaign from the forests, which continued in Lithuania until 1953. The western Allies did nothing to aid the Baltic States other than refusing to recognise Soviet sovereignty. Although there had been a Russian minority population in the Baltic States for centuries – mainly refugees from persecution in Russia – it was virtually exterminated by Stalin and a wave of new Russian settlement began in 1945. By 1989 the ethnic origin of the populations were: Lithuanians 79.6 per cent, Russians 9.4 per cent; Latvians 52 per cent, Russians 34 per cent; Estonians 61.5 per cent, Russians 30 per cent; the remaining numbers were made up of Poles, Jews, Belorussians, Ukrainians and Swedes.

Movement for independence began in Latvia in June 1987 when a group of dissidents, the 'Helsinki 86', demonstrated at the Freedom Monument in Riga on 14 June. Other demonstrations were held on 23 August, the anniversary of the Molotov–Ribbentrop Pact, and on 18 November, the anniversary of the Latvian declaration of independence in 1918. The police attacked the 2,000 protesters at Tallinn in November, and demonstrations subsequently spread to the other two states until attendance reached hundreds of thousands. By early 1990 all three Supreme Councils had passed a number of declarations but had not yet declared full independence from the Soviet Union.

On 11 March 1990 the Lithuanian Supreme Council declared its full independence and Vytautas Landsbergis was elected Head of State. The Soviet reaction was to arrest Lithuanian deserters from the Soviet army and to take over a number of Communist Party buildings; on 18 April it cut off the shipments of oil. The Soviet economic blockade was only called off after the Supreme Council agreed a moratorium on the declaration of independence. On 30 March the Estonian parliament voted for gradual secession from the USSR, and the Latvian Supreme Council made a declaration 'On the Restoration of Independence' on 4 May. The run-up to independence witnessed a number of attacks by Soviet airborne and OMON (Ministry of Interior) troops. In January 1991 paratroopers stormed the press centre and the television centre in Vilnius, leaving fifteen dead. OMON troops seized the Ministry of Interior in Riga and continually attacked Baltic border posts.

The map contains the following labels:

To Russia, 1945
From Germany to Lithuania, 1923
From Poland to Lithuania, 1937

FINLAND
Helsinki
Gulf of Finland
St Petersburg
Tallinn
ESTONIA
Baltic Sea
Parnu
Tartu
Lake Peipus
RUSSIA
Pskov
Gulf of Riga
Riga
Valmiera
Liepaja
Jelgava
LATVIA
Siauliai
Daugavpils
Klaipeda
Panevezys
Daugava
LITHUANIA
Kaliningrad
Kaunas
Vitebsk
RUSSIA
Vilnius
Elblag
BELARUS
Olsztyn
Suwalki
Nemunas
Minsk
POLAND
Grodno
100 km.
100 mi.
Baranovici
Bobrujsk

The Baltic States

The Baltic States did not help the situation by passing a number of laws discriminating against the ethnic Russian populations.

Following referenda in March 1991, Estonia and Latvia declared their independence on 20 and 21 August 1991 and Lithuania redeclared its independent status. These declarations were recognised by the USSR on 6 September. The three states were admitted to the UN in September.

For several reasons the withdrawal of Russian forces from the Baltic States took place slowly. The main reason was to maintain pressure on the Estonian and Latvian governments to grant full civil rights to the Russian minorities there. Russian forces had withdrawn from Lithuania by the end of 1993 and from Estonia and Latvia by 30 August 1994; agreement was reached for the Skrunda early warning radar to continue to operate until 1998 and then eighteen months was allowed for its dismantling, a process that was completed on 19 October 1999.

Russian influence during the Soviet Union's occupation of Estonia was greater than it was in the other two Baltic States. The Russian language was considered to be essential in the running of the country and so there was no incentive for Russians to learn Estonian. Around 28 per cent of the population were native Russian speakers and to achieve

Estonian citizenship they had to meet the requirements of the Language Law passed in 1995; they must also have been resident in Estonia for five years and have to pass an elementary test on Estonian history. Russians see the law as discriminatory. Estonia has come under considerable criticism from Russia and there are some Russians who have called for sanctions to be imposed. However, there is no movement of Russians out of Estonia as their standard of living there is better than it would be in Russia, even if they do not have Estonian citizenship. On achieving independence Estonia looked to recover the lands around Pskov and Ivangorod that had been awarded to them by the 1920 Treaty of Tartu and which the Russians took away in 1940. The claim appears to be in abeyance as Estonia agreed in 1994 to drop its insistence on the Tartu Treaty being upheld. A border agreement has been negotiated and was initialled in 1999 but has not yet been signed.

The present situation in Latvia is that those eligible for citizenship have to pass a language test and know the basic principles of the constitution; their children, if born in Latvia, get automatic citizenship. The public use of the Russian language is banned. There were about 523,000 non-citizens in January 2002. Latvia has also agreed to Russian sovereignty over Pitlavo, an area that Russia annexed from Latvia in 1940; a border agreement has been initialled but not yet formally signed by Russia.

Lithuania has passed a law on the rights of national minorities that guarantees all citizens, regardless of ethnicity, equal political, economic and social rights and freedom. Minorities can be educated in their native language and may establish cultural organisations. There are also minority language radio and television programmes. Lithuania has reached three agreements with Belarus including one on the state border. Lithuania has no border problem with Russia, nor are there any problems regarding the Russian minority population. Negotiations continue over Lithuanian electricity exports to Kaliningrad and gas and oil transit from Russia to Kaliningrad. Lithuania and Poland have formed a joint battalion for peacekeeping purposes and a Lithuanian detachment serves in the Polish battalion in Kosovo.

The Baltic States feel threatened by Russia and know that their very limited defence assets would be unable to halt any Russian invasion. They are therefore keen to join NATO and may well be allowed to do so in November 2002. This move will be opposed strongly by Russia, which is against any further enlargement of NATO and would regard the inclusion of any parts of the former Soviet Union as a hostile act. Finland and Sweden are also opposed to Baltic membership, seeing it as a destabilising influence. NATO has not ruled out further enlargement but should be wary and will probably be divided over membership for the Baltic States. It is not clear what action NATO could take should the Baltic States be invaded, given their geographical circumstances and the fact that, apart from the short stretch of border with Poland, there is no direct access from NATO territory. The Baltic States are indefensible from a surprise attack from the east; Pentagon and NATO planners believe that they could not be defended by conventional forces. A 1999 US Congressional study concluded: 'Because it is unlikely that NATO members would wish to ensure a country's protection through nuclear guarantee alone, it is doubtful that the Baltic States would be allowed into NATO.' NATO will invite new members into the alliance during 2002.

There is, of course, a fourth Baltic entity, the Russian *oblast* of Kaliningrad, which is cut off from Russia by Lithuania. Kaliningrad has had a troubled history as well, having been at times Polish, Lithuanian and East Prussian. Its current population of nearly a million is totally Russian, the German population having either fled or been massacred in 1944–5. There has been some return of an ethnically German population but they have come from elsewhere in the former Soviet Union; however, tourism from Germany is increasing. There are no German ambitions, apart from in some extreme neo-Nazi groups, to reclaim the region. However, it was reported in January 2001 that Germany had secretly suggested providing help to arrange an 'association agreement' between Kaliningrad and the EU in return for waiving part of Russia's debt to Germany. Such a trade deal would place the enclave in Germany's sphere of influence. Lithuania, which calls the territory 'Little Lithuania', has no serious intentions of claiming it – mainly because of fears of Polish and German reactions and the undesirability of taking over 900,000 ethnic Russians into Lithuania. Indeed, in 1999 the Lithuanians and Russians signed an agreement on cooperation between Kaliningrad and the regions of Lithuania However, should Lithuania and Poland join the European Union, there will be a requirement for Keliningrad residents to have visas if they wish to cross Lithuania; Russia objects to this.

Much has been made of the military strength deployed in Kaliningrad, but in fact it is as much reduced as elsewhere in Russia and does not, of itself, pose any threat to its neighbours' security. Reports that tactical nuclear weapons had been transferred to Kaliningrad have been categorically denied by the Russians.

BIBLIOGRAPHY AND WEBSITES

Blank, Stephen J., *NATO Expansion and the Baltic States*, US Army War College, 1997
Herd, Graeme, *Crisis for Estonia? Russia, Estonia and a Post-Chechen Cold War*, Centre for Defence Studies, 1995
Knudsen, Olav (ed.), *Stability and Security in the Baltic Sea Region*, Frank Cass, 1999
Lieven, Anatol, *The Baltic Revolution: Estonia, Latvia, Lithuania and the Path to Independence*, Yale University Press, 1993.

Estonian Ministry of Foreign Affairs: www.vm.ee
Latvian Ministry of Foreign Affairs: www.mfa.gov.lv/eframe
Lithuanian Ministry of Foreign Affairs: www.urm.lt

The North Caucasus

The Caucasian Mountains now form Russia's southern border while at the same time encompassing a region of six republics, all with greater or lesser ambitions of greater independence. It is populated by some eighteen different ethnic groups, most of which have a long history of opposition to the Russians who have, over the years, introduced settlers. While Russia has no intention of losing control of this strategic region, the experience of the Chechen war could be repeated elsewhere in the North Caucasus, though the harsh Russian reaction should warn others not to try to break away.

The first significant contact between Russia and the Caucasian people came in 1556 when Ivan the Terrible conquered Astrakhan and a stretch of the Caspian coastline. At roughly the same time Cossacks arrived in the Terek region and set up settlements south of the river; the indigenous population of Chechens who had lived there for centuries kept very much to the mountains and forests. Two Russian army defeats in the early 1600s led to the Cossacks withdrawing north of the Terek. They returned as part of the Imperial army a hundred years later and recolonised the area. Chechens who sided with the Russians against the East Caucasian leaders, Sheikh Mansur Ushurma, who revolted in 1785 and was captured in 1791, and Imam Shamil, who led the opposition to the Russians after the death of Qazi Mullah in 1832 until 1859, when he surrendered but was allowed to go to Mecca, were rewarded with land north of the Terek. The period between these two East Caucasian revolts witnessed a period of relative peace punctuated by raids and counter-raids by the Russians and the Chechens and Daghestanis.

Russia needed to control Daghestan and Chechnya, and committed some 300,000 troops to doing so in the 1850s, for much the same reasons as it is holding on to the territory today. The area lies on the edge of the two main routes from Russia to the Transcaucasus: the Caspian coastal road and the road from Vladikavkaz to Tblisi in Georgia. Today the oil pipeline from Azerbaijan to Novorossiisk on the Black Sea also crosses Chechnya.

At the same time as the Russians were fighting Shamil, they were also conquering the West Caucasus, where there was no such unified opposition. By 1870 the Russians had driven out the majority of the mountain people and their lands were taken over by settlers

The North Caucasus

from Russia and Georgia, together with some Armenians. Islam had far less influence in the west than in the east.

The East Caucasians took the opportunities offered by the Russian–Ottoman War of 1877–8, the 1905 revolution and the collapse of Tsarist Russia in 1917 to rebel and on the first two occasions were suppressed brutally. In May 1918 the Chechens and Daghestanis established a North Caucasus Republic and supported the Red Army against the White Russians who controlled most of the North Caucasus. Once the White Russians were defeated, the mountain people turned to fight the Bolsheviks, who took nine months to subdue them. In 1921 the Soviets set up the Soviet Mountain Republic which covered the whole region bar Daghestan, but it was soon broken up into separate autonomous regions; the Chechen–Ingush region became an Autonomous Republic in 1936.

During the Second World War the Germans invaded the Caucasus and were only halted by the Red Army within artillery range of Grozny; the Chechens rebelled again but only relatively few crossed over to join the Germans. In 1943 Stalin decided to deport the Balkar, Chechen, Ingush, Kalmyk and Karachai populations to Kazakhstan and Kyrgistan; the Karachai were sent in November 1943, the Kalmyks followed in December and the Balkars in March 1944. It was the turn of some 478,000 Chechens and Ingush in February 1944; it is suspected that some 78,000 died on the journey. The Chechen–Ingush Autonomous Republic was broken up and its land shared out among its neighbours. The Chechens were allowed back to the Caucasus in 1958 and the Chechen–Ingush Autonomous Republic was re-established but with two traditionally Cossack districts of Stavropol added. The Russian settlers remained mainly in the towns and in the north of the republic.

In August 1991 the (then) Chechen–Ingush Autonomous Republic, under the leadership of General Dzhokhar Dudayev, demanded complete independence. Little action was taken other than the declaration of a state of emergency – a decision quickly reversed by the Supreme Soviet – and the imposition of an economic blockade. In 1994 a covert operation was mounted backed by the Russian Federal Counter-Intelligence Service but fronted by Chechens opposed to Dudayev. Despite reinforcement from the Russian army it was unsuccessful. During an attack on the Chechen capital, Grozny, on 26 November 1994, a number of Russian soldiers were captured. They were then publicly paraded – much to the surprise of their divisional commander who did not know that any of his soldiers were in Chechnya. The parade was probably the final straw for President Yeltsin, who ordered military intervention in Chechnya.

The operation came at a particularly bad time for Russian forces, which were still in the process of reorganising after the massive changes forced on them by the break-up of the Soviet Union. Many divisions were either being disbanded or converted into independent brigades and as a result virtually all were well under strength, the soldiers' living conditions were abysmal and morale was understandably low. Little or no time was allowed for preparations for the operation and the initial force, presumably chosen from those most readily available and up to strength, was hastily assembled. On 11 December the force was deployed to Chechnya without any preliminary training. It comprised a miscellany of different units drawn from virtually every branch – mechanised troops, airborne forces, naval infantry and Ministry of Interior Troops – none of whom had ever operated together before.

This was the first time Russian (or Soviet) forces had had to operate watched by the world's media and this added to the political requirement for the operation to be completed as quickly as possible. This in turn led to the disastrous decision to try to take Grozny with an armoured dash. The attacking forces paid heavily for this major tactical error. The Russians had badly underestimated Chechen strength and determination. Before 1991 there had been an armoured training centre based at Grozny. To allow this to be withdrawn unhindered a deal was struck in which half its equipment would be left behind; this deal left the Chechens with some T-54 tanks, BMP infantry fighting vehicles and artillery (although these were not used in the battle for Grozny).

Grozny was finally captured in early February 1995, and in March and April the Russians took the remaining towns as the Chechens withdrew into the mountains. Fighting continued and peace talks arranged by the Organisation for Cooperation and Security in Europe broke down. On 14 June a group of a hundred Chechens raided Budennovsk in Stavropol, capturing the hospital and taking a thousand hostages; two attempts by the Russians to recapture the hospital were unsuccessful and eventually the Chechens were allowed free passage. They took with them a hundred hostages who were released on 20 June.

Chechnya

In January 1996 a group of two hundred Chechens infiltrated into Kizliar in Daghestan and seized three thousand civilians; again free passage was agreed. But the Chechen convoy was halted at Pervomaiskoe and attacked by Russian special forces. The Chechens managed to escape with some hostages. Following agreement on a cease fire President Yeltsin appointed General Lebed, who had successfully defused the situation in Transdneistr in Moldova, with full powers to negotiate a peace settlement. On 31 August he and the Chechen commander, Aslan Maskhadov, signed an agreement which provided for the withdrawal of Russian troops and confirmed that the future status of Chechnya would be agreed to by 2001. In May 1997 Maskhadov, now the elected president of Chechnya, visited Moscow. He and President Yeltsin signed a short peace treaty confirming the cease fire agreement of August 1996 and committing both sides to rejecting the use or threat of force.

Chechnya, meanwhile, became a virtually lawless place; many of the fighters who had defeated the Russian army turned to crime. Kidnapping, including that of foreign workers, was rife; in October the head of the anti-kidnapping police was killed when his car was blown up. The whole region could have slipped out of control as the many criminal gangs, each from a different ethnic group (of which there are thirty-four in Daghestan alone), competed against one another. Four ethnic groups – Avars, Dargins, Kumyks and Nogays – claim some form of autonomy. If the disorder in Daghestan had spread it would have threatened Russia's main transport link with the Transcaucasus, and had it broken away much of Russia's Caspian shoreline would have been lost, so reducing its share of Caspian resources. The Cossacks too are looking for the creation of a Cossack Federal Republic, a move that is opposed by all the peoples of the North Caucasus.

In August 1999 fighting broke out in Daghestan between Chechen-backed Daghestanis and Russian forces. The Russian government seized what it saw as an opportunity to teach the Chechens a lesson and entered the country, at first as far as the Terek river. The Russian army was eager to take its revenge on the Chechens and to restore some of its prestige. It seems to have been given the go-ahead to subdue Chechnya and it set out about this with massive air and artillery attacks, aping NATO's tactics against Serbia. By the end of 1999 Grozny was still holding out as the Russians remorselessly cleared the mountainous forests in the south of the country, and many Chechens had fled as refugees into Ingushetia. Intense fighting in Grozny continued throughout January until the rebels decided to abandon the city in early February. Large numbers of Chechen fighters managed to escape but there is considerable confusion as to the numbers involved. Heavy fighting continued elsewhere in Chechnya with the Russians suffering heavy casualties: 156 men were killed between 29 February and 10 March, for instance.

In November 2001 President Putin agreed to allow talks to take place between his government and the Chechen rebels. Both sides claimed that the other had instigated the talks – which, as yet, have had no visible results. A large-scale Russian operation took place in January 2002 around Argun; as usual the numbers of casualties claimed by both sides are questionable. However, the Russian fear that Chechnya's revolt would be repeated across the whole North Caucasus has not been realised. Moreover, international opinions regarding Russia's action in Chechnya have altered, particularly after 11 September, with President Bush demanding 'that terrorists with ties to Usama bin Laden should be brought to justice'. The attitudes of the Transcaucasian States have also changed, with statements being made such as 'Russian actions are justified, correct and in accordance with international law'. There is evidence both of Islamic fighters helping the Chechens and of Chechens fighting in Afghanistan. In March 2002 informal talks began to prepare the ground for direct talks between President Putin and the Chechen leadership. Meanwhile the fighting continues.

At the western end of the Caucasus are the autonomous republics of Karachevo-Cherkessia and Kabardino-Balkaria. Both have divided populations and regional disputes could emerge here. The Circassians called for an autonomous republic which would also include the

Adygei autonomous region (whose population are of the same ethnicity as the Cherkess) and the coastal districts of the Russian Krasnodar region. The Karachai leaders demanded the restoration of the territory they had held before their deportation in 1943. The Russians decreed in 1995 that the republic should be abolished and incorporated into the Stavropol region, but this has not yet been implemented. In Kabardino-Balkaria both the minority Balkars and the Kabardins declared separate republics in 1991, a move backed by the parliament, but this plan was dropped because of strong opposition from ethnic Russians. One problem solved, temporarily at any rate, is the dispute between Ingushetia and North Ossetia; these territories came to blows in 1992 when the Ingush population in Ossetia was expelled. The two republics signed a treaty normalising relations in September 1997.

TRAVEL ADVICE

FCO and State: Both warn against any travel in Chechnya, Ingushetia, Daghestan, North Ossetia, Karachevo-Cherkessia, Kabardino-Balkaria including Elrus, and eastern and southern parts of Stavropol Crai, where it borders Chechnya and North Ossetia.

BIBLIOGRAPHY AND WEBSITES

Bennington Broxup, Marie (ed.), *The North Caucasus Barrier: Russian Advance towards the Muslim World*, Hurst, 1993

Dawisha, Karen and Parrot, Bruce (eds), *Conflict, Cleavage and Change in Central Asia and the Caucasus*, Cambridge University Press, 1997

Lieven, Anatol, *Chechnya: Tombstone of Russian Power*, Yale University Press, 1998

Seely, Robert, *Russo–Chechen Conflict 1800–2000: A Deadly Embrace*, Frank Cass, 2001

Smith, Sebastian, *Allah's Mountains: Politics and War in the Russian Caucasus*, IB Taurus, 1998

Central Asia-Caucasus Institute (Nitze School of Advanced International Studies): www.sais-jhu.edu/caci

Government of the Chechen Republic: www.amina.com

North Caucasus Conflict Centre: www.cdi.org/issues/Europe/ncaucasus

The Transcaucasus

	Armenia	Azerbaijan	Georgia
Population:	3,464,000	7,752,000	4,891,000
	Armenian Orthodox 94%	Azeri 92%	Georgian 75%
	Russian 2%, Kurd 1%	Daghestani 3%	Armenian 8%
		Russian 2%,	Azeri 6%
		Armenian 2–3%	Russian 6%
			Ossetian 3%
			Abkhaz 2%
Armed Forces:	42,000	72,000	17,000
Opposition:		Nagorno-Karabakh 18,000	Abkhazia 5,000
			South Ossetia 2,000
Per Capita GDP:	US$ 3,703	US$ 2,181	US$ 5,289
Currency:	dram	manat	lari

The territory now forming the three Transcaucasian Republics – Georgia, Armenia and Azerbaijan – was taken into the Tsarist Russian Empire in the first half of the nineteenth century. Before this time the peoples of the region had inhabited a much wider area and today a good number of ethnic Transcaucasians live beyond their national borders. Each of the three republics has its own modern problem deriving from ethnic minorities who are demanding a degree of self-determination, if not independence.

The Romans and Persians had contested the region since the first century BC. Armenia and Georgia adopted Christianity under the Romans in the fourth century AD. After the Arab invasion of 642 the Azerbaijanis and the North Caucasians became Muslims. The Transcaucasus has always provided the route for invading forces marching between Central Asia and Asia Minor; many invaders conquered and partitioned the region regardless of the indigenous population. The Seldjuks ruled it from AD 1071, followed by the Mongols and then the Turks and finally the Russians, who began penetrating the region in the early 1700s.

Armenia

Armenia has a long history as a nation, going as far back as the eighth century BC, and was once a much larger country than it is now. At the height of its power, in 65 BC, it stretched from the Caspian to the Mediterranean and ruled the north-eastern part of Asia Minor. It was then split between the Byzantine and Persian Empires. By the start of the First World War Armenia was split between Turkey and Russia, which had controlled the country since the early nineteenth century. The war gave the Armenians the opportunity to support one side or the other in an attempt to regain Armenian territorial unity. However, they decided that they would support their respective governments and neither government repaid their loyalty. The Russians conscripted 150,000 soldiers, deploying some of them far away on the Polish and Galician fronts. The Turks blamed the Armenians in part for their defeat by the Russians and in 1915 began a massive ethnic cleansing operation which is believed to have resulted in the deaths of some 600,000 Armenians and the flight of 300,000–400,000 refugees into Russia, Persia and Mesopotamia.

At the end of the war it was thought that the Armenians would receive special treatment from the victorious powers but none was prepared to accept a mandate for governing Armenia. The powers compelled the Turkish government to recognise an independent Armenian state and the US was to arbitrate on its borders. In 1920 President Wilson gave back to Armenia virtually all the territory taken by Russia during the war, but his action came too late. In January 1920 the Turks had attacked the French garrison in Cilicia and driven them out of Marash, massacring some 50,000 Armenians. In May the Bolsheviks had taken control of Erivan and in September handed the area to the Turks, resulting in another massacre of Armenians. In October France withdrew from Cilicia. The

The Transcaucasus

Treaty of Lausanne, which finalised the peace between Turkey and the Powers, made no mention of an independent Armenia.

TRAVEL ADVICE
FCO and State: Take care in Armenian/Azerbaijan border areas. Danger of mines and sniper fire.

Azerbaijan

Azerbaijan or the land of the Azeris only became a state in 1918. It has had changing borders throughout its history; the Azeris (who for most of their history have been associated with Persia) were originally Zoroastrian but converted to Islam after the Arab invasion in the mid-seventh century. In the eleventh century, as part of the Seldjuk Empire, they became fused with a number of Turkic tribes who arrived, over many years, from Central Asia; gradually the language changed to become a distinct tongue. The Mongols under Hualagu conquered the Azeris in the thirteenth century. The region witnessed much of the fighting between the Ottoman Turks and the Iranians; in 1747, after the death of Nadir Shah, the Iranians lost control and the Azeris broke up into a series of *khanates*.

In the second half of the eighteenth century attempts were made to form a single nation. North-eastern Azerbaijan was dominated by Fath 'Ali Khan of Kuba who aimed to unite the whole region under his rule but he was forestalled by the Russians who viewed Kuba's ambitions as a threat to their own expansionist ambitions. The Russian commander, Pavel Tsitsianov, a Georgian, as part of his conquest of Georgia, decided that he must first control the Azeri *khanates* as far as the Caspian Sea; some accepted the Russian terms peacefully while others had to be conquered. The Treaty of Gulistan gave Russia control of a large amount of Iranian territory stretching from Baku to Georgia, but it did not end the Russian–Iranian fighting. The Iranians invaded in 1825 but were defeated at the battle of Ganja and the Russians went on to capture Tabriz. The Treaty of Turkmanchai, signed in 1828, gave Russia more Azeri territory as the country was divided between Russia and Iran along the line of the Araxes river. After the formation of the Soviet Union the Azerbaijan region became the Republic of Azerbaijan and on the break-up of the USSR gained its independence.

NAGORNO-KARABAKH
Armenia and Azerbaijan are both affected by the Armenian-populated enclave of Azerbaijan known as Nagorno- (Russian for mountainous) Karabakh (Azerbaijani black garden). Some Armenians have claimed that Nagorno-Karabakh was part of Armenia as early as the seventh century BC but Azeri historians believe that the indigenous Albanian population was assimilated by Armenian settlers in the eighth century. It became part of the Persian province of Albania (not to be confused with Balkan Albania) after the partition between Byzantium and Persia in AD 387; the inhabitants remained Christian. It fell to the Russians in 1805. The main settlement of Armenians in Karabakh took place in 1828–30, with another wave in 1877–8 following the Russo–Turkish war. There had been no borders dividing Georgia, Armenia and Azerbaijan between the Russian conquest of the Transcaucasus in 1828 and the Russian revolution in 1917. The three states materialised after the revolution but before their occupation by the Bolsheviks in 1920; during this time the Armenians fought the Azerbaijanis over territory including Nagorno-Karabakh. The Bolsheviks allocated to Azerbaijan both Nagorno-Karabakh and Nakhichevan, an Azeri enclave on the border with Iran; the former had the status of 'autonomous region' and the latter of 'autonomous republic'. At the same time Armenia was awarded the Azeri-populated regions of Zangezur and part of Gazakh. Separatist aims were encouraged in 1987 when Gorbachev's economic advisor, an Armenian, advocated that the enclave should become part of Armenia. In February 1988, after a series of strikes and demonstrations, the regional

Soviet of Nagorno-Karabakh appealed to the Supreme Soviets of the USSR, Armenia and Azerbaijan to agree to its transfer to Armenia. In February some two thousand Azeri refugees from Stepanakert arrived in Sumgait, sparking off two days of rioting in which both Armenians and Azeris were killed. This led to large-scale deportations from both Armenia and Azerbaijan, involving some 250,000 people.

The collapse of the Soviet Union exacerbated the situation and both Armenian and Azeri national forces gained in strength from inheriting weaponry from departing Soviet units. The scale of fighting increased dramatically with the Armenians taking over more Azeri villages and establishing at Lachin a corridor from the border to Nagorno-Karabakh, which had declared itself an independent republic but was not recognised as such. During the spring and summer of 1993 Azerbaijan lost control of Nagorno-Karabakh and seven neighbouring counties – amouonting to roughly one-sixth of its former territory. By the time the fighting subsided in May 1994 Azerbaijan had suffered 11,000 killed; some 750,000 people became refugees. Armenia lost 6,000 dead. A stalemate was reached. It was hoped the issue could be resolved but nothing was agreed, despite the efforts of Russia (which has liberally supplied the Armenians with arms), Turkey (which backed the Azeris), Iran and the Organisation for Cooperation and Security in Europe, which has prepared an observer force as yet undeployed.

Hopes have been raised of achieving a solution as talks between the two sides have taken place regularly since their two leaders, Robert Kocharian of Armenia and Heydar Aliyav of Azerbaijan, met President Bush separately in Washington in April 2001. The two leaders have held face-to-face talks frequently since 1999.

TRAVEL ADVICE
FCO and State: Avoid Nagorno-Karabakh and the Armenian-occupied areas around it.

Georgia

Since gaining independence Georgia has suffered far more disruption and is more likely to lose territory to ethnic minorities than Armenia or Azerbaijan, despite being the oldest nation of the three. Georgia is divided in two by the Likhi mountains, which in the past served as the frontier between Byzantium and the Arab Empire and later between the Ottoman Empire and Persia. The East Georgians were converted to Christianity around AD 330 and the West Georgians in the sixth century; with staunch Muslim neighbours on either side, religion probably held the Georgians together and led to their appeals for Russian support.

The Russian Empire first invaded Georgia in 1801 but did not complete its conquests until 1864, after two wars had been fought against the Turks. Between 1918 and 1921 Georgia regained its independence and was the scene of fighting between Red and White Russians and between Bolsheviks and Mensheviks. In 1921 the Bolsheviks took control and Georgia became part of the Soviet Union. The Soviets gave Abkhazia (a separate kingdom from the eighth century, which merged with West Georgia at the end of the century) and Adjara (inhabited by Sunni Muslims) the status of autonomous republics while South Ossetia (an area settled by Ossetians from across the Caucasus in the seventeenth and eighteenth centuries) became an autonomous *oblast*.

On attaining independence in 1991 Georgia found it had inherited three separate territorial/ethnic problems and a population of whom 30 per cent were not ethnic Georgians. The president, Zviad Gamsakhurdia, attempted to abolish the autonomous status of the three areas but Georgian nationalists deposed him in an armed coup in January 1992. A period of civil war followed until the end of 1993 when government forces took Gamsakhurdia's last stronghold, Zigdidi, and he committed suicide. Eduard Shevardnadze, the former Soviet Foreign Minister, was invited back to lead the country in March 1992 and was elected head of state in October.

Caucasians

///// Abkhaz

///// Georgian

\\\\ Dagestani

\\\\ Chechen, Ingush

Indo-Europeans

≡≡≡ Armenian (incl. Greek)

——— Kurd

=== Ossetian

▬▬▬ Talysh

Altaic

||||| Azeri

||||| Turk

||||| Kumyk

The Transcaucasus showing the ethnic populations

There had been friction between the Georgian government and the South Ossetians some years before Georgian independence. In August 1988 the Ossetian Popular Front protested to Moscow that Georgia's intention to make Georgian the only official language was unacceptable and called for South Ossetia's unification with North Ossetia. In September 1990 the Front declared an 'Independent Soviet Democratic Republic' which was shortly followed by the abolition of South Ossetia's autonomous status by the Georgian parliament. Violent clashes followed and Soviet Interior Ministry troops were sent to the region. In June 1992 the situation was defused after agreement between Yeltsin and Shevardnadze and a joint Russian–Georgian–South Ossetian peacekeeping force was established. It is still deployed.

Abkhazia was briefly a full Union Republic from 1921 until its status was downgraded to autonomous republic within Georgia in 1931; then followed a period of 'Georgianisation' with the forced resettlement of Georgians in Abkhazhia reducing the Abkhaz proportion of the population. In 1978 an attempt to secede failed but Russian policy allowed Abkhazians to gain a disproportionate influence in the Supreme Soviet and the local Communist Party. In the Soviet referendum of March 1991, which the Georgians boycotted, the Abkhazians voted overwhelmingly to remain in the Union. After Georgian troops had captured Sukhumi in August 1992 the Abkhazians appealed to Russia for protection. Fighting continued, interrupted only for short periods by cease fires, until the Abkhazians recaptured Sukhumi and the rest of the region in September 1993. At least 200,000 ethnic Georgians fled from their homes. In July the UNSC agreed to the deployment of observers and established the UN Observer Mission in Georgia (UNOMIG), which began to deploy in August but this process was suspended following the breakdown of the cease fire in September. Georgia joined the Commonwealth of Independent States (CIS) in October and obtained Russian assistance in exchange for the use of port facilities and agreement over the stationing of Russian troops.

A Russian peacekeeping force deployed along the Inguri river in June 1994 and established a 12km-wide demilitarised zone (DMZ) on both sides of the river. There is also a heavy weapons exclusion zone stretching a further 20km beyond the DMZ. Despite the presence of Russian troops and the UN observers, both sides have infiltrated armed groups from time to time into each other's territory, and the bulk of the refugees from both sides have not yet managed to return to their homes. A flare-up of the conflict occurred in May 1998 when Abkhazian forces launched an offensive against Georgian infiltrators, which caused some 30,000 ethnic Georgians to become refugees for a second time.

The situation in the Muslim region of Adjara has been far more peaceful, probably because of the presence of the Russian bases at Batumi and Medzhinistskari. However, though recognising Georgian sovereignty in principle, it is virtually independent and its president, Aslan Abashidze, is a potential political rival to Shevardnadze for the Georgian presidency. Elsewhere in Mingrelia, which borders Abkhazia, the population remains loyal to the late Gamsakhurdia and in the Armenian-populated area around Akhalkalaki, where there is another Russian base, there could be a further problem. Just how much Russia is influencing events in Georgia is unclear but it is strongly suspected by the Georgian government of provoking trouble. In October 1999 Shevardnadze said that he intended to apply for NATO membership. Russian border troops were withdrawn in November. Four Russian military bases remain in Georgia despite the Russian agreement in November 1999 to close two of them; Georgia has rejected Russian requests for the troops there to be used against Chechnya.

The conflict in Chechnya has spilled over into Georgia and Abkhazia. Chechen guerrillas have been using the Pankisi Gorge as a safe haven and training ground for some time; the gorge's population consists of Muslim Kistinians. It is also thought that al Qaida men have infiltrated to Pankisi possibly en route to Russia, Europe or America. As there are several thousand refugees in the gorge the Georgians are not prepared to clear it. In October 2001 some Chechens – the numbers reported differ considerably – were active in the Kodori Gorge in Abkhazia, together with Georgian paramilitaries. They are blamed for the shooting-down of a UN helicopter. The US has agreed to provide training for the Georgian forces and to supply some military equipment; US troops arrived on 27 May. The Georgians are calling for the withdrawal of the Russian peacekeepers in Abkhazia, while the Abkhazian prime minister said that they would apply for associate membership of the Russian Federation.

TRAVEL ADVICE

FCO: Strongly advise against travel in Abkhazia and South Ossetia, particularly around the Pankisi Gorge and the districts of Zugdili and Tsalenjika, bordering Abkhazia. Armed crime is prevalent in Svaneti (in north-west Georgia). State: Warn against visiting Pankisi Gorge and Akhmeta, also borders with Daghestan and Chechnya. Avoid Abkhaz border off main roads and after dark.

BIBLIOGRAPHY AND WEBSITES

Croissant, Michael, The Armenian–Azerbaijan Conflict: Causes and Implications, Praeger, 1971 and 1998

Gachechiladze, Revaz, The New Georgia: Space, Society, Politics, UCL Press, 1995

Gribincea, Mihail, Russian Policy on Military Bases in Georgia and Moldova, Cogito Publishing, 2001

Hewitt, George (ed.), The Abkhazians, Curzon Press, 1999

Hoiris, Ole and Martin Yurukel, Sefa (eds), Contrasts and Solutions in the Caucasus, Aarhus University Press, 1998

Hunter, Shireen T., The Transcaucasus in Transition: Nation-Building and Conflict, Centre for Strategic and International Studies, 1994

Wright, John, Goldberg, Suzanne and Schofield, Richard (eds), Transcaucasian Boundaries, SOASD/GRC Geopolitics Series, UCL

Armenian Embassy: www.armeniaemb.org
Georgian Parliament: www.parliament.ge
President of Azerbaijan: www.president.az

The Kurils or The Northern Islands

Fifty-five years after the end of the Second World War the ownership of a number of islands lying between Japan and the Kamchatka peninsula is still the subject of a dispute between Japan and Russia; the latter currently occupies the islands and has done so since the closing stages of the war in 1945. The disputed islands are the three closest to Japan–Shikotan, Kunaishiri and Etorofu – together with a group of smaller islands known as the Habomais group. There is no dispute over the islands further to the north-east which are known as the Kurils. Japan always refers to the islands that it claims as the Northern Islands.

The basis of the Japanese claim is that the islands are historically part of Japan and that Russian influence has never been exercised south of Uruppu. Also, the Japanese-claimed islands are different from those further north in terms of fauna, flora and climate, all of which equate to those found in Japan. The more northerly, Russian, islands are sub-arctic in character. Japan points to the Treaty of Commerce, Navigation and Delimitation of 1855 when Japan owned Karafuto (Sakhalin) and the border between Russia and Japan was agreed as being south of Uruppu. By the 1875 treaty Japan exchanged Sakhalin Island for the Kuril Islands. Both treaties confirm Japan's claim to the Northern Islands. The Russians argue that the treaties have no standing today and that they made concessions under duress; further, they say the agreements were nullified when Japan attacked Russia in 1904. In this war the Japanese gained the southern half of Sakhalin. At the Allied conference at Yalta it was agreed that 'the former rights of Russia violated by the treacherous attack of 1904 shall be restored', including Sakhalin and the Kurils. The Soviet Union declared war on Japan forty-eight hours after the first nuclear bomb had been dropped on Hiroshima and immediately occupied southern Sakhalin and all the islands between Kamchatka and Hokkaido. The 17,000-strong Japanese population was deported.

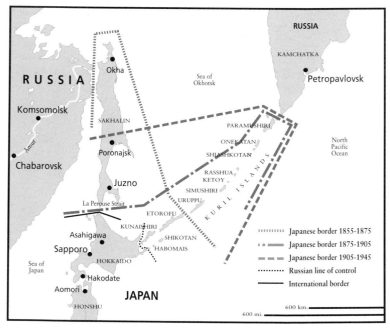

The Kuril or Northern Islands

Japan also claims – and has been supported in this claim by the US – that the Yalta agreement statements have no international legality and were purely statements of intent. Further, it says that Kunaishiri and Etorofu are not part of the Kuril Islands group. The US note to Japan also stated that 'the final disposition of territories as the result of war is to be made by a peace treaty'. The Soviet Union was not party to the Treaty of San Francisco in 1951 which was signed by forty-eight of the fifty-one wartime allies and Japan, and in which Japan renounced its claim to the Kurils. Negotiations for a Soviet–Japanese peace treaty were held in 1956 but no agreement was reached because although the Soviets were prepared to hand over the Habomais and Shikotan they would only do so in return for retaining Kunaishiri and Etofuru. However, both countries signed a joint declaration that ended the state of war between them. It included a paragraph stating agreement on continuing negotiations for a peace treaty and noting that after its conclusion the Habomais and Shikotan would be handed over to Japan. In 1960, following the signing of the US–Japanese Security Treaty, the Soviets said it was impossible for them to return the Habomais and Shikotan to Japan.

Soviet–Japanese relations improved when Gorbachev became president and it was rumoured that a large financial package of loans and grants had been offered for the return of the Northern Islands; however, the Soviet military were totally opposed to any handover. On coming to power, Boris Yeltsin expressed his desire to settle the dispute and Georgy Yavlinsky, then vice-chairman of the interim cabinet, suggested that the 1855 Treaty should be respected and the islands returned. His opinion was reinforced by the discovery of documents revealing that in 1853 Tsar Nicholas I acknowledged Japan's sovereignty over all four islands. At the Japanese–Russian Summit held in Siberia in November 1997 both sides pledged to achieve a peace treaty by 2000, but immediately before the next summit meeting in April 1998 the then Russian prime minister designate told the Duma that Russia would not hand over the islands. In September 2000 Prime Minister Yoshiro Mori and President Vladimir Putin met and discussed a number of issues. The question of the islands was not resolved but they agreed to continue negotiations; their joint statement, however, did not even mention the islands. Mori and Putin met again at Irkutsk in March 2001; in a joint statement they agreed to promote negotiations to conclude a peace treaty 'through the solution of issues concerning the attribution of the islands . . .'.

BIBLIOGRAPHY AND WEBSITE

Goodby, James, Ivanov, Vladimir and Shimotamai, Nobuo (eds), 'Northern Territories' and beyond: Russian, Japanese and American Perspectives, Westport, 1995

Japanese Ministry of Foreign Affairs: www.mofa.go.jp/region/europe/russia

The Middle East

Two of the most worrying issues now facing the world are found in the Middle East. They are the Arab–Israeli conflict, which has been the cause of five wars and numerous terrorist incidents, and the security of Persian Gulf oil, which has been threatened by two wars in the last twenty years. This section begins with an overview of the proliferation of nuclear, biological and chemical (NBC) weapons, the so-called weapons of mass destruction, and the long-range missiles that can deliver them. It then examines the confrontation between Israel and the Arab world before turning to the various problems in the Gulf. Finally there is a discussion about Islam and whether it presents a threat to world peace.

Middle East Proliferation

While the Middle East may not be the most dangerous place in the world at the moment it does hold the record for the number of major wars fought there in the last forty years. Although several Middle East states have had so-called weapons of mass destruction for some years, any fresh outbreak of war would probably see the use of long-range missiles with NBC and conventional warheads.

Range is not the most important requirement for missiles in the Middle East, as the range table shows. Syria's current missiles can reach any part of Israel, while their most accurate surface-to-surface missile (SSM), the Soviet SS-21, can strike as far south as Tel Aviv – a city that is only 500km from Iraqi territory and just over 1,000km from Iran. Similarly Tehran is roughly 600km from Iraqi territory and Baghdad not more than 100km from the border with Iran. Jordan, Lebanon, Oman and Qatar have no SSMs, nor do Bahrain and Kuwait but they have the 30km-range US MLRS and the 70km-range Russian Smerch rocket-launcher respectively.

However, some countries are developing missiles with ranges that could engage targets well beyond the immediate Middle East area. Iranian missiles were paraded for the first time on 25 September 1998 in Tehran. Three different, Iranian-built, short-range SSMs were on display. All have solid fuel propellant and two have ranges of around 150km; all are available for export. Also on parade was the Shahab 3, successfully tested in 1998 and most recently in 2002. It has a claimed range of 1,300km with a 1,000kg payload, but probably with a CEP 4000 metres of the missile will soon be operational. A Shahab 4 is known to be under development, probably based on the Soviet SS-4, and may have a range of up to 2,000km. Israel claims that versions with even longer ranges are being developed, and the Iranian defence minister has publicly mentioned Shahab 5. Iran has received ballistic missile-related equipment, technology and expertise from Russia, China and North Korea. The US has identified nine Russian institutes and firms that are assisting in the missile programme and imposed sanctions on them. Former Iranian president Hashemi Rafsanjani has claimed that Iran can now develop and manufacture missiles without outside help and that is certainly Iran's aim. The official US position on the missile threat to the US is that none is likely to emerge before 2010, but the Rumsfeld commission believed Iran could be capable of deploying inter-continental missiles in five years.

Before the Gulf War of 1991 Iraq was successfully producing intermediate-range missiles. After the war fifty-one Al-Hussein missiles were destroyed by the UN Special Commission(unscom); one Scud missile was also destroyed but it is strongly believed that Iraq had concealed other Scuds. Al-Hussein had a range of 650km and could carry both conventional and chemical weapon warheads (thirty of the latter were found by inspectors). The Al-Abass had been tested at a range of 850km. This was an upgraded version of Al-Hussein, which was itself an upgrade of the Soviet Scud short-range missile. Iraq also manufactured Scuds and fired these at Israel and targets in Saudi Arabia during the Gulf War. UN Resolution UNSCR 687 of April 1991 forbids Iraq from having missiles with ranges of more than 150km but it still has a number of elderly Soviet Frog missiles and has developed the Al-Samoud which has a range just below the 150km limit. It was test-fired several times in 2000 despite the bombing of its production facilities by the US and UK in December 1998. No doubt Iraq has the ability to produce longer-range missiles once UN controls are lifted; it would not be surprising if work has not already started on them since the UNSCOM inspectors left Iraq at the end of 1998.

Israel is known to have a nuclear arsenal and has been suspected of possessing operational nuclear weapons since at least the late 1960s. Whether it would ever use them in the 'Samson' mode is debatable, nor has the presence of these nuclear weapons deterred the Arabs from engaging in conventional war against Israel. If an Arab country or Iran were to obtain nuclear weapons the situation would be quite different, and as dangerous as that between India and Pakistan following their nuclear tests. Israel is not averse to employing pre-emption when it is threatened. Its nuclear weapons could be delivered by aircraft or by the Jericho missile; the range of the most recent version is thought to be over 7,000km. Its latest fighter-bomber, the US F-15I, can reach Iran, but not necessarily all of Iran's counter-force targets and this could cause Israel problems should Iran acquire nuclear weapons as is forecast. Israel's latest German-built class of submarines give it the capability to launch cruise missiles and so could provide Israel with a nuclear second-strike capability. Israel has never tested a nuclear weapon and has ratified the Comprehensive Test Ban Treaty; however, it has not signed the Nuclear Non-Proliferation Treaty. Israel is also considered to have both a chemical and biological weapons capability.

Several Middle East countries are suspected of having nuclear ambitions and the fear is that some could purchase nuclear weapons or fissile material stolen from the huge Russian stockpiles. After the Pakistani tests in 1998 it is now known that there is an Islamic bomb. The extent of Iraq's nuclear programme surprised the world when it was revealed soon after the end of the Gulf War; long suspected, it was far closer to fruition than anyone had imagined. Details of Iraq's nuclear facilities before 1991 are shown on p. 98. With the know-how and the designers and engineers still available, it should not take Iraq long to regain its previous position once sanctions are lifted and international attention turns elsewhere. Now that UNSCOM, the UN inspection organisation, has been withdrawn who knows what clandestine activities have begun. The US fears that Iraq may pass weapons of mass destruction to the Al-Qaida terrorist organisation. There have recently been hints that Saudi Arabia may be considering starting a nuclear weapons programme.

Iran is strongly suspected of having nuclear weapons ambitions, a suspicion based mainly on energy-rich Iran's plans for nuclear power reactors which many consider it does not need. Nuclear developments started under the Shah's regime in 1957 when an agreement was signed with the US on cooperation in the peaceful use of nuclear energy and a research reactor was completed in 1967. By the time of the 1979 revolution the most advanced project was the building of two 1,250 megawatt pressurised water reactors at Bushehr, which were roughly 80 per cent and 65 per cent complete. A large number of Iranians were sent abroad to study nuclear technology. Military research is believed to have comprised weapons design at the Amirabad centre; a laser enrichment programme; and an uncompleted plutonium extraction plant at Tehran. In 1992–3 there were a number of unconfirmed reports of the smuggling of a small number of nuclear warheads from

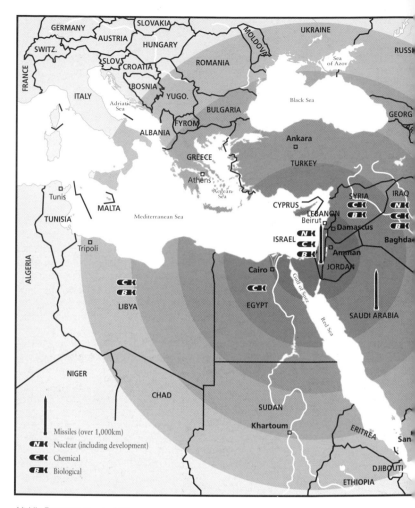

Middle East weapons capability

Kazakhstan to Iran. Kazakhstan denied the allegations but in April 1998 the Israeli newspaper *Jerusalem Post* claimed that it had been shown copies of Iranian government papers confirming the receipt of four warheads and supplies of enriched uranium from Kazakhstan in 1991. In January 1995 Iran signed a contract with Russia for the completion of the two reactors at Bushehr; later that month Iran commissioned a cyclotron accelerator at Karaj, ostensibly to produce radioactive material for medical scanners. The Russians resisted heavy US pressure not to complete the reactors; however, in August 2002, Russia announced it would build a further reactor at Alwaz. The US managed to dissuade Ukraine from supplying the turbines for the Bushehr reactors. Chinese officials are said to have assured the US that the proposed sale to Iran of anhydrous hydrogen fluoride needed for a uranium enrichment process would not take place. The IAEA inspects some but not all of Iran's nuclear facilities and as yet has not found any evidence of nuclear weapons development. Nevertheless there is a strong body of opinion in the US and Israel that Iran *is* developing nuclear weapons and could have a nuclear capability in a matter of a few years.

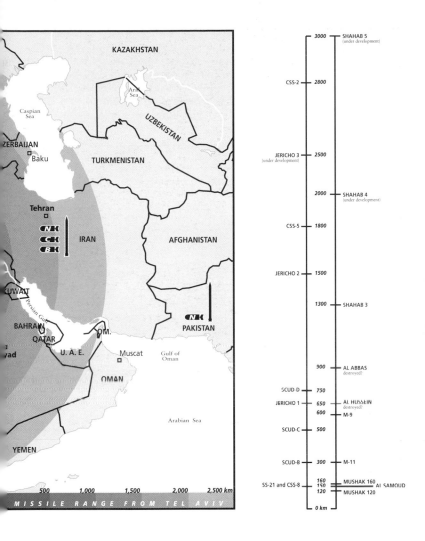

MISSILE RANGE FROM TEL AVIV

Chemical and biological weapons (CBW) are far easier and cheaper to develop than nuclear weapons; they would doubtless be considered as terrifying as nuclear weapons had the world experienced their full-scale use in modern war but they are unlikely to obtain the same political significance. As it is, the Middle East has witnessed the use of chemical weapons on several occasions, including by the Egyptians in Yemen in the 1960s. Iraq used them against Iran in the First Gulf War and later against Kurds at Halabaja, and Iran was forced to reply in kind against Iraq. Other Middle East countries credited with a CW capability are Israel, Syria and Libya. The latter constructed a chemical plant at Rabta and, after a fire at Rabta, built the underground complex at nearby Tarhuna.

Biological weapons (BW) have not yet been employed operationally, other than in assassination attempts, but it is believed that a number of Middle East countries have BW programmes. Certainly Iraq was known to have such weapons under development and was widely believed to have had some weapons loaded with biological agent, but not much of the programme was revealed by UNSCOM inspectors. Most information came from

General Hussein Kemal Hassan who defected to Jordan in 1995, and from an admission by Rihab Taha, a leading Iraqi germ specialist. After Hassan's defection there were further admissions about Iraq's biological warfare activities, which had included producing anthrax and botulinum toxin, testing delivery means and loading missile warheads with biological agents BW programmes are strongly suspected to be in progress in Iran, Israel, Libya, Syria and possibly Egypt. BW can be produced in small, hard to recognise facilities; far less agent is required than for chemical attack (CW) and biological agents disperse over a much larger area than chemicals. Moreover, biological weapons are more adaptable for terrorist use, as they can be more easily smuggled than CW or fissile material and can be effectively disseminated through water supplies.

In terms of future Middle East wars, it has to be emphasised that those most at risk from nuclear or CBW will be the civilian populations and not the fighting forces.

WEBSITES
Center for Strategic and International Studies, Middle East Programme: www.csis.org
Centre for Non-Proliferation Studies (Monterey Institute for Strategic Studies): www.cns.miis.edu

Lebanon

Population: 4,345,000 (excluding 500,000 Syrians and 500,000 Palestinian refugees)
Muslims 60%, Christian 30%, Druze 6%, Armenian 4%
Armed Forces: 63,500, Internal Security Force: 13,000
Non-government: Hizbollah 500
Foreign forces: Syria 22,000, UNIFIL 3,650 (reducing)
Per Capita GDP: US$ 4,900
Currency: Lebanese pound

Lebanon's long history begins with the Phoenician city states in the tenth century BC. It was then conquered by the Persians in the sixth century BC, by Alexander the Great in the fourth and by the Romans in the first. It was part of the Byzantine Empire until AD 641 and from then on, apart from short periods of Crusader rule, was held by Islam; from 1516 until the end of the First World War it was part of the Ottoman Empire.

The country has a multiplicity of religious beliefs. The Romans introduced Christianity and the Arabs Islam, and there are a number of branches and sects of each. The largest Christian sect is the Maronite, the next the Greek Orthodox. The most numerous Muslims are Shi'a but there are nearly as many Sunni. And there are the Druze, who also live in northern Israel and southern Syria.

A period of fighting between Druze and Maronites began in 1841 and eventually led to the establishment of two multi-faith district councils, each with a member from the Druze, Greek Orthodox, Greek Catholic, Maronite and Sunni communities; the councils' role was to advise the governors – the first time religious persuasion was accorded formal representation. A peasants' revolt in 1858 developed into conflict between the Druze and the Maronites in which both Sunni and Shi'a Muslims supported the Druze while the other Christian sects joined the Maronites. The fighting spread across the whole country with the Muslims, aided by the Ottomans, gaining the upper hand until France intervened and saved the Maronites in the northern Chouf Mountains from the massacres that had occurred elsewhere. As a result of European pressure the Ottomans created an autonomous governorate of Mountain Lebanon in which the religious sects were represented on the council not equally but in proportion to their percentage of the population.

The modern Lebanese state was created, along with other Middle Eastern countries, at the end of the First World War when the Ottoman Empire was broken up. Initially Lebanon

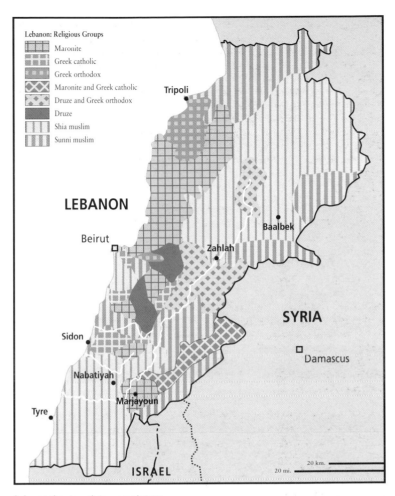

Lebanon showing religious populations

was a French mandatory territory, as was Syria; border changes effected during the mandate have left a legacy of problems that persist today. In 1920 the French created Greater Lebanon, which added Tripoli and the Akkar district in the north and the Bekaa Valley in the east from Syria. While Mountain Lebanon had been predominantly Christian, in Greater Lebanon the Christian and Muslim communities were of roughly equal strength. Independence was granted in 1941 but not achieved until 1943 when a 'national pact' was arrived at: the Christians renounced the protection of European powers, the Muslims the ambition of union with Syria. The multi-faith nature of the population was taken into account – the president was always to be a Maronite and the prime minister a Sunni Muslim.

Lebanon took little part in the Arab war against Israeli independence in 1948. There was some fighting along Israel's northern border but all territory won or lost was exchanged after the war. The Lebanese–Israeli border, though technically still an armistice line, follows the line of the Lebanese–Mandatory Palestine border. Lebanon did not carry out terrorist raids against Israel though the Palestine Liberation Organisation (PLO) continued its fight against Israel from Lebanese soil after its eviction from Jordan in 1970. Lebanon took no part in the 1967 or 1973 Arab–Israeli wars.

The massive increase in the Palestinian presence in Lebanon in 1970 had a number of consequences. First, it led to much deeper Israeli raids into Lebanon as they sought to hit the PLO leadership. Secondly, it brought about a strengthening of all the armed militia – the Christians purchased arms in Europe and received training from the Lebanese army while the Muslims received arms from the Palestinians. Clashes between the Palestinians and the Lebanese army on the one hand and between armed factions on the other had taken place since 1968, but full-scale civil war did not break out until 1975. Initially it was fought between Palestinians and left-wing Muslims against the Christian Phalangists. In 1976 an Arab peacekeeping force, mainly provided by Syria, deployed; the other Arab contingents soon withdrew while the Syrians have remained in strength ever since. PLO and later Hizbollah terrorist attacks across the border into Israel have provoked numerous retaliatory operations and several invasions by the Israelis. In 1978 the Israelis occupied a zone close to their border where there are frequent clashes between Hizbollah guerrillas and the Israeli Defence Force and the Israeli-backed South Lebanese Army (SLA). The Israeli Prime Minister, Ehud Barak, said he would withdraw from Lebanon in July 2000.

The first Israeli invasion took place in March 1978 in response, the Israelis claim, to an increasing Palestinian build-up in the south of the country and not as a direct retaliation for the PLO seaborne raid which resulted in the deaths of thirty-four Israelis. Southern

Southern Lebanon as it was before 21 May 2000

Lebanon was also the scene of conflict between Christian and Shi'a communities and the Israelis took the opportunity to destroy Shi'a villages and recruit the Christians into Major Haddad's militia. Israel withdrew its forces which had penetrated as far north as the River Litani by the end of April, and handed over control to the UN Interim Force in Lebanon (UNIFIL) except for a 10km strip along the border where Major Haddad took charge.

The attempted assassination of the Israeli ambassador in London was cited as the reason for the much larger and longer-lasting invasion in 1982 when the Israelis advanced as far north as Beirut and eventually caused the PLO to withdraw from the country. The Israeli forces remained in Lebanon for a further thirty months, which resulted in many Israeli casualties and led to the formation of the Shi'a Hizbollah. Hizbollah originated in a breakaway group of Amal (a Lebanese faction) and was backed by Iran. It was initially supervised by the small contingent of Iranian Revolutionary Guards who arrived in the Bekaa in July 1982 and was soon reinforced to some 2,000-strong.

Hizbollah was probably responsible for two suicide car bomb attacks on the French and US Marine units which caused massive casualties. The withdrawal of the western contingents from Lebanon was claimed as a victory by Hizbollah. Later a similar attack, which was certainly carried out by the group, was made on the Israeli HQ in Tyre. The Israelis' movements were continually harried by Hizbollah until they fought their way out of Lebanon in June 1985. After the Israeli withdrawal fighting continued in Lebanon with clashes between an alliance of the Shi'ite Amal and the Druze against the Christians, Amal against the Palestinians left in Beirut, and pro-Syrian militias against the fundamentalist Sunni in Tripoli. Civil war intensified in 1986; the tripartite agreement between the Maronites, Amal and the Druze collapsed within two weeks and the Syrians had to deploy troops in Beirut to halt the fighting between Amal and Hizbollah.

The civil war was only brought to an end in 1990 after the surviving members of Lebanon's parliament met in Taif and later in Lebanon to agree a new constitution. Initially most parties rejected the Taif Agreement. Nevertheless a new president was appointed, only to be killed two weeks later. This atrocity spurred the formation of a new government, composed equally of Christians and Muslims, which dismissed the army commander, General Aoun. Most of the army remained loyal to Aoun and it was not until October 1990 that the general surrendered to the Syrian army. The armed factions all agreed to leave Beirut and eventually consented to disarmament; only Hizbollah was allowed to continue to be armed.

Opinion in Israel was divided over whether it should withdraw unilaterally from South Lebanon. Argument in favour of withdrawal pointed to the ever-growing list of Israel casualties (39 killed in 1997 and 24 in 1998, not to mention the 73 who died in a disastrous helicopter collision en route for Lebanon in 1987). Also, Israel always earned (and still does) adverse publicity whenever it reacted to a terrorist attack (usually on the principle of ten eyes for one rather than an eye for an eye). Withdrawal could have had a positive effect on negotiations with Syria, which would no longer have been able to use Hizbollah as a surrogate force to provoke Israel. (Syria could easily curtail Hizbollah activity if it wished – both Syrians and Hizbollah are based in the Bekaa Valley and most of Hizbollah's arms and ammunition is flown in from Iran through Damascus airport.) UNIFIL said that it could redeploy up to the Israeli border within a week.

Withdrawal would also mean Hizbollah rocket attacks reaching further into Israel; they could already hit northern Israel from north of the Israeli security zone. Arrangements would have to be made to protect the members and families of the SLA, against whom reprisals were likely to be taken, and, of course, Israel was also reluctant to be seen to be making any withdrawal which could spur on its enemies. Eventually the withdrawal was completed on 21 May 2000. It had begun in a low-key way some weeks earlier but for the final few days it took place under widespread media coverage. The South Lebanon Army disintegrated. A number of its members surrendered and others deserted, while 6,000 soldiers and their families were allowed into Israel. The withdrawal was closely followed up by Hizbollah and by the original Lebanese inhabitants returning to the villages they had

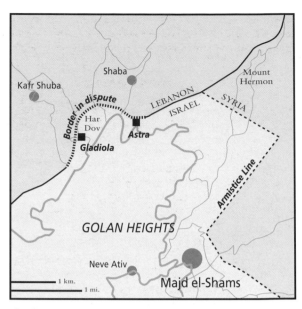

The Shaba Farms

been forced to leave, some as long ago as eighteen years previously. The IDF and the UN then demarcated the border again because over the years Israeli border defences had encroached into Lebanese territory. The UN announced that the Israeli withdrawal had been total and complete, but Hizbollah maintains that one area on the slopes of Mount Hermon, the Shaba Farms (Har Dov to the Israelis), was still occupied Lebanese territory. The Israelis maintain that the disputed area is in Syria. It has provided a useful excuse for Hizbollah to harry the Israelis and they kidnapped three Israeli soldiers there in October 2000. Hizbollah still holds the soldiers and is demanding the release of nineteen Lebanese prisoners in Israel in exchange for their release.

Israel expected, or rather hoped, that the Lebanese Army would fill the gap their withdrawal left and ensure there were no terrorist attacks across the border. However, the Lebanese army is loath to take on this responsibility and so only a few hundred soldiers have been sent to the south and they keep well away from the border. There have been very few border incidents, other than at the Shaba Farm, since the Israeli withdrawal. Israel replied to all these incidents as usual with an air strike or artillery fire. Israel has also attacked Syrian targets deep in Lebanon in April and July 2001, blaming the Syrians for not controlling Hizbollah.

The new Syrian president, Bashar Assad, Hafez Assad's son, responded to growing demands for Syrian withdrawal from Lebanon by redeploying Syrian forces from Mount Lebanon and from most of Beirut. In all, some forty-five sites were evacuated, most of the withdrawn troops going to the Bekaa Valley and only a few armoured units crossing into Syria. The Syrians are highly unpopular in Lebanon, not just because of their military presence, but because over half a million Syrian workers are taking the jobs in reconstruction and agriculture which the Lebanese badly need. The UN too is considering a draw-down of UNIFIL, its mission in Lebanon. UNIFIL strength will be cut from 5,800 to 2,000 by July 2002 and eventually it will become purely an observer force.

Hizbollah has been designated a terrorist organisation by the US which has threatened Lebanon with sanctions unless it freezes Hizbollah's funds and disarms its fighters. Since March Hizbollah has stepped up its attacks on Israeli positions along the border, has fired rockets towards Qiryat Shmona and on one occasion penetrated into Israel to attack kibbutz Metzuba, killing an army officer and five civilians. The Israelis believe the attacks are intended to provoke them while they are heavily engaged in operations in the West Bank.

TRAVEL ADVICE

FCO: Most visits are trouble-free. Avoid Palestinian refugee camps, do not visit the Israeli border, do not visit the northern Bekaa Valley.

State: Warns of risks to US citizens. No US airline uses Beirut airport. Avoid Palestinian camps, take special care in south Beirut and parts of the Bekaa Valley. Danger from landmines.

BIBLIOGRAPHY AND WEBSITES

Abul-Husn, Latif, *The Lebanese Conflict: Looking Inward*, Boulder, 1998
O'Balance, Edgar, *Civil War in Lebanon, 1975–92*, Macmillan, 1998
Saad-Gharayeb, Amal, *Hizbu'llah: Politics and Religion*, Pluto Press, 2002
Sirriyeh, Hussein, *Lebanon: The Dimensions of Conflict*, International Institute for Strategic Studies, Adelphi Paper 243, 1989

Hizbollah: www.hizballah.org
Middle East Intelligence Review: www.meib.org
Middle East International Online: http://meionline.com
Middle East Network Information Center: http://link/lania.utexas.edu
Middle East Research and Information Project: www.merip.org

Israel

Population: 6,336,000 (including Israelis in the West Bank, Gaza, East Jerusalem and the Golan)
Jews 82%, Arab 19% (of which 3% Christian, 2% Druse)
Armed Forces: 163,500
Foreign Forces: UNTSO 144
Per Capita GDP: $US 19,200
Currency: shekel

The land between the Mediterranean and the River Jordan is probably the most fought-over stretch in the world. It is the junction of the three continents of Europe, Asia and Africa and connects to a fourth area, the Arabian peninsula. A great number of powers have ruled the region since the Israelites settled there: Abbasids, Assyrians, Babylonians, Persians, Romans and Ummayids. The Crusaders captured Jerusalem in 1099, but lost their last stronghold in the Holy Land in 1291 to the Mamelukes who were defeated in their turn by the Ottomans. They ruled a vast Middle Eastern empire until the First World War when it was broken up and Palestine became a British mandate. Throughout all this time there had always been a small Jewish presence; by 1882 it totalled some 24,000, when the Palestinian population was about 300,000. There were waves of immigration, *aliyah* in Hebrew, both at that time and between 1904 and 1914. Despite the Balfour Declaration of 1917 which promised a Jewish national home in Palestine, the British controlled Jewish immigration very strictly, even after the Second World War and the Holocaust.

When Israel gained its independence on 15 May 1948 it was immediately attacked by five Arab armies. Since then it has only signed peace treaties with two of its attackers, Egypt and Jordan. Fighting between Arab and Jew had occurred much earlier – in 1920, 1929 and 1936; serious conflict broke out after the United Nations General Assembly passed a resolution in November 1947 to establish Jewish and Arab States in a partitioned Palestine.

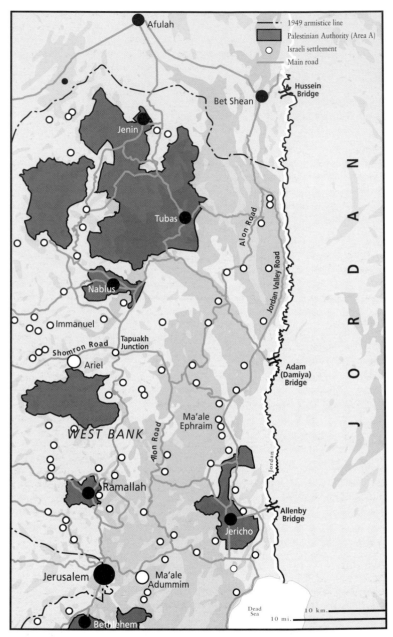

The Jordan Valley

By May 1948 the Jews had roughly trebled the territory they controlled. The fighting ended after the Israeli capture of Elat on the Red Sea on 10 March 1949; as Armistice agreements were signed Israel withdrew from Lebanon and Iraqi troops from west of the Jordan. Some exchanges of land took place along the cease fire line between Israel and Jordanian-controlled West Bank. The Israelis controlled the bulk of Palestine, with Egypt taking the Gaza Strip; Syria took some small areas in the Yarmouk Valley and along the border to the north, while Jordan occupied East Jerusalem and the West Bank.

There have been three major Arab–Israeli wars. The first came in 1956 when Israel, in collusion with France and Britain, invaded Egypt and then withdrew from the Sinai which it had over-run. In 1967, provoked by the closure of the Straits of Tiran and an Egyptian build-up in Sinai, Israel launched a pre-emptive air strike that destroyed most of the Egyptian, Syrian and Jordanian air forces. During the six days of fighting Israel captured Sinai, the Golan Heights, the West Bank, Gaza Strip and East Jerusalem; it did not withdraw from these territories after a cease fire was agreed, although it was called upon to do so by the UN Security Council. Surprised by the Arab attack in 1973 Israel nearly lost the Golan and the Egyptians managed to cross the Suez Canal; eventually Israel regained the Golan, crossed the Canal and surrounded the Egyptian army, trapped on the east bank. In addition to the major wars there have been outbreaks of fighting on all of the armistice lines and terrorist attacks, made mainly by Palestinians across all Israel's borders.

Israel has now signed peace treaties with Egypt and Jordan, and had made considerable progress towards reaching agreement with the Palestinians. Israel withdrew from the whole of Sinai and from small areas along the border with Jordan. The Israeli government under the late Yitzhak Rabin began talks with the Syrians on a peace treaty; although nothing was signed or formally announced it would appear that Rabin agreed to withdraw from the Golan in return for a resumption of normal relations. Although the principles which it would follow were agreed, no conclusion was reached on matters such as the final border; the timing and phases of withdrawal; separation and limitation of forces clauses; and confidence-building measures. Israeli–Syrian peace talks reopened in December 1999 but were broken off in February by the Israelis, claiming it was impossible to negotiate while Israeli soldiers were under attack in Lebanon. Israeli involvement in Lebanon is described on pp. 78–81.

Despite the progress made towards peace with all its neighbours Israel still feels threatened and faces three quite separate forms of threat: conventional war, missile attack and terrorist attack. Each threat has to be countered by different forces with different equipment and training. The question of missile attack and defence is covered in the section entitled Middle East Proliferation on pp. 72–6, while terrorism is covered in the Palestinian section on pp. 85–93. At present Israel is best prepared to meet the least likely threat – conventional war launched by its Arab neighbours. Egypt remains an existential threat on account of its large armed forces which are increasingly equipped with more modern weapons paid for by US aid. The Limitation of Forces agreement means that Egypt can station few troops east of the Suez Canal and it likely that Israel will act fast enough to meet any attacking force deep in Sinai and halt it there.

Balance of Forces

	Egypt	Jordan	Syria	Total	Israel
Tanks	5,000	1,060	4,700	10,760	3,930
Artillery	3,500	830	3,020	7,350	2,340
Attack Helicopter	105	20	87	214	130
Combat Aircraft	580	100	590	1,270	450

Israel's main fear is a surprise attack on the Golan but Syria could recover the Golan through negotiation. Syria would then be in an even better position to attack Israel despite the demilitarised zone and limitations on forces that would undoubtedly be included in any peace treaty. However, as long as Israel holds on to the Golan a Syrian attack is always a possibility. From the east Israel fears an Iraqi rather than a Jordanian attack, although the Jordan Rift (not the river) is an effective tank obstacle and there are few crossing points; nor are there many east–west routes through the West Bank. The Israeli air force could hold up any attempt to cross the Jordan Rift, but nevertheless Israel has deployed an

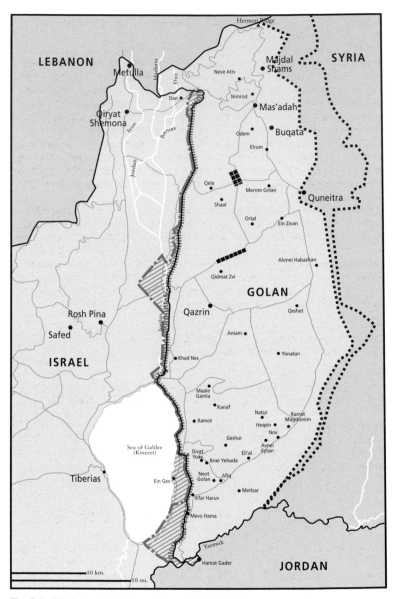

The Golan Heights

Note: At the north-east coast of the Sea of
Galilee the 1923 border and the 1949 armistice line both
run 10 meters inland from the high water mark

———	Demarcated boundary 1923
▬ ▬ ▬	Armistice line 1949
/////	Demilitarized zones 1949-1967
‖‖‖‖‖‖	Syrian line of control, 4 June 1967
● ● ●	Disengagement lines 1974
■ ■ ■	Anti-tank mines fired by battery of 4 MLRS

armoured division in the West Bank poised to cross the River Jordan and meet any Iraqi force in the desert east of Mafraq.

Many Israelis see giving up the Golan as throwing away their country's security on the Syrian front but the situation has changed radically since the pre-1967 days when Syrian troops overlooked Israel's Hula Valley. Attacking up the Golan Heights will be less difficult as there are now many more tank-passable roads and tracks up the Heights and modern tank engines have much greater power. Syrian artillery can, in any event, now hit targets in Israel from its present positions on the Golan. The peace treaty could include restrictions on the development of minefields and anti-tank obstacles on the Golan. The political fall-out of withdrawal would be far less than would accrue from abandoning settlements in the West Bank. There are far fewer settlers, with only some 17,000 living on the Golan, nor are there the same emotional ties as there are to the biblical areas of Judaea and Samaria (though there was Israelite settlement there during the reigns of David and Solomon).

At one time, when Ehud Barak was prime minister, there was some optimism that the Arab–Israeli confrontation might be close to an end but that optimism has now disappeared, mainly owing to the scale of the Israeli–Palestinian fighting. After so many years of violence Israelis will continue to feel threatened even if peace treaties are reached with all its neighbours, and with Iraq and Iran which are still implacably opposed to Israel's very existence. Of course, Israel's neighbours feel equally threatened, having lost all wars with Israel. Sadly there are extremists both in Israel and in the Arab world who do not want peace and who will always attempt to upset the peace process.

TRAVEL ADVICE
FCO: Warns against travel in the Israel/Gaza border area and along the Lebanese border.
State: Advises travellers to defer their visit.

BIBLIOGRAPHY AND WEBSITES

Karsh, Ephraim (ed.), *Between War and Peace: Dilemmas of Israeli Security*, Frank Cass, 1996
Schiff, Ze'ev, *A History of the Israeli Army: 1874 to the Present*, Sidgwick & Jackson, 1985

Haaretz (newspaper): www.haaretz.co.il/eng
Israel Ministry of Foreign Affairs: www.israel-mfa.gov.il
Jaffee Centre for Strategic Studies: www.tau.ac.il/jcss/start
Jerusalem Report: www.jrep.com

A Palestinian State (West Bank and Gaza)

Population: West Bank: Palestinians 2 million, Israelis 206,000; Gaza: Palestinians 1.1 million, Israelis 7,000
Security Forces: Presidential Security (Force 17), Special Security Forces, National Security Force, National Intelligence, Preventive Security Force, Military Intelligence. Strengths unknown.
Paramilitary: Tanzim
Islamic Groups: HAMAS, Islamic Jihad

The name Palestine was given to the region lying between the Mediterranean and the River Jordan by the Romans after their conquest in 64 BC. Before then the indigenous population of numerous tribes had been generally known as Canaanites, who were joined by the Israelite and Philistine invaders. The region was conquered or fought over on numerous occasions both before and after the Roman conquest but since then the original inhabitants have been known as Palestinians, whether Christian or Muslim, and these people included

Jews until Israel gained its independence. There has not been an independent indigenous state in the region since the Israelite invasion.

In 1880 the Jewish population of Palestine numbered some 24,000, compared to an Arab population of 300,000. The Jewish repopulation of Palestine began in 1882 as a result of the pogroms in Russia and the persecution in Poland and Romania; 25,000 emigrated then and a second *Aliyah* took place between 1904 and 1914 when 40,000 Jews came from Europe and Yemen. During the First World War the British Foreign Secretary Arthur Balfour, in a letter to Lord Rothschild, stated that 'the government would use its best endeavours to establish a National Jewish Home in Palestine, but this was not to prejudice the rights of the Palestinian population'. After the defeat of the Turks in 1918 Britain received a mandate to govern Palestine. However, it restricted the immigration of Jews. In the 1920s there were several instances of Arab attacks on Jewish settlements, the worst being the killing of fifty-nine people, including women and children, in Hebron in August 1929.

The Arab revolt of May 1936 was aimed as much at British authority as it was at the Jewish population; by October eighty Jews had been killed and the British Army had killed over a hundred Arabs in suppressing the revolt. A commission, the first of several and headed by Lord Peel, was tasked with examining the future of the British mandate; the commission recommended partition but with a British-controlled sector from the Mediterranean as far as and including Jerusalem. A number of other investigating organisations were appointed until finally a UN Commission reported in November 1947. This too recommended partition into Arab and Jewish states but with a UN-controlled international territory around Jerusalem. The Jews accepted the UN recommendation but the Arabs did not. The UN General Assembly passed a resolution on 29 November 1947 recognising Israel's independence. Fighting between Jews and Arabs had begun well before this and after the resolution was passed elements of five Arab states entered Palestine to attack the Israelis. The war continued until 10 March 1949 when Israel captured the Red Sea port of Um Rashrash, now called Elat; armistice agreements with Israel's four neighbours were signed between February and July 1949. In the war the Israelis had seized considerably more territory than had been recommended in the UN partition proposal but they had also lost the Jewish Quarter of Old Jerusalem and a number of settlements to the north and south of the city. The Egyptians gained control of a strip along the Mediterranean coast around Gaza and Jordan controlled what became known as the West Bank. Large numbers of Palestinians fled or were forced to leave the areas now controlled by Israel, many being housed in refugee camps in the West Bank and Gaza Strip. Only in the north did a considerable Palestinian population remain under Israeli control, as did the Bedouin who lived in the Negev.

In the 1967 war Israel captured the remaining parts of Palestine, the West Bank and the Gaza Strip, as well as Sinai and the Syrian Golan Heights. Many of the refugees in camps in the West Bank fled to Jordan. Despite the resolutions of the UN Security Council Israel remained in control of these territories and retained them after the 1973 war.

In the early days of their occupation the Israelis were seen as no worse governors than the Jordanians; many Palestinians were inured to occupation: 'Before the Jordanians it was the British, before them the Turks, so what's new?' The Gaza Strip became a hotbed for Palestinian terrorism until 1971 when General Ariel Sharon eradicated the terrorists using Draconian methods. In the West Bank there were demonstrations from time to time and some amateur attempts at terrorist attack. The Israelis established a number of settlements in both Gaza and the West Bank; they were carefully sited so as to enhance the defence of the areas, mainly along the border with Egypt, in the Jordan Valley and on the high ground overlooking it. Also they were thought necessary to justify the Israeli army's continued presence so that it would be protecting civilians and not just occupying land.

The 'Allon' plan avoided establishing settlements close to centres of Arab population. The Likud government changed this policy when it was elected in 1977; it was dedicated to the dogma that Judaea and Samaria formed the 'God-given land' known as 'Erez Israel'. Settlement activity increased enormously from the 33 settlements with 20,000 inhabitants in the West Bank and Gaza in 1977 to the current 146 settlements and some 213,700 settlers (excluding East Jerusalem). Many are ardent supporters of 'Erez Israel' who are unlikely to leave their settlements even when they are totally surrounded by Palestinian-controlled land.

By 1987 the Palestinians' resentment was growing. First, their problems appeared to have been relegated to a position of secondary importance at the Arab League summit in Jordan in November. Secondly, Palestinians in the Occupied Territories felt abandoned to some extent by the PLO hierarchy. Palestinian youth was becoming disenchanted with the apathy of their elders, particularly when compared with the success of the Southern Lebanese Shiites against Israeli forces there. The example of the lone Palestinian who flew by hang-glider into northern Israel and killed six Israeli soldiers before being killed himself did much to encourage belligerence. The spark which led to the Intifada, or uprising, in December 1987 was a traffic accident at a Gaza crossing point in which four Arabs were killed by an Israeli vehicle. Initially, the Intifada was spontaneous and essentially home-grown; it quickly spread from Gaza to East Jerusalem and the West Bank. The Israelis were caught by surprise and reacted with ill-conceived measures of violence, which were soon broadcast across the world. Palestinian morale was boosted and a good deal of sympathy was generated worldwide. Coping with the Intifada was not what the Israeli army had been trained or equipped for, nor did they see it as their proper role; the general staff soon made it clear that there was no military solution and that a political one must be found. A number of Israelis realised for the first time that they could not occupy the territories forever.

The first moves towards solving the Palestinian problem came as part of the Camp David Accords of 1979, when the Egyptian–Israeli peace treaty was negotiated, in which the Israelis committed themselves to moving towards autonomy for the Palestinians. However, the Shamir government made no attempt to implement this. Next, at the end of the Gulf War a conference jointly chaired by the US and Russia was held in Madrid, which the Palestinians attended as part of the Jordanian delegation. At the conference the US assured all parties that it sought a Palestinian autonomy agreement lasting five years and that in its third year talks on its final status would start. The main conclusion of the conference was that bilateral talks should be initiated between Israel and Arab countries, and it was agreed to hold a number of follow-on conferences, including one to be held in Washington involving Israel, Jordan and the Palestinians. Despite all the effort no progress was achieved.

At the end of August 1993 it was revealed that secret talks had been taking place between the Israeli government and the PLO in Oslo, and that they had agreed to recognise each other. In September Prime Minister Yitzhak Rabin and Chairman Yasser Arafat exchanged letters in which the PLO recognised Israel's right to exist in peace and security and renounced the use of terrorism and violence. Rabin responded by saying that Israel recognised the PLO as the representative of the Palestinian people and would start negotiations with them. On the 13th a 'Declaration of Principles on Interim Self-Government Arrangements' (Oslo I) was signed at the White House.

The aim of the Declaration was to establish a Palestinian Interim Self-Government Authority and to hold elections for a council to govern the West Bank and Gaza in respect of all matters except those being reserved to the permanent status negotiations. These included: Jerusalem, settlements, refugees, security arrangements and borders. The transitional period was not to exceed five years. The principles also included provisions for the handover of certain civil responsibilities such as health and education; the redeployment of Israeli forces; the formation of a Palestinian police force; and the withdrawal from the Gaza Strip and Jericho area. Despite a number of horrifying terrorist incidents – which included the killing of thirty Palestinians at prayer in the Hebron Tomb of Abraham Mosque by an Israeli extremist, followed by two bombs which killed thirteen Israelis – an 'Agreement on the Gaza Strip and Jericho' was signed in Cairo on 4 May 1994. Israeli troops withdrew and Jericho was handed over to the Palestine National Authority (PNA) on the 15th and Gaza the next day.

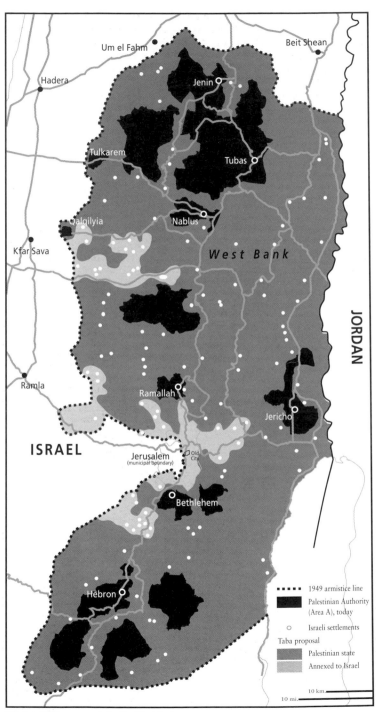

The Israeli/Taba proposals for the West Bank

'The Israeli–Palestinian Interim Agreement on the West Bank and Gaza Strip' (Oslo II) was initialled in Washington on 28 September 1995. The agreement divided the West Bank into five zones: East Jerusalem (annexed by Israel), Israeli settlements to remain under Israeli control and Areas A, B and C. In Area A the PNA is responsible for security and all Israeli troops were withdrawn; in Area B responsibility for security is shared by Israel and the PNA; and in Area C Israel retains full security control. The PNA is responsible for civil administration in Areas A, B and C. Initially Area A comprised six of the main Arab towns, which were handed over by the end of 1995. The inclusion of Hebron was delayed while negotiations took place on how much of the city Israel would retain so as to protect the small Jewish settlement in its centre.

The process was then interrupted by two events. First came the assassination of Prime Minister Rabin on 4 November 1995 by an Israeli extremist, following which his successor, Shimon Peres, decided to call elections. Secondly, there was the killing of the leading Palestinian bomb-maker, Yehiya Ayash, 'the Engineer', on 5 January 1996 by means of a booby-trapped mobile telephone; this led to a series of reprisal attacks by suicide bombers who killed fifty-six Israelis. Voting for safety rather than security, the Israelis elected Benjamin Netanyahu as prime minister and the Likud returned to government; the peace process came virtually to a halt. Not until January 1997 was the main part of Hebron handed over to the PNA, nine months after the scheduled date. Israel retained control of Abraham's Tomb and about 20 per cent of the city, where some 30,000 Palestinians live, so as to protect 500 Israeli settlers. The Hebron agreement included, among other matters, the withdrawal of Israeli forces in three stages from the whole West Bank except for Israeli settlements, the

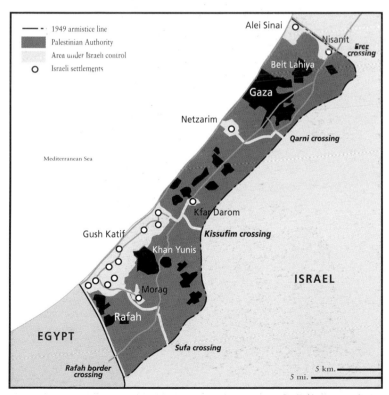

The Gaza Strip

security roads linking them to Israel, and as yet undefined military areas. Two Israeli offers for the first stage of withdrawal were rejected by the PNA as being too small.

The deadlock appeared to be broken by the Wye Memorandum agreed to by Netanyahu and Arafat on 23 October 1998 after a week of hard negotiating at President Clinton's insistence at the Wye Plantation in Maryland. The agreement included: an Israeli release of several hundred Palestinian prisoners; a timetable for the arrest by the Palestinians, supervised by the CIA, of alleged terrorists and confiscation of illegal weapons; an Israeli troop withdrawal from a further 13 per cent of the West Bank, of which 3 per cent is to be declared a nature reserve; and the opening of Gaza airport, which took place on 3 November. Most importantly for Israel the Palestinian National Council was to meet and vote to confirm the annulment of the anti-Israeli clauses in the PLO Charter; this took place in the presence of President Clinton on 14 December. Initially there was a two-week delay while Netanyahu insisted that the Wye Memorandum be ratified by the Israeli cabinet and then by the parliament, the Knesset. The Memorandum was ratified in the cabinet by 7 votes to 5 with three abstentions and two absences and in the Knesset by 75 to 19 with nine abstentions and sixteen members not voting.

The first stage of the troop withdrawal took place on 20 November when the PNA took full control (Area A) of 7.1 per cent more of the West Bank. The Wye Memorandum was then halted following a speech by Yasser Arafat in which he proclaimed his intention of declaring Palestinian independence on 4 May 1999, the date the five-year transitional period ended. Despite the efforts of President Clinton to hold the Israelis to the deal, the Israeli cabinet set three conditions for the resumption of the Wye agreements. The Palestinian Authority had to renounce its intention of unilaterally declaring an independent state; halt violence and incitement; collect and destroy illegal weapons; detain murderers; and cooperate with Israel.

The Palestine peace process took on a new lease of life with the Israeli election of May 1999 which made Ehud Barak prime minister. A summit meeting was held at Sharm el Sheikh in September 1999 at which Barak committed Israel to carrying out the withdrawals agreed to at Wye by the Netanyahu government. The final-status talks were to begin straight away with the aim of establishing a framework agreement by 15 February 2000 and getting final agreement by September. It was now clear that there would be a Palestinian state, although its borders were yet to be decided. This would depend on Israeli demands to retain most but by no means all of the settlements under Israeli sovereignty; land in Israel might be handed over to the Palestinians in exchange. The Palestinians did not reject this principle but did not agree to the proportionality of the exchange. Israel would also have to decide on whether it wants to have a 'hard' border with Palestine or one that allows freedom of movement for workers and for trade. In the latter case Israel would need to have an element of control on the borders between Gaza and Egypt and the West Bank and Jordan (a much shorter distance to control).

There was much optimism as President Clinton chaired another Israeli–Palestinian summit at Camp David in July 2000. However, the summit ended in failure when Yasser Arafat refused the package offered by the Israelis. It is still not entirely clear exactly what was on offer, as Israeli sources tend to exaggerate some elements while Palestinians insist that the offer was not nearly as generous as is commonly thought. Certainly many Israelis, and not just those on the right wing, thought Barak had gone too far; the most generous offer is claimed to have been total withdrawal with Israel annexing 9 per cent of the West Bank, leaving some sixty settlements with 40,000 inhabitants in Palestinian territory. A much smaller area of Israel would be transferred to the Palestinians in compensation for the annexation. Withdrawal from the Gaza Strip and the Samarian Mountain range settlements is thought to have been included in the package. Whatever the truth of the matter, Arafat was blamed for the failure, particularly by Clinton who had regarded the summit as his last chance to achieve Middle East peace. Of course, Arafat would have been condemned by the Palestinians if he had accepted a package they felt was unsatisfactory in respect of refugees and the Haram ash Sharif (Temple Mount) in Jerusalem. The Israelis are criticised for not realising that Arabs will react favourably to agreement of principle and then will negotiate, for example, a watered-down implementation of the principle – but will not talk further when the principle is rejected.

In Israel Barak lost even more political support, mainly because of the concessions he was prepared to make, and Israelis had their view that Arafat did not want peace confirmed. The negotiators did not give up and met at Taba, in Egypt, in August in an attempt to bridge the gaps, but the talks were overtaken by events. On 28 September Ariel Sharon, now the Likud party leader, made a much-publicised visit to the Temple Mount, protected by a large force of police who clashed with Palestinians on the Mount. The next day Jewish worshippers at the Western Wall were stoned from the Temple Mount. Israeli reaction left 7 dead and 220 wounded. The second Intifada (though many Israeli officials claim it was not an 'intifada' which is an uprising of the people but a declaration of war by Arafat) then began. Sharon's visit may have lit the fuse but many believe that the uprising had been planned earlier and was just waiting for the spark to set it off. Others say the uprising had been inevitable for some months as Palestinians became more and more frustrated by the conditions imposed on them by Israel.

This time it was different; the Palestinians had weapons and were prepared to use them. Over the months the violence escalated and at one stage spread to involve Israeli Arabs who rioted across a wide area; ten were killed by Israeli police. By now Barak no longer had a coalition majority in the Knesset and failed in a move to bring the Likud into the coalition. In December he announced that he would resign as prime minister and hold an election for the post; many saw this as a move to ensure that his predecessor, Benjamin Netanyahu, could not stand (and most likely win), as he was not then a member of the Knesset. To quell the criticism Barak called a general election which was won by Sharon and the Likud party.

With Sharon in charge the Israelis expected a massive clamp-down on the Palestinians but he behaved, initially, for him, with commendable restraint, even after the murder of twenty-two young people outside a discotheque by a suicide bomber. A number of cease fires were agreed and all were violated. There was an increase of firing at Israeli settlers motoring in the West Bank. The Israelis, for their part, concentrated on taking out suspected terrorist leaders, many of whom were murdered by undercover soldiers, and responding to Palestinian violence by attacking PA offices and police buildings with highly accurate missiles fired from helicopters, and on occasions by F-16 fighters. Using aerial attack allowed the Israelis to reach targets deep inside Palestinian built-up areas but must have been dependent on intelligence provided by collaborators, a number of whom have been executed by the PA. The Israelis could therefore claim to be making controlled responses to Palestinian terrorist attacks (though often there are inevitably some civilian casualties as well as those targeted), while Palestinian attacks are designed to cause maximum casualties among the Israeli people. However, it is clear that Sharon has no intention of offering the Palestinians anything like as much as that offered by Barak.

Following the Middle East Peace Summit held at Sharm el Sheikh in October 2000, President Clinton organised an international fact-finding committee headed by former Senator George Mitchell, who had conducted a similar inquiry in Northern Ireland. The committee's report, released in May 2001, made a number of recommendations: both the Palestinians and Israelis were to end the violence and resume talks as a matter of urgency; they should resume security cooperation; and establish a 'cooling-off period'. The Palestinians were to make a 100 per cent effort to prevent terrorist attacks. The Israelis were to freeze all settlement activity, including the 'natural growth' of settlements; the IDF should consider withdrawing to positions held before 28 September in order to avoid friction, and should refrain from the destruction of houses, trees and agricultural property. Israel should lift all closures, pay all tax revenues owed to the Palestine Authority and permit Palestinians employed in Israel to return to their jobs. In May a further agreement was reached called the Tenet plan, named after the US Central Intelligence chief who brokered it. Its clauses included, among other matters, the resumption of security cooperation; the Palestinian Authority was to arrest terrorists and Israel was to release all those arrested who had no association with terrorist activities; and Palestinian incitement to attack Israeli targets would end, while Israel was to take action against those inciting or engaging in violence against Palestinians. Needless to say, the Mitchell Report has not been implemented. Some observers claim it is flawed by the absence of any reference to the end result required for peace – the establishment of a Palestinian state. The Tenet plan has also not been implemented.

Sharon has called several times for a week free of violent incidents as a precursor to resuming talks; on every occasion the week has been interrupted by a Palestinian attack or an Israeli reprisal or undercover assassination. A suicide bomber killed fifteen Israelis on 9 August at a Jerusalem pizzeria. In response Israel occupied Orient House in Jerusalem which houses the Palestinian Authority offices and which is the focal point for the Palestinian cause; they also occupied a number of buildings in the Palestinian compound in Abu Dis. On 17 October Rehavem Ze'evi, the Minister of Tourism, was assassinated in an East Jerusalem hotel; Israeli troops and tanks entered a number of West Bank towns and remained there despite US calls for their withdrawal.

The violence has continued to escalate, with each terrorist attack resulting in further Israeli destruction of Palestinian Authority security bases – which in turn provokes yet another suicide bomber. In the early months of the second Intifada Palestinian casualties far outnumbered those suffered by Israel, but by 2002 the numbers were levelling out as the Palestinians adopted the Hizbollah tactics that led to Israel's withdrawal from Lebanon. The Israelis have begun re-entering Palestinian refugee camps in their search for terrorists. Israel's reaction to the attacks on 11 September was to say 'now the Americans know what we have had to put up with for many years'. A number of Palestinian organisations have been designated as foreign terrorist organisations, including Harakat al-Muqawamah al-Islamiyya (HAMAS), the Palestinian Islamic Jihad and, in Lebanon, Hizbollah. On 22 March the US added the Al Aqsa Martyrs Brigade, a militant off-shoot of Fatah, to its list of terrorist organisations following their claims of responsibility for a number of suicide bomb attacks. The Israeli Kahane Chai (Kach) has also been listed. The US government appeared loath to become involved in the situation in Israel because they are too committed to the war on terrorism and the axis of evil, and they do not seem to realise that success in that war would be more likely if the Palestinian–Israeli conflict could be finally settled.

A suicide bomb attack at a Passover supper (*seder*) that killed 29 and wounded 130 Israelis on 27 March 2002 was the final provocation for Sharon, who ordered the Israeli Defence Force to search the West Bank and destroy the terrorist infrastructure. The operation, named 'Defensive Wall', caused widespread damage – devastation might be a more accurate word – and an unknown number of casualties; several thousand Palestinians were arrested and every west Bank town bar Jericho invaded. The resumption of negotiations will be impossible for some time. The US has been powerless to halt the Israeli operation despite the visit of Secretary of State Colin Powell to the region. Some claim President Bush's policies have inflamed the situation. On 12 March 2002 the US voted at the UN Security Council for a resolution that called for a Palestinian state; the UN Secretary General said they must end the illegal occupation and must stop the bombing of civilian areas, the assassinations . . .'. The Palestinians saw these reports as support for their cause with no criticism of their use of terror. Following the passover bombing President Bush has said: 'Suicide bombings in the name of religion is simple terror,' and he defended Israel's right to defend itself, so giving some encouragement to Sharon's plans.

Israel has now decided that the only way to reduce the number of suicide bombings is to construct a fence/wall to keep the bombers out. This course had been avoided for many years as it would have been a form of border – so delineating Israel's claims on West Bank territory; it would also complicate matters concerning settlements stranded to the east of the fence (there has been a fence around the whole Gaza strip for many years). Another two suicide bombs, this time in Jerusalem on 18 and 19 June, led to the Israelis re-entering a number of towns with the possibility of a more permanent stay. Both the Israelis and US President George Bush called for the replacement of Arafat as the head of the PNA. By the end of July 2002, 1,660 Palestinians and 575 Israelis had been killed since September 2000.

TRAVEL ADVICE

FCO: Advises against all travel to Gaza and the West Bank.

State: Warns that the situation in Gaza and West Bank is extremely volatile. US citizens residing in the territories should consider moving.

BIBLIOGRAPHY AND WEBSITES

Karmi, Ghada, and Eugene Cotron (eds), The Palestinian Exodus 1948–1998 [pub?date? AQ]

Safieh, Afif, *The Peace Process: From Breakthrough to Breakdown?*, Palestinian General Delegation to the UK, 1997

Schiff, Ze'ev, Khalidi, Ahmad and Agha, Hussein, *Common Ground on Redeployment of Israeli Forces in the West Bank*, Initiative for Peace and Cooperation in the Middle East, 1995

Israel, The West Bank and Gaza: Toward a Solution, Jaffee Centre for Strategic Studies, 1989

Report on Israeli Settlement in the Occupied Territories (bi-monthly), Foundation for Middle East Peace, Washington

West Bank and Gaza: Israel's Options for Peace, Jaffee Centre for Strategic Studies, 1989

Applied Research Institute for Jerusalem: www.arij.org

Council for Palestinian Restitution and Repatriation: http://rightofreturn.org

Foundation for Middle East Peace, Settlement Report: www.fmep.org

Hamas (Islamic Resistance Front): www.Hamas.org

Israel/Palestine Center for Research and Information: www.ipcri.org

Palestinian Academic Society for the Study of International Affairs: www.passia.org

Palestinian Authority: www.pna.net

Peace Now: www.peacenow.org.il

PLO Negotiations Affairs Department: www.nad.gov.ps

Jerusalem

Population: Greater Jerusalem 622,000 (Jews 429,000, Muslim 151,000, Christian 42,000)

The future status of Jerusalem, claimed by both Israelis and Palestinians as their historical capital, had been deliberately left as the final problem to be solved in the Arab–Israeli peace process. The hope was that if everything else had been satisfactorily solved then all that had been achieved would not be thrown away because agreement could not be reached over Jerusalem.

Jerusalem is holy to all three monotheist religions and all three have fought to regain it for their faith: the Crusaders recovered it from the Fatimids for Christianity in 1099; Saladin and the Saracens regained it for Islam in 1190, following the defeat of the Crusaders at the Battle of Hattin; and the Israelis held the western half of Jerusalem in 1948 during the War of Independence and completed its capture in 1967. Ever since they have maintained it is the indivisible capital of Israel.

The origins of Jerusalem have not been firmly established. The earliest evidence of occupation is pottery found in tombs in the area now known as Ophel and dated to 3200 BC. It became a Canaanite city and at some stage was inhabited by people whom the Bible calls Jebusites. Inscriptions on broken vases found at Luxor and dated to 1878–42 BC provide evidence that the city was called Rushalimum. Any dispute over the ownership of Jerusalem must begin with its capture, probably around 1000 BC, by David, who was the

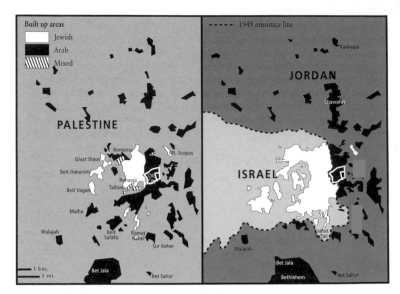

Jerusalem 1948

Jerusalem 1967

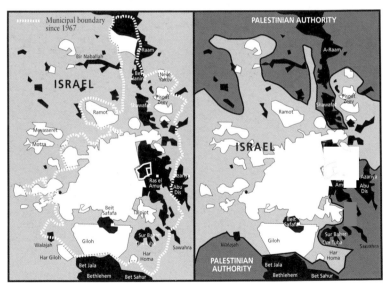

Jerusalem 2002

Taba proposals for Jerusalem

first king of both Israel and Judah, the two nations established by the Jews after their arrival in the 'promised' land.

Jewish control of Jerusalem, whether under a united Israel or a separate Judah, lasted until its capture by the Babylonian king Nebuchadnezzer, in 597 BC. Control of Jerusalem and the Holy Land then passed in turn to the Persians, Alexander the Great, the Ptolemies and the Seleucids. In 167 BC the revolt by the Maccabeans recovered Jerusalem for the Jews, but only until 63 BC when it was taken after a siege by the Romans. With the exception of the two Jewish revolts – the first in AD 66 and the second, the Bar Kochba revolt, in AD 131 – the Romans and their Byzantine successors ruled the Holy Land until the Muslim conquest and the fall of Jerusalem in the winter of 636/7.

The Crusaders drove out the Muslims in 1099 and Christians ruled Jerusalem until 1187 when Saladin took the city. Muslim rule by the Ayyubids, Mamelukes and Ottomans continued until the First World War, when General Allenby entered Jerusalem at the end of 1917. The British were given a mandate to govern Palestine and they did so until May 1948 when Israel gained its independence. The United Nations partition plan envisaged Jerusalem becoming an international zone. In 1948 Jerusalem was the scene of bitter fighting both in the city and on the supply route from Tel Aviv, and it was at times cut off from Israeli-held territory; the Arabs captured the Jewish Quarter in the Old City. An armistice was reached with the Jordanians in 1949 which left Jerusalem divided, the western or modern part being held by the Israelis and the eastern half and the Old City by the Jordanians. It is claimed that some 60,000 Palestinians were displaced from their homes in West Jerusalem. A number of Jewish settlements around Jerusalem were over-run by the Jordanians and destroyed; they have now been re-established.

In 1967 the Israelis sent a message to the Jordanians: 'We shall take no action against Jordan unless Jordan attacks us first' – but it was ignored. King Hussein said later that 'he knew he would lose but had no alternative but to join the Arab assault'. Nevertheless, after heavy fighting, Israel captured and reunited Jerusalem. In June 1967 Israel extended the municipal boundaries in all directions; the Jewish Quarter was reoccupied, extended and rebuilt. The Haram ash Sharif, or Temple Mount, was left under the charge of the Islamic Waqf and Jews were forbidden to pray on the Mount. Since then Israel has built a circle of dense housing virtually all round the city, most of which is on land that formed part of the West Bank. Some 176,000 Israelis now live there. Israelis have also managed to buy property and land in Palestinian quarters of Jerusalem such as Silwan and Ras al Amoud. In 1995 permission was given for development on one of the few remaining open spaces around Jerusalem – Har Homa (to Israelis) or Jabal Abu Ghneim (to Palestinians) – between the outskirts of Jerusalem and Bethlehem. The Labour government halted the development after land clearance had begun but the Likud government gave the go-ahead in late 1996. The development is now inhabited by Israelis.

The international community does not share Israel's view of its right to rule over an undivided Jerusalem, as can be seen from the fact that virtually no foreign embassies have been opened in Jerusalem; these remain firmly in Tel Aviv, requiring their ambassadors to make frequent journeys to Jerusalem. Most consulates in Jerusalem have always seen themselves as embassies to the Palestinian population, whether in Jerusalem or the West Bank. The US Congress, however, supports Israel's claim and in June 1997 voted almost unanimously in favour of a resolution declaring Jerusalem to be the eternal and undivided capital of Israel; it also voted $100 million to fund the move of the US embassy from Tel Aviv to Jerusalem. As yet, however, the embassy has not moved.

There is no doubt that the Palestinian population of Jerusalem has been badly treated by the Israeli authorities. East Jerusalem has been starved of funds to update public utilities, planning permission for new building by Palestinians is hard to get and many unauthorised buildings have been demolished. A welcome development is the decision by the Israeli Interior Minister, Nathan Scharansky, to rescind the regulation that deprived Palestinian Jerusalemites of the right to reside there once they had been absent for seven years.

It will not be easy to mediate an equitable solution to the problem of Jerusalem that will be acceptable to both moderate Israelis and Palestinians, let alone to any of the hard-liners. In mid-1999 it was rumoured that Prime Minister Barak and Chairman Arafat had reached a provisional agreement over Jerusalem in which no land would be handed to the Palestinians. They would, however, have authority over Jerusalem's 150,000 Palestinians there and over the Islamic holy sites. In return Israel would not oppose Palestinian statehood and would agree to the town of Abu Dis, 2 miles east of Jerusalem, becoming the Palestinian capital. Agreement on these terms is unlikely under the Sharon leadership.

TRAVEL ADVICE

FCO: Do not visit the Old City on Fridays.
State: Only visit the Old City in daylight.

BIBLIOGRAPHY AND WEBSITES

Armstrong, Karen, *A History of Jerusalem: One City*, Three Faiths, HarperCollins, 1996
Karmi, Ghada (ed.), *Jerusalem Today: What Future for the Peace Process?*, Garnet Publishing, 1996
Segal, Jerome M., Levy, Shlomit, Izzat Sa'id, Nadar and Katz, Elihu, *Negotiating Jerusalem*, SUNY Press, 2000
Wasserstein, Bernard, *Divided Jerusalem: The Struggle for the Holy City*, Profile Books, 2001
Jerusalem File, The International Campaign for Jerusalem, bi-monthly

International Christian Embassies in Jerusalem: www.cdn-friends-icej.ca
Jerusalem Report: www.jrep.com
Palestine Report (Jerusalem Media and Communications Centre) http://mail.jmcc.org

Iraq

Population: 22,300,000 Arabs 80% (of which 55% Shi'a, 45% Sunni Muslim) Kurds 20%
Armed Forces: 424,000
Opposition Forces: KDP 15,000, PUK 10,000, SCIRI 4,000–8,000 (in Iran)

Iraq has only been a state since the end of the First World War, when the Ottoman Empire was broken up. The territory between the Euphrates and the Tigris rivers has been important throughout history, whether as Sumeria, Assyria, Babylonia or Mesopotamia ('the land between the rivers') in Alexander's Empire, and it was just as crucial for the invading British forces in the First World War.

In the early third century AD the Persians had driven back the Romans to the west of the Euphrates. In 651 the Persians were defeated by the Arabs and Mesopotamia and Syria became a single Arab province. The Persians reoccupied Baghdad in 945 and Shi'a Islam dominated Mesopotamia until the Sunni Seldjuks were invited by the then Caliph to end the Shi'a domination. Following a period of rule by the Mongol leader Tamerlaine, the Persians took Baghdad and then Mosul in 1508 and an attempt was made to re-establish the Shi'a persuasion. In 1534 the Ottoman Sultan Suleiman failed to conquer Persia but, encouraged by a Sunni revolt, marched on Baghdad, leaving only Basra and the extreme south to be occupied four years later. In the first three centuries of Ottoman rule the three provinces were governed as one entity from Baghdad, Mosul becoming separated in 1879 and Basra in 1884.

In 1865 the Turks attempted to gain more power in Arabia following a conflict over the Saudi succession, and Britain strengthened its ties with Bahrain. By the end of the century Britain, whose aims were to protect communications with its Indian Empire and to safeguard supplies of oil to fuel the navy, had realised the strategic importance of Kuwait and in 1899 signed an agreement to protect the sheikh. He promised that neither he nor his heirs would in any way hand over any part of the sheikhdom to another power without British consent. The seeds of the Iraqi–Kuwait dispute were sown.

The French and the British divided the Middle East between them in the Sykes–Picot Agreement of 1916, the provisions of which were kept secret from the Arabs who were being encouraged to revolt against the Turks. The British captured Baghdad in March 1917 and Kirkuk in May, but withdrew two weeks later as priority had been given to General

Allenby's campaign in Palestine. Kirkuk was reoccupied in October 1918 and the Armistice came into effect at noon on 31 October. The Armistice terms included the surrender of all Turkish troops in Mesopotamia but immediately there was disagreement as the Turks claimed that the Mosul province was not part of Mesopotamia. At a conference held on 7 November the Turks reluctantly agreed to withdraw from Mosul.

The Cairo conference of 1921 confirmed the basic elements of the Sykes–Picot agreement. Mesopotamia was renamed Iraq and Feisal, who had expected to rule Syria, agreed to be the Iraqi king but under strict British supervision. The British retained full control over the Kurdish area that had been recognised as an independent state by the Treaty of Sèvres in 1920. Britain, particularly the India Office, hoped to keep Iraq as a colony with a compliant ruler; the first Anglo-Iraqi Treaty was signed in October 1922. However, before the agreement there were numerous revolts and the British forces were too weak and too dispersed to defend all their garrisons. After reinforcement, and using air power and gas, the British crushed the revolt.

At the end of 1922 the Turks advanced into Mosul but were driven back by the British air force. At the Allied-Turkish Peace Conference at Lausanne the Turks made demands to recover Mosul, but were unsuccessful. In the Treaty there was no mention of Kurdistan and the Kurds were split between five states. Iraq was therefore formed by the Treaty of Lausanne from three Ottoman provinces: Mosul, Baghdad and Basra. In the south the population were mainly of the Shi'ite persuasion while elsewhere they were Sunnis; in the north-east lived the hated Kurds, numbering some 700,000.

In 1925 the League of Nations, after a commission of inquiry whose recommendation was backed by the Court of International Justice, awarded Mosul to Iraq on condition that the British protected the Kurds until 1950. A second Anglo-Iraqi Treaty in 1930 allowed that Britain would continue to oversee foreign policy and army training. The Treaty protected British oil interests and allowed two military bases to be maintained. At the same time many of the mandatory responsibilities were dropped on account of their cost. In the 1930s there were a number of coups, culminating in General Nuri al-Said seizing power in 1938; he was pro-British and broke off relations with Germany at the start of the Second World War. In March 1940 Nuri was replaced by the anti-British Rashid Ali al-Gilani, who refused to give Britain more bases in Iraq. In 1941 fighting broke out between the British and Iraqis who had a small amount of German air support. Eventually Rashid fled to Iran and Nuri was reinstated as prime minister. He remained part of the government until 1958. Brigadier Abdul Karim Kassem formed a 'Free Officers' organisation similar to that formed in Egypt. On 14 July 1958 Kassem entered Baghdad and seized power, killing both the king and Nuri. He declared Iraq a republic.

The Ba'ath movement had been founded in Syria in 1947 and was devoted to the cause of pan-Arabism. The Iraqi Ba'ath Party was founded in 1951 but was slow to gain support. In March 1959, with Syrian and Egyptian backing, it fostered a revolt in Mosul that was brutally crushed by the Iraqi army. This was not the only attempt at revolt between 1958 and 1963.

In June 1961 Kassem claimed Kuwait to be part of Iraq and demanded its return. Only the support given by other Gulf States and the deployment of British troops and armour ended Kassem's plan to invade Kuwait. Kassem was overthrown in February 1963 in a coup led by the Ba'ath Party, accompanied by a wave of mass arrests and executions, particularly of communists. The new regime did not last long and was overthrown in an army coup in November.

Saddam Hussein had joined the Ba'ath Party in 1957 and in 1958 he was a member of a team which attempted (but failed) to assassinate General Kassem. Saddam was wounded and escaped to Syria. He then remained in Egypt until 1963, returning to Iraq after Kassem's death. He went underground in November 1963 but was arrested and imprisoned in October 1964. He later escaped. By 1966 he had become the deputy secretary of the party and in 1968, after a second, this time successful, Ba'ath coup, he became Deputy Chairman of the Revolutionary Command Council responsible for internal security. As such he built

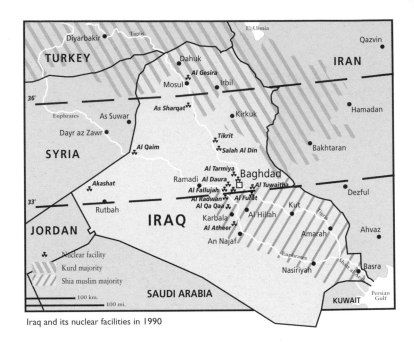

Iraq and its nuclear facilities in 1990

up a number of security organisations and orchestrated a series of purges. He declared himself president on 17 July 1979 and carried out a massive purge of the party.

Nuclear Facilities pre-1991

Baghdad: research and development for lithium no.

Al Gesira: production of uranium peroxide, uranium tetrachloride and feed material for electromagnetic isotope separation (EMIS)

As Sharqat: EMIS

Tikrit: weapon components

Salah Al Din: weapon components

El Quim: phosphate plant producing uranium concentrate

Akashat: uranium mine

Al Daura: reactor components and high pressure equipment

Al Furat: centrifuge production, planned site for experimental cascade

Al Fallujah: high temperature ovens

Al Radwan: weapon components

Al Qa Qaa: explosives including bridge wire detonators and storage of HMX

Al Atheer: main research and development site, computer simulation, uranium metallurgy

Al Tuwaitha: research reactor, enrichment research and development

Al Tarmiya: EMIS (8 units operational before bombing)

After the successful completion of the Gulf War, when Iraq invaded and occupied Kuwait, the people of Iraq were encouraged to rise up and overthrow Saddam and his regime. Initially the uprisings were successful both in the northern Kurdish area and among the Shi'a in the south who, it was suspected, received help from Iran. But the rebels found that they had no support from the US whose president had encouraged them to overthrow Saddam, The Iraqi leader then brutally put down the insurrection, first in the south, where the rebels had managed to seize a number of cities, before turning to deal with the Kurds. His repression resulted in a mass movement of refugees. The Shi'a fled to Iran and into the marshes south-east of Basra. The Kurds fled in large numbers into the mountains on the Iraq–Turkey–Iran borders; television pictures of their plight led to the deployment of an international force to establish 'safe havens' for them. After the ground troops were withdrawn, Allied air units were based in Turkey to monitor a 'no-fly zone' declared north of the 36th Parallel. A similar 'no-fly zone' south of the 32nd Parallel is monitored by aircraft based in Kuwait and Saudi Arabia. Although the Iraqis were forbidden to fly in these two zones, thus protecting the populations from air attack, no action was taken to prevent tanks and artillery being used against them. The 'no-fly zones' are still in force and Allied planes attack any Iraqi air defence elements that threaten them. The southern 'no-fly zone' boundary has been altered to the 33rd Parallel.

As part of formal cease fire terms agreed at the end of the Gulf War Iraq had to declare the extent of its nuclear, chemical and biological warfare and missile programmes and facilities and allow these to be destroyed. Its compliance was to be monitored by teams from the International Atomic Energy Agency (IAEA) and the UN Special Commission (UNSCOM). Despite the success achieved by these teams in eliminating Iraq's capability, now that UNSCOM no longer carries out its monitoring mission there are concerns that Iraq is attempting to reacquire chemical and biological weapons. The extent of Iraq's weapons of mass destruction and missile programmes is discussed on p. 73 in the section entitled 'Middle East Proliferation'. The UN Security Council's Resolution 1284 of December 1999 authorised the establishment of the UN Monitoring, Verification and Inspection Commission (UNMOVIC) to replace UNSCOM, which left Iraq in 1998. The commission is preparing itself for deployment, carrying out training and analysing information, including imagery provided by commercial satellites.

Iraq had said it would not accept an inspection regime unless all sanctions were lifted; in surprise moves in August 29002 Iraq offered to hold talks with Hans Blix, the chief UN weapons inspector, and to allow a US Congressional delegation to spend three weeks in the country. The US immediately turned down the offer to Congress.

While virtually everyone agrees that Saddam Hussein should be removed from office there is no one outside his own clique who could take over and hold the country together. The replacement would, presumably, have to be even more ruthless than Saddam himself in order to establish his leadership. There have been reports of several attempted coups by generals but on each occasion they have been betrayed and it will be a brave man who tries again. There are numerous opposition parties, said to number ninety-one, all based abroad, but there is no agreement between them. Nor is there any single leader with the charisma needed to mount a successful opposition campaign from abroad, despite the backing of $97 million in credit and surplus military equipment voted by the US Congress for this purpose. In November 1999 the US administration announced the provision of the first $5 million of military equipment and training for the Iraqi opposition. In the last days of his presidency Bill Clinton approved a $12 million plan for the Kurdish opposition which, though split, has the greatest strength – but it already has a virtually autonomous region and, given Turkish opposition to any Kurdish state, is likely to be content with that.

For the moment it seems that Iraq and the world are stuck with Saddam Hussein, and this is perhaps preferable to the conflicts that might break out should he lose control and the country break up into its three component parts. However, President Bush put Iraq at the head of his 'axis of evil' and the world waits to see how the US will tackle the problem of Saddam's overthrow, which Secretary of State Colin Powell confirmed that Bush was 'set on' and 'might have to do alone'. Iraq, though, is naturally keen to be reconciled with its Arab neighbours and to have sanctions lifted. In April 2002 Iraq suspended oil exports for one month as a protest against Israeli operations against Palestinians. It also sought to get other Muslim countries to join the oil ban. Sanctions would be lifted if Iraq is prepared to apologise for its invasion of Kuwait, accept the blame and pay the necessary reparations. But even that is unlikely to satisfy the US which is determined to see the end of Saddam Hussein.

In June 2002 President Bush revealed that he had authorised the CIA to mount an operation to take Saddam Hussein 'dead or alive', with the help of opposition groups and, if necessary, special forces. The move has been criticised but would certainly be much less destabilising than a full-scale invasion which the US military believe is the only realistic but hard to achieve option.

TRAVEL ADVICE
FCO: UK nationals should not attempt to travel to Iraq.
State: Urges all US citizens not to travel to Iraq.

BIBLIOGRAPHY AND WEBSITES
Longrigg, Stephen, *Iraq: 1900 to 1950*, Oxford University Press, 1953
Simons, Geoff, *Iraq: From Sumer to Saddam*, Macmillan, 1994
Tripp, Charles, *A History of Iraq*, Cambridge University Press, 2000

The Kurds

Population: about 25 million
Armenia 0.05m, Azerbaijan 0.2m, Iran 5.5m (10%), Iraq 4.1m (23%), Syria 1m (8%), Turkey 10.8m (19%) (percentages of national population)

The Kurds are probably the descendants of the Indo-European tribes that migrated westwards probably during the second millennium BC; some claim they are descendants of the Medes who lived to the north-east of Persia, between the Zagros Mountains and the Caspian Sea, until they were conquered by the Persians in 550 BC. The wild tribes settled in the mountainous region which now covers eastern Turkey, south-west Armenia, north-west Iran, northern Iraq and north-east Syria. From the relative safety of the mountains their communities survived unassimilated under the various empires that controlled the area in turn, but were probably joined by both Arab and Turkoman tribes that later came to be considered Kurds. They are not ethnically identical and have no common language. The term Kurd has had a number of meanings: as *Cyrtii* or mercenary slingers in the Seleucid regime of 300 BC, and as the nomads of the Iranian plateau at the time of the Islamic conquest. The name Kurdistan for the region inhabited by the Kurds was first used by the Seldjuks in the twelfth century, but it has never had identified borders and its extent has changed over the centuries.

By the time of the First World War the Kurds were mainly living under Ottoman rule; the creation of a Kurdish state was promised, but never implemented, by the 1920 Treaty of Sèvres (which also recognised the Kurdish claim to exist as a people). The Treaty of Lausanne of 1923, which realigned Turkey's borders, made no reference to the Kurds, although it over-ruled Turkey's claim to retain Mosul Province whose population at that time had the same number of Turks as Kurds. The Europeans considered that a Sunni Kurdish state would act as a useful buffer between Turkey and the Turkmen people of Central Asia; between Turkey and the newly formed Soviet Union republic of Azerbaijan; and between the Shi'a populations in Azerbaijan and the Azeri provinces of northern Persia. In the event British control of the newly independent Iraq and the exploitation of oil in Mosul Province would have been threatened by Kurdish nationalism and the plan was dropped.

Since then the Kurds, who number as many as 25 million, have been unhappy residents of the region. There have been many Kurdish uprisings, for example against the Turks in 1924, 1930 and 1937, in Iran in 1880, 1920 and 1944, and in Iraq from 1931 to 1935, in 1945 and from 1961 to 1970. With few exceptions the Kurds in neighbouring countries have never managed to cooperate against their rulers. Indeed, often the ruling power has enlisted the help of a neighbouring Kurdish population against their own rebelling Kurds.

Kurdish rebellions led to a number of officially agreed border changes in the region (borders arbitrarily imposed by the Allies after the defeat of the Turks in 1918). Following the 1930 rebellion, during which Turkey accused the Persians of supporting the Kurds, the Turks exchanged strips of land near Kotur and Bazirgan (and later near Maz Bicho) in return for the eastern slopes of Mount Ararat, which had been a Kurdish stronghold during the rebellion.

In 1945, for a period of one year, the Soviet Union during its occupation of northern Iran established a small Kurdish Republic of Mahabad (south of Lake Urmia). Mahabad lay within the also separatist province of Azerbaijan populated by ethnic Azeris initially supported by the Soviet Union. Once the Soviets confirmed their intention of withdrawing the Azerbaijanis soon came to terms with the government. There were some skirmishes between Kurds and the Iranian army but Kurdish unity was fragile and began to break up; in December Iranian control was re-established. The importance of this event was to bring the Kurdish question to international notice again. However, it was then to be forgotten for some years.

TURKEY

In more recent times the Kurds have been highly active in opposing their rulers but once again failing to act in concert. Turkish Kurdish militancy increased throughout the 1980s as the PKK – Partiya Karkaren Kurdistan (Kurdistan Workers' Party) – intensified its insurgency and the government took counter-measures. With Iraq busy with its war with Iran, the Turkish army, alarmed by the growing liaison between Kurdish nationalists and left-wing political parties, staged a coup and took control of Turkey. An alliance between the PKK and the Iraqi-based Kurdistan Democratic Party (KDP) led to a Turkish incursion into Iraq, with the agreement of the Iraqi government.

Since 1984 the Turkish authorities have battled against the PKK both in eastern Turkey and across the border in northern Iraq. During that time some 30,000 people, mainly PKK guerrillas but also some civilians, have died. A large proportion of the Turkish army has been deployed in south-eastern Turkey in its efforts to suppress the revolt. Ironically this region coincides to some extent to that portion of Turkey excluded from the Conventional Forces in Europe Treaty – an exclusion granted in recognition of the threats faced by Turkey from its southern neighbours. The PKK receives assistance from both Syria and Iran; Syria allows PKK camps and training to take place over the border from Hatay (the province returned

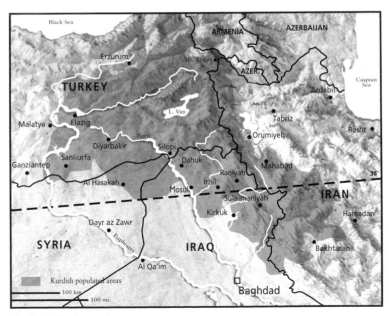

The Kurdish lands

to Turkey in 1938 after being part of the French mandate and which Syria claims) and in Lebanon. Syria also remains suspicious of Turkish plans for the use of Euphrates waters in the GAP irrigation project (see pp. 298–9) as this could reduce Syria's vital water supply.

In February 1999 the PKK leader, Abdullah Ocalan, was extradited to Turkey from Kenya where he had been hiding in the Greek Embassy. He was tried by a military court and sentenced to death; the sentence has not yet been carried out. Ocalan then called for an end to the Kurdish rebellion, a move that was supported by the PKK but they considered it depended on the government's response. The PKK guerrillas have started to pull out of Turkey but at the end of September the Turkish army sent 5,000 men, backed by air support, into northern Iraq to hunt down those who had vowed not to give up the struggle. In October, with their strength reduced to about 1,000 fighters in Turkey from a peak of 10,000, the PKK agreed to end their insurgency and to withdraw from Turkey. In December it was announced that the curbs on the use of the Kurdish language were to be lifted, but the bans on Kurdish broadcasting and education remain. In August 2000 Turkey signed two UN conventions that guarantee the social and political rights of minority populations. In January 2001 Turkish troops entered Iraq again at the request of the Iraqi Kurdish Kurdistan Workers' Party, which claimed that the PKK had occupied forty-five of their villages. At the moment the PKK is quiescent with 6,000 armed men in Iraq; the Turkish government line is that as there is no war so there can be no cease fire, nor will they negotiate with terrorists. The PKK is included in the US list of designated foreign terrorist organisations. In April 2002 the PKK announced that it had 'fulfilled its mission', had disbanded and that a new group called the Kurdistan Freedom and Democracy Congress would henceforward represent Kurdish interests; the Turkish government remains sceptical.

IRAQ

Iraqi Kurds came to prominence after the Gulf War of 1991 when, with encouragement from President George Bush, they rebelled against Saddam Hussein, only to be viciously repressed by the remnants of the Iraqi army because they received no military support from the coalition. The uprising began in Raniyah on 4 March 1991 and rapidly spread across the Kurdish region. Within a fortnight Kurds had taken control of virtually the whole area, including the city of Kirkuk. Iraqi reaction was swift and a major offensive backed by the whole spectrum of Iraqi heavy weapons was launched on the 28th; within a matter of days the Iraqis had recovered control and hundreds of thousands of refugees fled to the mountains on the Turkish–Iraqi border and into Iran.

The plight of the Iraqi Kurdish refugees caused a public outcry that 'something must be done'; the British prime minister, John Major, was responsible for persuading the coalition to set up a 'safe haven' for them protected by troops. Mainly from the UK and the US, they deployed on Operation Provide Comfort, which also helped to deliver food aid and to construct camps. A 'no-fly' zone north of the 36th Latitude was established to protect the Kurds from Iraqi air attack and this is still monitored by British and US, but no longer French, aircraft based at Incirlik in Turkey. By July the bulk of the refugees had returned home and most of the coalition ground forces had withdrawn, leaving a 'rapid reaction force' based at Silopi in Turkey and a UN 'guard' force set up along the southern edge of the 'security zone'. Both have now been withdrawn.

Iraqi Kurds are split between the supporters of Massoud Barzani and the Kurdistan Democratic Party (KDP) and those of Jalal Talibani and the Patriotic Union of Kurdistan (PUK). The pro-KDP Kurds live in the north-east of Iraq and are mainly tribal, whereas the PUK supporters generally live further to the south and are mainly townspeople. By the second half of 1996 the KDP had lost the support of both Turkey, because of the truce with the Turkish PKK, and Iran. The KDP had invaded the PUK region to attack the Kurdistan Democratic Party of Iran (KDPI); in 1994 it lost the city of Arbil to the PUK. Fighting between the two factions escalated in August and Barzani called on Saddam Hussein for help, which was willingly supplied. Some 30,000 Iraqi troops overran Arbil and turned it over to the KDP; the KDP went on to take the city of Sulaimaniya. Iraqi security forces hunted down those who had backed the US CIA operation based in Arbil and who had not been hurriedly evacuated by the Americans. The US swiftly mounted a series of cruise missile attacks on air defence targets in southern Iraq and strongly reinforced their forces in the Gulf, but found little support for further military action against Saddam, the French withdrawing their contribution to the force monitoring the northern no-fly zone. The US took the opportunity to extend the southern no-fly zone northwards to the 33rd Parallel, bringing a number of air bases into it.

In February a leading member of the KDP was murdered in a move that was seen as an attempt to precipitate renewed fighting between the KDP and PUK. However, the two leaders cooperated and both parties condemned the killing, which was carried out by a break-away group of a third Kurdish party, the Al-Tawhid, which split from the Islamic Movement of Kurdistan (IUM) in 1998.

IRAN

The Kurdish Democratic Party in Iran (KDPI, to distinguish it from the Iraqi KDP) was formed in 1945 but hardly existed until 1951 when the Shah lost much of his power to the liberal prime minister, Muhammed Musaddiq, and membership then rose. The US-backed army coup in 1953 restored the Shah to power and the KDPI lay low. When Qasim came into power in Iraq in 1955 he courted the Kurds and Mustafa Barzani returned there from exile in Iran. He proposed the amalgamation of the Iraqi KDP with the KDPI but before anything could be arranged the Shah's secret police arrested some 250 Kurdish activists and once again the KDPI was reduced to a few exiles in Iraq. Mustafa Barzani now made his peace with the Shah in return for aid against the Baghdad government. A new Kurdish campaign began in 1967 but with no support from the KDP it was soon defeated by the army.

The Kurds, who are Sunni Muslims, welcomed the overthrow of the Shah but became involved in fighting with local Shi'a forces within weeks of Ayatollah Khomeini's return. The new Iranian government employed the Pasdaran or Revolutionary Guard Militia rather than the regular army against the Kurds and this resulted in a brutal pacification campaign in which some 10,000 Kurds were killed in fighting or were executed. Nearly half of Iran's population is not Persian and so giving autonomy to the Kurds was not considered an option. The Kurds are divided: a second major group materialised in 1978 (though they claim they were formed in 1969), known as Komala or the Organisation of Revolutionary Toilers of Iranian Kurdistan. Komala was a Marxist organisation but was more democratic than the KDPI and aimed to provide education and health services. It was more determined to fight than the KDPI who attempted to negotiate with the government.

The KDPI and Komala agreed to cooperate in late 1982 and enjoyed two years of military success, but when they split again after a murder, four years of bitter infighting helped the Iranian forces to drive the KDPI into Iraq. Komala began to disintegrate after joining the Communist Party of Iran and lost members as it was no longer a Kurdish entity. Both KDPI and Komala continue with camps in Iraq where they have been attacked but not evicted by the Iraqi Kurds.

The prospect for Kurdish freedom and a Kurdish state is highly improbable at present but if the world community takes a stronger interest in minority rights, as it did in Kosovo and East Timor, that situation could change.

BIBLIOGRAPHY AND WEBSITES

Arfa, Hassan, The Kurds: An Historical and Political Study, Oxford University Press, 1966
Gunter, Michael, The Kurds and the Future of Turkey, Macmillan, 1997
Kreyenbroek, Philip G., and Stephanie Sperl (eds), The Kurds: A Contemporary Overview, Routledge, 1992
MacDowall, David, A Modern History of the Kurds, IB Tauris, 1997

Olsen, Robert, *The Kurdish Question and Turkish–Iranian Relations*, Mazda, 1998
——, *The Kurds: A Nation Denied*, Minority Rights Publications, 7th edn, 1997

Kurdistan Observer: www.kurdistanobserver.com
Kurdistan Regional Government: www.krg.org
Turkish Ministry of Foreign Affairs: www.mfa.gov.tr/ac/acf
Washington Kurdish Institute: www.clark.net/kurd

Iran

Population: 68,281,000
Persian 51%, Azeri 24%, Gilaki/Mazandarani 8%, Kurd 7%, Arab 3%, Lur 2%, Baloch 2%, Turkman 2%
Armed Forces: 513,000, including 125,000
Revolutionary Guard Corps (Pasdaran Inqilab)
Opposition Forces: NLA up to 8,000 (Iraq-based)
KDP-Iran 1,200–1,800
Per Capita GDP: $US 7,400
Currency: rial

Iran, or Persia as it was called before 1906, has a long history as an independent state. The Persians came from Central Asia at much the same time, the third millennium BC, as the Medes and the Hindus. The time of greatest Persian power came in the fifth century BC when their empire stretched from the Indus in the east to Thrace and Cyrenaica in the west, and from Samarkand in the north to Elephantine, on the Nile, in the south.

The Persians were conquered by Alexander the Great and after his death Persia became part of the Seleucid Empire. The Roman Empire did not advance into Persia, which broke away from the Seleucids around AD 250. The Arabs conquered the Persians between 642 and 652. When the Persians were converted to Islam they were initially Sunni; in the early sixteenth century the Safavids, who followed the Sufi form of Sunnism, took power and adopted Shi'ism.

In more modern times Iran under the Shah was a strong supporter of the West, being a member of the Central Treaty Organisation, with Turkey, Pakistan, the US and UK, which formed an eastern extension to NATO. The Shah was overthrown in 1979 and the rule of the ayatollahs began with the return from exile of Ayatollah Khomeini, who led the country until his death in 1989. Khomeini instituted a new Islamic constitution that split power between the president and his government and the Leader of the Islamic Revolution, who is also Commander-in-Chief of the Armed Forces, and the Council of Guardians. Khomeini was succeeded by Ayatollah Ali Khamenei as Supreme Leader and Ayatollah Hashemi Rasfanjani as president, the latter being a pragmatist who revised the constitution, creating more presidential power. The Supreme Ruler remains head of the Revolutionary Guards. The election held in 1997 produced a landslide victory for Mohamad Khatami, a moderate cleric who gained the support of the young and of women. President Khatami has begun a movement to improve relations with both Iran's neighbours and the West, but ultimate power remains in the hands of Khamenei.

Do the ayatollahs now in power in Iran present a threat and if so, to whom? The Gulf Arab states feel threatened not only militarily but also by the Islamic extremism of the Shi'a ayatollahs, although their relations with Iran are improving. Americans and to a lesser extent Europeans perceive a threat from Iran's development of long-range missiles armed with nuclear, chemical and biological warheads and from Iranian-inspired terrorism. The military threat posed by Iran's armed forces today can be overstated; the forces are large in number but as yet are not equipped with modern armaments. The air force is credited with

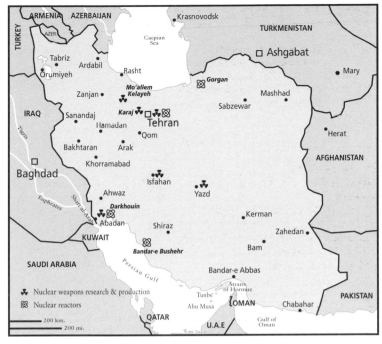

Iran showing nuclear facilities

some 300 combat aircraft but serviceability is considered to be less than 50 per cent and by now there must be a grave shortage of spares for the 200 aircraft supplied by the US to the Shah over twenty years ago. The Gulf States have twice as many aircraft and these are more modern, better maintained and better armed. The three Iranian submarines acquired from Russia between 1992 and 1997 do represent a threat to shipping in the Persian Gulf and could make transiting the Straits of Hormuz dangerous. However, the Iranian navy lacks the amphibious shipping to transport the size of force that would be needed to mount an invasion across the Gulf; at present it could lift no more than 1,000 men and 50 tanks. The Iranian navy is the service that can best challenge the Gulf States but it can never match the force that could be deployed by the US.

Iran has been aggressive in the past. In 1971 it occupied the Tunbs, which belonged to Ras al-Khaimah. With the agreement of Sharjah it also occupied half of the island of Abu Musa; in April 1992 it unilaterally occupied the whole island. During the Iran–Iraq war, begun by Iraq over the control of the Shatt al-Arab waterway, Iranian Revolutionary Guard naval units regularly attacked tankers, mainly those of Saudi Arabia and Kuwait, normally by laying mines in their path. In September 1998 Iran deployed as many as 270,000 troops and Revolutionary Guards on the border with Afghanistan in a show of strength after the murder of Iranian diplomats in Mazar-i-Sharif. Although Iranian troops clashed with Taliban forces, the deployment did not escalate into war.

The threat posed by Shi'a extremism is less easy to quantify. There are Shi'a majorities in southern Iraq and Bahrain and sizeable minorities in Saudi Arabia and Kuwait. There is evidence of Iranian support for Shi'a dissidents in Bahrain, Kuwait and Saudi Arabia but these have made little impact. Iran has had more success in supporting Hizbollah in Lebanon and Hezb e Wahdat in Afghanistan. It has rarely managed to forge alliances with Sunni movements, the only exception being the government of Sudan with whom it reached agreement in April 1995. The agreement included the supply of arms and assistance in training by Iran, the sharing of intelligence, and an increase in cultural exchanges. Since the election of Mohammed Khatami as president Iranian relations with Saudi Arabia and other Gulf states are much improved. However, the president's hands are tied as the ultimate power lies with the Supreme Leader, Ayotollah Khamenei, who controls the army, the Revolutionary Guards and the judiciary. While Khatami is seen as a reformist, Khamenei is a hard-line conservative; between the two is former president Rafsanjani, now the chairman of the influential Expediency Council, a body with a policy-making role.

At the time of the Iranian Revolution the US Embassy in Tehran was occupied and the staff held hostage for 444 days. The US mounted a rescue mission which went disastrously wrong. There is therefore no love lost between the Iranian regime and the US government, the latter invariably claiming that Iran supports international terrorism (naming Mujahidin Khalq, Hizbollah and HAMAS) and is actively developing weapons of mass destruction. It could be said that the US is more of a threat to Iran than Iran is to the US; the US has imposed seventeen separate sanctions on Iran since 1979. The Iran–Libya Sanctions Act penalises foreign firms that invest more than $20 million a year in Iran's energy industry. The US has blocked the construction of an oil pipeline from the Caspian Sea, and opened Radio Free Iran.

Once Iran has fully developed and deployed long-range missiles, with or without nuclear warheads, it will be able to threaten its neighbours more directly but at present the latter are making efforts to improve their relations with Iran. As great a threat could be Iranian backing for opposition groups opposed to the feudal rulers in the Arabian peninsula, but they are unlikely to support democratic groups and most extremist Islamist groups are Sunni rather than Shi'a. The US has named Iran as part of the 'axis of evil' and its phobia regarding Iran will ensure American protection for the Gulf States for many years yet. The ayatollahs pose a threat but it should not be overstated.

TRAVEL ADVICE

FCO: Only travel to Bam and Kerman, in the south-east, in government-approved tour groups.
State: Consider carefully the risks of travel. The Kurdish north-west and
Baluchistan, near the Pakistan border, are not safe for tourism.

BIBLIOGRAPHY AND WEBSITES

Chubin, Shahram, *Whither Iran? Reform, Domestic Politics and National Security*, IISS Adelphi Paper 342, 2002

Iran Daily: www.iran-daily.com
Iranian Embassy, London: www.iran-embassy.org.uk
Iran Weekly Press Digest: www.neda.net/iran.wpd
Net Iran (Iranian News): http://netiran.com
Tehran Times: www.tehrantimes.com

Islam

Professor Samuel Huntingdon, in *The Clash of Civilisations* (1996), forecast that future conflicts will take place between the seven main civilisations he identifies in today's world: Western, Latin American, African, Islamic, Sinic, Hindu and Japanese. Although he does not say so overtly, the tenor of his analysis is that the most likely civilisation to indulge in conflict is Islam. He quotes various sources to show that already a very high proportion of current and recent conflicts have involved Islam either on one side or both. He clearly sees Islam as a threat, pointing to its resurgence and the numbers of Muslims turning to a more Islamist way of life and eschewing secularism. Islam is the only religion that is also a political, social and cultural way of life. He also points to the growing success of Islamist movements in becoming the only alternative to existing regimes and, where they have taken power, to the reintroduction of *sharia* or Islamic Law. Islam is pro-modernisation but against westernisation. Islam has its own international organisation, the Organisation of the Islamic Conference; no other religion has such a similar body, nor has there ever been, for example, a conference of Christian Defence Ministers or of Buddhist Agricultural Ministers. Following the events of 11 September 2001 rather more credence is being given to his thesis; eighteen of the organisations named by the US government as 'foreign terrorist organisations' are Muslim and virtually all operate from the Middle East.

An alternative view is set out by Professor Fred Halliday, who considers the threat posed by Islam to be a myth. He acknowledges that there are two 'Islams' – the religion, and the social and political system. He clearly believes there is no unitary Islamist political force. He does not discuss the religion of Islam but states that it is not unitary; it may not be as fractured as Christianity but it is certainly not unitary, as the different philosophies of the Sunni and Shi'a persuasions show. Which professor is right?

If Professor Huntington is right, to whom is Islam a threat and what is the nature of that threat? The answer, of course, is that there are many different entities which see Islam as a threat, and the threat to each entity is generally different. Most non-Muslims feel threatened by 'fundamentalism' probably without understanding what fundamentalism is. A better word is 'extremism' and the people most threatened by extremist Islam are those who are less extreme or secular Muslims. In most but not all intra-Muslim conflicts one side is more extreme in its pursuit of Islam than the other. Examples include the Iran–Iraq war, the Algerian and Afghanistan civil wars, the rivalry between HAMAS and the Palestinian Authority, and Islamic terrorists in Egypt, Lebanon, Yemen and Karachi. The most notorious terrorist organisation, Usama bin Laden's al Qaida, is an example of Islamic extremism; it is still a threat to the US despite the operations to eliminate it from Afghanistan. The Iraqi invasion of Kuwait and its use of chemical weapons against its own people at Halabja, and the Syrian massacre of the Muslim Brotherhood in Hama are examples of intra-Muslim conflict without religious connotations. In the Arabian peninsula the contenders for power in place of the feudal rulers are democracy and Islam, with the latter being firm favourite. Certainly Islamic extremism is the enemy of true democracy. In Iran there is a growing split between the extremists and those looking for modernisation. So Islam is as much a threat to itself as to anyone else.

In the wider world there are many examples of Muslim versus non-Muslim conflict. However, a good many of these are more concerned with land than with religion. 'Natives versus Immigrants' is the theme of the conflicts between Israel and the Palestinians, in Bosnia, Kosovo and East Timor. There are of course similar conflicts over land with no Muslim participation, as in Northern Ireland and Croatia for instance. The United States is an ally to some Muslim states but is opposed to the regimes in others. It feels threatened by Islam more on account of terrorism and the proliferation of weapons of mass destruction. It is true that Islamic extremists see the US as their major enemy and have carried out a number of successful terrorist attacks against US targets. However, a number of Muslim states feel equally threatened by the US and are probably more at risk. The US has bombed Afghanistan, Libya, Sudan and Iraq and imposed sanctions on them and others. It has placed sanctions on Russian firms suspected of supplying Iran with nuclear and missile technology and has strongly warned companies not to invest heavily in the Iranian energy industry. The world of Islam cannot understand, and strongly resents, the apparent unfairness of US policy at the UN in respect of its and Israel's non-compliance with UN resolutions. (It must be said that Usama bin Laden never mentioned the Palestinians in any of his utterances before 11 September.) The US–Israeli strategic partnership seems fine in theory but should the US obtain Israeli military support or use Israeli facilities in any conflict then the whole Muslim world is likely to side with its opponents.

The likelihood of a pan-Islamic alliance being formed to confront one or other of the non-Muslim civilisations is very remote, and the experience of Arab alliances is not encouraging in this respect. Examples include the Gulf Cooperation Council's consistent failure to implement

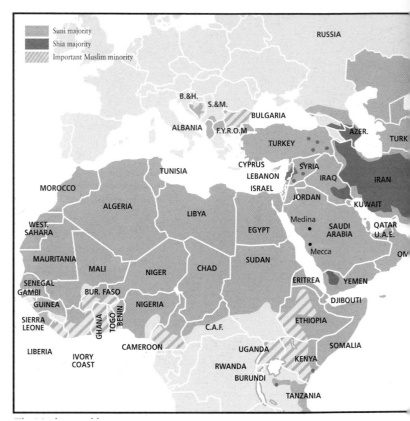

The Muslim world

the measures agreed for their common defence; the split in the Muslim world of those supporting the US-led coalition and those more sympathetic to Iraq after its invasion of Kuwait; and Egypt's apparent deception of Syria over its true objectives in the 1973 Yom Kippur war. Then there is the split between those countries which actually want to make peace with Israel and those who remain implacably opposed to any concessions being made to the Israelis.

While the general public and, in some countries, governments undoubtedly see Islam as a threat it is very much a self-induced one brought about through ignorance and the bias of the media. Islam is far more of a threat to Muslims and Muslim states than it is to the West. Muslims who have experienced a degree of democracy and have enjoyed the fruits of modernisation are fearful of being subjected again to the rigours of *sharia* and the loss of freedom in strict Muslim behaviour; witness the pleasure and relief of ordinary Afghans at the fall of the Taliban. The Islamic tendency is gaining ground in a number of previously secular states, in Turkey, Malaysia and Pakistan for example, and the Islamic opposition appears to be gaining acceptance in Algeria. On the other hand the development of missiles, chemical and biological weapons and possibly nuclear weapons in a number of Muslim countries and the propensity for Islam to employ terrorism, especially suicide attacks, is a threatening factor for non-Muslim states. A more worrying aspect is the increased immigration of Muslims to non-Muslim countries and the Islamic missionary work being carried out there.

There will doubtless continue to be relatively minor clashes between civilisations along the traditional faultlines of the world where Islam and other civilisations meet: in the

Balkans, the Caucasus, Central Asia, the Middle East and the Indian sub-continent to name a few. There appears to be a growing Islamist movement in far western China. However, the likelihood of a major war between Islam and, say, the West still remains highly unlikely, although America's 'War on Terrorism' is being played up by some as the start of just that; two of the three countries forming the 'axis of evil' and three of the top suspects for sheltering al Qaida (Somalia, Sudan and Yemen) are all Muslim states.

BIBLIOGRAPHY AND WEBSITES

Dekmejian, R. Hrair, *Islam in Revolution: Fundamentalism in the Arab World*, Syracuse University Press, 1995

Huntingdon, Samuel P., *The Clash of Civilisations and the Remaking of World Order*, Simon & Schuster, 1996

Halliday, Fred, *Islam and the Myth of Confrontation*, IB Taurus, 1996

Keppel, Giles, Allah in the West: Islamic Movements in America and Europe, Polity Press, 1997

Lewis, Bernard, What Went Wrong? the Clash between Islam and Modernity in the Middle East, Weidenfeld & Nicolson, 2002

Tibi, Bassam, *The Challege of Fundamentalism: Political Islam and the New World Disorder*, University of California Press, 1998

The Islamic Interlink: www.ais.org/~islam
The Wisdom Fund: www.twf.org

North Africa and the Horn of Africa

This chapter covers the countries north of the Sahara Desert and those to its east in the Horn of Africa. The problems of North Africa include the civil war in Algeria and the long-term dispute over the Western Sahara between Morocco, the Polisario and the United Nations. An earlier version of this book was criticised for not including a section on Libya. In many ways Libya is a reformed character: it has given up the men accused of organising the Lockerbie plane disaster and has even suggested that it will pay compensation to the victims' families (but only if all sanctions are lifted), although compensation will only be accepted if it is accompanied by a full admission of responsibility; it has already paid compensation for the murder of a London policewoman. On the other hand the US still considers Libya to be a supporter of terrorism, to have nuclear weapon ambitions and to have produced 100 tons of chemical weapon agents. In the Horn of Africa the civil war in Sudan, the confrontation between Ethiopia and Eritrea and the failed state of Somalia are discussed.

Algeria

Population: 32,136,000, Berbers 20%
Armed Forces: 124,000, Para military: 80,000
Opposition: Groupe Islamic Armée (GIA) 1,500; Groupe Salafiste Pour la Prédication et le Combat (GSPC) 500
Per Capita GDP: $US 7,300
Currency: dinar

In Algeria's municipal and departmental elections in June 1990 the Front Islamique du Salut (FIS, or Islamic Salvation Front) polled some 65 per cent of the votes cast, winning in thirty-two out of forty-eight provinces and in over half the municipalities. This caused the Algerian government to postpone the national election due in June 1991 – and since the elections Algeria has suffered an almost daily series of violent incidents in which as many as 100,000 people may have died.

Western North Africa was originally inhabited by the Berbers (*Imazighen* in their language, meaning 'free men'). The region was part of the Roman and Byzantine Empires until it was invaded by the Ummayid Arabs in the seventh century AD when it was converted to Islam. After a brief period of Spanish rule in the sixteenth century it became part of the Ottoman Empire; the Ottomans formed the frontiers of Algeria. By the eighteenth century Ottoman rule was only nominal: Algeria had become a pirate state and its attacks on shipping provoked a European reaction – an Anglo-Dutch fleet bombarded Algiers in 1816. The French captured Algiers in 1830 following a three-year blockade imposed after the French consul was assaulted, and then went on to occupy the whole North African region from today's Tunisian–Libyan border in the east to Agadir on the Atlantic in the west. The French introduced large numbers of settlers into Algeria; the European population, 109,000 in 1847, rose to 984,000 by 1954, of whom 70 per cent had been born in Algeria. The northern *départmentes* of Algiers, Constantine and Oran

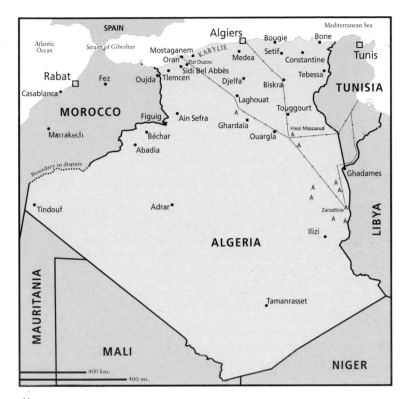

Algeria

were incorporated into metropolitan France in 1881; the remainder of the country was under military control.

The Algerian War of Independence began with an insurrection in the Aurès Mountains on 1 November 1954. The Front de Libération Nationale (FLN) (National Liberation Front) was founded and offered to negotiate as long as the principle of self-determination for the Algerian people was accepted. The French responded that Algeria was the heart of the French republic and would be defended by all possible means. During the eight-year war some 1.5 million people are believed to have died.

From the start Algerian independence, gained in 1962, was marred by dispute. Its first president, Ahmed Ben Bella, was removed in a military coup after only three years. The army remained the main power throughout the next two presidencies because when the bulk of the French settlers left, so did most senior civil servants. The only political party – the Front de Libération Nationale which had collapsed in 1962 – was revived but never gained the independent influence and power that could have united the country. A number of trends then emerged: modernisation, initially funded by oil revenue, took place but the agricultural sector was allowed to stagnate and Algeria had to import food to feed its fast-growing population (which was increasing by roughly 3 per cent per year). As oil prices fell so the new heavy industries became more of a burden on the state because they operated at a loss. Under President Chadli Algeria became a multi-party democracy in 1989 and although a large number of political parties were formed the main threat to the governing FLN came from the Islamists, in the form of the FIS, which had widespread appeal and was supported by over 10 per cent of the population within a year of its formation.

The FIS made substantial gains in the local elections of 1990, winning 54.3 per cent of the vote. Ahead of the scheduled national election of June 1991 the FLN-dominated National Assembly changed the election rules in order to weaken the FIS's chances and forbade electioneering to take place in mosques. In early June two squares in Algiers were occupied by several thousand Islamists; they were dispersed by troops who killed six and wounded over a hundred more. The elections were postponed until December when the FIS gained 188 of the 430 Assembly seats and seemed certain to gain control in the second round due to be held in January 1992. But these elections never took place: the army suspended them on the grounds that an FIS-controlled Assembly would mean the end of democracy. The FIS was banned in March and by the end of the month some 9,000 members had been arrested and sent to camps in the Sahara.

The following years have seen widespread violence with a breakdown of law and order. Members of the banned FIS formed an underground group, the Armed Islamic Movement, later renamed the Islamic Salvation Army (AIS). A splinter group of disaffected AIS formed the Groupe Islamique Armée (GIA), which has emerged as the strongest element of the various Islamist guerrilla groups. In 1993 the Islamist terrorists turned their attention to foreigners in an attempt to undermine the economy and a number were murdered, including engineering and electricity workers, priests and Russian military advisers. The murders have not deterred foreign investment in the oil and gas industries, which seem to have been spared from attack. Estimates of the number of dead – including soldiers, police, GIA and innocent civilians – vary but could be as high as 100,000.

There have been two elections while the FIS has been banned. In 1995 a former general, Liamine Zéroual, became president in an election seen as an attempt to return to democracy. In 1997 the Rassemblement National Démocratique, a new party sponsored by the government and formed that year, won 38 per cent of the vote in national elections compared to the FLN's 16 per cent. It gained a higher percentage in the provincial and municipal elections. Soon after there came growing allegations of government involvement in a wave of killings in August and September said to have been committed by the GIA. The army claimed to have killed several hundred of the rebel GIA, but there were allegations that the army had taken no action to stop some of the massacres.

In the presidential elections held in April 1999 Abdelaziz Bouteflika replaced Zéroual when the other six candidates withdrew immediately before the election. He promised to continue to fight insurgency but also invited Islamic militants to engage in political talks. He intended to tackle unemployment, corruption and inefficiency. The AIS said it was giving up the armed struggle, and in return some three thousand imprisoned FIS members were released. The amnesty was to end in January 2000 and Bouteflika said that after that date every effort would be made to 'neutralise' any rebels who refused to give up the struggle. In January 2000 the government estimated that some five thousand rebels, mainly GIA men, had spurned the amnesty offer and the army began its campaign to end the revolt on 18 January.

The government then revised its figures, saying that 4,200 rebels had surrendered but that at least 1,500 remained active. In early February the AIS accepted the amnesty and over 1,100 of their men surrendered. However, the violence was not over: twenty people were massacred one night in February and twenty-seven were reported killed in various incidents in the east and south of the country in April. This pattern continued throughout 2000 and in early 2001. The army then instituted new tactics involving the use of special forces, who claimed to have killed three hundred rebels in early 2001, including thirty-three members of the Salafist Group for Preaching and Combat (GSPC) near Tizi Ouzou, and seventy members of the GIA near Setif.

In April and May 2001 violence broke out in Kabylie after a young Berber man died in police custody. In two months of riots and demonstrations some eighty people have been killed by the police in the Berber heartland. The main causes of the disaffection are the Berbers' lack of civil liberty and the poor economy which has caused high unemployment. They have spent many years unsuccessfully campaigning for the recognition of their language and culture. On 14

June a massive demonstration involving several hundred thousand people, not all Berbers, took place in Algiers; five were killed and nearly a thousand injured in clashes with police. A second march was planned for 5 July, Algeria's independence day, but the police prevented most of the demonstrators from entering Algiers. Around one thousand finally reached 1 May Square, where the march was due to start; they dispersed peacefully. Another Berber protest march was blocked by police in October. Also in October the president agreed to meet Berber leaders and to grant Berber Tamazight the status of a national language.

In October 2001 the violence flared up again but after 11 September US and Western opinion was more supportive of the government, recognising that perhaps there was more to the Algerian claims that they were dealing with terrorists rather than it being a human rights issue. However, it is still maintained that the terrorist activity was originally provoked by the way the country was run. Some Algerian Islamists fought in Afghanistan against the Russians and some have joined al Qaida. The GIA, but not the GSPC, has been designated a foreign terrorist organisation by the US. In February 2002 Antar Zouabri, the leader of the GIA since 1996, was killed in a clash with security forces. His death has not ended the violence, which is particularly prevalent in the Berber areas.

TRAVEL ADVICE

FCO: Advises against all holidays and non-essential travel except to the Sahara desert.
State: Strongly recommends that US citizens always travel in the company of a reputable Algerian.

BIBLIOGRAPHY AND WEBSITE

Ageron, Charles-Robert, *Modern Algeria: A History from 1830 to the Present*, Hurst, 1991
Fuller, Graham, *Algeria: the Next Fundamentalist State?*, Rand, 1996
Quandt, William, *Algeria's Transition from Authoritarianism*, Brookings Institute Press, 1998
Shah-Kazemi, Reza (ed.), *Algeria: Revolution Revisited*, Islamic World Report, 1997.
Spencer, Claire, *The Maghreb in the 1990s*, IISS Adelphi Paper 274, 1993
Willis, Michael, *The Islamist Challenge in Algeria: A Political History*, Ithaca, 1997

World Algeria Action Coalition (Washington): www.waac.org

Morocco and Western Sahara

Population: 28,476,000
Armed Forces: 198,000
Paramilitary: 48,000
Opposition: POLISARIO Front ±5,000
Foreign Forces: MINURSO 230
Per Capita GDP: $US 8,200
Currency: dirham

The North African coastal region was conquered by the Ummayid Arabs and the population converted to Islam between AD 622 and 750. Until the twentieth century Morocco was inhabited by a collection of tribes with the Sultan only exercising real control over the towns and plains. The Spanish captured the Canary Islands in the first few years of the fifteenth century and their interest in the African coastline stemmed from their need for fishing rights and the opportunity to trade with Saharan caravans. After the Spanish–Moroccan war of 1859–60 the Moroccans conceded land on the Atlantic coast to Spain so that it could establish its fishing industry but this was not set up at Ifni until some years later.

Spain's negotiations with the French over its control of Western Sahara were dependent on the recognition of France's influence in Morocco. This was not finally given assent until

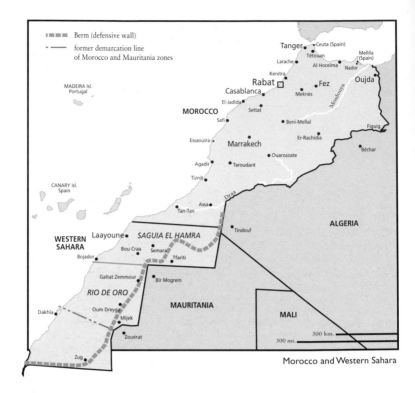

Morocco and Western Sahara

the Franco–German agreement of 1911 and the Treaty of Fez of 1912 when the Sultan placed Morocco under French protection. A number of Franco–Spanish conventions in the early twentieth century demarcated the border between their areas of interest; the final convention of 1912 gave Spain only a small area of Morocco split from its enclave at Ifni. Saguia el-Hamra and Rio de Oro were recognised as Spanish colonies. However, Spanish control of the interior was not established until 1934.

As Africa became decolonised after the Second World War both Morocco, from which the French had withdrawn in 1956, and Mauritania, which had been a French colony from 1920 to 1960, claimed the territory of Western Sahara. At the same time the Popular Front for the Liberation of Saguia el-Hamra and Rio de Oro (POLISARIO) was formed, and duly claimed independence for the territory. When Spain finally withdrew in February 1976 the *Djema* (the Saharawi body formed by Spain in 1967 and named after the traditional *djemas* that had controlled tribal life) approved the reintegration of Western Sahara with Morocco and Mauritania. Serious fighting broke out between the POLISARIO guerrillas and the forces of Morocco and Mauritania. The latter agreed that Morocco should have the northern two-thirds of the territory. The POLISARIO withdrew over the border into Algeria where it has had bases ever since. To defend against the POLISARIO guerrilla attacks that took place regularly in the years before 1982 the Moroccan government ordered the construction of a 2,500km-long earth wall (the *berm*) and deployed nearly half its army along it.

In 1979 Mauritania and the POLISARIO signed a peace agreement in which Mauritania, which had been driven out by POLISARIO, gave up its claims to Western Saharan territory. Morocco refused to recognise the treaty and its troops occupied the southern part of the country. The United Nations has been involved in Western Saharan affairs since 1963, and the General Assembly has on several occasions affirmed the right of people to self-determination. In 1975 the International Court of Justice advised that although there were legal ties of allegiance to the Sultan of Morocco by some of the tribes (at the time of Spanish colonisation) and that there were some land rights between Mauritania and the territory, these did not establish any tie of territorial sovereignty. In 1979 the Organisation of African Unity (OAU) called for a referendum on self-determination and established a committee with the UN. At the OAU summit in 1981 King Hassan II agreed to a cease fire and a referendum but refused to talk directly to the POLISARIO. In 1982 twenty-six OAU members recognised the Saharan Arab Democratic Republic and admitted it to the Council of Ministers; Morocco withdrew from the OAU. After several years of negotiating by a joint UN/OAU mission of good offices, the UN appointed a special representative in 1988 who reported proposals for a settlement to the UN in 1990.

The UN plan was for a UN Mission for the Referendum in Western Sahara (MINURSO) that would monitor the cease fire, the reduction of armed forces and the confinement of those forces remaining in specified locations. It would also make the arrangements for the referendum, including the identification of those eligible to vote, and supervise a repatriation scheme for refugees. In April 1991 the UNSC decided to establish MINURSO and an agreed cease fire was to come into effect on 6 September; however, a number of preliminary tasks could not be completed before this date. Fighting restarted after an unofficial cease fire of two years; 228 UN monitors with helicopter support were deployed. A cease fire has held since September 1991 but progress towards holding the referendum has been painfully slow with a number of interruptions caused by both sides. Timetables have been amended and MINURSO's mandate extended repeatedly. Disagreement continues over who is eligible to vote in the referendum, with the Moroccan authorities arguing for the inclusion of some 65,000 tribesmen who were not included in the Spanish census of 1974. The POLISARIO opposes this on the grounds that it is intended to increase the pro-Moroccan vote – a view that UN officials tend to agree with. Some 150,000 Saharawi refugees and the POLISARIO guerrillas remain in camps in south-west Algeria.

Both Morocco and the POLISARIO agreed on 31 July 2000 as the date for the referendum but it did not take place, again because of disagreements on who was eligible to vote. The UN and its special envoy, former US Secretary of State James Baker, began to lose patience. Baker drew up a new plan in 2001. It would postpone the referendum for five years, during which time the Saharawis would enjoy a very limited form of autonomy. In the referendum *all* residents of Western Sahara, including the army, would be entitled to vote. Naturally POLISARIO rejected the plan, leaving its members with no alternative but to remain in their camps in Algeria, although that country will no longer support their military ambitions. Two other events have made the POLISARIO's situation worse. President Chirac in December 2001 described Western Sahara as 'the southern provinces of Morocco', and King Hassan has given the go-ahead, for the first time, for oil exploration to take place off Western Sahara's coast. Contracts were agreed with a French consortium and a US oil company.

POLISARIO has also enlisted the help of an oil company but to obtain its services has had to agree to allowing it one third of Western Sahara's territorial waters should independence be gained. In April the UN Security Council delayed consideration of an American-drafted resolution backing Morocco's annexation of Western Sahara by three months.

TRAVEL ADVICE
FCO and State: No restrictions in Morocco. Warn of risk of Roundmines in Western Sahara.

BIBLIOGRAPHY AND WEBSITES
Hodges, Tony, *Western Sahara: Roots of a Desert War*, Lawrence Hill, 1983

Moroccan Ministry of Communications: www.mincom.gov.ma
Western Sahara: www.arso.org

The Sudan

Population: 29,632,000
Muslim 70%, Christian 10%
African 52%, Arab 39%
Armed Forces: 117,000
Opposition Forces: SPLA 20,000–30,000
Per Capita GDP: $US 1,709

Sudan has always been divided in two separate ways: by its people and their religions, and by the nature of the territory. In the north, covering roughly two-thirds of the country, it is dry; north of the capital, Khartoum, lies the Nubian Desert – the eastern end of the Sahara – which continues over the border into Egypt. The people here are largely of Arab descent and are Muslims; there are also Nubians living along the Egyptian border, Bedouin tribes in the west and Beja tribesmen in the Red Sea Hills to the east. The three southern provinces are quite different in terrain: they consist mainly of equatorial forests with the vast swamps of the Sudd. The people, who are either Christian or Animist, are of Nilo-Hamitic and Negro ethnicity and are closer in origin to the African peoples found in neighbouring Congo, Kenya and Uganda than to the northerners.

Accounts of the history of Sudan come mainly from the words of travellers. Nubia, in the north, was conquered by the Egyptians sometime after 2000 BC. The Romans sent a small expedition that reached the Sudd and then reported that the country was not worth conquering. Around AD 1500 the north was converted to Islam though pockets of Christianity remained. The only interest in the south was in the search for ivory and slaves, both of which were ruthlessly extracted, particularly after the Turkish-Egyptian penetration from 1820. The Egyptian conquest of Mohammed Ali in 1821 was driven by the lure of gold thought to be there and the desire to overthrow the last of Egypt's earlier rulers, the Mamelukes. After a short period of Egyptian rule the local tribal leaders were allowed to continue under the supervision of a governor-general in Khartoum. Taxation and corruption became excessive after General Gordon had resigned as governor-general in 1880, having failed to eradicate the slave trade, and became the causes of a revolution led by the Sheikh Muhammed Ahmed, the Mahdi. After the Mahdi had taken control of Kordofan and Dafur, a British force (Egypt was then a British protectorate while still nominally part of the Ottoman Empire) under General Gordon was dispatched to quell the rebellion in 1884. But the garrison of Khartoum was overwhelmed and Gordon murdered, and the Mahdi and his successor ruled Sudan from 1885 to 1898. After the battle of Omdurman in 1898 Sudan became an Anglo-Egyptian Condominium but was in effect ruled by the British governor-general. British interest in southern Sudan intensified as the French pressed eastwards from Central Africa, culminating in the Fashoda incident in 1898, a clash between British and French troops that nearly resulted in an Anglo-French war. During Kitchener's governorship the south was subject to missionary activity to convert the people to Christianity, a process which further separated the southern provinces from the north.

Sudan gained its independence on 1 January 1956. In 1958 a military coup took place but civilian rule was restored in 1964. Another military coup in 1969 led by Colonel Gaafar Mohammed el-Nimeiri established the Revolutionary Command Council; Nimeiri became President in 1971.

Opposition to Nimeiri's policies arose in both the north and the south and among Muslims and non-Muslims. Initially the Sudan People's Liberation Army (SPLA) addressed national issues rather than purely southern Sudanese problems. The dissidents in the south were now actively supported by Ethiopia following Nimeiri's support for anti-Derg forces there. The opposition was split into numerous groups but Ethiopian influence helped to bring them together, as did the cooperation of army defectors. In May 1983 two battalions

Sudan

in Jonglei were persuaded to defect en masse with their arms and equipment. The SPLA emerged in July 1983 under the command of a former colonel, John Garang, who ensured that all operations were authorised and that all recruits were sent for training in Ethiopia. The late 1980s saw a series of SPLA victories as they grew in strength, captured smaller garrison towns, bottled up the army in the larger ones and took control of much of the south. In 1985 Nimeiri was deposed and a year later Sadiq el-Mahdi, leader of the Umma party, was elected prime minister of a coalition government. A peace treaty was signed with the SPLA, which split the coalition and led to another military coup. General Ahmed el-Bashir became president and the Umma party was outlawed.

The SPLA suffered a major reverse in 1991 when the overthrow of Mengistu, the Ethiopian dictator, deprived them of Ethiopian support and the organisation fragmented again. There was a split between those, like Garang, looking to overthrow the Khartoum government and those simply wanting independence for the south. The SPLA commanders in the Upper Nile region complained of being isolated and the last in line for supplies and reinforcements. In August 1991 they renounced their support for Garang and their aim of independence for the south. They did not receive the support they had expected from the northern elements of the SPLA, and later accepted arms from the government, which further alienated them from the mainstream SPLA. They did, though, tie down numbers of

Garang's forces, which allowed the government to recover considerable territory during the period 1992–4.

In due course the SPLA recovered and by the end of 1995 was regaining the ground lost; a number of factors helped to bring this about. New forces – the National Democratic Alliance in the north and the Sudan Allied Forces along the Eritrean and Ethiopian borders from Kassala to Kurmuk – allied themselves with Garang and opened up new fronts against the government. The Sudanese government's support of Islamist dissidents led to the SPLA alliance gaining support from the Ethiopian, Eritrean, Kenyan and Ugandan armies. At the same time a regional intergovernmental body, formed originally to cooperate over drought and desertification and renamed the Intergovernmental Authority for Development, attempted to mediate in the civil war which was seen as destabilising the region. One of its recommendations was the separation of religion from the state in Sudan, but the government was unable to accept secularism and remained committed to *sharia*. By now Sudan was playing host to a number of Islamist groups such as HAMAS, Hizbollah, Islamic Jihad, a number of Egyptian terrorist groups and even at one time Usama bin Laden, providing them with arms and training camps.

A new development in the south has been the discovery of oil in Eastern Upper Nile in 1999. The new oilfields are around the town of Benitu and so lie astride the boundary between north and south Sudan. By mid-2001 production stood at around 200,000 barrels a day; reserves could total up to 2 billion barrels. To protect oil workers and facilitate new exploration, the government has been systematically depopulating the area; the UN estimates up to 30,000 people may have been displaced but local chiefs claim the true figure is twice that number. The government's militias are also attacking aid agencies.

Although Sudan is named by the US as a state that sponsors international terrorism, nevertheless President Bush, under pressure from Congress, appointed a special envoy to Sudan to help broker peace. In fact Sudan had begun cooperating with US agencies over terrorism some time before 11 September. Since then the US has been given permission for military overflights, and the Sudanese government has handed over details of suspected al Qaida allies and allowed the US envoy to visit southern Sudan.

The civil war continued, inflamed by the oil exploration, but the SPLA's supporters were now concerned elsewhere, Eritrea and Ethiopia with their own war and Uganda having joined the civil war in the Congo. President Bashir and the Eritrean president have signed a treaty agreeing not to support each other's rebels. The government's finances have improved because of the oil exports, and the oil companies' investment in roads and airstrips helps the government's forces to move around more easily.

In January 2002 John Danforth, the US special envoy, Clare Short, the UK Minister for Overseas Development, and Hilde Johnson of Norway all held talks with the Sudanese government and the SPLA, and are hopeful that peace talks might follow. After five weeks of talks, agreement has been reached which should end the civil war. There is to be a six-year transition period ending with a referendum in the south offering it independence. Sharia will be confined to the north with the south being guaranteed freedom of religion. However, the transition period will not begin until a ceasefire is agreed and this seems unlikely given the large-scale casualties caused by a government attack only days after the agreement had been signed.

TRAVEL ADVICE

FCO: advises against *all* travel, except for relief work, to southern Sudan and the Nuba Mountains.

State: advises against all travel to Sudan.

BIBLIOGRAPHY AND WEBSITES

Clapham, Christopher (ed.), *African Guerillas*, James Currey, 1998

Gurdon, Charles (ed.), *The Horn of Africa*, SOAS/GRC Geopolitics Series, UCL Press, 1994

Lesch, Ann Mosely, *The Sudan: Contested National Identities*, James Cirrey, 1999
Sidahmed, Abdel Salam, *Politics and Islam in Contemporary Sudan*, Curzon, 1997

Sudanese Embassy, Washington: www.sudanembassyus.org
The Sudan Foundation (London): www.sufo.demon.co.uk
Sudan People's Liberation Movement and SPLA: www.newsudan.com

Ethiopia and Eritrea

	Ethiopia	Eritrea
Population:	63,659,000. Oromo 40%, Amhara and Tigrean 32%, Sidamo 9%, Shankella 6%, Somali 6%, Afar 4%	3,905,000. Tigrinya 50%, Tigra and Kunama 40%, Afar 4%, Saho 3%
Armed Forces:	252,000	172,000
Foreign Forces:	UNMEE 3,860	
Per Capita GDP:	$US 571	$US 441
Currency:	Birr EB	Nafka

Ethiopia and Eritrea have suffered war almost continuously since 1970. There were five years of peace between the end of the civil war that overthrew the regime of Mengistu Haile Mariam and led to Eritrean independence in May 1993, and the renewed outbreak of fighting between the two countries in 1998 which did not end until December 2000.

The original inhabitants were the Agau, a Cushite people. Around 700 BC there was a wave of immigration of Semite people from southern Arabia who settled in what is now north-east Ethiopia and Eritrea. They established the kingdom of Axum, which was converted to Coptic Christianity in the fourth century. Its power declined as that of Islam expanded and it became isolated from the Christian world. The region first became Independent in the eleventh century. Between the fourteenth and seventeenth centuries the Christian state expanded after its conquest of the sultanates of the south-east escarpment, the Cushite Gibe region and Senaar in Sudan. In the late nineteenth century Menelik II took control of the area now constituting southern Ethiopia. As the kingdom of Abyssinia it suffered a number of invasions but never fell to European colonisation as the rest of Africa did. The northern province of Eritrea had fallen to the Turks in the mid-sixth century and was then taken by Italy in 1889; it became a colony in 1900. The Italians invaded Ethiopia in 1935 and occupied it until they were defeated by the British in 1941, when Emperor Haile Selassie, who had first come to power in 1916, returned. After the war the British administered Eritrea until 1952 when it became an autonomous part of a federal Ethiopia. In 1961 the emperor revoked Eritrea's autonomous status and disbanded its government; the resulting armed resistance continued inconclusively until 1991. The army deposed Haile Selassie in 1974 and the country became a socialist state ruled by the Dergue or military council.

A rebellion by the non-Amharic Oromo people took place in 1964 as a result of governmental repression. The uprising spread and declared its aim to be independence as Western Somalia; the revolt tended to merge with that in the Ogaden region of Somalia. The Ethiopian uprising ended in 1970 but the Somali revolt continued. In 1977 another attempt to secure independence was made during the Ethiopian–Somali war but all resistance had petered out by the early 1980s.

Before Colonel Mengistu Haile Mariam took power in a coup in 1977, the Dergue had lost its first two leaders from assassination. After Mengistu came to power any rival or opponent suffered a similar fate. Ethiopia moved closer to the Soviet block and was, with Soviet and Cuban help, able to repulse the Somali invasion of 1977. At their peak Soviet advisers in Ethiopia numbered some 1,400 and Cubans over 11,000. The Soviet–Ethiopian

Eritrea and Ethiopia border region

agreement ended in January 1991 and Soviet military aid ceased; Mengistu had to flee the country less than five months later. The main opposition groups were the Eritrean People's Liberation Front (EPLF) and the Tigray People's Liberation Front (TPLF); they were allied against Mengistu but had different long-term aims – the EPLF's aim of independence was not supported by the TPLF, though initially it was looking for autonomy for Tigray.

In May 1991 the EPLF defeated the Ethiopian army in a battle some 50km south of Asmara which it then occupied and set up a provisional Eritrean government. At the same time the army was also beaten by the Ethiopian People's Revolutionary Democratic Front (EPRDF), which installed a new government in Addis Ababa. Following an internationally monitored referendum Eritrea formally declared its independence in May 1993. Earlier the provisional governments of Ethiopia and Eritrea had agreed to cooperate over security, trade and immigration; landlocked Ethiopian access to the port of Assab was guaranteed.

Border disputes between Ethiopia and Eritrea erupted in May 1998 after years of disagreement as to its legal line, which had never been officially demarcated. Fighting first took place over the Yigra triangle a barren 250 sq. mile area around Badme. Ethiopia claimed it had been administering this area for some time but Eritrea insisted that Italian maps showed the area as its own. It is unclear which side began the fighting but both sent large-scale forces to defend their rival claims. By mid-June the war had spread to four other disputed zones, three to the east of Badme at Zalambessa, and one close to the Djibouti border where the main road to Assab crosses the frontier. Accurate reports of the fighting are scarce but all indicate a heavy toll of casualties on both sides. A three-day battle fought at Tsorona has been described as resembling the First World War with mass attacks being beaten off by machine-gun fire. The Eritreans claim to have killed some ten thousand Ethiopians and to have destroyed or captured about eighty of their tanks. A moratorium on aerial bombing was agreed in 1998 but the Eritreans claim that Massawa was bombed in May 1999. The war continued, largely unreported, after a pause during the rainy season.

In May 2000 the UN Security Council passed a resolution calling on both sides to halt the fighting or face an arms embargo. This led to a violent demonstration in Addis Ababa against the US and UK. The embargo was enforced on 18 May after the Ethiopians had taken Barentu; they then pushed deeper into Eritrea. Peace talks at Algiers began as the fighting continued. The Organisation of African Unity had prepared a peace plan and pressed both sides to accept it: the Eritreans did so on 9 June but the Ethiopians waited until the 15th before agreeing. A peace treaty was signed on 12 December. The UN deployed a peacekeeping force, the UN Mission to Ethiopia and Eritrea (UNMEE), established a 25km-wide buffer zone (the Temporary Security Zone) between the two countries and began to demarcate the border.

TRAVEL ADVICE

Ethiopia

FCO: Avoid area of Ethiopian/Eritrean border and within 20 Kilometres of it in Tigray and Afar (Djibouti border) regions. Banditry in all border areas, check before crossing into Somalia by road or travel east of the line Harer to Gode. Do not cross Djibouti border by road or train.
State: as for FCO but stay 50km from border. Ogaden region is dangerous.
Avoid the western tip of Gambella Province (in south-west Ethiopia)

Eritrea

FCO: Avoid area of Eritrean/Ethiopian border and don't go south of Barentu–Dekemahara. Keep to main roads. Warns of piracy. Avoid Eritrean/Sudan border.
Keep to main roads. Warns of piracy.
Do not travel south, south-east or west of Barentu on account of mines and banditry. Avoid Eritrean/Sudan border

BIBLIOGRAPHY AND WEBSITES

Gurdon, Charles (ed.), *The Horn of Africa*, SOAS/GRC Geopolitics Series, UCL Press, 1994
Henze, Paul B., *The Horn of Africa: From War to Peace*, Macmillan, 1991.
Iyob, Ruth, *The Eritrean Struggle for Independence: Domination, resistance, nationalism 1941–1993*, Cambridge University Press, 1995
Makinda, Samuel, *Security in the Horn of Africa*, International Institute for Strategic Studies Adelphi Paper 269, 1992.
Woodward, Peter, and Forsyth, Murray, *Conflict and Peace in the Horn of Africa*, Dartmouth, 1994.

Eritrean government: www.netafrica.org/eritrea
Ethiopian government spokesman: www.ethiospokes.net/index
Ethiopian Information Service: www.ethemb.se
Horn of Africa Review: www.sas.upenn.edu/Africa

Somalia

Population: 10,317,000
Somali 85%
Armed Forces: official nil
Per Capita GDP: US$ 1,100
Currency: shillings

The Somali people were originally nomadic tribesmen living on the east coast of Africa; they are divided into clans which are grouped together in clan-families. It is claimed that they are descended from Noah's son Ham and that his son Cush founded the Cushite race whose original kingdom was in northern Sudan. The Cushites migrated southwards after their defeat by the Auxumites around 300 BC. Legend has it that the Somali clans were formed by Arab settlers who married the local Oramo women. Two clans are still named after the settlers Darod and Isaq, while the Hawiye and Gadabursi clans can be traced to even earlier settlers. Their traditional enemies are the Christian Amhara to the west of the Rift Valley, who in the fourteenth and fifteenth centuries made efforts to control trade routes to the sea. The Somalis reacted to the increased extent of the raids in the sixteenth century by crossing the Rift and penetrating as far west as the Abyssinian highlands.

After European colonisation the Somalis found themselves in four separate entities. In the north the French established the colony of the Isa, a Somali clan, and the Afars, an Ethiopian people; this has now become the independent state of Djibouti. The British established the Somaliland Protectorate in 1884–5, signing treaties with the Isa and Gadabursi clans and the Habr Awal, Habr Garhajis and Habr Tojaala sub-clans. The area southwards to the border of the British colony of Kenya, in which a number of Somalis lived, became Italian Somalia. Inland to the west lay the Ogaden, also populated by Somalis but claimed by the Ethiopians; the British agreed to draw a boundary giving Ethiopia the northern Ogaden in 1897. Similarly the Italians and Ethiopians came to an agreement but no official boundary was drawn.

British Somaliland and Italian Somalia gained their independence and merged as the Somali Republic in 1960. In 1969 the elected prime minister was overthrown in a military coup by the army commander, Mohammed Siad Barre, who instituted a 'scientific socialist' state based on Marxist-Leninist principles that overrode the clan culture. One of the country's early aims was to create a greater Somalia embracing all the Somali people. In 1977 the Somalis invaded and overran the Ogaden but were beaten back by the Ethiopians after the latter had received Cuban and Soviet support. The war caused several hundred thousand Ogadeni Somalis to become refugees in Somalia. The refugees formed 'militias' and committed atrocities against the Isaq population in the northern border region. This, coupled with the northerners' feeling of being left behind in terms of political and social development, led to the formation of the Somali National Movement (SNM). Other clans formed opposition groups.

In 1982 the north, or former British Somaliland, attempted to gain a degree of autonomy but its efforts were crushed by the central government: Hargheisa and Burao were bombed and badly damaged. In April 1988 Barre agreed to an Ethiopian–Somali Accord that called for the demilitarisation of the border area and appeared to give up Somalia's claim to the Ogaden. Ogadenis, many of whom had joined the army, felt betrayed. In the north the SNM, encouraged by Ethiopia, was waging a civil war but now had to leave its bases in the Ogaden. It briefly captured Hargheisa and Burao but the government recovered them in 1989. At the same time the SNM received substantial reinforcements from deserting troops.

In 1989 former General Mohamed Farah Aidid, after six years in prison and working as the Somali Ambassador in India, returned to the country and took charge of the Hawiye United Somali Congress (USC). Also in 1989 the US withdrew its military assistance on account of the regime's poor human rights record; other western donors, except Italy, also cut their aid. The UNHCR, attempting to help the many refugees, was ordered out after disagreements over the numbers of refugees and the routes for supplying aid; food supplies ended in November 1989. Somalia then suffered a widening civil war as the government was reduced to little more than Barre's clan militia. Hunger spread, caused both by the fighting and by a drought. By mid-1992 some 4.5 million people faced starvation and some 300,000 may have died. Barre was forced out of office and left Mogadishu in January 1991. The interim president, Ali Mahdi Mohammed a Hawiye, was not supported by Aidid, the SNM or the Ogadeni group called the Somali Patriotic Movement (SPM); the country was thus ungovernable. In May Northern Somalia announced its independence as Somaliland, although as yet this has not been recognised.

In March 1992 the UN brokered a cease fire and embarked on a large-scale humanitarian relief operation. The United Nations Operation in Somalia (UNOSOM) was established but it took two months of negotiations before fifty unarmed observers were deployed to monitor the cease fire. It became obvious that aid convoys required military escort, but

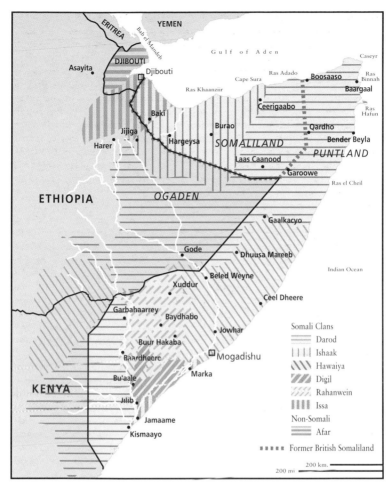

Somalia

again it took some months before the first troops, from Pakistan, arrived in September to guard the UN depot in Mogadishu. By September the UN had authorised a total of 4,200 infantry and logistical troops but only 900, including the Pakistani battalion, ever deployed. The UN situation in Somalia was untenable: its operations at the airport and seaport came under fire and its aid convoys were hijacked with increasing frequency as UN supplies became the only acceptable currency.

In November the US offered to lead the Unified Task Force (UNITAF) to create a secure environment for the delivery of humanitarian aid. On 2 December the UN accepted the offer and the first US contingent landed on the beaches of Mogadishu on 9 December 1992. US forces were built up to a strength of 28,000 with another 17,000 troops being provided by 29 other countries. In January 1993 the UN Secretary-General chaired a meeting attended by 14 Somali political groups, which agreed to a ceasefire, disarmament and the holding of a conference at Addis Ababa on national reconciliation.

UNITAF had always been planned as a short-term mission and in May 1993 UNOSOM II took over the task. The US took responsibility for part of the logistics and provided a 'quick reaction' force that remained under US national command. Most other UNITAF contingents remained as part of UNOSOM II. Serious fighting broke out in Mogadishu in June with 25 Pakistani soldiers being killed by Aidid's men and their bodies mutilated. The US began attacking arms depots, and street battles between Somali gangs and the UN forces took place. In the following three months the fighting escalated and efforts were made to arrest Aidid. On 3 October two US special forces helicopters were shot down; a relief column had great difficulty in reaching the survivors and suffered many casualties, as did a second rescue column. In all, 18 were killed and 75 wounded. The bodies of the dead US soldiers were shown on television as they were dragged around the city. The US immediately reinforced their troops with tanks and armoured vehicles, at the same time announcing their total withdrawal by the end of March 1994. The incident was the first defeat of a 'high tech' force by a 'low tech' enemy. A number of countries withdrew their UNOSOM II contingents in late 1993/early 1994. UNOSOM II adopted a far less confrontational posture and although it remained on the defensive there was no reduction in the number of attacks made on it and other international agencies.

UNOSOM II continued its mission in Somalia until March 1995 but without success in its aim of creating a secure environment. An international task force including US Marines covered the final withdrawal. UNOSOM II left Somalia with no central government and with the clans and their militia still competing for control of important assets such as the port and airport, but with no ambitions to take control of the whole country. Attempts to broker a settlement have been made, notably at Sodere in Ethiopia in January 1997 but the Somali National Association (SNA) did not attend; in December that year the SNA and the National Somali Congress (NSC) met in Cairo.

In July 1998 another breakaway entity was established. Puntland, populated by the Darod clan, covers the north-eastern part of the country. Subsequently the Darods in the south formed Jubaland on the coast in the province of Jubabada and Hoose, and the Digil and Rahawein clans in the provinces of Bay and Bakool followed their lead. In August 2000 the regional organisation for the Horn of Africa, the Intergovernmental Authority on Development, hosted a conference at Djibouti at which it was agreed to form a Transitional National Assembly (TNA) as the start of a reunification process. Only Somaliland has declared its independence but Puntland withdrew from the TNA in October 2000.

The situation in Somalia is still very unstable. The Transitional National Government (TNG) controls very little of the country, about half of Mogadishu and a small coastal strip; it is primarily backed by the president's sub-clan, the Hawiye-Ayr. The rest of the country, bar Somaliland, is under the control of opposition 'warlords' in various alliances. Ethiopia backs the Somali Reconciliation and Reconstruction Council (SRRC). A complicating factor is the presence of an Islamic group allied to Usama bin Laden's al-Qaida, the al-Itihaad al-Islamiya, which is known to have training camps in southern Somalia and which was declared a terrorist organisation by the US Executive Order 13224 of September 2001.

Since 1995 Somaliland has enjoyed stability and security but has not yet received any international recognition, mainly because this is unacceptable to Somalia. There is a modest level of government and some rebuilding of the infrastructure; education has been organised, law and order restored and a degree of commerce achieved. Northern Somalia is the most stable part of the country as there is strong clan leadership and no freelance warlords. The South remains in crisis, and much land is still occupied by outside clans which weakens the influence of local clan leaders. There is a good deal of lawlessness with looting and kidnapping. Mogadishu itself remains split. Perhaps the war on terrorism is what is needed to solve the problems in Somalia. Indeed, Somalia is at the top of the US list for future intervention. The TNG is being supportive and has welcomed a US reconnaissance party; there are reports of the deployment of US special forces.

Ships and aircraft from the US, Britain, France and Germany are patrolling Somalia's coastline and overflying its territory.

TRAVEL ADVICE

FCO and State: Advise against all travel to southern Somalia and Puntland, also Sool and Sanaag regions of Somaliland.

BIBLIOGRAPHY AND WEBSITE

Gurdon, Charles (ed.), *The Horn of Africa*, SOAS/GRC Geopolitics Series, UCL, 1994

Hirsch, John and Oakley, Robert, *Somalia and Operation Restore Hope*, US Institute of Peace Press, 1995

Lyons, Terence and Samatar, Ahmed, *Somalia: State Collapse, Multilateral Intervention, and Strategies for Political Reconstruction*, Brookings Institute, 1995

Woodward, Peter and Forsyth, Murray (eds), *Conflict and Peace in the Horn of Africa*, Dartmouth, 1994

Horn of Africa Review: www.sas.upenn.edu/African

Note: For further up-to-date travel advice on African and other destinations, see 'Departure Lounge', page 315.

Sub-Saharan Africa

Africa has now replaced Latin America as the most violent continent in the world. In this section the civil wars and massacres that have taken place – and are still taking place – in Angola, Rwanda and Burundi, Liberia, the Democratic Republic of Congo and Sierra Leone are examined in more detail. There has been some good news, though: the civil war in Mozambique that lasted for over fourteen years has been resolved successfully with United Nations' assistance. Africans would not agree with those who consider that the end of the Cold War made the world a safer place: in the period since it ended thousands of people in Africa have been killed by AK-47 rifles and machetes. The UN General Assembly has adopted a protocol aimed at halting the illegal manufacture and trade in firearms. The UN estimates there are over five hundred million small arms in the world, and the value of illegal trading in small arms is put at anything between $2 and $10 billion a year.

The first colonists to settle in Africa were the Dutch who established themselves at the Cape of Good Hope in 1652. When the British occupied the Cape Colony in 1806 the Boers moved north to found the Republics of Transvaal and the Orange Free State. The next state to be established was Liberia: this was not a colony but an area bought by the American Colonisation Society in 1822 as a home for freed slaves. Although Britain and France had established some colonies earlier, the real race for Africa began in 1880 and continued until 1904 when the Entente Cordiale settled the final disputes between the French and British. The last territories to become European colonies were the French Protectorate of Morocco, and Tripolitania and Cyrenaica, captured by Italy from Turkey in 1912. Belgium, Germany, Portugal and Spain also had African possessions. The only countries to remain totally independent were Liberia and Ethiopia, though Italy occupied the latter in 1935.

Before colonisation there were few African states as the term is now understood. Families coalesced into tribes and from time to time tribes were dominated by stronger neighbours; a number of kingdoms emerged. Today the term 'tribe' is seen as a relic of the past and so the term 'ethnic groups' has been used to denote people with a common historic community. Colonisation took little account of the indigenous inhabitants and borders were decided largely on the whim of the colonisers and a convenient compass bearing, though sometimes a conveniently placed river was used as a boundary. Colonial borders often drove a wedge between people of the same ethnic group, and many are still a cause of discord today.

After the end of the First World War Germany lost its colonies and these were then administered under League of Nations' mandate by other European states. Similarly, after the Second World War Great Britain administered the former Italian colonies until they received their independence. (The Italians were given back the administration of Italian Somaliland in 1950 under a UN mandate.)

The bulk of decolonisation took place in the 1960s and 1970s. While most states gained their independence peacefully, a number dissolved into civil war soon afterwards. The worst of Africa's civil wars have occurred in the former colonies of Belgium and Portugal and in the never-colonised countries of Liberia and Ethiopia. Britain and France have maintained links with their former colonies. The UK has preserved contact through membership of the Commonwealth, which has been joined by two states that were never actually British possessions, Cameroon and Mozambique. French links are both cultural and economic. France has defence agreements with eight francophone states and technical military

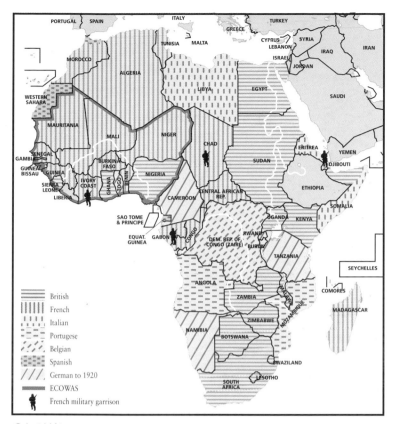

Colonial Africa

assistance agreements with twenty-three others; French forces are still stationed in Chad, Côte d'Ivoire, Djibouti, Gabon and Senegal. In 1996 France announced plans to reduce its presence to only two or possibly three garrisons; it withdrew its garrison from the Central African Republic in 1998.

Africa is currently racked by violence with over a third of its countries involved either in civil war or in border disputes with neighbours. Like people throughout the world, the African considers his most prized asset to be his land, whether personal or communal. The value of the land is, of course, much increased if it lies above important minerals, including gems or oil, and much African conflict is focused on the control of such assets. A growing number of states are, with European encouragement, providing peace-keeping forces but some of these are taking sides in the civil wars and are becoming part of the problem rather than helping to solve it. Many African leaders have become dictators, acquiring massive riches at the expense of their people – following the example of some of their former colonial masters. A number of the current civil wars are about acquiring wealth as much as power.

In addition to war and civil war Africa is beset by a further major problem: AIDS. It is claimed that as many as twenty-eight million Africans are infected by HIV, the virus that causes AIDS. It is said that 6,300 are dying every day – a figure that could rise to 13,000 by 2005. Another horrific statistic is the estimate that there may be as many as forty million AIDS orphans by 2010. The global problem of AIDS is covered on [pp. 289–92].

In July 2002, at a summit meeting in Durban, African heads of state decided to end the Organisation of African Unity and, in its place, establish the African Union. The new organisation will have the right to intervene in member states to halt genocide and to punish war crimes and gross violations of human rights. Whether it will do so is another matter.

BIBLIOGRAPHY AND WEBSITES

Diamond, Larry and Plattner, Mark F. (eds), *Democratization in Africa*, John Hopkins University Press, 1999

Pakenham, Thomas, *The Scramble for Africa*, Weidenfeld & Nicolson, 1991

Africa News Online: www.africanews.org

Africa Peace Information Locator: http://sdrc.lib.uiowa.edu/ceras

Africa Policy Information Center: www.africapolicy.org

African Conflict Journal: www.africanconflict.org

Electronic Network for Understanding Conflict in Africa: www.accord.org.za/accnet

Organisation of African Unity: www.oau-oau.org

Angola

Population: 13,326,000 Ovimbundo 37%, Kimbundu 25%, Bakongo 13%
Armed Forces: 130,000
Opposition: UNITA 20,000 fully equipped, plus 30,000 supporting militia
Per Capita GDP: US$ 1,600
Currency: kwanza

Portugal, which had already established trading settlements on the West African coast, notably at Luanda and Benguela, was allotted what is now Angola by the Berlin Conference of 1884–5, which divided African territory between the European powers. Portugal had long viewed the region as an economic replacement for its loss of Brazil. However, Portuguese interest in Angola was purely for trade and it only administered the hinterland after the conference for fear that it would lose the colony if it did not do so.

Initially Portugal's colonies had a high degree of autonomy and were ruled dictatorially by governors who were free to gain investment from any source. After the appointment of António de Oliveira Salazar to organise Portugal's economy following the military coup of 1926 the colonies were brought very much under direct control from Lisbon; by 1951 they had become part of the Portuguese nation, just at the time when other European powers were shedding their African colonies.

Anti-colonial activity – attacks in Luanda and in the northern coffee-growing area – in early 1961 led to a new wave of development and investment, as well as a military clamp-down, in an attempt to both hold on to the colonies and maintain the Salazar regime in power in Portugal. Coffee dominated the Angolan economy and the demand for labour effected the ethnic divisions between the northern people, the Bakongo and Mbundu, and the southern Ovimbundo brought in to work on the new coffee plantations. The Bakongo are the most northern of the Angolan people; they also live in Zaire and the Angolan enclave of Kabinda. The Mbundu live along the River Kuanza which flows from the Cassanje Mountains to Luanda and was the main access route from the coast to the interior. There is a fourth group, the Lunda-Chokwe, who inhabit the north-east and central parts of Angola.

In 1954 the rights of indigenous colonial populations were defined and two categories were given preferential treatment. 'Mestiço' were those of Portuguese-native descent and 'civilizado' was the status given to those who were literate, had no criminal record, paid tax and had acquired an undefined degree of Portuguese culture; this process further divided the Angolan population. The first anti-colonial political movements were the Popular

Movement for the Liberation of Angola (MPLA), established in 1956, which recruited both 'Mestico' and 'civilizado', mainly in the towns, and the National Front of Liberation of Angola (FNLA), which was supported by the unprivileged Angolans. The MPLA was supported mainly by the Mbundu, the FNLA by the Bakongo. A third party, the National Union for the Total Independence of Angola (UNITA), led by Jonas Savimbi, represented the interests of the more populous Ovimbundo and Lunda-Chokwe. The ethnic make-up of the political movements was not absolute and there was some movement between the groups.

The war for independence began in 1961 but the Portuguese managed to maintain control of the whole country until the military coup in Portugal in 1974. Fighting continued for some weeks but the army was unwilling to continue the struggle and over the next six months cease fires were signed with the three nationalist movements. In January 1975 the leaders of the three movements met and signed an agreement for independence from Portugal and set up a transitional government, with the movement leaders forming a joint presidency alongside the Portuguese High Commissioner; independence would follow on 11 November. Before November, however, fighting broke out between the movements, each of which had gained international support. The Soviet Union and Cuba, who had sent several hundred military advisers to Angola during the summer, backed the MPLA which had become a Marxist organisation. The US, naturally, backed the other two groups. The West generally supported UNITA. The South Africans provided military support for the FNLA.

As the strongest of the three groups the MPLA established the government; the FNLA eventually disbanded but UNITA continued to fight and to control territory. In 1988 the Cuban involvement reached its peak with some 50,000 troops deployed. Negotiating a peace settlement was made more difficult by the presence of up to nine thousand men from the South West African People's Organisation (SWAPO) who used Angolan territory as a base for their fight to achieve independence for South West Africa (now Namibia). The African National Congress (ANC) also had training bases there and, as a result, there were frequent incursions of South African forces from South West Africa. At the end of 1988 agreement was reached between Angola, Cuba and South Africa over the withdrawal of foreign troops and the UN was requested to monitor the process. (Namibia gained its independence on 1 April 1989.) The United Nations Angola Verification Mission (UNAVEM) of sixty observers from ten countries deployed in January 1989 with a mandate that was to last until August 1991, by which time the Cuban withdrawal would be complete. UNAVEM was concentrated at the ports and Luanda airport, and had two mobile teams checking that Cuban redeployment was taking place as agreed. The withdrawal was interrupted twice by UNITA forces and after the second attack in January 1990 was suspended for one month. Withdrawal was completed on 25 May 1991, just over a month ahead of schedule.

In April 1990 the government and UNITA began talks, mediated by Portugal and with the US and Soviet Union as observers, which resulted in a peace agreement signed at Estoril in May 1991. The agreement provided for a cease fire and it was arranged that the forces of both sides would collect in specified areas for demobilisation, with twenty thousand troops from each side going on to be trained for the new joint Angolan army. There was also provision for a general election in which UNITA would participate. The cease fire came into effect on 15 May 1991 and the UN was invited to monitor the demobilisation process. The first of UNAVEM II's 350 military and 60 police observers arrived on 2 June and deployed to the fifty assembly areas and to ports, airports and border crossing points. While there were no violations of the cease fire for fifteen months only 45 per cent of the government forces and just 24 per cent of UNITA had been demobilised by September 1992. Progress in forming the new army was behind schedule and there was a lack of food and transportation.

In September 1992 both sides announced the disbandment of their armies but neither had completed demobilisation and a much higher proportion of UNITA remained under arms. The elections took place at the end of September and the results, despite UNITA claims of widespread fraud, were declared by the UN monitors as 'generally free and fair'. As neither side had won over 50 per cent of the vote a second round was necessary.

Angola, showing sources of its riches

Fighting broke out again. Another cease fire was arranged but it did not last long. Through 1993 and most of 1994 fighting continued and there was a series of peace talks, mostly held at Lusaka. At the same time a serious humanitarian problem had developed, with many people approaching starvation and the UN relief efforts being halted from time to time by the war.

The Lusaka Protocol was signed on 20 November 1994, delayed by the continued fighting including the capture of Huamba, and a cease fire came into effect on the 22nd. The protocol comprised ten annexes covering a wide range of topics including the cease fire, the demilitarisation of UNITA, the disarming of civilians, the UN mandate and completion of the electoral process. A much stronger UN force, UNAVEM III, replaced the observers of UNAVEM II with an increased number of observers and police, and in due course units of infantry, engineers, transport and medical personnel were deployed. At its peak UNAVEM III numbered 6,500 troops, 336 military observers and 226 civil police. The UN also took on a new role clearing land mines; this work is now mainly carried out by demining NGOs.

The cease fire held until the summer of 1998 with only minor local violations; demobilisation took place although UNITA sent only the older men and young boys to the collection centres. UNITA representatives duly took their seats in the National Assembly. UNITA still held a number of strategic areas and some important diamond mines but it lost its main conduit for exporting its gems when President Mobuto lost control of Zaire in 1997. In July 1997, at the end of UNAVEM III's extended mandate, a new UN group, the UN Observer Mission in Angola (MONUA), was formed. During 1998 UNITA failed to hand over a number of its strongholds and by October the civil war had re-erupted, this time with fears that it could spread over Angola's borders into the Democratic Republic of Congo (Zaire). All attempts to halt the fighting failed and in February 1999 the UNSC voted unanimously to end its operations in Angola, and MONUA and most other UN agencies withdrew, having spent eight years and some $1.5 billion trying to make peace in this troubled country.

In June 1998 the UN placed trade sanctions on UNITA and insisted that no one should buy Angolan diamonds unless they had a government-approved certificate of origin. However, UNITA have managed to continue to smuggle diamonds out and to purchase arms with the proceeds, estimated in 1998 as $200 million out of the Angolan total of $700 million. This has enabled them to continue the war with some degree of success. The government mounted a large-scale operation in September 1999 and recaptured a number of towns including Andulo, which had been UNITA's military headquarters for five years. The lack of damage in the captured towns has led to the belief that UNITA had made a tactical withdrawal. Namibia, which with Angola was supporting the Congolese president, Laurent Kabila, agreed to allow the Angolans to use its territory to mount attacks against UNITA from the south.

By the end of 2001 UNITA had been driven back mainly into border areas and had lost control of most of the diamond-producing areas. Its fighting strength has been badly hit and it is now only capable of mounting hit-and-run attacks. But it is not yet defeated and probably has both financial reserves and stocks of diamonds with which it can purchase arms and fuel – but only if it can bring these in over Angola's borders. The government is attempting, with some success, to force UNITA away from areas bordering the Democratic Republic of Congo and Zambia. Corruption and inefficiency are ensuring that the money earned by oil and diamond exports is not being used to support the population, many of whom are starving and lack the proper medical care to cope with the growing incidence of diseases such as polio, tuberculosis and malaria, as well as AIDS.

The situation changed dramatically with the death of Jonas Savimbi in a clash with government troops on 22 February 2002. Within three weeks peace talks had begun. The UNITA delegates were tired and under nourished, and some leaders were too sick even to attend the talks. The negotiations include points from previous talks: an amnesty for those who surrender and the integration of some UNITA troops into the Angolan army. Whether full-scale peace will be achieved is doubtful; not all UNITA fighters may obey the leadership and the Angolan army is also guilty of looting and privately selling diamonds from the mines recovered from UNITA.

A new account of how the civil war began has emerged with the release of recently declassified US documents. These reveal that the US sponsored an anti-communist intervention in Angola, in cooperation with South Africa, some weeks before the Cubans arrived. The intervention failed – the Marxist government was established – and so began the civil war that lasted from 1975 until 2002.

TRAVEL ADVICE

FCO: Advises against all holiday and non-essential travel; warns of landmines and danger of crime.
State: Warns of dangers of travelling.

BIBLIOGRAPHY AND WEBSITES

Anstee, Margaret, *Angola: The Forgotten Tragedy*, David Davies Memorial Lecture published by International Relations, 1993
Gleijeses, Piero, *Conflicting Missions: Havana, Washington and Africa, 1959–1976*, Chapel Hill, 2002
Guiarães, Fernando Andresen, *The Origins of the Angolan Civil War*, Macmillan Press, 1998
Hodges, Tony, *Angola from Afro-Stalinism to Petro-Diamond Capitalism*
Klingshoffer, *The Angolan War*, Westview, 1986
Maier, Karl, *Angola: Promises and Lies*, Serif, 1996

Angolan government: www.angola.org
UNITA Kwacha Press: www.kwacha.com

Liberia

Population: 3,309,000
Armed Forces: 11,000–15,000
Opposition: LURD (numbers not known)
Per Capita GDP: US$ 600

The first American-freed African slaves landed on the coast of West Africa in 1822, sent by the American Colonisation Society. It had purchased 60 miles of coastline between Cape Mesurado (St Paul, now Monrovia) and the River Junk for $300 worth of trade goods. At that time the territory, now Liberia, was the home of sixteen ethnic groups. In the following years a number of other US states obtained land and sent their freed slaves there: Maryland at Cape Palmas and Virginia between the Junk and Farmington Rivers, both in 1827, and Pennsylvania in 1835 from Bossa Cove to the mouth of the St John River. In 1838 Mississippi acquired from Greenville to the mouth of the Sinoe. In 1847 these territories united as the Republic of Liberia. The constitution and flag copied that of the US; of the population, 5 per cent were former American slaves. After the end of the American civil war there were no further immigrants to Liberia. In 1883 the British annexed the territory north-west of the River Mano and in 1892 France annexed the land east of the River Cavallo; the French also annexed territory in the north of the country in 1911.

In 1912 the US sent three African-American former army officers to train the Liberian Frontier Force, which was responsible for defending the borders and suppressing internal opposition. In 1915 the Kru people who lived on the coast rebelled against the government and demanded that they be annexed by Sierra Leone. An American warship was diverted to assist in quelling the rebellion.

In 1944 William Shadrach Tubman became president and remained in power until he died in 1971. He was succeeded by William Tolbert, who had been vice-president for twenty years. His administration was corrupt and he was killed in a coup mounted by indigenous non-commissioned army officers led by Master Sergeant Samuel Doe in April 1980. The coup ended the rule of the 50,000 Americo-Liberians over the 2.5 million indigenous Africans. The Doe regime was notoriously savage, practising imprisonment without trial and summary execution for little reason. The US turned a blind eye to his excesses because it needed Liberia as an entry point into Africa to counter growing Soviet influence. Liberia was also a conduit for US arms to the anti-communist forces in Angola and was the site chosen for the Voice of America radio transmitters. Doe was re-elected in 1985 in a fraudulent election that was in fact declared fair by the US Secretary of State.

Another army coup was attempted soon after the 1985 election but its leader was soon caught and killed. A number of opponents to Doe's rule found it necessary to leave the country; one of these was a notably dishonest junior minister, Charles Taylor, who fled to Burkina Faso and then received military training in Libya. At the end of 1989 a previously unknown group, the National Patriotic Forces of Liberia (NPLF), sent a force of two hundred men over the border from Côte D'Ivoire to attack soldiers, police and other officials. They had expected to be supported by the people of Nimba Province but they lost all backing when Taylor assumed command of the NPLF. Taylor's men were mainly Gio tribesmen and they targeted the Krahn, Doe's group. The army was sent in and killed some 1,500 young men and caused 150,000 people to flee either to Côte D'Ivoire and Guinea or into the bush when their villages were looted and burnt. However, the NPLF was not defeated and Taylor's 10,000 men overran most of the country other than Monrovia where Doe remained in control.

Taylor's NPLF then split, with Gio Prince Yarmie Johnson leading the breakaway group that entered Monrovia in February 1990, fighting both Taylor and Doe. In June Taylor captured the international airport, forcing Doe to barricade himself in his residence with several hundred bodyguards. The Economic Community of West African States (ECOWAS) held an emergency meeting, which was attended by only seven of the sixteen member states; calling themselves the Economic Community Monitoring Group (ECOMOG), they decided to send in a peace-keeping force of three thousand men to enforce a cease fire and supervise elections. The force deployed in early September with contingents from Gambia, Ghana, Guinea, Nigeria and Sierra Leone. Taylor established himself in Kakata as a temporary capital, from which virtually the whole Madingo population had been evicted or massacred.

ECOMOG arranged a cease fire between Doe and Taylor. Doe, believing he was safe, left his residence to visit the ECOMOG commander, but Johnson's men, the United Liberation Movement in Liberia (ULIMO), attacked and captured Doe, killing him and all his escort. ECOMOG did nothing to prevent the massacre and was threatened by Taylor, and Johnson took prisoner fifty of its men. ECOMOG managed to evacuate around a thousand of Doe's supporters and their families but several hundred stayed behind in the residence. This was attacked by both Taylor and Johnson separately; they also attacked each other. The three groups met in Mali, agreed a cease fire and later, in February 1991, signed a formal agreement to hold a reconciliation conference. Sadly, the agreement made no progress. Doe's supporters were now known as the Armed Forces of Liberia (ALF). The rest of 1991 saw further fighting between the three factions and new attempts to broker a cease fire, but no progress was made throughout most of 1992. It was not until November 1992 that the UN imposed an arms embargo on Liberia and appointed a special representative.

In July 1993 a meeting was held at Cotonou in Benin, attended by the three Liberian factions, the UN special representative, the chairman of the Organisation of African Unity (OAU) and the executive secretary of ECOWAS. A peace agreement was reached and

Liberia

signed. It allowed for a cease fire from I August followed by disarmament, the deployment of a further four thousand (non-West African) peacekeepers, and the establishment of a UN observer force (UNOMIL). In 1994 some slow progress was made: further agreement was reached, the Council of State of the Transitional Government was installed and three demobilisation centres were opened. ECOMOG and UNOMIL were deployed but not in all the regions because of local resistance. A new faction, the Liberian Peace Council (LPC), emerged in the south-east of the country and opposed ECOMOG deployment there. Of the sixty thousand soldiers in all factions, only some two thousand were disarmed and demobilised in the first month.

Fighting broke out in May 1994 within the ULIMO, between Krahn and Mandingo men, and also in the east between the NPLF and the LPC. ECOMOG became increasingly mistrusted. A further agreement was reached at Akosombo, Ghana, in September but the military situation worsened. The Mandingo faction of ULIMO captured the NPFL headquarters and a coalition of the ALF, LPC and Krahn ULIMO attacked the NPFL in the northern and eastern regions of the country. The fighting created some 200,000 refugees and UNOMIL, unable to fulfil its mandate, withdrew to Monrovia. In December those groups who had signed at Akosombo together with the newly formed factions and breakaway groups signed another agreement in Accra. During 1995 the political stalemate continued and the attitude of the factions prevented essential relief from being delivered to the 1.5 million people estimated to need it. Fighting still continued, with four different conflicts between differing factions ravaging most of the country. Another meeting was held, this time at Abuja, at which most of the outstanding issues were settled. A new cease fire was agreed, the humanitarian situation addressed and improved and a new council of state installed – its membership plus some ministerial posts ensured that all the factions and sub-factions were represented.

The situation deteriorated at the end of 1995. Disarmament and demobilisation were behind schedule, as was the deployment of ECOMOG throughout the country. Inter-faction skirmishing continued and in April 1996 major fighting broke out between two coalitions in Monrovia, which was systematically looted by both sides and half its population made refugees. ECOMOG concentrated its forces in a number of locations but had to withdraw completely from several provinces. By now it was a mainly Nigerian force whose soldiers had been in Liberia for two years and were poorly paid; morale was understandably low and their effectiveness doubtful. US forces helped to evacuate foreigners from Monrovia. Another meeting in August produced another agreement signed by the four leading warlords, including Taylor and Johnson. Heavy fighting resumed in Monrovia in May. In August ECOWAS imposed a number of sanctions on Liberia, the non-governmental aid agencies announced that they were curtailing their efforts to 'minimal life-saving activities' and the UN Secretary-General warned that the international community would disengage from Liberia if the factions did not make peace.

By January 1997 the situation had changed dramatically. ECOMOG and UNOMIL reported that ten thousand men had been demobilised and over five thousand weapons handed in. Following the end of the arms amnesty ECOMOG recovered nearly four thousand additional weapons. By April the disarmament process was considered to be 90 per cent complete, though it was suspected that many weapons had been hidden. An election was held in July and was won by Taylor. His National Patriotic Party gained 21 of 26 Senate seats, and 49 of 64 seats in the House of Representatives. UNOMIL's mandate ended on 30 September and ECOMOG began its withdrawal in December. Some 150,000 people are thought to have died in the civil war, which was one of the first to see the large-scale employment of boys as young as twelve as soldiers. Possibly as many as three thousand were involved.

Violence re-erupted in August 1999 when rebels entered the country from Guinea, taking hostages and occupying a number of villages. By 2001 it was obvious that Taylor was supporting the Revolutionary United Front (RUF) in Sierra Leone and was supplying arms in return for diamonds. In March the UN Security Council imposed an arms embargo on

Liberia and warned it that an embargo on diamond sales and a ban on travel by senior officials would be imposed if Liberia continued to support the RUF. In May the additional sanctions were imposed. In early 2001 the civil war re-erupted in the Lofa province in north-east Liberia with rebels entering the country from Guinea. Arms are being smuggled in to the government through Cote D'Ivoire.

A new opposition group has emerged, Liberians United for Reconciliation and Democracy (LURD), made up of an assortment of previous rebels. They attacked Kley Junction on 7 February 2002 and then the Bong mines. In May they threatened Monrovia and were fighting for Gbarnga, a Taylor stronghold. There are those who claim the rebellion is a government ploy to have the sanctions imposed by the UN lifted; they say they have not yet seen a rebel. However, it is hard to tell the difference between a soldier and a rebel and many soldiers are both.

TRAVEL ADVICE

FCO: Advise against all holiday and non-essential travel. Warns against all travel to Lofa Province.

State: Warns against all travel.

BIBLIOGRAPHY AND WEBSITES

Nelson, Harold D., *Liberia: a Country Study*, The American University, 1984

African Conflict Journal: www.africanconflict.org
Liberian Embassy, Washington: www.liberiaemb.org

Sierra Leone

Population: 1,880,000 Mendes 32%, Temnes 31%, Limbas 8%, Krios 2–3%
Armed Forces: 6,000
Opposition: RUF 8,000
Foreign Forces: UK 600, Russia 100, UNAMSIL 17,400
Per capita GDP: $US 712
Exchange Rate: $US 1 = 1,894 L

Sierra Leone has long been protected from invasion by its geography. The coastal plain was thickly wooded and to the east lay mountains. Even the rivers running from the mountains were not navigable. The major African kingdoms did not penetrate into the area but there were numerous waves of migrating people and some separate ethnic groups settled there. The first Europeans to visit, in 1462, were Portuguese who named it Serra Lyoa because to them the small mountainous peninsula that juts out into the Atlantic resembled a lion. The estuary of the River Scarcies provided a safe harbour for European ships that came to collect cargoes of gold, ivory and slaves and also to take on water and wood for fuel.

An African people invaded the area in the 1560s and captured the estuary but were unable to penetrate far inland. While the Portuguese were the first settlers, the British too had begun to settle in the country south of the estuary by the early seventeenth century. The Crown gave the Royal African Company a monopoly in 1663; it built two forts but health problems and the destruction of one fort caused the company to abandon Sierra Leone by 1730. There was no further British government involvement until it outlawed the slave trade in 1807 and took over the Sierra Leone Company, which had been set up in 1791 by individual traders opposed to the slave trade. Earlier Granville Sharp, another opponent of the slave trade, proposed founding a settlement of free slaves, most of whom had escaped from America to Nova Scotia and New Brunswick, and he persuaded the British government to transport them to Africa. There were clashes between the settlers and the local Temne people until a peace treaty was signed in 1807. Freetown became a Crown Colony in 1808.

After the abolition of slavery the British government took over the colony and set up a Vice-Admiralty Court to try the crews of slave-ships captured by the Royal Navy; the released slaves stayed to settle in the colony. They were educated and converted to Christianity by missionary societies funded by the government. Merchants replaced the trade in slaves with exports of timber, palm oil and groundnuts. The Krios (released slave) population wanted to see the colony expanded but the government opposed this until it realised that Sierra Leone was being hemmed in by the colonies being established by the French. A protectorate was created in 1896 in the areas of British influence, where the local chiefs advised by British District Officers would have autonomy. To pay for this administration, the so-called 'Hut Tax' was introduced in 1896: this prompted an uprising of the Mende people aimed at driving out the colonists completely. The rebels were soon subdued by the military, but many Krios were massacred.

The movement for the end of colonial rule in West Africa began in 1920. A new constitution introduced to Sierra Leone in 1924 increased the number of indigenous people on the Legislative Council, including representatives from the protectorate for the first time, but still British officials were in control. After the Second World War decolonisation took on a new urgency and a new constitution was proposed. This would treat the colony and the protectorate as a single entity, and although the colonists would be given special representation the majority of voters would be from the protectorate and so would hold power. The Creoles objected to this plan. A revised constitution was accepted in 1951 and slowly Sierra Leone advanced towards independence, which it gained in 1961.

The first two elections were won by the Sierra Leone People's Party, controlled by the southern Mendes and led by the much-respected Milton Margai. The All People's Congress led by Siaka Stevens, backed by the northern Temnes and Limbas, won in 1967 but the army, disputing the result, took control. In a counter-coup the army brought Stevens back as prime minister in 1968 and he was sworn in as president when Sierra Leone became a republic in 1971. Stevens remained in power and introduced a one-party state; he stepped down in 1985. His successor was the army commander, General Joseph Momoh, who returned the country to multi-party politics in 1991 but he was attacked by the Revolutionary United Front (RUF) and the Sierra Leone civil war began. Charles Taylor in Liberia, where several Sierra Leone opposition parties were based, is seen as having had a hand in the rebellion. The RUF concentrated their operations in the south-east province. Corruption and appointments decided on political and ethnic grounds seriously weakened the army's capability – probably the most competent element had been sent to take part in the West African peacekeeping force in Liberia. Large-scale conscription of the unemployed took place but the new soldiers were poorly equipped and unpaid; they resorted to the same tactics as the RUF, using looting and intimidation to survive. The army stepped in again in 1992 to overthrow Momoh, with Captain Valentine Strasser leading the interim National Provisional Ruling Council (NPRC). The RUF expected a deal to be made with the NPRC but public opinion was opposed to this and so Strasser continued the war. The first Nigerian troops were deployed in Freetown in March 1993. A number of civil militia were formed because of lack of faith in the army, the most important being the 'Kamajors'. Strasser agreed to the involvement of the South African mercenary company Executive Outcomes, which was brought in by two mining companies because RUF rebels were affecting their operations. The mercenaries teamed up with the Kamajors and made significant progress until Strasser was overthrown by his deputy, Julian Maada Bio, in January 1996. Bio opened negotiations with the RUF and a peace process involving Côte d'Ivoire, the OAU and the UN was set in motion. The army wanted to achieve peace before holding elections but was over-ruled by popular opinion and an election was held in March 1996. It brought into power Ahmed Tejan-Kabbah, a former UN official, and the Sierra Leone People's Party.

Sierra Leone

Kabbah made a number of mistakes: he blamed the north for allowing former army corporal Foday Sankoh to start the civil war and demanded an apology; in an unpopular move he brought All People's Congress (APC) members into his administration; his liaison with Nigeria with whom he agreed a defence arrangement was equally unwelcome. His worst mistake was to end the contract with Executive Outcomes, the only disciplined force in the country. The Kamajors were greatly strengthened in numbers and their leader became deputy minister of defence. The army was further disaffected and strengthened its alliance with the RUF. A peace accord was signed in Abidjan in November but it was upset by the arrest of Sankoh during a visit to Nigeria in March 1997 and his overthrow as leader of the RUF. This was too much for the army, which saw a conspiracy to bring in Nigeria forces to destroy the RUF. In May an army coup released Major Johnny Paul Koroma, who had been arrested after leading a failed coup. He overthrew the government and Kabbah went into exile.

The new army regime faced opposition from the civil population, as well as from the OAU meeting at Harare and the Commonwealth, but little action was taken by its opponents. The RUF was brought into the government. Sankoh, though still in Nigeria, was appointed vice-president and was able to encourage his men to back the military regime. Kabbah now openly enlisted Nigerian support and at a meeting with the military junta and the British high commissioner a date was set for his return to power. To emphasise their determination the Nigerians bombarded Sierra Leone from the sea. This provoked the capture of some three hundred Nigerian soldiers who were assisting in the evacuation of foreign civilians. They were released but Nigeria was set on intervention. ECOWAS was split, with five members opposed to military action, and Liberia refused to allow its territory to be used as a base for operations. Several reasons have been advocated for Nigeria's involvement: one was the need to keep the army occupied now that the Liberian operation was over; another was the aim of the RUF and elements in the Sierra Leone army of gaining control of some of the country's natural resources, particularly the diamond mines.

At a meeting held at Conakry in October 1997 the junta agreed to Kabbah's return to power by April 1998. ECOMOG would supervise the demobilisation of the forces, and Koroma and his officers would not be charged with treason. Koroma then demanded that the army and the RUF men incorporated in it should not be disarmed, as they were the national army. He also objected to Nigeria's leading role in ECOMOG and demanded the release of Sankoh. These demands led the Nigerians to decide to remove the junta. An attack on Nigerian troops was all the excuse they needed and the signal for an all-out attack on Freetown, which fell after three days' fighting in February 1998. The army and the RUF fled into the countryside.

The RUF, however, was not defeated and its members went on a rampage of terror, mutilating hundreds of civilians. In July, while feigning surrender, they attacked the northern town of Kabala. The UN authorised a military observer force (UNOMSIL) to observe and report on the situation. In early January 1999 the rebels managed to fight their way into Freetown where they caused widespread damage. Kabbah and the still-imprisoned Sankoh ordered a cease fire, which the rebels said they would honour once Sankoh was released. Kabbah countered by saying he would release Sankoh only after the cease fire had held for a week. ECOMOG troops were still attempting to clear Freetown of rebels two weeks later. UN observers reported that both sides had committed atrocities and that 150,000 refugees had been created. In July 1999, after several weeks of negotiations, a power-sharing deal known as the Lomé peace accord was agreed at Abidjan; the rebel leader, Foday Sankoh, will be vice-president, responsible for the mineral industry and for reconstruction. By October ECOMOG was planning the gradual withdrawal of its 12,000 troops and the UN had authorised the deployment of a 6,000-strong peacekeeping force that will help the disarmament and demobilisation of some 45,000 militia of both sides. The UN mandate authorised by UNSC Resolution 1270 was to assist the government with disarmament, demobilisation and reintegration; to establish a presence throughout the territory; to ensure the security and freedom of movement of UN personnel; and to facilitate the delivery of humanitarian aid.

The first contingent of the UN Mission in Sierra Leone (UNAMSIL) arrived on 30 November 1999. At the end of April 2000 UNAMSIL took over from ECOMOG; at the same time some four thousand ECOMOG Nigerian troops came under UN command. The programme of disarmament and demobilisation did not go well and only about a quarter of the RUF's 15,000 men had been disarmed. Sankoh remained in control of the Kono diamond-mining area, using its output to obtain arms and to fund the RUF. UNAMSIL was slow to deploy. Its mandate was enhanced in February and a strength increase of five thousand men was approved but by the end of April only 8,700 out of the 11,100 authorised had actually deployed. The UN commander announced that disarmament in the diamond-mining area was to begin in June; this provoked the RUF into confrontation with the UN. In the first week of May the RUF seized some five hundred UNAMSIL soldiers from Zambia and Kenya and took their weapons and vehicles; they also recovered the five thousand weapons surrendered earlier.

A mass demonstration took place outside Sankoh's house in Freetown, and the UNAMSIL guards were swept aside as the crowd surged forward to attack the house. Sankoh's bodyguards opened fire and killed about 20 demonstrators. The British government sent a force of naval ships with a Commando embarked and flew in a battalion of the Parachute Regiment whose main task was to guard the international airport. They also carried out patrols and in a clash with RUF men inflicted casualties on them. The Sierra Leone army managed to arrest a number of RUF leaders in Freetown. Sankoh was spotted at his house, attacked and beaten by civilians; rescued by British troops he was handed over to the Sierra Leone authorities who still hold him in prison. The deployment of British troops stabilised the situation but the UK would not place them under UN command. The bulk of the force was withdrawn in June leaving a large training mission which began a series of month-long sessions to retrain the Sierra Leone army which it also rearmed and re-equipped.

In August 2000 a group of soldiers from the British training mission found themselves taken prisoner by a group of former Sierra Leone soldiers calling themselves the West Side Boys. After a period of careful reconnaissance the prisoners were rescued by the SAS supported by men of the Parachute Regiment. One SAS man was killed in the operation; the West Side Boys suffered serious casualties.

The training of a new Sierra Leone army by the British has allowed the government to take much firmer action against the RUF. The British also provided an operational headquarters to advise the Sierra Leone government on operations, and equipment for the new army and kept a brigade in the UK on standby should it be needed.

The last few years of the civil war saw a vast increase in the atrocities committed by the rebels and to a lesser extent by government forces. A worrying aspect of the civil war has been the large number of children who have been forced into the units of both sides. In November 2000 a cease fire was signed in Abuja and the disarmament process began. In May 2001 nearly six hundred children were released by the RUF as part of their disarmament process. By February 2002 some 47,000 armed rebels and government militia had surrendered their weapons to the UN. However, the RUF still controls the diamond mines and despite the UN ban on the trading of diamonds without a government certificate large numbers (said to be worth $138 million in 1999) are being smuggled out of the country. In January 2002 a symbolic bonfire of handed-in weapons was lit to celebrate the end of the civil war. The presidential election on 14 May was won by Kabbah but showed the country was divided with the Sierra Leone People's Party gaining 90 per cent of the votes in the south of the country and the main opposition, the All People's Congress, taking 60-70 per cent in the north; the army and police overwhelmingly voted for Koroma who came third. A war crimes court and South African-style 'truth and reconciliation' commission are to be established. After sucgh a long period of war it is too early to sday whether peace really has, or will, be maintained in Sierra Leone; nobody is overoptimistic; diamonds are still the main cause of corruption. A war crimes court and South African-style truth and reconciliation commission are to be established. After such a long period of war it is too early to say whether peace really has been achieved, and can last, in Sierra Leone; nobody is over-optimistic.

TRAVEL ADVICE

FCO: Advises against all holiday and non-essential travel.
State: Urges caution outside Freetown.

BIBLIOGRAPHY AND WEBSITES

Fyfe, Christopher, *Sierra Leone Inheritance*, Oxford University Press, 1964
Hirsch, John L., *Sierra Leone: Diamonds and the Struggle for Democracy*, Lynne Rienner Publishers, 2000
Malan, Mark and Phenyo Rekate and Angele McIntyre, Peacekeppeing in Sierra Leone; UN AMSIL hit, the home straight, Institute for Security Studies, 2002

African News Online: www.africanews.org/west/sierraleone
Diamond Trade Network: www.diamonds.net
Integrated Regional Information Networks: www.reliefweb.int/iron/archive/sierraleone
Sierra Leone government: www.sierra-leone.gov.sl
Sierra Leone News: www.sierraleone.org/slnews
Sierra Leone Web: www.sierra-leone.com
UN Mission in Sierra Leone: www.un.org/Depts/dpko/unamsil

Democratic Republic of Congo

Population: 53,297,000
Armed Forces: 81,000
Opposition Forces: Rallye pour le Congo Démocratique:
Liberation Movement (RCD-ML): 2,000–3,000
Goma (RCD-Goma) up to 20,000
Movement for the Liberation of the Congo (MLC) 18,000
(The MLC and most RCD-ML formed the Front for the Liberation of Congo (FLC) in January 2001)
Foreign Forces: Pro-government: Zimbabwe 8,000 (Angola 8,000, Namibia, 1,400, both withdrawn)
Angola 8,000; Namibia 1,400 withdrawn, Zimbabwe 8,000
Pro-opposition: UNITA (Angola) 2,000, Burundi 1,000,
Rwanda 15,000–20,000, Uganda 2,000
UN (MONUC): 3,400 out of 5,500 authorised
Per Capita GDP: US$ 400
Currency: Congolese franc

This vast region of central Africa has had many names. Originally the Kongo Kingdom, it was claimed by Belgium as the Congo Free State until annexed as the Belgian Congo; after independence its name was changed to Zaire and it is now called the Democratic Republic of Congo (DRC). The region had a complex pre-colonial history and a number of quite different societies lived there. Much of the area was inhabited by small-scale communities, originally based on villages that expanded by conquering neighbours and developing into tribes. The Mongo people of the central basin had no unifying political focus, nor did the '*gens d'eaus*', living along the north of the River Congo. The people living between the Congo and River Ubangi had a more hierarchical social system based on lineage. In the east there were Muslim/Arab traders and in the north-east, in the forest of Ituri, there were groups of 'hunter-gatherers'. A number of kingdoms were formed over the centuries. In the late 1300s the Kongo Kingdom began to expand, a process that continued until the mid-seventeenth century. In the late fifteenth century the Luba Empire was formed; around 1500 the Zande people appeared in the north; and about 1630 the Kuba Kingdom was set up.

The first European explorers, the Portuguese, arrived in 1483. Dr Livingstone explored the Congo Basin between 1840 and 1872. In 1878 King Leopold II of Belgian formed a consortium of bankers to finance exploration and colonisation and by 1887 Sir Henry Stanley, under the auspices of the Belgian government, had obtained some 450 treaties with local chiefs. At the Congress of Berlin Leopold claimed the region as the Congo Free State and turned it into a private fiefdom, taking the profits of the state for himself. The Belgian military expelled the Afro-Arab slave traders between 1890 and 1894 and slavery was banned. In 1908 Belgium annexed the territory as the Belgian Congo. Between 1885 and 1908 some ten million people are said to have died of exhaustion, famine and disease as the king extracted a fortune from the country.

As late as the 1950s measures were introduced to allow Africans to own land, to have the right to trial and to participate in politics. In 1956 the Alliance of Congo People (Alliance des Bakongo-Abako) called for immediate independence. The Katangan independence party, the Confédération des Associations du Katanga, under the leadership of Moise Tshombe, was formed. By 1959 the Belgians had recognised the goal of total independence for Congo. In July that year the Congolese National Movement (Mouvement National Congolais) split, with Patrice Lumumba leading the radical group, and in May 1960 he was appointed prime minister. Joseph Kasavubu, an Abako, was elected president and independence was gained on 30 June.

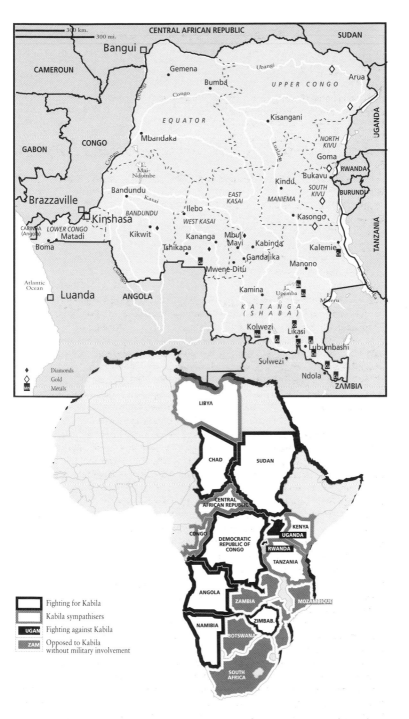

Democratic Republic of Congo and its African allies and opponents

In July 1960 the army mutinied against its European officers and Joseph Mobuto, later to be known as Mobuto Sese Seko, became chief of staff. An unratified treaty allowed Belgium to maintain two military bases in the Congo and as disorder spread the Belgian government, without the agreement of the Congolese government, ordered its troops to restore law and order and protect its nationals. A number of serious clashes between Belgian and Congolese troops occurred. Katanga declared its independence on 11 July and UN military assistance was called for. The UN Security Council agreed a Resolution on the night of 13 July which called on Belgium to withdraw its forces and authorised a peacekeeping force. Within forty-eight hours the advance party of the United Nations Operation on Congo (ONUC) had arrived. Within six weeks Belgian forces had withdrawn from the country but the secession of Katanga had not been resolved.

Following fighting between Baluba and Lulua tribesmen the Southern Kasai seceded and there was increasing opposition to the government in the provinces of Equateur and Leopoldville. In September a constitutional crisis developed when President Kasavubu decided to dismiss the prime minister; he refused to go and in turn dismissed the president. Mobutu mounted a less than successful coup and the army backed a council of commissioners who supported Kasavubu but the council was opposed by Lumumba, who was imprisoned. After his release he was murdered in 1961: the Belgian government apologised in February 2002 for the role it played in this incident. ONUC managed to remain neutral. It also negotiated an end to the fighting in Katanga and set up a number of protected areas for both Europeans and Africans. Katanga's secession ended in February 1963; ONUC remained in the Congo until the end of June 1964 assisting with the reorganisation and training of the army and with the restoration of civil activity in a wide range of services.

In July 1964 Tshombe returned from exile and was appointed prime minister, and the country adopted the name of the Republic of Congo. Kasavubu and Tshombe were soon embroiled in a power struggle until Mobutu and the army intervened, establishing a 'second republic'. Mobutu was elected president in 1970; the country's name was changed to Zaire and all provincial names were also changed. Zaire suffered rebellions in Shaba in 1977 and 1978; the first was put down with the help of Moroccan troops and the second by French and Belgian soldiers.

Zaire is rich in natural resources, with industrial diamonds, gold, copper, cobalt, manganese and tin. There is also offshore oil. Like his Belgian predecessor, Mobutu built up a personal fortune but at the same time the country suffered from massive inflation and its infrastructure began to collapse through lack of maintenance. In 1994 close on a million refugees – Hutus from Rwanda – camped in eastern Zaire where they were fed by the UN; among them were Rwandan army and Hutu militiamen who both controlled the camps and mounted raids against Rwanda and Burundi.

A new rebellion broke out in late 1996 in Kivu Province. It was sparked off by the attempted expulsion of the Tutsi population known as the Banyamulenge, who had lived in Kivu for generations. They turned on the Zairean Army and beat them. They then turned on the Hutus, who had been encouraging the army. The Hutus fled their camps. Some 600,000 crossed back into Rwanda in a mass movement while another 300,000 went deeper into Zaire, where thousands are thought to have been massacred in the forests. The rebellion was led by Laurent Kabila, a Luba from Shaba, who had taken part in earlier failed uprisings. The Zaire army was unpaid and ill-equipped, and Kabila's men crossed the country remarkably swiftly, reaching Kinshasa in six months and taking it in May 1997. Kabila became president and Zaire's name changed again to the Democratic Republic of Congo (DRC).

The change of regime did not bring peace to the country. Both Uganda and Rwanda supported Kabila and were disappointed that he failed to secure the east of the country – a failure that allowed insurgent Hutus to continue their cross-border attacks. The two countries therefore began to support a new rebel force opposed to Kabila, the Rallye pour le Congo Democratique (RCD). The Rwandan element of Kabila's forces left Kinshasa in

July 1998 as they felt they had been insufficiently rewarded and Kabila took the opportunity to replace senior army officers with his own men. This in turn led to a mutiny in Goma and elsewhere and the rebellious units soon took Kivu Province and most of Haut Zaire, and even threatened Kinshasa until Angolan troops drove them off. The RCD had active support from the Rwandan and Ugandan armies, while Kabila had military support from Chad, Angola, Namibia and most importantly Zimbabwe, which supplied most of Kabila's air support. Most of the intervening countries eyed the DRC's wealth but only individuals became rich while the cost of intervention had to be borne by the already impoverished governments. The UN Security Council has condemned the illegal exploitation of the DRC's natural resources.

In August the RCD split, with one faction being supported by Rwanda and the other by Uganda, and the troops of these two countries came to blows in three days of fighting in the city of Kisangani. A peace agreement had been ready for signing since July 2000 when it was agreed by the Foreign and Defence Ministers of the African countries involved in the war, but the two factions of the RCD could not agree on who should sign on their behalf. Eventually the agreement was signed by fifty founder members of the RCD on 1 September in Lusaka.

Kabila was assassinated on 16 January 2001. He had not been a reforming leader, and he was incompetent and unpopular. He opposed the deployment of African and UN observers, and frustrated the efforts of former Botswana president, Ketumile Masire, to broker talks between the government and the rebels. He was succeeded by his son Joseph who vowed to seek peace and restore the Lusaka Accords, although he wants these revised. An early success was the holding of a meeting in Lusaka in February, attended by all the intervening countries bar Rwanda. In March the Ugandan and Rwandan armies began to withdraw their troops; all foreign troops are committed to withdrawing, initially by 15km to allow the UN to monitor the cease fire. In July 2000 the DRC and Rwanda reached agreement on the withdrawal of Rwandan troops and the disarming by the Congolese, monitored by the UN, of Rwandan rebels.

The UN has deployed across the country which is still divided, with the northern part controlled by the FLC, the eastern part by the RCD and the southern and western parts by the DRC government. A complicating factor is the emergence of the Mai Mai and other militia in a strip running north–south through the eastern part of the RCD-controlled region. The Mai Mai (meaning 'water water') are members of the Hunde tribe, and they and similar groups are razing numerous villages as they murder and loot.

TRAVEL ADVICE

FCO: Advises against all holiday and non-essential travel. Do not walk the streets of Kinshasha after dark.
State: Warns against travel, particuarly in the Eastern provinces.

BIBLIOGRAPHY AND WEBSITES

Cilliers, Jacklie and Mark Malan, Peacekeeping in the DRC: MONUC and the Road to Peace, Institute of Security Studies, 2001
International Crisis Group Central Africa Project: www.crisisweb.org/projects/cafrica
Republic of Congo and the Civil War (International Relations Security Network): www.isn.ethz.ch/congo

Rwanda and Burundi

	Rwanda	Burundi
Population:	8,823,000	6,773,000
Armed Forces:	60,000–70,000	45,000
Opposition:	Hutu rebels 15,000	FDD 16,000
	(in DRC)	FNL ±2,500
Per Capita GDP:	$US 627	$US 600
Currency:	franc	franc

The origins of the terms 'Hutu' and 'Tutsi' are unknown owing to the lack of written records in ancient Africa. The Hutu are a Bantu people while the Tutsis, who are taller and have lighter skin, are thought to be a Hamitic people who probably came from Ethiopia in the sixteenth century. The original colonists, the Germans, followed by their successors after the First World War, the Belgians, considered the Tutsis to be the more intelligent and as a result the Tutsis gained most of the jobs in the colonial administration and were also favoured by the educational system. There were, though, no tribal distinctions nor any traditional tribal lands; Hutus and Tutsis lived intermingled and often inter-married; they speak the same language. As the colonists 'separated' the two, so animosity developed and turned to enmity; what had previously been more of a caste system became an explosive ethnic one. The first violence between the two took place in Rwanda, before independence, in 1959, when the Hutus, backed by the Belgians, threw out the Tutsi royal family and committed a number of massacres a causing large numbers of Tutsis to flee to Burundi and Uganda.

Burundi achieved independence in 1962 and for several years there was a balance between Tutsis and Hutus in the Burundi government even though 85 per cent of the population were Hutu. The Tutsis made every effort to control both the government and the army and ethnic divisions assumed greater importance following the assassination of Prince Rwagasore (a member of the Ganwa feudal elite) in October 1961. In 1965 there was an attempted coup by Hutu army officers which led to a purge of Hutu officers and the killing of several thousand Hutus, not just in the army but also most of their civil leaders. The same thing happened again in 1969. Widespread Hutu uprisings took place in 1972 and the army, now entirely Tutsi, is estimated to have killed 250,000 Hutus plus a number of rival Tutsis and to have caused 150,000 refugees to flee the country. Incidents of Tutsi provocation in 1988 led to the massacre of hundreds of Tutsis in the north; the army responded by massacring some 20,000 Hutus and driving many more into Rwanda.

A Hutu president of Burundi was elected in 1993 and for the first time a Hutu government was appointed. A Tutsi military coup four months later failed to take power but it sparked an outbreak of ethnic violence in which 200,000 died and over a million people were driven from their homes. The next Hutu president was killed in a plane crash together with the Rwandan president. This set off the Rwandan crisis and led to a mass of refugees crossing into Burundi, but this did not provoke a fresh outbreak of violence there. In July 1995 former President Buyoya, a Tutsi, regained power in Burundi in a military coup. Burundi did not agree to any form of peacekeeping force deploying in the country but the UNHCR has played a major humanitarian role.

Until 1959 the Tutsis dominated political and economic life in Rwanda. When the king died extremist Tutsis attempted to fill the power vacuum but provoked a Hutu revolt. To avoid increasing ethnic violence a large number of Tutsis left the country, most going to Uganda. Rwanda gained its independence in 1961. The Tutsis made a number of unsuccessful attempts to make an armed comeback but the Hutu remained in control of the country.

In October 1990 Rwanda was invaded by the Tutsi Rwandan Patriotic Front (RPF) from Uganda, where it had been formed among the refugees. Many were serving in the Ugandan National Resistance Army. Although its advance into Rwanda was halted and

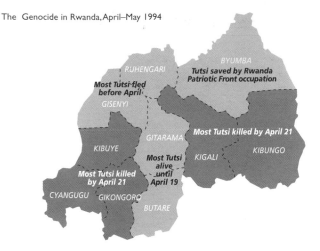

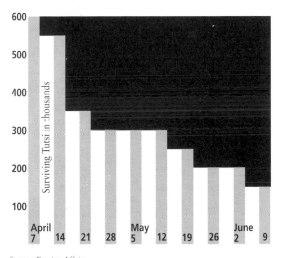

Source: Foreign Affairs

Estimated pace of genocide

pushed back, the RPF claimed to have taken control of the Rwandan–Ugandan border. After a conference at Dar-es-Salaam Rwanda agreed to accept back Tutsi refugees, to scrap the one-party system and to allow the Tutsis to form a political party. Fighting continued along the border and Tutsi gains caused thousands of Hutu refugees. A cease fire was agreed to in July 1992 and the Neutral Military Observer Group, supported by the OAU, monitored the agreement. Hostilities in the north resumed in February 1993 with the Rwandans accusing Uganda of assisting the RPF. As a result, in July the UN agreed to deploy a mission, the UN Military Observer Mission Uganda–Rwanda (UNOMUR), along the border to ensure there was no reinforcement of the RPF. In August the Arusha Accords were signed and the UN agreed to deploy the UN Assistance Mission in Rwanda (UNAMIR) to maintain security in Kigali and establish a DMZ; this force incorporated UNOMUR.

On 6 April 1994 the aircraft carrying both the presidents of Rwanda and Burundi crashed, killing all on board. Two days later the RPF renewed their attacks. At the same time a series of mass murders of Tutsis amounting to genocide took place across the country. It was evident that the murders carried out by the Hutu army and militias known as the 'interahamwe' had been long prepared and only the signal to start had been awaited. At least 500,000 Tutsis and 'moderate' Hutus are known to have died. By the end of May the RPF had captured half the country and had surrounded Kigali. The Belgian government decided to withdraw its battalion from UNAMIR and the UN debated its future operations in the area. It was decided that it should withdraw, leaving only 270 men in Kigali to continue mediating between the two sides. The only alternative would have been to rush in several thousand troops with a Chapter VII enforcement mandate.

It was now the Rwandan Hutus' turn to suffer and over 250,000 refugees crossed into Tanzania in twenty-four hours. At the end of May 1994 the UN Security Council was told that some 1.5 million people had been displaced in Rwanda and a further 400,000 refugees had crossed its borders. On 8 June the UNSC resolved to reinforce UNAMIR to 5,500 men. In the first week of July the French, in Operation Turquoise, established a 'humanitarian protected zone' in south-western Rwanda. It is now claimed that the French action allowed a large number of the Hutus responsible for the earlier killings to escape to the Democratic Republic of Congo, worsening the situation there. By 18 July the RPF had taken control of virtually the whole country and unilaterally declared a cease fire; on the 19th a broad-based government of national unity was formed. During July the refugee crisis grew and an estimated 1.5 million Hutus, often driven on by the Hutu army, crossed into Zaire; they were followed by the remnants of the army.

In Zaire former Hutu officials and military personnel forced the refugees to remain in the camps; they were suspected of preparing for a counter-attack into Rwanda and were responsible for the state of lawlessness. The UN recommended deploying both police and military forces to control the camps but few nations were prepared to risk their troops in such an operation. The Zaire government and humanitarian agencies did their best; a number of nations sent military units to support humanitarian efforts, including the US, the UK, Australia and Israel. They concentrated on the supply of food and water, medical arrangements, road building and the repair of UN vehicles.

In August 1995 the Zaire government began the forced repatriation of refugees. By the time the policy was abandoned because of international pressure some 130,000 people had been returned to Rwanda, but as many as 170,000 fled into the forests to avoid repatriation. The UNHCR then took on the task of organising the return of refugees, but the results were too slow for the Tanzanian and Zairean governments. UNAMIR's mandate ended in March 1996 and UN troops withdrew from Rwanda. The total cost of UN operations there was over $4 billion.

In October 1996 fighting in eastern Zaire between the government and the ethnic Tutsi Banyamulenge who have inhabited Kivu for many years led to panic in the refugee camps. Some 600,000 people fled back to Rwanda and a further 300,000 went west, deeper into Zaire. In December 1996 the UNHCR reached agreement with the Tanzanian authorities for the total repatriation of the remaining 540,000 refugees. On hearing of the plans most refugees attempted to hide in the bush but were turned back by the Tanzanian army and then shepherded to the border.

In recent years there has been some admission that the genocide in Rwanda could have been prevented but for the lack of support, particularly from the US, for further action by the UN. In a visit to Kigali in March 1998 President Clinton apologised for not having 'fully appreciated ... this unimaginable terror'. An international criminal tribunal has been established and is dispensing justice to those accused of genocide in Rwanda. The Rwandan government is also holding trials; there are 115,000 suspects in prison but Rwanda has no experienced judges as these, being Tutsi, were victims of the crimes about to be tried.

In November 2001 Rwanda and Uganda were close to war. The two countries were at first allies intervening in the DRC in support of the anti-Kabila rebels; however, fighting between their soldiers broke out in Kisangani in 1999. The two governments ended by supporting rival rebel factions, and both are operating in North Kivu Province. A solution, perhaps only temporary, was brokered by the British government, by which both sides would extradite each other's rebels. Both Uganda and Rwanda are dependant on British aid.

A civil war has been in progress in Burundi since the newly – and democratically – elected Hutu president, Melchior Ndadaye, was assassinated by Tutsi soldiers in 1993. Pierre Buyoya, a Tutsi, seized power for the second time in 1996 and became president, despite several attempted coups by army officers who disagreed with his policy of negotiating with the Hutus. However, a power-sharing agreement was reached at Arusha, in Tanzania, in November 2001; Buyoya continues as president for eighteen months after which he will hand over to a

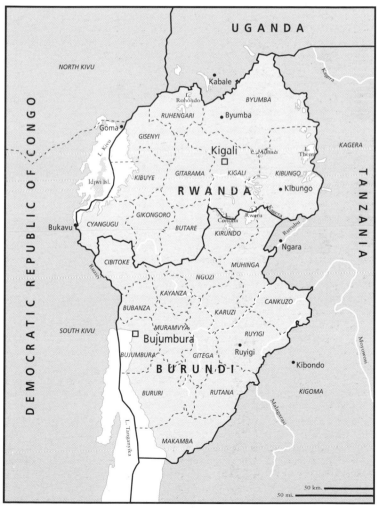

Rwanda and Burundi

Hutu. The agreement does not please everyone. There are two Hutu armed opposition factions in Burundi both containing a number of returned fighters from the DRC; they were not represented at Arusha and do not accept its conclusions. The Forces pour la Défense de Démocratie (FDD) is mainly based in South Kivu in the DRC with smaller numbers in the Kigoma region of Tanzania. The Forces Nationales de Libération (FNL) is also based in the DRC north of Lake Tanganika. South Africa has sent a small force into Burundi primarily to protect Hutu politicians returning from abroad and to train Burundian bodyguards.

TRAVEL ADVICE

Burundi		Rwanda	
FCO:	Advises against all travel	FCO:	Advises against travel in the rural areas of Cyangogu, Gikongaro and the Nyungwe Forest.
State:	Advises all travel deferred.	State:	Advises against travel in Nyungwe Forest.

BIBLIOGRAPHY AND WEBSITES

Gourevitch, Philip, *We Wish to Inform You that Tomorrow We Will be Killed With Our Families*, 1998
Le Marchand, René, *Burundii Ethnic Conflict and Genocide*, Cambridge University Press, 1994
Melvern, Linda, *The People Betrayed: The Role of the West in Rwanda's Genocide*, Zed Books, 2000
Prunier, Gerard, *The Rwandan Crisis 1959–1994: History of Genocide*, Hurst, 1995

Burundi Information: http://burundi@burundi
Rally for the Return of Refugees and Democracy in Rwanda: www.rdrwanda.org
Rwanda Information Exchange: www.rwanda.net

Zimbabwe

Population: 11,781,000
Whites 70,000, Asians 20,000
Shona 70%, Ndebele 20%
Armed Forces: 39,000
Paramilitary: 22,000
Per Capita GDP: US$ 2,300
Currency: dollar

Zimbabwe ('stone house' in Bantu) was the scene of an early African civilisation. Ruled first by the Shona and then by the Rwozi it was annexed and colonised by the British in the late nineteenth century.

Southern Africa was originally inhabited by Bantu-speaking people. The Dutch East India Company established Cape Town as a port en route to the Indies in 1652. The British purchased Cape Town and its hinterland in 1814; they also established a colony in Natal on the south-eastern coast. In 1836 the Dutch began their Great Trek, which led to the forming of the Boer provinces of Transvaal and the Orange Free State, areas where there was little indigenous population. The country to the west of the Orange Free State became a British protectorate in 1885 as the local rulers feared a take-over by the Boers; it was called Bechuanaland and today is Botswana. Cecil Rhodes became prime minister of the Cape Colony in 1890; he was a leading shareholder in the British South Africa Company and his aim was to colonise all of Africa for Britain, from the Cape to Cairo.

The first step had to be the annexation of Barotseland, the territory north of Bechuanaland, to forestall Boer, French and German colonisation. Rhodes bought it for £19,000 in 1889; it later became part of Northern Rhodesia. The next acquisition was Matabeleland, and Rhodes obtained a concession in October 1888 from Chief Lobengula, a concession the chief unsuccessfully appealed against later. The British South Africa Company received a charter in 1889 giving it the authority to extend its operations north of the Limpopo without limit except for the Bechuanaland Protectorate. The new territory was to be called Zambesia and Rhodes dispatched a column of 'pioneers' and police under Frederick Selous to raise the Union Jack at 'Fort Salisbury' in Mashonaland. Uprisings against the Chartered Company in 1893 and 1896 were all suppressed vigorously, and to some extent were provoked by the Company so that it could consolidate its authority. The Company now claimed ownership of the land and when the 'pioneers' were disbanded allowed them to make claims to 3,000 acres each. Southern Rhodesia was established by an Order in Council in 1898 which also required the Company to 'assign to the natives land sufficient for their agricultural and pastoral requirements'.

Southern Rhodesia became a self-governing colony in 1923 (while Northern Rhodesia and Nyasaland became protectorates) following a referendum which rejected union with South Africa. However, only the white community had any say in the governance. In 1930 a Land Apportionment Act was passed that confirmed the policies of driving Africans off their land to live in reserves. Africans could vote if they met certain conditions of income and property value, but the levels were set so high that only thirty-nine out of over a million Africans were able to vote in 1936; the level of the restrictions was raised from time to time. The Central African Federation, comprising the two Rhodesias and Nyasaland, was established in 1953, a move opposed by the African politicians of Northern Rhodesia and Nyasaland, but promoted by the British government for a number of reasons. One was to keep the Union of South Africa in the Commonwealth; others were to keep Southern Rhodesia separate from South Africa and to prevent Africans turning to communism. African opposition was to some extent restrained by the covert funds given to their political leaders by the UK government. But African opposition developed during the 1950s; the African National Congress was formed in 1957. Robert Mugabe emerged as an African who did not accept British finance and believed that power came from a gun. The Land Apportionment Act was debated and not repealed in 1960, as had been suggested by a select committee, despite there being ten million acres of unused land still reserved for whites only.

Led by Southern Rhodesia, the Central African Federation sought independence but the British government would not contemplate this before the two protectorates had shown they were totally in support of the Federation. The Monckton Report published in October 1960 agreed that there was a right of secession from the Federation; it also recommended an eventual parity of African and white representation in the Federal Parliament. The Central African Federation broke up in 1963 with Northern Rhodesia and Nyasaland gaining their independence as Zambia and Malawi..

In the 1960s a number of African political parties were formed and successively banned. The African National Congress was banned in 1959; its leader, Joshua Nkomo, then formed the National Democratic Party in exile; this was banned in 1961. Nkomo then created the Zimbabwe African People's Union (ZAPU) which was banned in 1962. A group split from ZAPU and formed the Zimbabwe African National Union (ZANU) under Ndabaningi Sithole; its secretary-general was Mugabe.

In 1965 Ian Smith's government made a Unilateral Declaration of Independence which led to the imposition of international economic sanctions, a naval blockade and civil war. Some argue that if the British Labour government had made some show of force the problem would have been solved, but Prime Minister Harold Wilson ruled out the use of force and opted instead for sanctions, which achieved nothing until 1974 when Portugal withdrew from Mozambique. South Africa's attitude was ambivalent; it foresaw that African rule was inevitable but it wanted a moderate pro-Western government in Harare and so supported the Rhodesians sufficiently to allow time for a peaceful solution to be achieved. Neither white nor black Rhodesians wanted this outcome. The war dragged on for fourteen years, helped along by South African circumvention of sanctions and by the internal fighting among the African parties.

ZAPU and ZANU, whose military wing was the Zimbabwe African National Liberation Army (ZANLA), began launching a series of small-scale attacks in 1966; ZAPU's military

Zimbabwe

wing, the Zimbabwe People's Revolutionary Army (ZIPRA), tried three rather larger-scale incursions, all of which resulted in disaster for the guerrillas. The years between 1969 and 1972 were relatively quiet while the African movements revised their strategy and built up their military strength, much aided by support in training, finance, arms, and indoctrination from the Soviet Union, China and Frelimo in Mozambique..

The guerrilla war started in earnest in 1972 and lasted until 1980; for the first four years the white Rhodesians were winning but the tide turned during 1976 and if a settlement had not been reached at the Lancaster House conference they might have been defeated. By the end of 1974 the white Rhodesians thought they had won, but a combination of Vorster, Kenneth Kaunda of Zambia (whose country was suffering both economically and from ZANLA and ZIPRA in-fighting in Zambia) and Julius Nyere, the president of Tanzania, persuaded the Rhodesians to agree to a cease fire. Joshua Nkomo and Robert Mugabe (ZANU) were released from prison but not all nationalists were freed. Vorster promised to withdraw his forces from Rhodesia. The cease fire collapsed and infiltration resumed, but the nationalists' inexperience led to greater Rhodesian success. ZANU/ZAPU and tribal rivalry led to many African self-inflicted casualties; ZANLA withdrew from Zambia and concentrated its efforts from Mozambique. Following a raid in August 1976 by Selous Scouts against a ZANLA camp in Mozambique, where over a thousand Africans were killed, President Vorster of South Africa withdrew South African air force units from Rhodesia, held up the supply of ammunition and oil, and openly declared his support for majority rule in Rhodesia. Guerrilla strength grew and many more infiltrated into Rhodesia. Under pressure from Vorster and the US Secretary of State Henry Kissinger, Smith conceded the principle of majority rule.

Both sides intensified their military operations and both gained successes. Smith persuaded Bishop Muzorewa and Sithole, both of whom had their own private armies, to join a new-style government. An election was held in April 1979 and Muzorewa won 51 of the 72 African reserved seats and became, nominally, prime minister. The Lancaster House conference opened while fighting continued but the white Rhodesians were being much less successful, suffering casualties and losing helicopters. The Lancaster House conference finally led to constitutional change and an Interim UK Administration, headed by Lord Soames, governed the country while a Commonwealth force supervised the disarming and rehabilitation of the guerrillas. Elections were held in March 1980 in which Mugabe's party (Zimbabwe African National Union) won 57 of the 80 seats reserved for black candidates. In April 1980 Zimbabwe became independent.

The early years of independence were not peaceful; South Africa was not helpful, and the civil war in Mozambique created difficulties for the transit route to Zimbabwe.

Internally ZANU and ZAPU were at loggerheads. In 1986 the abolition of the reserved parliamentary seats for whites was announced. In 1987 the posts of president and prime minister were combined and held by Mugabe and in 1989 a one-party state constitution was proposed. ZANU and ZAPU had merged in 1987. There was no mention in this period of land reform although there was a considerable amount of unused land owned by white farmers which could have redistributed; much of what *was* redistributed ended up in the hands of Mugabe's cronies.

The system of land tenure in Zimbabwe has four components. Large commercial farms, of which there were some 4,500, occupied 11.2 million hectares. A total of 1,100 small commercial farms took 1.4 million hectares. There was 16.4 million hectares of communal land where some 900,000 families farmed; their land had little irrigation and no machinery. Some resettlement had taken place on 3.3 million hectares providing small farms for 50,000 families. Farmers on communal land had a right of tenure and their farms could be inherited. The large commercial farms produced 100 per cent of the tobacco, which represented one third of all exports while utilising only 2 per cent of harvestable land. In 1993 the tobacco crop of 171,000 tonnes earned $325 million.

The first farms were seized as early as 1998 after Mugabe had announced plans to seize twelve million acres for redistribution. The Commercial Farmers Union responded with a plan to sell some three hundred farms. In September 1999 the Zimbabwe Congress of Trades Unions formed the Movement for Democratic Change (MDC) which has now become the main opposition to Mugabe. Two events occurred in early 2000. A referendum was held on the adoption of a new constitution devised by Mugabe's government, which was voted out by 54 per cent. A parliamentary election was held in June that, despite pre-election intimidation and the 'serious flaws in the electoral process' reported by European Union monitors, gave Mugabe only a small majority of 62 seats compared to the MDC's 57. The MDC won all the urban constituencies and won a majority of seats in Manyika and Masvingo provinces. ZANU-PF won only one seat in Matabeleland, where in the 1980s the Korean-trained 5th Brigade carried out a massacre of so-called Ndebele dissidents.

Mugabe could clearly see the threat to his hold on power and so became determined to use the land issue to gain popularity. The invasion of farms by squatters, nominally war veterans, began with much violence; it was not only the white farm owners who were evicted but also the black workers whom the farmers housed and allowed to work part of the land. Some six hundred farms had been seized by the end of April and 1300 by the end of May, and 90 per cent of all white-owned farms are now scheduled for seizure.

In September 2001 a conference was held in Abuja, chaired by President Olusegun Obasanjo of Nigeria and attended by a number of Commonwealth representatives, to discuss the problems of Zimbabwe's land reforms. After ten hours of talks it was agreed that land ownership needed to be rectified (but in a transparent and equitable manner) on account of historical injustices. A compensation fund would be administered by the UN Development Programme. Continued implementation of the reform scheme would be preceded by a review of land seizures. ZANU-PF unanimously endorsed the Abuja agreement.

The economy has been in crisis for some time, a situation not helped by the high cost of the Zimbabwean intervention in the Democratic Republic of Congo which cost £175 million between August 1998 and August 2000. There has been a loss of income and hard currency by the reduction in tobacco exports, and tourism has virtually ended. Prices have risen enormously and there are serious shortages of food and fuel.

In the run-up to the presidential election in March 2002 there was massive and blatant intimidation. Independent monitors from the European Union have withdrawn, but the Commonwealth did not vote to expel Zimbabwe. In the election considerable obstacles were placed in the way of MDC supporters by reducing the number of voting stations and closing some stations while large numbers of voters were still queuing to vote. Even so the MDC leader, Morgan Tsvangirai, obtained 1,258,401 votes (42%), with Mugabe winning with 1,685,212 votes (56%). There were instances of electoral fraud, with more votes being cast for Mugabe than the number of people who voted. The Commonwealth election observers reported that 'the conditions in Zimbabwe did not adequately allow for a free expression of will by the electors' and the Commonwealth then suspended Zimbabwe for one year. Violence against MDC members has continued since the election with the paramilitary National Youth Service Force being primarily responsible. They have created some 50,000 refugees.

In June 2002, Mugabe ordered a further 2,900 white farmers to stop farming, despite the severe shortage of food, and to leave their farms by 10 August; the takeover of these farms would have left some 100,000 black workers and their families, numbering perhaps 700,000 all told, jobless and homeless; however in August successful legal challenges were mounted that delayed the evictions in some cases; while Mugabe voiced his defiance of Western opinion at the Earth Summit in Johannesburg at the beginning of September.

Travel Advice

FCO: Exercise cautin, seek advise, avoid demonstrations.

State: avoid large gatherings, demonstrations and seized farms. In Nyanga avoid Pungwe Falls, Mterazi Falls and Honde Falls on account of the risk of armed robbery.

Bibliography and Website

Kriger, Norma J., Zimbabwe's Guerrilla War: Peasant Voices, Cambridge University Press, 1992

Meredith, Martin, *Mugabe,* Perseus Press, 2002

Moorcroft, Paul L., *African Nemesis: War and Revolution in Southern Africa 1945–2010*, Brassey's, 1990

Verrier, Anthony, *The Road to Zimbabwe 1890–1980*, Jonathan Cape, 1986

Zimbabwe Agricultural Trust: www.zawt.org

Zimbabwe Democracy Trust: www.zimbabwedemocracytrust.org

Nigeria

Population: 113,700,000

Armed Forces: 78,000

Per Capita GDP: US$ 1,359

Currency: naira

Nigeria has been inhabited since 700 BC and it developed some of the earliest states in Africa in the twelfth to the fourteenth centuries. In the north were the Hausas (city-states of Kano, Katsina and Zaria) and the Kanuri kingdom of Borno. In the south and centre were the Yoruba, Aja, Borgu and Nupe kingdoms. In the Islamisation of Africa the Borno were converted to Islam first, being the closest to the Arab world and having the most contact with it. Europeans first visited the west African coast some time after Arab traders had reached the region overland. The western African coastline had been explored by the Portuguese since 1418. Although the slave trade had already been in existence for some time, there was a huge increase in demand after the European conquest of South and Central America in the sixteenth and seventeenth centuries; a number of slave-trading stations were established on the west African coast.

Serious European colonisation did not begin in the area until the nineteenth century. Lagos is said to have been bought in 1861 and became a colony in 1886. After exploration by the National African Company, the protectorates of North and South Nigeria were established in 1900. The three regions established by Britain each had a dominant ethnic group: in the colony the Yoruba; in the north the Hausas; and in the south the Igbos. Each region also had numerous other smaller ethnic groups, totalling over 350. They had all had differing relations over history; in the north the Hausa Kingdom reached its peak in 1804 when the Fulani 'jihad' brought the north and part of the central belt under the Sokoto Caliphate; in the west the territory was split between the Benin and Oyo Empires but they declined at the end of the nineteenth century; there was no central power in the east though the city-states of Calabar and Opobo gained importance through their trade in slaves with Europeans.

In 1906 the southern protectorate and the colony were joined together for administrative purposes and the whole united as a British colony in 1914. As usual in Africa the European-imposed borders bore little relation to the local communities, and the need to satisfy minority groups led to many changes of internal organisation. Despite unification the civil administration in the north and south continued, as before, on their separate ways, mainly because the northern administrators considered the south corrupt. The north had less contact with European influence and Christian missionaries, and as a result the south gained in terms of superior education and political development. Each region developed a main, ethnically based, political party and all called for regional autonomy in a weak federal system; their weaker political opponents took the other view, wanting a strong federal government but allowing the formation of more ethnic states. In 1960 Nigeria gained its independence and in 1963 became a republic within the Commonwealth; at the same time the western region was divided in two

Nigeria

The constitution was changed in 1976 to divide the country into 12 states, in 1976 into 19 states, in 1991 into 30 states and finally in 1996 into today's 36 states. The north of the country is predominantly Muslim with the south being Christian; a broad band across central Nigeria has a mixed population. However, many Christians have moved to northern cities and Muslims have gone south. The question of the introduction of *shari'ah* (traditional Islamic law) is of concern to Christians. Twelve mainly Muslim states enforce shari'ah. In Kono it has been on and off, with each change leading to widespread rioting by the disappointed community. Recently, there have been several occasions when the prosecution sentence of death by stoning has been awarded; the Federal government has declared shari'ah to be unconstitutional.

The first military coup, led by mainly Ibo junior officers, took place in 1966 but the new government was soon overturned by a counter-coup led by Colonel Yakubu Gowon, who restored the federal system and appointed a military governor for each region. In 1967 disagreement over the share of oil revenues led to the eastern region of Biafra declaring itself an independent Igbo state. The civil war lasted until 1970 and one million lives were lost in the war and through famine. In the 1970s and early 1980s a series of bloodless coups took place, all bar one resulting in a military-led government. President Ibrahim Babangida made strenuous attempts to end corruption and began by banning previous office-holders from standing for re-election; he was overthrown by another general, Sani Abacha. Most presidents have been northern Muslims. The first civilian president after sixteen years of military role was Olusegen Obansanjo, who was elected in May 1999. He is a Christian Yoruba southerner and was president from 1976 to 1979.

A long-standing problem has been the unrest in the oil-producing states of the Niger Delta, which see little of the wealth created returned to the region. The oil companies employ few locals and cause considerable pollution. Threatening the oil companies and kidnapping employees has become a major source of income. For many years Nigeria failed to benefit from oil revenues as these were appropriated by the president's cronies who had been granted export licences.

Nigeria is bedevilled by ethnic and religious differences made worse by the high levels of corruption and violent crime. However, most incidents of violence are caused by politicians seeking popularity by stirring up jealousy between differing groups, and by disputes over land or when a small community feels threatened by another. Religious and ethnic differences inevitably make such outbursts worse. When the army intervenes there are usually large numbers of casualties. It is claimed that over six thousand people have been killed since May 1999, when civil rule was re-established, including two thousand in Kaduna in February 2000 and five hundred more killed by the army in Benue in October 2001. Democratic leaders worry that the US War on Terrorism may inflame inter-religious conflict in Nigeria.

TRAVEL ADVICE

FCO: Beware of violent crime, mainly in Lagos. Avoid travel in Bakassa. Kidnapping and hostage-taking is frequent in Delta, River and Bayelsa States.

State: Warns of the danger in travelling. Commercial fraud is a major problem. Similar advice to FCO on danger of kidnapping.

BIBLIOGRAPHY AND WEBSITES

Crowder, Michael, *The Story of Nigeria*, Faber & Faber, 1980

Maier, Karl, *This House Has Fallen: Nigeria in Crisis*, Allen Lane, 2000

Osaghae, Eghosa E., *Crippled Giant: Nigeria Since Independence*, Hurst, 1998

Tamuno, N. Tekena and Ukpabi, Samson C. (eds), *Nigeria Since Independence: The First 25 Years*. Volume VI: *The Civil War Years*, Heinemann (Nigeria), 1989

Africa News Online – Nigeria: www.africanews.org/west/nigeria

Association of Concerned African Scholars: www.prairienet.org/acas/siro

Federal Republic of Nigeria: http://tribeca.ios.com/~n123/nigerldr

Nigerian High Commission London: www.nigeriahighcommissionuk.com

Central and South Asia

This section includes both Central Asia and the area known as South Asia. It covers from Kazakhstan in the north to Sri Lanka in the south, and from Pakistan in the west to Myanmar in the east. It is a region with many problems, mainly internal but including the long-standing India–Pakistan confrontation over Kashmir. Afghanistan has been a dangerous area throughout its history and not just since 11 September 2001. Internal problems covered include the thirty-year civil war in Sri Lanka, possibly now at an end, the Maoist rebellion in Nepal, and the uprisings in India, Pakistan and the newly independent Central Asian states.

Central Asia

	Kazakhstan	Kyrgyzstan	Tajikistan
Population:	16,115,000	4,733,000	6,225,000
	Kazak 51%	Kyrgyz 56%	Tajik 67%
	Russian 32%	Russian 17%	Uzbek 25%
	Ukrainian 5%	Uzbek 13%	Russian 2%
	Uzbek 2%	Ukrainian 3%	
Armed Forces:	64,000	9,000	6,000
Foreign Forces:			Russian 22,000
Per Capita GDP:	US$ 3,700	US$ 2,300	US$ 1,000
Currency:	tenge	som	rouble

	Turkmenistan	Uzbekistan
Population:	4,450,000	24,576,000
	Turkmen 77%	Uzbek 73%
	Uzbek 9%	Russian 6%
	Russian 7%	Tajik 5%
	Kazak 2%	Kazak 4%
Armed Forces:	17,000	50,000
Opposition Forces:	IMU ±2,000	
Per Capita GDP:	US$ 2,600	US$ 3,000
Currency:	manat	som

The histories of the Central Asian states share many common strands, including their invasion by powers such as the Arabs, Mongols and Russians, their conversion to Islam, and in more recent history the changes to their names and borders. The present situation stabilised after the Russian revolution and the five states had all become republics of the Soviet Union by 1929. It is preferable to describe their history collectively rather than individually.

In the fifth century BC the area that is now Uzbekistan was peopled by Bactrians, Soghdians and Tokharians. Samarkand and Bukhara were cities and the region was enriched by the silk route. Alexander the Great reached Samarkand, Tashkent and Bukhara in 328 BC. The Arab conquest came in AD 750. Between then and the Mongol conquest of 1219–25 a

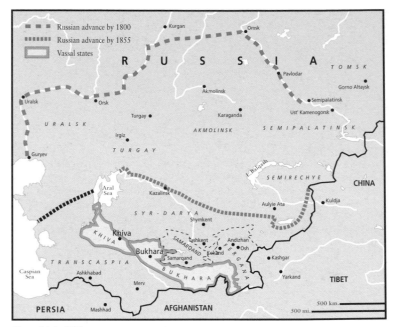

Central Asia 1908

number of different Turkic peoples entered the region; the term Turkmen came to be applied to the southern Oghuz tribes who were pushed westwards by the Mongols and settled in today's Turkmenistan. In 1500 the Uzbek nomadic tribes, which came from Transoxiana, established the Khanate of Bukhara which included the Fergana Valley. In 1511 the Kazakh tribes were unified by Khan Kasym. Around 1700 Bukhara lost the Fergana and another Uzbek Khanate, the Kokand, was established there. Russian influence appeared as a result of a Kazakh appeal for protection from the Kalmyks in 1726; in 1785 the Kyrgyz similarly appealed for protection from Kokand. Russian settlement began after the abolition of serfdom in 1861. The Russian conquest began in 1865 and lasted until the defeat of Kokand in 1876. By 1867 the Russians had established the Guberniya (governate-general) of Turkestan, which covered the area that is now Kyrgyzstan, Tajikistan, Turkmenistan, Uzbekistan and southern Kazakhstan; the remainder of Kazakhstan belonged to the Guberniya of the Steppes.

After the Russian revolution in 1918 the whole of Central Asia became the Turkestan Autonomous Soviet Socialist Republic (ASSR). Two years later the Soviet Bukharan People's Republic and the Kyrgyz ASSR (comprising Kyrgyzstan and Kazakhstan) were established; Kyrgyzstan and Kazakhstan split into two separate ASSRs in 1925. In 1924 the ASSRs of Turkestan and Uzbekistan were formed, and finally in 1929 Tajikistan became a Soviet Socialist Republic, incorporating the area that is now north Tajikistan, but the Tajiks lost the cities of Samarkand and Bukhara where most of Uzbekistan's nearly a million Tajiks live. In 1936 Uzbekistan was given Karakalpak.

Stalin sought to impose nation-state identities on these newly formed ASSRs, dividing the ethnic populations between ASSRs and attempting to destroy pan-Turkic and pan-Islamic loyalties. One move which may yet provoke conflict in the region was the splitting of the Fergana Valley between three ASSRs, Tajikistan (25%), Uzbekistan (60%) and Kyrgyzstan (15%). The valley is surrounded by mountains which cut off each state's share of the valley from the remainder of its territory. Some ten million people live there, three-quarters of

Central Asia today

them Uzbeks. All three states depend heavily on the valley: Uzbekistan for most of its water; Tajikistan for 65 per cent of its industry; and Kyrgyzstan for half of its industrial and agricultural production. Following the collapse of the Soviet Union there has been a religious revival in the area.

The war in Afghanistan after the 11 September attack has had implications for all Central Asian countries. US forces have deployed in Uzbekistan and Kyrgyzstan, in the latter for at least one year. So far Kazakhstan and Turkmenistan are free of the security concerns that threaten the other three Central Asian states, though Kazakhstan has always worried that there could be a secession by the Russian majority population in the north of the country. A small group of US special forces are training Kazakh troops. Both countries are rich in natural gas reserves: Kazakhstan has 65–70 trillion cubic feet and Turkmenistan 101 trillion. Kazakhstan also has reserves of 5–6 billion barrels of crude oil. Uzbekistan also has gas reserves of 66 trillion cubic feet.

Ever since it gained independence Tajikistan has been threatened by internal conflict between communism and Islam, which has resulted in the continued presence of a Russian division, composed of Russian officers and mainly Tajik conscripts, and Russian Frontier Forces. The communists won the first election after independence, but the opposition – a coalition of democratic, nationalist and Islamic groups – did not accept the result; efforts were made to form a coalition government but these proposals were not accepted by the communists. The first fighting occurred in June 1992 when communists from Kuliab attacked farms in Kurgan Tube belonging to members of the Islamic Renaissance Party (IRP). In the civil war that followed over twenty thousand were killed and several thousand fled into Afghanistan. The Tajik community in Afghanistan has supported the IRP with training and weapons.

Uzbekistan is named after Uzbek Kahn, the leader of the Golden Horde. Islamists formed the Islamic Movement of Uzbekistan in 1998 and immediately established links with Usama bin Laden and the Taliban which gave the IMU a safe haven and allowed it to set up training camps around Kunduz. The IMU is one of the US's designated foreign terrorist organisations. Its members have carried out terrorist attacks, including the kidnapping of foreign nationals for ransom, in Uzbekistan and have raided Kyrgyzstan. They have camps across the border in Tajikistan. The threat posed by the IMU has been much reduced by their fighting alongside the Taliban in northern Afghanistan. However, the former communist regime that rules Uzbekistan bears down harshly on its Islamic community and so a resurgence of support for the IMU is always possible.

Kyrgyzstan has a number of problems with its neighbours. In its Fergana Valley territory there are three enclaves, two belonging to Uzbekistan and one to Tajikistan. Uzbekistan is keen to establish a corridor linking it to the Sokh enclave, and is willing to exchange this for Uzbek territory; Kyrgyzstan is resisting the proposal as it might lead to the creation of a Kyrgyz enclave in Uzbekistan. The large Uzbek population in the town of Osh, in Kyrgyzstan, rioted in June 1990 because of the unfair allocation of land and housing and their exclusion from local government.

The Central Asian countries that border China also face potential security problems. This is mainly because a million Kazakhs and smaller numbers of Tajiks and Kyrgyz live in western China and because the indigenous Chinese, the Uighurs, are Muslim. Border disputes inherited from the Soviet Union have been addressed and solved on the Kazakhstan border. Kyrgyzstan has signed two border agreements with China but the fairness of these is now being questioned. China and Tajikistan still have to resolve their dispute over some 20,000 square kilometres in the Pamir Mountains. However, Kazakhstan, Kyrgyzstan, Tajikistan, China and Russia signed an agreement on confidence-building measures at Shanghai in April 1996 ('the Shanghai five'). Further agreements on force reductions in border regions and on cooperation to fight separatism, religious extremism, terrorism and drug and arms trafficking were signed in 1997 and 1998.

Central Asia also faces water problems. The southern provinces of Kazakhstan and virtually all of the other four Central Asian states (and parts of Afghanistan and Iran) lie in the Aral Sea Basin. Most water originates in Kyrgyzstan and Tajikistan. Uzbekistan and the two Kazakhstan provinces depend for over 50 per cent of their water on upstream states, while 98 per cent of Turkmenistan's water originates from outside the country. Water supply is essential in Uzbekistan and Turkmenistan for irrigation of the cotton crop, a crop established by Soviet central planning, and also in Kyrgyzstan and Tajikistan for hydroelectricity. Population growth, particularly in the Fergana Valley, exacerbates the problem. Independence has made the

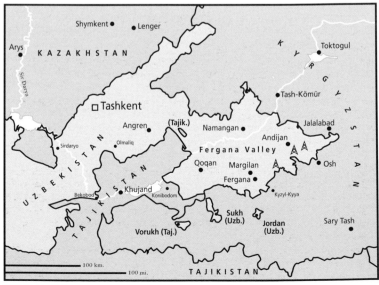

The Fergana Valley

158

solving of problems more difficult. Soviet era water allocations remain in force and the status quo is backed by Turkmenistan and Uzbekistan who see renegotiation as likely to reduce their allocations, while Kyrgyzstan and Tajikistan, which have the smallest allocations of the water of which they are the source, support allocation revision.

TRAVEL ADVICE

Kazakhstan: Both FCO and State warn of general increased threat to citizens owing to global terrorism. This warning also applies in Kyrgyzstan, Turkmenistan and Uzbekistan.

Tajikistan: FCO and State both advise against all travel.

Uzbekistan: Avoid border areas with Afghanistan, Tajikistan, Turkmenistan and Kyrgyzstan.

Kyrgyzstan: FCO and State both advise against travel to the south and west of Osh. Avoid Uzbek and Tajik borders and Ferghana Valley. There is a danger of landmines in Batken Oblast and on the Kyrgyz–Uzbek border.

BIBLIOGRAPHY AND WEBSITES

Alison, Roy and Jonson, Lena (eds), *Central Asian Security: The New International Context*, Royal Institute for International Affairs, 2001

Allworth, Edward (ed.), *Central Asia: 130 Years of Russian Dominance, A Historical Overview*, Duke University Press, 1994

Dannreuther, Roland, *Creating New States in Central Asia*, IISS Adelphi Paper 288, 1994

Grousset, René, *The Empire of the Steppes: A History of Central Asia*, Rutges University Press, 1970

Roy, Olivier, *The New Central Asia: The Creation of Nations*, IB Tauris, 2000

Weisbrode, Kenneth, *Central Asia: Prize or Quicksand*, IISS Adelphi Paper 338, 2001

Calming the Ferghana Valley: Development and Dialogue in the Heart of Central Asia, Council on Foreign Relations and the Century Foundation, 1999

'Central Asia: Border Disputes and Potential Conflict', International Crisis Group Asia Paper 33, 2002

Central Asia – Caucasus Analyst: www.cacianalyst.org

Central Eurasian Project: www.soros.org/central_eurasia

Afghanistan

Population: 25,590,000 (including refugees in Pakistan, Iran and Kyrgyzstan)
(Ethnic groups) Pushtun 38%, Tajik 25%, Hazara 19%, Uzbek 12%, Almaq 4%, Baluchi 0.5%
(Religion) Sunni (mainly Hanafi sect) 84%, Shi'a 15%, some Hindu and Sikh
(Language) Pushtun 35%, Afghan-Persian 50%, Turkic 11%
Armed Factions: Taliban (before US operations started) maybe 45,000, including some 5,000–7,000 Pakistanis, some Arabs and Chechens
Northern Alliance or United Islamic Front for the Salvation of Afghanistan 25,000
Currency: Afghani

Afghanistan is another country that suffers from having an ethnically and religiously mixed population. The dominant ethnic group is the Pushtuns who inhabit the southern half of the country (and also northern Pakistan); they are mainly Sunni Muslims. The Hazaras in central Afghanistan are Shi'a Muslims. In the north there are three ethnic groups, each related to their neighbours in Central Asia: Turkomen in the north-west, Uzbeks to their east and Tajiks in north-east Afghanistan.

Afghanistan has always been made up of small, fiercely independent tribal kingdoms. The country has seen a series of invaders over the centuries, some more successful than others at controlling the region. Darius, Alexander, Genghis Khan and Tamerlaine all held sway there for periods, as did the Persians and Moghuls. In 1719 it was the turn of the Afghans to become the conquerors. At various times they held Persia, northern Pakistan and India, and Kashmir. At the end of the eighteenth century the 'Great Game' began with Russia and Britain seeking to gain influence, but neither conquered the region (though Russia took control of what are now the Central Asian Republics).

The British invaded Afghanistan on a number of occasions. The force that occupied Kabul for two years from 1838 withdrew and was annihilated during its winter retreat. Other invading forces purely carried out punitive measures before withdrawing. After the war of 1878–80 Afghanistan became a buffer state between Britain and Russia who agreed Afghanistan's borders and forced the Amir to take responsibility for the Wakhan Corridor so that there would be no common border between the two. The British supplied the Pushtun Amir with arms and finance, which enabled him to crush tribal revolts and establish a totalitarian state. Afghanistan severed its ties with Britain in 1919.

During the Cold War Afghanistan received aid from both East and West but the Soviets provided nearly five times as much as the US and trained and equipped the army. The US did not supply military aid as this was opposed by Pakistan, a member of the Central Treaty Organisation (CENTO) and the South-East Asia Treaty Organisation (SEATO), both US-led alliances. Both superpowers attempted to influence the ruling regime rather than, as elsewhere, supporting rivals. In 1973 the ruler Mohammed Zahir Shah was deposed by his cousin Daoud Khan, who was supported by Soviet-trained army officers and the Parcham wing of the communists – the People's Democratic Party of Afghanistan (PDPA). Daoud proclaimed himself president. The abolition of the monarchy before a tested alternative was put in place worried not only the superpowers but also Afghanistan's neighbours, who feared that a period of instability could overflow their borders.

Jamiat-I-Islami, the Islamic movement led by Burhanuddin Rabbani and Ahmad Masoud, was suppressed and its leaders fled to Pakistan where they received support from both Pakistan and the CIA. They attempted an uprising in 1975 which was quickly put down. The Islamists then split into two parties: the Jamiat-I-Islami, comprising mainly those with a Tajik background, and the predominantly Pushtun Hizb-I-Islami led by Gulbuddin Hekmatyar. In April 1978 the communist PDPA took power in a military-backed coup following the arrest of a number of its leaders; US aid was suspended and Soviet influence was greatly expanded. The communist coalition soon split and the Khalq wing took charge and imposed a brutal regime that led to a number of revolts across the country, some aided by Islamist refugees in Pakistan. In March 1979, following the overthrow of the Shah in Iran, an attack by Jamiat-I-Islami captured Herat and killed the Soviet advisers there. The Soviets decided on limited intervention into Afghanistan to forestall an expected American move in reaction to the Shah's fall (in fact none was contemplated) and to assist in controlling the internal disorder. The Soviets secured Kabul, killing the Khalq leader, and installed the Parcham leader Babrak Karmal. Restoring government control required large-scale Soviet military reinforcement so that by 1981 there were over 100,000 troops deployed. The Soviets initially employed the wrong troops – motor rifle units that were neither trained nor equipped for counter-insurgency operations – and the wrong tactics.

The invasion had automatically provoked US assistance for exiled Afghan groups known as the Mujahedin (meaning 'holy warriors') and weapons were soon reaching them through Pakistan. As the number of opposition parties increased dramatically, the Pakistan government decided to restrict the supply of arms to only seven groups which formed, in May 1985, the Ittehad-I-Islami Afghan Mujahedin and later the Afghan Interim Government. The Soviet army never managed to pacify the country and suffered heavy casualties; the supply of US Stinger SAMs ended Soviet air superiority. Soviet policy changed when Gorbachev became president in 1985. President Karmal was eased out of office in 1986 and was replaced by Muhammed Najibullah. In April 1988 agreement was reached at Geneva over Soviet withdrawal and by 15 February 1989 the Soviet army had left, admitting to having lost 15,000 men killed and 35,500 wounded.

The PDPA government was expected to fall quickly but it was three years before it gave up power, though it only had control of the main cities during this time. The Soviet withdrawal did not end the civil war as the Mujahedin coalition fractured and clashes occurred between Hizb-I-Islami and other Mujahedin groups. Their backers, Iran and Saudi Arabia, accentuated the differences between the Persian-speaking and Pushtun Mujahedin. The government was forced to concentrate its forces on defending the major cities, allowing the Mujahedin to take control of most of the countryside where they reverted to their habitual rivalry and abandoned their fight with the government.

The entry into Kabul in April 1992 of the Uzbek militia of Rashid Dostam, who had deserted Najibullah, in alliance with Jamiat-I-Islami, was peaceful but fighting soon broke out between the various parties and the destruction of Kabul began. Alliances were formed and broken; the main power struggle was between Rabbani, now president, and Hekmatyar, the prime minister, who had been joined by Dostam. They concentrated their efforts on Kabul while the other groups established their own territories across the country.

The strife and corruption within the Mujahedin movement is believed to have been the main reason behind the formation of the Taliban in Kandahar in early 1994. They first came to notice in October when two hundred men from the madrassas in Kandahar and Pakistan arrived at Spin Baldak on the Pakistan border and attacked the troops of Gulbuddin Hekmatyar. With Pakistani help they captured a large dump of weapons that had been assembled by the Pakistanis but not yet distributed; the dump contained some 18,000 Kalashnikov automatic rifles and many pieces of artillery. On 3 November the Taliban, at Pakistani request, rescued a convoy that had been hijacked by another group of Mujahedin; they then went on that evening to take control of Kandahar. Taliban appealed to the young and to the religious student community (*talib* means student). Their initial progress was breathtaking and by February 1995 they had reached the outskirts of Kabul; they were then held up there for the rest of that year and most of 1996. They made progress elsewhere, though, taking Herat in September 1995. A year later they took Jalalabad and then, after forcing their way through the Sarobi Gorge, they attacked Kabul from the east and took it on 26 September. They continued their advance northwards until they reached both the Salang Pass held by Dostam and the Panshir Valley held by Masoud. Dostam and Masoud made a pact and pushed the Taliban forces back to Kabul. Fighting continued in 1997 with as many as 200,000 refugees arriving at Kabul. The situation changed briefly when one of Dostam's lieutenants, Abdul Malik, defected to the Taliban, which quickly moved into Mazar-I-Sharif after the town had been taken by Malik. The Taliban then attempted to disarm the Shi'a fighters who resisted and, aided by Malik, killed three hundred Taliban and captured a thousand more. Following this, the Taliban was recognised as the legitimate government of Afghanistan by Pakistan, followed by Saudi Arabia and the United Arab Emirates but not by the United Nations.

In August 1998 the Taliban took the northern city of Mazar-I-Sharif and then massacred perhaps as many as five thousand Shi'a Hazara men in reprisal for prisoners executed there in 1997. The murder of nine Iranians in Mazar-I-Sharif caused the Iranian government to amass troops and hold exercises on the border but it did not, as was expected, attack the Taliban. The Taliban now ruled the whole country apart from the far north-east and the Panjshir Valley where Masoud still held out and in three enclaves: one to the west of Herat; another around but not including Maymenah; and the third north-west of Bamyan. They made Kandahar the centre for their government. This imposed a strict Islamist regime, turning back the clock in many respects but particularly over the treatment of women who were not allowed either to work or to go to school. Education generally suffered, as most teachers had been women. Other examples of the Taliban's extremist behaviour included the destruction of two huge, 1,500-year-old statues of Buddha at Damian; the threat to oblige Hindus to wear an identification sign; and the continual harassment of UN and NGO workers, forcing many to leave the country.

The world has two major quarrels with Afghanistan: its increasing export of opium and the threat it poses to international peace and security. Afghanistan has become the largest

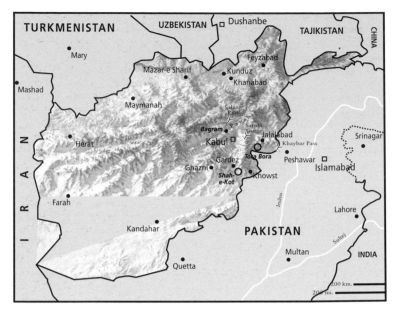

Afghanistan

producer of opium, which is refined into heroin, producing 72 per cent of the world's crop in 2000. In 1992 opium-poppy cultivation covered some 20,000 hectares, mainly in Nangarhar Province; next it was widely grown in Helmand Province which had previously been Afghanistan's main food-producing area. By 2000 some 64,510 hectares were under poppy cultivation and some 3,656 tonnes were harvested. This increased production resulted in a drop in farm-gate prices for fresh opium from $40 per kg in 1999 to $30 in 2000. On a number of occasions the Taliban tried to prevent opium cultivation; their leader, Mullah Omar, banned it and trafficking in July 2000 and once again in October. Although there were reports of some arrests and of the public ploughing in of some crops, there was little noticeable effect on exports.

Secondly, the Taliban had a history of fostering international terrorism by providing a safe haven for terrorists, training facilities and other support. In October 1999 the UN Security Council unanimously passed Resolution 1267 which deplored the giving of shelter and support to international terrorists, most notably to Usama bin Laden. The Resolution imposed the limited sanctions of freezing Taliban assets and banning flights of the Ariana Afghan Airline Afghanistan. As the Taliban had not complied with UNSC Resolution 1267, the Security Council passed Resolution 1333 on 19 December 2000. This directed them to cease to provide training and support for international terrorists; to hand over Usama bin Laden; and to close all terrorist camps within thirty days. Until full compliance was achieved additional sanctions came into effect. These were an arms embargo, including training and advice; the closure of all offices overseas; restriction on the travel of senior officials; and the banning of the export to Afghan territory of acetic anhydride, the precursor chemical used to manufacture heroin.

Following the attacks on the World Trade Centre in New York and the Pentagon in Washington on 11 September 2001, which were carried out by bin Laden's al Qaida organisation, the US demanded that the Taliban must hand over bin Laden to them. When they failed to do this the US decided to launch air attacks on Taliban military assets and the first air raids and cruise missile attacks began on 7 October. Usama bin Laden responded in a pre-recorded television programme which was broadcast by the Al Jazeera television station based in Qatar only two hours after the bombing began. 'I swear to God that America will not live in peace,' he said. The Taliban leadership said it would fight 'to the last breath' and that they would never surrender bin Laden.

The US, with support from the UK and other nations, deployed special forces to Afghanistan to operate with the United Front or Northern Alliance, the mainly non-Pashtun anti-Taliban coalition. They assisted in planning the campaign and directed us air support against Taliban positions. This allowed the United Front to make large gains; Mazar-I-Sharif fell after heavy fighting but the Taliban abandoned Kabul after their positions had been heavily bombed. A number of war lords who had supported the Taliban changed sides. It was thought that the cave complexes in the Tora Bora mountains were the main hiding places of al-Qaida, and special forces led anti-Taliban forces in clearing these; many al-Qaida are thought to have escaped over the border into Pakistan despite the Pakistanis' deployment of troops to prevent this.

After a conference held in Bonn in December 2001, Afghan faction leaders agreed on a new interim government and appointed Hamid Karzai as its leader. United Front leaders fill the key posts of foreign affairs, defence and home ministers. This government was replaced in June 2002 by another transitional government chosen by a *loya jirga* or tribal assembly, which elected Hamid Karzai as head of State. Elections will follow in eighteen months. There are already signs that unifying Afghanistan will be difficult. An attempt was made on Karzai's life in September. The Uzbek general Abdul Dostum threatened to boycott the new administration as he had only received the agriculture, mining and industry portfolio but now supports it as he is the deputy defence minister. At Gardez a battle broke out between the supporters of the interim government-appointed regional governor and those

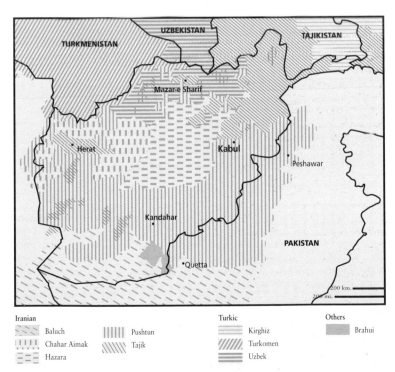

Afghanistan showing ethnic populations

of the previous incumbent; both men are Pashtuns and both claim to support the Karzai administration. Fighting has also been reported in the north between Uzbek and Tajik militias. Further fighting between the forces of rival war-lords is expected and these could turn on peacekeepers.

In December 2001, a British General was sent to Kabul to reach agreement over an international force to maintain stability, initially in the capital. British troops, which had been at Bhagram airbase for some weeks, deployed into Kabul and protected the 'swearing-in' ceremony of Hamid Karzai. By February 2002 some 4,000 troops from 15 countries had joined the International Security Assistance Force (ISAF) and were patrolling Kabul – though not elsewhere in Afghanistan, which is considered essential if peace is to be established. Outside the capital, security is being maintained by local 'warlord' militias supervised by US special forces; the US was happy to support this arrangement; however, in August 2002 it indicated a change in policy when the Administration signalled that ISAF should be expanded and deployed beyond Kabul. The US found that it had to deploy more ground troops, in particular to destroy Taliban and al Qaida forces in the mountains south of Gardez; they were joined by British mountain warfare-trained Royal Marines and special forces from a number of countries. British troops, bar some logistical units, have now been withdrawn and the peacekeeping lead has been taken over by Turkey. Most al Qaida men are believed to have crossed the border into Pakistan's tribal areas.

TRAVEL ADVICE
FCO and State: Strongly warn against any travel in Afghanistan.

BIBLIOGRAPHY AND WEBSITES
Griffin, Michael, *Reaping the Whirlwind: The Taliban Movement in Afghanistan*, Pluto Press, 2001
Magnus, Ralph and Eden, Naby, *Afghanistan: Mullah, Marx and Mujahid*, Westview, 1998
Maley, William, *Fundamentalism Reborn? Afghanistan and Taliban*, Hurst, 1998
Marsden, Peter, *The Taliban: War, Religion, and the New Order*, Oxford University Press/Zed Books, 1998
Rashid, Ahmed, *Taliban: Islam, Oil and the New Great Game in Central Asia*, IB Tauris, 2000
Rubin, Barnett, *The Search for Peace in Afghanistan*, Yale University Press, 1995

Jamiat-e-Islami: www.jamiat.com
Omaid Weekly: www.omaid.com
Online Center for Afghan Politics: www.afghan-politics.org
Taleban Islamic Movement: www.taleban.com

India and Pakistan: Proliferation and Disputes

Indian and Pakistani enmity entered a new dimension when the two countries exploded nuclear devices in May 1998. That India and Pakistan had a nuclear capability came as no real surprise but the tests have confirmed that capability and have given cause for worry over the situation in South Asia. However, the first Indian–Pakistani war erupted immediately after each received its independence on the British withdrawal and partition of the Indian Empire in 1947. The predominantly Muslim state of Kashmir opted for India and Pakistan occupied the north and western parts of it; the Kashmir problem, discussed on pp. 168–70, has bedevilled their mutual relations ever since. There have been two wars since then, in 1965 and 1971. The two armies exchange fire over the Kashmir line of control frequently. To the north-east, forces face each other over the Siachen Glacier, at 20,000ft above sea level, where the line of control has never been delineated. Clashes began in 1984, when India deployed troops to the mountain passes, mainly because Pakistani maps showed the territory as theirs, and have continued ever since. The Indians see their possession of

India showing nuclear facilities (see page 177 for Pakistan nuclear facilities)

the glacier as essential on the grounds that with China now in control of both Shaksam Valley, ceded by Pakistan in 1963, to the west and Aksai Chin, taken from India in 1962, to the east, Pakistani control of the Siachen would threaten Ladakh and the route to Leh down the Nurba Valley. The Chinese have military roads connecting Siachen with Tibet, through Aksai Chin and with Havelian. Neither side will allow the other to claim the territory that is still undemarcated. In February 1999 the two prime ministers agreed that the future of Siachen should be negotiated.

The world was taken by surprise when India exploded three nuclear devices at its Pokhran test site in the Rajahstan Desert on 11 May 1998. Two days later India announced that it had carried out two more tests. It was no surprise, therefore, when Pakistan carried out five nuclear tests on 28 May and two more on the 30th. The Indian tests took place only two months after the Hindu nationalist Bharatiya Janata Party (BJP) government had been elected; they could probably have taken place much earlier had the political decision to authorise tests been taken by the previous government.

International reaction to the tests centred on the implications for non-proliferation and whether they would encourage other states to embark on nuclear weapons programmes. The Comprehensive Test Ban Treaty (CTBT) was seen to be weakened by the failure of seismic stations to record India's tests on 13 May.

The real outcome of the tests is that they confirmed the widely held suspicion that both India and Pakistan were pursuing nuclear programmes and probably had all the components needed to produce nuclear weapons, even if these had not been assembled. In 1974 India had exploded a so-called 'peaceful' nuclear device and so was known to have the ability to

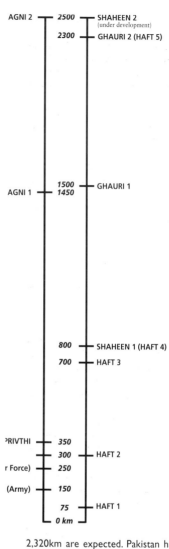

AGNI 2	2500	SHAHEEN 2 (under development)
	2300	GHAURI 2 (HAFT 5)
AGNI 1	1500 1450	GHAURI 1
	800	SHAHEEN 1 (HAFT 4)
	700	HAFT 3
PRIVTHI	350	
	300	HAFT 2
r Force)	250	
(Army)	150	
	75	HAFT 1
	0 km	

make nuclear weapons. In many ways the tests could have positive results: India and Pakistan have both said they will consider joining the CTBT and may support a fissile material production ban that is being discussed in Geneva. India has also said it might join both the Nuclear Suppliers Group and the Missile Technology Control Regime. Neither country can join the Nuclear Non-Proliferation Treaty, which recognised five nuclear states when it came into force in 1970, as no other nuclear-armed state can be admitted. However, there is no reason why some form of trilateral treaty with the United Nations could not be drafted which would legally and politically bind them to the same commitments to non-proliferation as the recognised nuclear states have undertaken. So far neither state has joined any of these arms control treaties. The Indian government has committed itself not to carry out any more tests.

Both India and Pakistan are also developing surface-to-surface missiles (SSMs) capable of delivering nuclear warheads. India already has the Privthi in two versions: for the army a 150km-range missile and for the air force a 250km-range version. The air force missile was successfully test-fired in December 2001. The Agni I was tested to a range of 1,450km in 1994 and is reported to be ready for production. Agni 2 is a 2,500km-range version being developed with a solid-fuel propellant. It was test-fired on 11 April 1999 despite pressure from the US and China not to precipitate a missile race on the sub-continent; a second test took place in January 2001. Another Indian missile test took place on 25 January 2002, which Pakistan found provocative and which was criticised by the US and a number of European states. An Agni 3 is also being developed, with possibly a 5,000km range carrying a 1,000kg payload. India is also developing a cruise missile and a sea-launched ballistic missile. Pakistan quickly responded to the Indian test by trialling its Ghauri 2 (HATF-V) missile on 14 April, achieving a 1,120km flight; further full-range tests over 2,320km are expected. Pakistan had tested its Ghauri 1, with a 1,450km range, in April 1998. Both these missiles are strongly suspected of being North Korean No-dong as Pakistan is thought to have acquired twelve of these missiles in 1998. Pakistan also has a series of short-range missiles. HATF II are believed to be Chinese M-11s which were left unboxed between 1991 and 1997 when they were issued to the army. The Shaheen (HATF-IV), which has a 700km range with a 1,000kg payload, was also tested in April 1999. HATF-III (Ghaznavi) was first tested on 26 May 2002. It has a 290 km range.

India maintains that its nuclear and missile developments are not designed to threaten Pakistan but are intended to be a deterrent to possible Chinese incursions. Not that this is any comfort to Pakistan, which sees the developments as a distinct threat that it must counter with its own capability. There have been two positive developments. First, the Indian–Pakistani agreement not to attack each other's nuclear installations was reached in 1985, but not signed until 1988 nor ratified until January 1991. Secondly, in February 1999 the two prime ministers agreed a package of confidence-building measures that included an exchange of information on nuclear doctrine and on nuclear weapon and missile holdings and deployment. Advance warning of missile test flights would be given. The required warning was given by both states for the 1999 tests. Both countries' missiles will threaten other countries: Agni 2 will be able to reach the south-east corner of Iraq and most of Iran, but Israel will be just out of range of Pakistan's Ghauri 2. Pakistan has made it clear that it will use nuclear weapons if necessary while India has said several times that it would not be the first to use them.

After three wars over Kashmir, where the issue is no nearer to being solved and where artillery fire is regularly exchanged, the possibility of a fourth war cannot be discounted. In August 1999 the Indians shot down a Pakistani surveillance aircraft which they claimed had intruded into Indian air space. The next day Pakistan fired on Indian military aircraft and helicopters, without shooting any down, close to where its plane had come down. Fortunately the incident did not escalate. The most recent crisis in December 2001 was sparked off by the terrorist attack on the Indian parliament building in which twelve people were killed, including the five attackers. Kashmiri militants are strongly suspected of being behind the attack but both Lashkar-e-Tayyiba and Laish-e-Mohammad (the former designated a foreign terrorist organisation by the US) have denied responsibility. Nevertheless, Pakistan has arrested the leader and a number of activists of the latter group in an attempt to ease the tension as both India and Pakistan deployed troops and heavy weapons including missiles that could be nuclear armed.

The dispute over the maritime border in the Sir Creek estuary remains unresolved. The Indians want the boundary to be equidistant from both shores while Pakistan maintains that it should be closer to the Indian side. (The border's extension out to sea would give Pakistan a larger continental shelf in an oil-rich area.) As the tidal channel keeps shifting, thus altering the physical shape of the two coastlines, neither side will agree on the line of the maritime border. If the claims are not resolved by 2004 the matter will be decided by the UN. Another difference has emerged over the Tulbul Navigation Project. This concerns the Indian construction of a barrage on the River Jhelum for, it is claimed, navigational purposes. The Pakistanis claim it is for storage purposes and is therefore a violation of the Indus Waters Treaty of 1960.

In May 2002 Pakistan carried out tests of three of its missiles (HATF-II/Abdali, HATF-III/Ghaznavi, HATF-V/Ghauri). Pakistan claimed the tests were not linked to the tension with India, while India claimed they were a PR exercise. Given India's preponderance in conventional strength, a future war could involve the use of nuclear weapons, perhaps first by Pakistan and then inevitably by India. However, the possession of nuclear weapons by both India and Pakistan could act as useful deterrent not just to nuclear war but to any war. In this light perhaps the nuclear tests have served a useful purpose.

BIBLIOGRAPHY AND WEBSITES

Budania, Rajpal, *India's National Security Dilemma: The Pakistan Factor and India's Policy Responses*, Indus, 2001

Perkovich, George, *India's Nuclear Bomb: The Impact on Global Proliferation*, University of California Press, 1999

Quinlan, Sir Michael, *How Robust is India–Pakistan Deterrence?*, Survival Winter 2000–01, International Institute for Strategic Studies

Tellis, Ashley J., 'India's Emerging Nuclear Posture: Between Recessed Deterrent and Ready Arsenal', RAND

Indian Ministry of Foreign Affairs: www.meadev.gov.in
Pakistan government: www.pak.gov.pk

Kashmir

Terrorist Groups:

Hizb-ul-Mujahideen	1,000
Harakat-ul-Mujahedin	500
Lashkar-e-Tayyiba	300
Laish-e-Mohammad	300
Al Badr Mujahedin	50

Kashmir has been claimed by both India and Pakistan since the end of the British Indian Empire on 15 August 1947. It is the main source of dispute between the two countries, and has been the cause of three wars between them. Any fourth war is likely to be provoked by the continuing dispute over Kashmir and indeed was close to breaking out after Kashmiri militants made a suicide attack on the Indian parliament in December 2001. There is also an Indian claim to Aksai Chin which lies in north-east Ladakh and which was occupied by the Chinese in 1962.

The Valley of Kashmir is bounded by three mountain ranges: the North Kashmir Range to the north, the Great Himalayan Range to the east and the Pir Panjal Range to the south and west. There are twenty passes leading into Kashmir over the mountains and so it is not invulnerable to hostile movement. In ancient times Kashmir's independence rested on the strength of its king: under a strong monarch it remained secure from foreign intervention but under a weak one, who failed to guard the passes, it fell to conquerors. The original inhabitants were Nagas and other lesser tribes, but in AD 800 Aryans from today's Uttar Pradesh became the dominant people in the region. Brahmin priests played an influential role throughout Kashmir's history.

The population is religiously mixed. Muslims predominate but there are also Hindus and Sikhs, who live mainly in Jammu, and some Buddhists in Ladakh. Kashmir was originally Hindu, but Islam was introduced in the early fourteenth century. The persecution of Hindus began in the late fourteenth century when Genghis Khan demanded tribute of Kashmir. At first the Muslims were of the Sunni persuasion only but the Shi'a faith was introduced in 1492, further complicating Kashmir's religious tensions.

Kashmir's status as an independent kingdom ended in the mid-sixteenth century when it was brought into the Mughal Empire. As the power of the Mughals declined, Kashmir was ruled by tyrannical governors; this led to Kashmiri nobles turning to Afghanistan for help. The Afghans took over in 1751 but the Kashmiris soon found they were as cruel as the Mughals had been. After fifty years of rebellion and two unsuccessful attacks by Sikhs, Kashmir finally fell to the Sikhs in 1819. Sikh rule lasted for only twenty-eight years and was as harsh as that of the Afghans, with the character of the governor determining the lot of Kashmiris.

The Dogras, a hill Rajput people, ruled Jammu by the beginning of the nineteenth century but they lost this to the Sikhs in 1808. Gulab Singh was the great-great-nephew of the Dogra leader Ranjit Dev. He had fought against the Sikhs when only sixteen. He then joined the Sikh army and took part in the Sikh capture of Kashmir in 1819; after leading the Sikhs in putting down the revolt in Jammu in 1820, he was made the Rajah of Jammu. He and his two brothers acquired control of numerous small hill territories around Kashmir and in 1835 had made Ladakh a vassal to Jammu. Gulab deserted the Sikhs in their war with the British to avoid losing his domain should the British annex Sikh territories. After the British had defeated the Sikhs at the Battle of Sobraon in February 1846, they accepted Kashmir in lieu of the indemnity they demanded of the Sikhs; a week later the British had sold Kashmir to Gulab Singh for the same sum: one krore of rupees. Jammu and Kashmir remained loyal to the British during the Indian mutiny in May 1857. Dogra rule of Kashmir and Jammu was maintained until British rule in India ended.

At partition, the rulers of princely states were asked to accede to either India or Pakistan; the ruler of Kashmir, who was a Hindu, despite British advice to take account of

Kashmir

▨ Princely State of Kashmir		⧸⧸⧸⧸ Ceded by Pakistan to China in 1963	
‒ ‒ ⌃ ‒ Line of Control		⦀⦀⦀ Occupied by Indian since 1983 (no defined boundary)	
⟋⟋⟋ Claimed boundaries			

the majority Muslim population, chose to accede to India after attempting for two months to remain independent. The decision sparked off an immediate war between the newly independent states of India and Pakistan. If the former viceroy Lord Wavell's advice had been taken, Britain would have retained control of the Muslim areas until agreement had been reached over boundaries, at which point Britain would have withdrawn; in this way the war would have been avoided and Kashmir might have survived in peace.

Fighting ended after the UN Security Council set up the UN Commission for India and Pakistan (UNCIP) which visited Kashmir in July 1948 and achieved the agreement of the Indian and Pakistani governments to order a cease fire immediately before midnight on 1 January 1949. The cease fire has been monitored by the UN Military Observer Group India and Pakistan (UNGOMIP) ever since.

Hostilities broke out in August 1965 after disagreements over claims to the Rann of Kutch. Fighting began along the Kashmir cease fire line and by September had spread to the Indian–West Pakistan border. The UN adopted a number of resolutions and finally demanded in UNSC 211 that a cease fire take effect from 0700 GMT and that all troops were to be withdrawn to the positions held before 5 August. The UN established another monitoring mission, the UN India–Pakistan Observer Mission (UNIPOM) to monitor the cease fire along the international border. Following a meeting in Tashkent, agreement was reached on troop withdrawal; it was effected by 25 February 1966. UNIPOM was disbanded on 22 March.

Hostilities broke out again in early December 1971, this time initially on the Indian–East Pakistan border. Both sides reinforced their forces in Kashmir in violation of the Karachi Agreement (reached in 1949) and fighting broke out there on 3 December. A cease fire came into effect on 17 December, by which time a number of positions had changed hands. Pakistan continued to report Indian violations to UNGOMIP but India argued that the UN mandate had lapsed on account of the war and UNGOMIP had no responsibility for the new cease fire line, which had come into existence in December. UNCIP was also responsible after the 1971 war for assisting in the establishment of a cease fire line that became known as the 'line of control'. Pakistan retained control of the Northern Areas (Baltistan and the Gilgit Agency) and a strip of land west of the Pir Panjal Range now known as Azad Kashmir. In December 1972 the two governments agreed a new line of control which with some small differences followed the line of the 1949 cease fire line.

The current uprising in Indian Kashmir began in July 1989 when bombs exploded in Srinagar, followed by sporadic outbreaks of violence. The revolt was prompted by the realisation that Pakistan was unable to hold and India had no intention of holding the plebiscite on Kashmir's future as agreed by both countries at the 1949 cease fire. The kidnapping of the daughter of the Indian home minister and her exchange for five Kashmiri militants from prison was the signal for demonstrations of victory throughout Kashmir. With weapons acquired from Pakistan and Afghanistan, a 'jihad' was launched against the Indian authorities. The Indians responded by appointing a hard-line governor with instructions to put down the revolt; he was sent some 250,000 men from the army and a number of paramilitary forces. Both sides have been guilty of atrocities and it has been estimated that as many as twenty thousand people have been killed since 1989.

Indian and Pakistani troops still face each other all along the 776km-long line of control and regularly exchange fire across the line. In ten days in June 1998 it is estimated that some 400,000 rounds, including artillery, had been fired, killing about a hundred people from both sides of the line. In May 1999 the most serious clash for some years erupted when several hundred 'fighters' (the Indians claimed they included Pakistani troops) occupied the mountains in Indian Kashmir around Kargil. Militants in Indian Kashmir get support from a number of Muslim countries, including volunteer fighters. The Indians accuse Pakistan of actively supporting the militants.

After 11 September the US designated two Kashmiri groups, Lashkar-e-Tayyiba and Harakat-ul-Mujahedin as terrorist organisations. Following the terrorist attack on the Indian parliament building in December 2001, President Pervez Musharraf of Pakistan, in a speech to his nation, said that Pakistan would continue to give diplomatic, moral and political support to Kashmiris; he then banned Lashkar-e-Tayyiba and Laish-e-Mohammad signalling the end to terrorist support. Incidents of violence continue in Kashmir with casualties to both the Indian security forces and terrorist organisations.

While both India and Pakistan claim Kashmir, its inhabitants would prefer complete independence. UNSC Resolutions 38 and 39 of 1948 declare that Jammu and Kashmir are disputed territories whose final status has yet to be decided. Kashmir is one of the world's longest-lasting disputes and a solution appears unlikely.

TRAVEL ADVICE

FCO: Advises against all travel to Kashmir and Jammu except for Ladakh.

State: Advises against travel to Kashmir Valley, Doda district and Srinagar. The terrorist organisation Harakat al Mujahedin banned US citizens from visiting Kashmir in 1999.

BIBLIOGRAPHY AND WEBSITES

Ganguly, Sunit, *The Crisis in Kashmir*, Cambridge University Press, 1997

Lamb, Alastair, *Incomplete Partition: The genesis of the Kashmir Dispute 1947–1948*, Roxford Books, 1997

Malik, Hafeez (ed.), *Dilemmas of National Security and Cooperation in India and Pakistan*, Macmillan, 1993

Schofield, Victoria, *Kashmir in the Crossfire*, Tauris, 1996

Wirsing, Robert, *War or Peace on the Line of Control? The India–Pakistan Dispute over Kashmir Turns 50*, International Boundaries Research Unit, 1999

International Boundaries Research Unit: www.ibru.dur.ac.uk
India: www.meadev.gov.in/opn/kargil
Pakistan: www.pak.gov.pk/kashmir/index-kashmir

India

Population: 1,029,548,000
Hindu 80%, Muslim 14%,
Christian 2%, Sikh 2%
Armed Forces: 1,263,000
Paramilitary: 1,089,000
Per Capita GDP: US$ 1,900
Currency: rupee

India's chief security concerns are Kashmir (see pp. 168–171) and possible nuclear and missile confrontation with China and Pakistan (see p. 166). In a state that was derived from the territory of 592 princes, that has a population of over a billion, with four main religions and fifteen major languages, it is not surprising that there are a number of internal issues that have security connotations. Fortunately, a number of these appear to be resolved but there is always a chance, given changes in government policy, that they might re-erupt.

Assam's importance lies in its control of the Siliguri corridor which links the north-eastern provinces (which are rich in natural resources) with the main body of India, losing Assam would mean the loss of the north-east. Historically Assam was never part of India at any stage and was only incorporated into India by the British after the Burmese invasion of 1874. Until then it had been independent for over 700 years despite numerous invasions from east and west. Assam is the meeting place of three major ethnicities – Aryan, Dravidian and Mongoloid – and its people are more ethnically varied than in any other state in India. Early causes of dissent were the introduction by the British of Bengali professionals and clerks to the administration, and the economics of the tea industry built by the British, who took the profits, and worked by labourers from north-east India, who sent their wages home.

Dissidence in Assam began as a student movement. It was highly successful and following the boycotted elections in 1983 it developed into a political wing, the Assam Gana Parishad (AGP) and a military wing, the United Liberation Front of Assam (UFLA). The UFLA made contact with Pakistani Inter-Services Intelligence (ISI) and the Afghans and sent men for training in Myanmar. It gained considerable power when the AGP formed the government and used this to extract large sums from business. At its peak in 1990 its strength reached some three thousand. After Unilever decided to abandon its tea-plantations rather than pay the UFLA's demands, the Indian government decided to dismiss the state government and the army launched an operation against the UFLA. The army withdrew when the situation was considered stable enough to hold elections, which were won by the Congress Party. Immediately the UFLA kidnapped a number of managers and engineers of the oil industry. The army returned and conducted a more successful campaign, and the UFLA agreed in January 1992 to political talks.

An AGP government was re-elected in 1996 but UFLA aggression increased; in 1998 considerable progress was made in containing the violence and UFLA groups withdrew across the border to camps in the jungles of Bhutan. The Indian government knows there is no military solution and have been encouraging the militants to join talks but they insist on three pre-conditions: talks must take place out of India; UN representatives must take part;

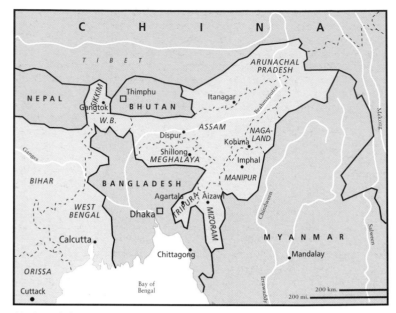

North-east India

and only the sovereignty of Assam is to be discussed. These conditions are unacceptable; nevertheless the government began a development plan for the region. Its policy of continuing both military operations and economic development appears successful, but the rising tide of violence since April 2001 makes Assam one of the most dangerous places in India.

Another issue in Assam is the separatist movement of the Bodos, a major tribe living in the north of territory. They claim to be the original inhabitants of Assam and believe that both the Assamese and the Indians are discriminating against them. They formed the National Democratic Front of Bodoland (NDFB) which claims the land north of the Brahmaputra for the six million Bodos. In 1993 the governments of India and Assam signed an agreement with the Bodos creating an autonomous Bodo Council but its geographical boundary has not yet been decided. The Bodo Liberation Tiger Force and the National Democratic Front of Bodoland still campaign for independence from Assam within the Indian Federation and have carried out some instances of ethnic cleansing. In 1996 the Bodos launched a campaign of violence, killing some seven hundred non-Bodos and attacking the railways.

To the east and south of Assam lie six states. Three – Nagaland, Manipur and Tripura – have a long record of insurgency; the first two are fighting for independence while the last hopes to obtain a separate tribal homeland. Insurgency in Arunachal Pradesh ended with the surrender of the leader of the United People's Volunteers of Arunachal Pradesh. The opposition movements in Meghala and Mizoram, both formerly part of Assam, currently operate within the Indian constitution.

The Naga National Council (NNC) was formed in 1946 when Nagaland was still part of Assam and under British rule. Nagas, immigrants from eastern Tibet, also settled in Manipur, Arunachal Pradesh and upper Myanmar. Before Indian independence an agreement was reached between the NNC and the Governor of Assam that recognised 'the right of the Nagas to develop themselves according to their freely expressed wishes'. The agreement was to be reviewed ten years later. The Nagas believed this would lead to independence while the Indian government saw it as leading only to a revision of the administrative arrangements. When the NNC realised the situation it declared Nagaland's independence in August 1947. Negotiations between the Nagas and the Indian government continued for ten years without agreement and with security operations taking place against the growing underground Naga army. In 1960 agreement was finally reached and by December 1963 Nagaland had become a state within the Indian Union.

The Naga dissident movement split in 1980 following an agreement with the government known as the Shillong Accord, and the Nationalist Socialist Council of Nagaland (NSCN) was formed in the jungle of the Naga Hills where fighting continued. In 1986 a joint Indian-Myanmar offensive was launched but it did not break the Nagas. Peace talks were instituted but distrust and misunderstanding split the NSCN into two factions – NSCN-IM and NSCN-K. The government and the NSCN-IM agreed to a cease fire in late 1997. Since then the insurgents have turned to crime. In January 2001 the Indian government and the NSCN-IM extended their cease fire for a further year. At the same time the government extended the area covered by the cease fire to include all Naga-inhabited areas in the north-east. This gives the states of Assam, Manipur and Arunachal Pradesh, which all have Naga populations, a voice in future talks.

Manipur, from which the Burmese were expelled in 1824 during the First Anglo-Burmese War, came under British rule in 1891 as a princely state after a conflict prompted by the execution of British officers. In October 1949 it became part of the Indian Union, gaining State of the Union status in 1972. In 1975 a group of young dissidents made their way to Tibet where they received training and political indoctrination. On their return to Manipur they began recruiting others and set up the Peoples Liberation Army, Eastern Region (PLA). Guerrilla operations consisted mainly of attacking police in order to capture their weapons.

A report in January 1999 assessed that four of the seven north-east states were seriously affected by insurgency, while in the other three there was simmering unrest. The Indian Home Ministry claims that there are ten dissident groups operating in Assam, Manipur, Nagaland and Tripura. Because of the long and hard-to-control borders with neighbouring countries, the groups are able to withdraw to safe areas where they can also acquire modern weapons. They also have contacts with the drugs trade. The dissident groups are concentrating on recruiting and on raising funds through extortion and ransom demands. None of these groups has been identified as a terrorist organisation by US Executive Order 13224.

A growing worry for the Indian government is the increasing incidence of Maoist-inspired terrorism in other parts of the country. The movement began in the Naxalbari district of West Bengal in 1967 and its supporters are often referred to as the Naxalites. Two organisations have been identified – the People's War Group (PWG) and the Maoist Communist Centre (MCC). The origin of both groups can be traced to the Communist Party of India, a Marxist-Leninist organisation that was formed in the mid-1960s. The two have combined to form a People's Guerrilla Army that has established a number of military-type action groups. The PWG was first formed in the Telengana region of Andhra Pradesh and has been responsible for a number of murders, including some two hundred police, and for cases of abduction and extortion in Andhra Pradesh and in the neighbouring regions of Madhya Pradesh, Maharashtra and Orissa. Similar acts of terrorism are committed in Bihar and Jharkhand by the MCC, which is allied to the Maoist rebel movement in Nepal. The government is currently treating the incidents as a local law and order problem to be tackled by provincial armed police, but there is a possibility that insurgency could develop on the scale of that in Kashmir and the north-east.

The Sikh religion evolved from Hinduism in the late fifteenth century when the Guru, Nanak, began teaching a faith that took in elements of both Hinduism (reincarnation and karma) and Islam (brotherhood). He was also much influenced by mysticism or the search for the heart of religion. Nanak was a Punjabi and it was in this area that the Sikh religion developed over some fifty-five years. It was recognised as a separate entity by the Mughal Emperor who gave it land where the first shrine was built. This shrine developed into today's holy city of Amritsar. The fifth Sikh Guru, Arjun, became the faith's first martyr when he was tortured to death by the Mughal Emperor in 1606.

Banda Singh, son of the ninth Guru, Tegh Bahadur, who was tortured to death by the Mughals for refusing to convert to Islam, introduced the custom of unshorn hair and gave all Sikh men the surname Singh or Lion. From 1709 until his capture at the end of 1715 Banda Singh led the Sikhs in a campaign against the Mughals. He won many victories but also suffered several defeats from which, until the siege of Gurdas Nangal, he always managed to escape to raise another army. Mughal persecution of the Sikhs continued until 1748 when the Afghans invaded India.

The Afghans claimed the Punjab, now totally under Sikh control, as part of Afghanistan. Large numbers of Muslims and Hindus accepted the security offered by the Sikhs in Punjab. Fighting between the Afghans and Sikhs continued until 1799 with both sides suffering disasters. During this period an estimated 200,000 Sikhs were killed by the Afghans but the Sikhs still remained in control of Punjab and other areas. The Sikhs were defeated in the two Anglo-Sikh Wars of 1845 and 1848, though the British lost two battles in the wars. The Sikhs did not side with the mutineers in the Indian Mutiny of 1857 and soon became the backbone of the British Indian Army.

As independence approached the Sikhs made it clear that they were opposed to the concept of Pakistan, the 'P' of which stood for Punjab, even though Muhammad Jinnah hinted that they would get full autonomy. The partition of Punjab was a disaster for the Sikhs: thousands in West Punjab were massacred both before and after partition and many more became refugees. The Sikhs in East Punjab turned on the Muslims in the area. The Sikh separatist movement was based on the Akali Dal, a religious political party set up in the 1920s. Realising that neither of the two options proposed for Punjab – partition or incorporation into Pakistan – was acceptable to Sikhs, it called for the creation of a Punjabi state. Nehru was opposed to this, seeing it as a communal demand rather than a linguistic one – the basis for the creation of other states in India. Indira Gandhi did grant the creation of a Punjabi state but at the same time created two other states from the original territory.

Sanjay Gandhi, Mrs Gandhi's younger son, attempted to engineer a split within the Sikhs and encourage opposition to the Akali Dal; Jarnail Singh Bhindranwale, a deeply religious teacher, led this opposition. His movement began to stir up hatred between Sikhs and Hindus but the government deliberately did nothing stop him. However, the Sikh split did not materialise because the supporters of the Akali Dal allied themselves with Bhindranwale and the two causes merged. Bhindranwale called for an armed uprising to achieve Sikh demands.

After several months of terrorist attacks by Sikhs, the government imposed presidential rule on Punjab but the new arrangements did little to halt the terrorism. Eventually, on 5 June 1984 the army was ordered to 'flush out the extremists from the Golden Temple using the minimum of force and causing as little damage as possible'. The temple area was strongly defended; tanks had to be brought in to effect an entrance and much damage was done. Army casualty figures were 83 killed and 249 wounded. There is no accurate estimate for losses on the Sikh side, and the total could have been as high as 1,500. After the assault several Sikh army units mutinied and on 31 October 1984 Indira Gandhi was assassinated by one of her Sikh bodyguards. This was followed by four days of anti-Sikh rioting in Delhi. Her son Rajiv, who succeeded her, quickly made a settlement with the Sikhs, giving them most of their original demands. Sikh violence continued for a couple of years but by 1997 separatist Sikhs lived mainly in North America and the UK. Today the Punjab is as peaceful as it has ever been and there is no talk of Khalistan or a Sikh independent state.

There have been other separatist movements in other states, for instance in Tamil Nadu in the 1950s and early 1960s. The 55 million Tamils are descendants of the original Dravidian inhabitants, not of the Ayrans who arrived later. The movement for Dravidastan ended when the nationalist Dravida Munnetra Kazagham gained power in Tamil Nadu in 1962, only to find he had no support from other Dravidian people in southern India. Other movements calling for separate states based on language have had little success; neither in Maharashta where the Marathi-speakers demanded a Vidharba state, nor in Andhra Pradesh where the Telegu speakers called for the creation of Telengana.

India

India is proud of the fact that it is religiously tolerant. Nevertheless, and unsurprisingly, inter-faith violence does occur from time to time. An incident that still has to be resolved is the destruction of the mosque at Ayodhya in Uttar Pradesh. It is claimed that here, some 400 years ago, the first Mughal Emperor destroyed the Hindu temple commemorating the birthplace of the Hindu god Rama and replaced it with a mosque. Hindu–Muslim clashes began in November 1989 and occurred regularly until Hindu extremists tore down the mosque in December 1992; this was followed by communal fighting which left two thousand people dead. For some years stonework for the new temple has been prepared at Karsewakpuram 2 miles away. In February 2002 the site was purified before the start of construction of the new temple; twenty thousand people attended the purification ceremony. Two days later Muslims attacked a train taking Hindus home from the ceremony, burning the train and killing fifty-eight people in Gujarat. The attack provoked several days of inter-faith violence at Ahmadabad and neighbouring villages in which at least six hundred were killed. The government deployed army troops to restore order.

A more recent feature has been the growing incidence of Hindu–Christian clashes that have taken place in Gujarat, Maharashta, Orissa and Uttar Pradesh. The number of attacks on Christians has risen steadily since 1996, when there were only seven, to eighty-six in 1998; there were sixty-seven in 1999 and eighty-one in the first nine months of 2000. In June 2000 the Pope told the visiting Indian prime minister that he was disturbed by the violence that had seriously damaged India's tradition of religious tolerance. The attacks are blamed on missionary work which is concentrating on the poorest in the community and has had some success.

India also has disputes with its other Muslim neighbour, Bangladesh. Even after the border was demarcated there remained a large number of enclaves whose inhabitants were citizens of the other side. Indian officials blame illegal Muslim immigrants for inflaming sectarian tensions in Bengal, Assam and Tripura. India and Bangladesh both claim the island of New Moore or South Talpatty in the Bay of Bengal. The island itself is unimportant but ownership greatly affects the extent of the owner's continental shelf.

TRAVEL ADVICE (NOT INCLUDING KASHMIR) (PRE-13 DEC 2001)

FCO: Advise against holiday and inessential travel in Manipur and Tripura. Warns against rural travel in Gujarat. There is an increased risk to British institutions and organisations from global terrorism.

State: in north-east India do not travel outside major cities at night. Do not travel alone, as this encourages crime.

22 July 2002, FCO and State: Advise against all travel close to the border with Pakistan in Gujarat, Rajistan and Punjab states.

BIBLIOGRAPHY AND WEBSITES

Kaviraj, Sudipta (ed.), *Politics in India*, Oxford University Press, 1997
Singh, Patwant, *The Sikhs*, John Murray, 1999
Tarapot, Phanjoubam, *Insurgency Movement in North Eastern India*, Vikas Publishing, 1993
Tully, Mark and Jacob, Satish, *Amritsar: Mrs Gandhi's Last Battle*, Jonathan Cape, 1985
Varshney, Ashutosh, Ethnic Conflict and Civic Life: Hindus and Muslims in India, Yale University Press

Hindustan Times: www.hindustantimes.com
Indian Ministry of Foreign Affairs: www.meadev.gov.in
Indian Ministry of Home Affairs: www.nic.in
Institute for Defence Studies and Analyses: www.idsa-india.org
Institute for Peace and Conflict Studies: www.ipcs.org

Pakistan

Population: 161,838,000
Armed Forces: 620,000
Paramilitary: 288,000
Per Capita GDP: $US 2,400
Currency: rupee

Pakistan's macro-problems are well known: both the development of nuclear arms and missiles, and the confrontation with India over Kashmir are considered elsewhere in this section. The Kashmir issue was recently seriously exacerbated by the Kashmiri terrorist attack on the Indian parliament which led to both countries going on to a war-footing. Of more general concern are the state of the economy and, since the military coup of October 1999, the re-establishment of democratic government. President Pervez Musharraf has promised an election in October 2002.

Pakistan is used to military rule. Field Marshal Ayub Khan governed the country from 1958 to 1969 and General Zia ul-Haq seized power in 1977 and ruled until his death in 1988. Nor has the record of civil rulers been a happy one: Zulfiqar Ali Bhutto, prime minister from 1973 to 1977, was hanged for murder, and his daughter Benazir, prime minister from 1988 until her dismissal in 1990, has been convicted of corruption. Now the deposed prime minister, Nawaz Sharif, is awaiting trial and his government is also accused of incompetence and corruption. There are, though, a number of internal issues that must give the government concern.

Pakistan showing nuclear facilities

Pakistan is divided into four provinces: Baluchistan, North West Frontier (NWF), Punjab and Sindh. All have at one time or another caused problems for the central government. Each province has its own linguistic group; the people of the NWF Province are Pathans and speak Pushtun. There are also large numbers of Urdu and Gujerati speakers known as Mohajirs; Muslims who emigrated from India on partition, they mainly settled in Sindh. At the national level there are three main political parties: the Pakistan Muslim League (there are several other Muslim League factions but none is as successful electorally), whose heartland is the Punjab, was led by Nawaz Sharif; the Pakistan People's Party (PPP), the party of Benazir Bhutto, whose main support comes from Sindh; and Muttahida (originally Mohajir) Qaumi Mahaz (MQM), which is also strong in Sindh and Karachi.

There have been separatist movements in three out of the four provinces; at various times these have aimed to form the independent states of Baluchistan, Pushtunistan and Sindhudesh. The Baluchistan independence movement, actually more like tribal resistance to central government, was crushed by military force in the early 1970s after Prime Minister Bhutto had been told that a Baloch Liberation Front had been formed and that the provincial governor was plotting secession. The Russian invasion of Afghanistan and the arrival of three million Pushtun refugees in northern Pakistan halted the drive for Pushtun independence.

Karachi is the scene of political unrest that has degenerated into terrorism between the two factions of the MQM and a breakaway group called the MQM-Haqiqi or Real MQM. Naturally the indigenous population and security forces became caught up in it. The violence began in 1994 and by mid-1995 was responsible for over two thousand deaths.

Over-reaction and suspected 'judicial' killings of MQM leaders by security forces in encounters led to the hardening of positions and an increase in violence.

There is also a fifth 'province' in Pakistan known as the Tribal Areas. This consists of a strip of land running for 720km along the Afghanistan border, varying between 100 and 25km wide. Only the road through the area between Peshawar and the Khyber Pass is subject to government control. Troops have entered the Tribal Areas in the search for al Qaida and Taliban escaping from Afghanistan. The tribal leaders are fiercely anti-American and are happy to shelter al Qaida and Taliban fugitives.

Pakistan also suffers from religious intolerance, both between Sunni and Shi'a Muslims and within the Sunni community between Islamists and Secularists. About 10–15 per cent of Pakistanis are Shi'a Muslims and their political parties have gained support and funds from Iran. Inter-faith violence was sparked off by the Iran–Iraq war. It began with political assassinations and led to the forming of terrorist organisations such as the Shi'a Sipah-e Mohammad Pakistan (SMP) and the Sunni Lashkar-e Jhangvi (neither identified under the US Executive Order 13224). Most of the inter-faith violence has taken place in Punjab, Karachi and the Kurram Agency on the Afghan border, where the Tori and Mangal tribes clash. The fighting in Afghanistan and Kashmir has encouraged the resort to violence in Pakistan and also made weapons easily available. There has been a large increase in the number of boys educated in *madrassah* or Islamic seminaries: several thousand joined the ranks of Taliban while others went to al Qaida. The government is to restrict the numbers of foreign students, currently put at thirty-six thousand.

After 11 September 2001 President Musharraf had to decide whether to support President Bush and the American people and risk a civil war, or to continue to support the Taliban (which Pakistan had helped to establish) and to risk being treated as 'against us' and possibly to see US military action against those considered terrorists in Pakistan. With war against India already a possibility he chose the first course and banned five of the most virulent Islamic groups, arresting some two thousand of their supporters. He also tackled the pro-Taliban elements in the intelligence services and armed forces, sending a number of senior figures into early retirement. This has earned him US friendship and the lifting of a number of sanctions; the international community has rescheduled 12.5 billion dollars-worth of Pakistani debt. While Musharraf's popularity has grown, his opponents have resorted to violence, such as the killing of Shi'ite Muslims in a Rawalpindi mosque and of five people including two Americans in the international Protestant church in the diplomatic district of Islamabad. Perhaps a strong military government is just what Pakistan needs at this moment.

TRAVEL ADVICE (PRE-13 JUNE 2002)
FCO: Advise against all but essential travel.
State: Defer all travel, residents advised to leave.

BIBLIOGRAPHY AND WEBSITES

Cloughley, Brian, *A History of the Pakistan Army: Wars and Insurrections*, Oxford University Press, 1999
Rushbrook Williams, L.E., *The State of Pakistan*, Faber & Faber, 1962
Talbot, Ian, *Pakistan: A Modern History*, Hurst, 1998
Ziring, Lawrence, *Pakistan in the Twentieth Century: A Political History*, Oxford University Press, 1997

Pakistan Daily: www.pakistandaily.com
Pakistan government: www.pak.gov.pk
Pakistan; a country study: lcweb2.loc.gov/frd/cs/pktoc

Nepal

Population: 24,434,000
Hindu 90%, Buddhist 5%, Muslim 3%
By location: Pahad 48%, Terai 44%, Mountain 9%
Armed Forces: 46,000
Opposition Forces: Communist Party of Nepal: 2,000–10,000
Per Capita GDP: US$ 1,500
Currency: rupee

Nepal has a multi-ethnic population sub-divided not just by ethnicity but also by caste, tribe and area of dwelling. The main groups are the Mongloid Tibeto-Burmans who had migrated from the north and who traditionally lived in the mountains and the hills known as the *pahad*. To the south of the *pahad* lay the *terai* or lowlands, which in earlier times consisted mainly of jungle. The tribes that lived here were also of Tibeto-Burman extraction but spoke Indo-European languages; they have always been considered the indigenous race. They were originally Buddhists, Buddha having been born at Lumbini in 563 BC. Known as Siddharta, he preached the equality of all people. About two thousand years ago an Indo-Aryan people, the Khas, came from the west and south and settled in west Nepal. They held faiths that coalesced into Hinduism. Over the years they established a number of small principalities in the Himalayas. Later the Khas moved into eastern Nepal and colonised that area. Over time the Buddhists turned to Hinduism while retaining some features of Buddhism and the principle of equality was reversed. The Hindus practised a caste system which became enmeshed with the tribal system so that today there is a 'pecking order' among the main tribes. Separate from both *pahad* and *terai* was the valley of Kathmandu, normally known just as 'the valley'. The people there were the Newars, also Tibeto-Burmans; they had adopted Hinduism (or rather pre-Hindu faiths) far earlier than the others as the valley lay on the trans-mountain trade route and so attracted migrants and traders. The hillmen were considered to be below the caste system.

The unification of the disparate elements in the region into the state of Nepal began in the eighteenth century and was brought about by the ruler of the principality of Gorkha, Privthi Narayan Shah. By the early nineteenth century Gorkha influence extended over

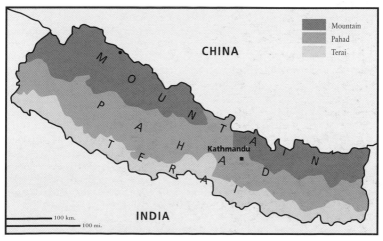

The topographical divisions of Nepal

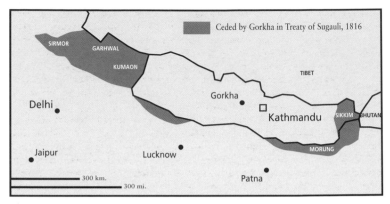

The Empire of the Gorkhas

today's Nepal and the whole country was ruled from Kathmandu. But the descendants of two of the valley principalities, Patan and Bhaktapur, still call the ruler the 'King of the Mountains'. The Gorkhas were ambitious and conquered land to the north-west and south-east of today's Nepal; they invaded Tibet but were driven out by the Chinese in 1792. Expansion southwards brought them into conflict with the East India Company. The Anglo-Nepali war began in 1814 and ended with the Treaty of Sugauli in 1816, by which Nepal gave up Sirmur, Garhwal and Kumaon in the north-west, Sikkim in the east and a southern strip of the *terai*. It also agreed to a British Resident in Kathmandu. The British respect for the Gorkhas' fighting ability led to their recruitment into the Indian Army, where they were known as Gurkhas.

In 1846 Jung Bahadur Kunwar (who later changed his name to Rana) became the dictator of Nepal after murdering his opponents. The royal family handed all but their title to him, and the Rana dynasty, as hereditary prime ministers with the title of Maharajah of Kaski and Lamjung, ruled Nepal for just over one hundred years. Bahadur further integrated Nepal and imposed a legal code (the *Muluki Ain*) under which each ethnic group was assigned a caste with a specific rank within the hierarchy. Eastern Nepal did not fit easily into the unified Nepal; it had a different system of land ownership, for instance. The government encouraged high caste Hindus to move to the east and over the years, as they were so much richer, they acquired land from the Limbu inhabitants. There remained a split between the *terai* and the *pahad* in terms of both communication and culture. As the *terai* was developed and the jungle cleared away it was settled by Indians rather than Nepalis, who were loath to leave their hill country. The Indians intermarried with the lowland Nepalis but not with the hillmen.

In 1951 power was returned to the monarchy, which had co-existed alongside the Rana dynasty, not through the coincidental civil uprising mounted by the Nepali Congress Party but as the result of an agreement reached by the Ranas, King Tribhuvan and the Indian government. The king and his successor, Mahendra, had massive public support and were revered. There were several reasons for the change. First, thousands of Nepalese had served in the Gurkhas in the two world wars and had their horizons widened by service abroad. Secondly, as there were no political parties in Nepal, the Nepalis could only turn to India for political guidance and from the 1920s onwards were influenced by the Indian Nationalist Movement. Thirdly, the Rana family had become too large for all its members to receive appointments. Members of the family began to be classified according to their degree of legitimacy; this fractured the family and some joined the anti-Rana movement.

The Nepalese constitution had been revised in 1948; this did not affect Rana hereditary rights but it did allow for freedom of speech. The prime minister was forced to resign by disaffected members of his family and his successor cancelled the constitution. The Nepali

Congress was formed in 1950 by the merger of two nationalist parties, and its military wing, the Mukti Sena (or Liberation Army), began an uprising against Rana rule. The rebels received little help from India other than moral support from Indian Nationalists who supported the principle of democracy for Nepal; nor did the king give the political or military movements any encouragement. The Congress Party was brought into the talks during the final stage and had no alternative but to agree to the conclusions. The full facts about which of the various parties conspired with whom will probably never be known.

A Rana/Nepali Congress coalition government was formed but it only lasted for nine months and was followed by a succession of other governments; at each change King Mahendra acquired more power. In 1960 the king suspended the constitution and imposed direct rule. He dispatched a fact-finding team to study the political systems in Egypt, Indonesia, Pakistan and Yugoslavia. Combining the team's findings with Nepal's history led to the *panchayat* constitution which aimed to establish democracy from the bottom upwards. Village assemblies elected district assemblies which in turn elected zonal assemblies, and they elected the members of the National Assembly to which the king nominated 20 per cent of its membership. No political parties were involved; they were banned. In fact, the country was governed by an alliance of the palace, army, police and rural elites who all relied on the king for their positions and prosperity.

The first communist party in Nepal was formed in 1949. Since then, others have formed, coalesced and split. In January 1990 seven communist parties, including the two largest, combined to form the United Leftist Front (UFL). Later, the other smaller communist parties that had not joined the UFL came together as the Joint National People's Movement. The *Jana Andolan* (people's movement) was also formed in 1990; this was a bloc of the many left-wing parties which, with the Nepali Congress Party, established an anti-*panchayat* alliance. After a major demonstration in February, followed by a general strike and clashes between the alliance supporters and the government, talks with the palace were held and the king agreed to end the ban on political parties. The *Jana Andolan* was a middle-class urban movement, active mainly in the valley of Kathmandu.

The Communist Party of Nepal (Maoist) was set up in 1995, its members coming from the Unified Marxist-Leninist CPN and the UFL. The Maoist appellation first emerged in Rukum where by coincidence an Indian Gurkha regiment, the 1/8th Gurkha Rifles, was traditionally recruited. In the Indo-Chinese war of 1962 the 1/8th were nearly annihilated and twelve men were taken prisoner and presumably brain-washed. However, the CPN

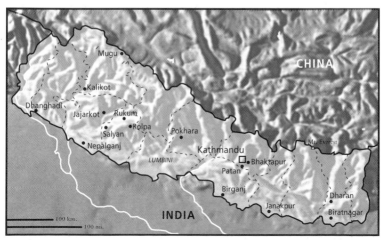

Nepal

(Maoist) does not follow Maoist philosophy. Communist influence spread further when the Tribhuwan University in Kathmandu was established in the 1950s. The first professors came from the Indian Patna University (known as the red heart of India), still a hot-bed of anti-establishment and anti-British influence.

The Maoist campaign of violence in western Nepal was provoked by a police operation to terrorise the people in the mountain district of Rolpa. It began with attacks on police stations in Rolpa, Rukum and Arghakhanchi districts and spread to Salyan, Jajarkot and Kalikot. The insurgency, which began in 1996, was caused by the uneven spread of development in Nepal that left the western provinces behind the rest of the country in terms of education, the eradication of poverty and road communications to the east. The 2.1 million people living there feel isolated and neglected, and two-thirds of them live below the poverty line. While slavery was abolished in 1928 bonded labour was not until 2000. The only source of income is labouring in the neighbouring Indian province of Kumaon. Initially the king and the National Defence would not allow the army to put down the rebels, believing it was a job for the police; however, they proved inadequate for the task and the army was unleashed in November 2001 when the king declared a state of emergency. A cease fire had been agreed to in July but was broken by the Maoists in November when they attacked a series of army and police posts, killing about a hundred men. A further weekend of violence took place on 16/17 February 2002 when the rebels killed over 150 police and soldiers and provoked a serious army counter-attack that left nearly two hundred rebels dead by the end of the month. The violence continues. Since February 1996 3,600 people are estimated to have been killed, over half of them since November 2001.

TRAVEL ADVICE
FCO: Does not warn against travel but advises exceptional caution as no area is completely safe. Only trek on established routes.
State: Reports threats to US interests. Check with Embassy before travelling.

BIBLIOGRAPHY AND WEBSITE
Brown, T. Louise, *The Challenge to Democracy in Nepal: A Political History*, Routledge, 1996

Kantipur Publications: www.kantipuronline.com
Nepal News: www.nepalnews.com
Nepal Online: www.nepalonline.org
Royal Nepalese Embassy London: www.nepembassy.com

Myanmar (Burma)

Population: 45,381,000
Burmese 68%, Shan 9%, Karen 7%, Rakhine 4%, Chinese 3%, Other (eight groups) 9%
Armed Forces: 344,000
Paramilitary: 100,000
Opposition Forces: Shan State Army 3,000, KNLA 4,000, All Burma Students Democratic Front 2,000; Karenni Army 1,000
Per Capita GDP: $US 1,400
Currency: kyat

Myanmar, formerly Burma, is a country with a number of ethnically different people. There is virtually no trace of the original aborigine population. The Burmese peoples came from eastern Tibet and western China and are believed to have come down from the Shan hills into the plains of lower Burma in about AD 840. The largest non-Burmese groups are the

Shan and the Karens, the former arriving by the thirteenth century while the latter had not completed their migration until after the British annexation of Bhamo in 1886. In many ways Burma is cut off from the rest of Asia either by the mountains to its north-west and east, or by the sea; within Burma, the Arakan is similarly isolated. Burmese history features a series of kingdoms, often at war, coalescing and then breaking up. The French and British started to take a hand in Burmese affairs in the eighteenth century, with the British supporting Alaungpaya who had rebelled against the French-backed ruler Talaing. Alaungpaya united the country and was succeeded in due course by his three sons who held the throne between 1760 and 1819. They invaded Siam twice, conquered the Arakan, repelled a Chinese invasion and took control of parts of Assam.

The First Anglo-Burmese War took place in 1824 and resulted in the Burmese being expelled from Assam, Manipur and Cachar; they were also forced to cede Arakan and Tenasserim, the southern coastal province, to the British. After the second war in 1852 the British annexed the remaining coastal province of Pegu. In the Third Anglo-Burmese War of 1885 the British completed their conquest of the country but it took five years and 35,000 troops to pacify Upper Burma. Burma became a province of the Indian Empire until 1937 when it was made a Crown Colony with a degree of self-government. Burma has nearly 4,000 miles of land border with five countries; the border areas are inhabited by a number of ethnic minorities.

During the 1930s the main hostility to British rule came from the Thakin movement led by Aung San and U Nu; it was violently opposed to the million-strong Indian population brought in as labour by the British (there are still some 1.5 million Indians and Chinese in Burma). At the start of the Second World War Aung San escaped British arrest and went to Japan where he received military training. The Japanese invasion led to the formation of a number of guerrilla groups among the tribes living along the borders with China and Thailand – the Kachins, Shans and Karens; they, with other minorities, continued the fight against the Burmese after independence was gained in 1948. During the Second World War, when the Japanese reneged on their promise of Burmese independence, Aung San formed a coalition – the Anti-Fascist People's Freedom League (AFPFL) – to fight the Japanese and then worked for independence from the British. Although Aung San was murdered in 1947 the AFPFL became the government in 1948.

The government's first act was to outlaw the Burmese Communist Party (BCP), whose 'White Flag' guerrillas were based in Wa Province along the border with China, which supported them. The BCP launched a rebellion in 1948 and in this they were joined by the Karens. At other times the Kachins and Shans have been in alliance with the BCP. All the non-Burmese minorities – the others being the Mons, Chins and Arakanese – have attempted to win some form of autonomy; they all considered the Burmese as much a colonial power as the British. The fortunes of the various dissident groups ebbed and flowed. In 1962 a military coup led by General Ne Win took power. Attempts to reach political agreement with the minorities were unsuccessful, as were more determined military campaigns. The minorities were by now involved in drug production and trafficking. In 1980 an amnesty was offered but only a few thousand accepted its terms. Nine dissident groups formed the National Democratic Front (NDF) which never united with the BCP against the government. Today a third of the population, inhabiting about half the country, are from ethnic minority, communist and other opposition groups.

In 1988 Ne Win resigned after twenty-six years in power and was replaced briefly by a civilian government that was overthrown the same year by Saw Maung, a retired soldier. The fighting continued and dragged in the Thai army, which did not want the guerrillas to establish themselves on Thai territory. The new government named itself the State Law and Order Restoration Council (SLORC). Elections held in 1990 were won by the National League for Democracy (NLD) led by Daw Aung San Suu Kyi, even though she was under arrest at the time. The military regime annulled the elections and arrested members of the NLD. The SLORC, known as the State Peace and Development Council (SPDC) since

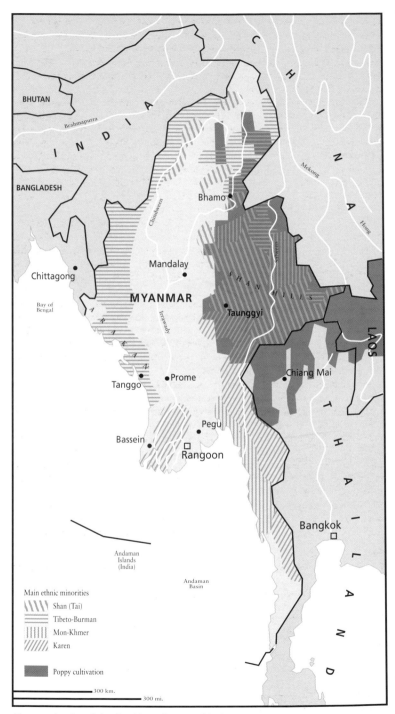

Main ethnic minorities

░ Shan (Tai)

▤ Tibeto-Burman

▥ Mon-Khmer

▨ Karen

■ Poppy cultivation

─ 300 km.

─ 300 mi.

Myanmar showing ethnic minorities and poppy cultivation

November 1997 but without a change of leadership or policies, greatly expanded the size of the army and received large quantities of military hardware from China. It managed to agree terms with nine of the expanding number of dissident groups; today there are four groups (the Shan State Army, the Karen National Liberation Army (KNLA), the All Burma Students Democratic Front and the Karenni Army) still continuing armed opposition with around ten thousand guerrillas all told.

The Burmese government's human rights record is one of the worst in the world. The UN Commission on Human Rights appointed a Special Rapporteur but he has not been allowed to visit the country. His report contained a long list of human rights violations that included arbitrary executions, political detentions, torture, rape, forced labour, forced relocation and no freedom of expression. Aung San Suu Kyi was released from house arrest in 1995 but put back under house arrest in September 2000. She has had talks with the government. Some 180 members of the NLD were released but another 1,700 remain in prison. The European Union has suspended all non-humanitarian aid to the country and imposed an arms embargo and the US has imposed sanctions on American investment in Burma.

In the late 1990s Burma was the world's leading supplier of opium, with a potential production in 1998 of 1,750 tons. Drug production rose dramatically from 170 tons in 1980 to a peak of 2,790 tons in 1997 but has been reduced since then and Afghanistan has now taken over as the world's prime producer. The United Wa State Army (UWSA) entered a cease fire agreement with the government in May 1989 and was given permission to set up various commercial ventures. By 1992 these were predominantly drug-related, at first with heroin production and later with the manufacture of methamphetamine ('speed'). By 1996 they had taken over the territory of the Mong Tai Army. Some fifty laboratories have increased production from 200 million tablets to an expected 700 million in 2002, all of them shipped to Thailand. The effect on Thailand has been disastrous, with large increases in crime, violence and corruption. The Burmese army is strongly suspected of assisting in the drug trade and taking a cut of the profits.

In 1997 the government came to an arrangement with the drug warlord Khun Sa, allowing him to continue trading in return for payment of tax on his profits. In 1998 the *Sunday Times* reported that the regime was actually expanding opium farming while claiming to be destroying it. In one instance some five thousand villagers in the Arakan were evicted to make way for drug farmers. Aung San Suu Kyi is reported to have had further talks with the SPDC, possibly to gain more prisoner releases. The outside world is divided about how to influence the SPDC and the best way to achieve the return of democratic government. At present the emphasis is on the isolation of Myanmar but a growing body of opinion believes that engagement will have more success. For its part the SPDC and its generals fear giving up control as they would most probably face trial for atrocities: they are likely to demand a total amnesty in the event of a democratic election. Aung San Suu Kyi was released from house arrest after 20 months; no one is at all confident that her release will lead to a quick return of the country to democracy.

TRAVEL ADVICE
FCO: Avoid border areas. Do not criticise the regime. Warns of bomb attacks on eastern border.
State: Advise on general caution. Contact the US Embassy.

BIBLIOGRAPHY AND WEBSITES
Carey, Peter (ed.), *Burma: The Challenge of Change in a Divided Society*, St Martin's Press, 1997
Christian, John, *Modern Burma*, University of California, 1942
Cocks, S.W., *A Short History of Burma*, Macmillan, 1910
Smith, Martin, *Burma: Insurgency and the Politics of Ethnicity*, Zed Books, 1991

Free Burma Coalition (Washington): www.freeburma.org
Myanmar (government site): www.myanmar.com
SOROS Foundation Burma Project: www.soros.org/burma

Sri Lanka

Population: 19,035,000
By Race: Sinhalese 74%, Tamil 18%, Moor 7%
By Religion: Buddhist 69%, Hindu 15%, Christian 8%, Muslim 8%
Armed Forces: 150,000 (including recalled reservists); Police (under Ministry of Defence) 60,000; National Guard 15,000
Opposition: Liberation Tigers of Tamil Eelam (LTTE) 6,000
Per capita GDP: $US 4,200
Currency: rupee

Sri Lanka, known as Ceylon during the British era, is a beautiful island – 'the pearl of the Indian Ocean' – and a popular tourist destination, plagued by a vicious civil war since 1983. There are two main ethnic peoples: the Sinhalese, the original inhabitants, who make up 74 per cent of the population; and the Tamils (18 per cent), most of whom migrated from southern India before the fifteenth century (others were brought in by the British after 1825 to work the tea plantations). The Sinhalese are mostly Buddhists, the Tamils are Hindu, and both communities have Christian minorities. There is also a Muslim population (about 8 per cent) who either came from south India or are the descendants of Arab, Persian and Malay traders and seamen.

Little is known of Sri Lanka's early history; first mentions of it came in Buddhist records begun in the first century AD. The island was divided into three kingdoms: Kitte on the west and south coast, Jaffna in the north and east, and inland Kandy; each was separated from the others by jungle. The Dutch and Portuguese colonised coastal strips between 1505 and 1796, after which the British governed the whole island until 1948 when it gained its independence. During all these years there was very little inter-community friction. The only serious clash arose between the Sinhalese and the Muslims in 1915 and it was quickly crushed by the British. The British, who needed an English-educated administrative class, and the Christian missionaries, who also set up a number of schools teaching in English, created an educated elite in both the Sinhalese and Tamil communities. The latter, who came mainly from the relatively barren area in the north, were eager to gain 'white collar' work. The constitutions devised by the British were based on territorial and demographic considerations which gave the Sinhalese an electoral advantage.

It was only after independence that violence broke out between Sinhalese and Tamils. The first outbreak occurred in 1956 after the passing of the 'Sinhala Only Bill' and the announcement that the leading teacher training college would be reserved for Sinhalese only. A non-violent Tamil demonstration near the House of Representatives was broken up by force and was followed by riots. The next round of violence came in 1958 when the Tamils attempted to gain autonomy in a federal state. Tamils were attacked, mainly in Colombo. Prime Minister Solomon Bandaranaike was assassinated in 1959 and was succeeded by his widow Sirimavo. The name Sri Lanka (meaning 'Resplendent Island') was adopted in 1972. In the elections of 1977 the Tamil United Liberation Front, formed in 1976, campaigned for an independent Tamil state of Eelam and again there were anti-Tamil riots. At the election Junius Jayawardene was elected president.

The long civil war began in 1983. The trigger is said to have been the ambush, killing and mutilation of thirteen soldiers on 23 July by the Liberation Tigers of Tamil Eelam (LTTE) in the Jaffna district. After the bodies had been taken to Colombo and displayed, there were widespread attacks on Tamils and their property in the city. Fifty-three Tamils were murdered in Colombo jail. The anti-Tamil attacks spread to other areas; the army and the police stood by and in some instances took part in the violence.

In June 1987 the army mounted a successful campaign to clear the Tamil rebels from their strongholds and had reached the outskirts of Jaffna when India intervened, fearing a massacre of Tamils in the city. Sri Lanka was forced to accept Indian monitoring of an agreement for the

INDIA

Palk Strait

Jaffna

Elephant Pass

NORTHERN

Vavuniya

Trincomalee

Anuradhapura

NORTH
CENTRAL

NORTH
WESTERN

Batticoloa

Indian Ocean

EASTERN

Kurunegala

Kandy

Ampara

CENTRAL

Radulla

Colombo

UVA

WESTERN

Ratnapura

SABARAGAMUWA

SOUTHERN

Galle

100 km.

100 mi.

Sri Lanka

army's withdrawal and the handing-in of Tamil weapons. A referendum was to be held in the Eastern Province on whether it should join the Northern Province permanently – a vote which the Sinhalese majority were confident of winning. Tamil extremists murdered many Sinhalese in the Eastern Province with the aim of frightening them into voting for the union. The Indian army presence, now over 30,000 strong, launched an attack on the LTTE in the north in October 1987. The Indians had some success but suffered heavy casualties. The Sri Lankans now had also to contend with the anti-Indian Janatha Vimukti Peramuna (JVP) insurgency in the south of the island. The president demanded the withdrawal of the Indian force: India refused, having already made a number of phased withdrawals from territory that was reoccupied by the LTTE, who now agreed to talks and to a cease fire.

The Indians pulled out of Jaffna in January 1990 and their withdrawal as a whole had been completed by the end of March; they had lost more than 1,200 soldiers killed. In June a number of clashes between the Sri Lankan army and the Tamil Tigers occurred. A cease fire was arranged but was soon broken by the Tamils who captured an army base. The army launched a major offensive and managed to relieve the garrison of Jaffna Fort, which had been besieged for three months, but then abandoned it. The civil war has continued with occasional breaks for talks ever since. The LTTE assassinated the president in May 1993 and the opposition candidate in October 1994. The Tigers managed to shoot down some air force planes and had considerable success against the Sri Lankan navy. In December 1995 the army captured Jaffna but the Tamil Tigers continued to operate and carried out terrorist attacks in Colombo. Since May 1997 the army has been attempting to clear the 74km-long road between Vavuniya at the southern end of LTTE-controlled territory and Elephant Pass just south of Jaffna, so that it no longer had to be supplied by air and sea. On 27 September 1998 Kilnochchi was attacked and over-run by the Tigers, who killed over six hundred soldiers. In December 1998 the LTTE offered to restart peace talks but the government refused.

In December 1999, just before the presidential election, a bomb blast killed 22 people and wounded another 110, President Chanrika Bandaranaike Kumaratunga was also wounded. The conflict, now in its eighteenth year, had claimed over sixty thousand lives, and on the eighteenth anniversary of the start of the civil war the Tamil Tigers carried out their most daring and successful raid. On 24 July 2001 they attacked Colombo airport, destroying three civil airliners and damaging three others; in addition, the air force lost three fighter aircraft, three trainers and two helicopters, with six more aircraft and six more helicopters being damaged. The fourteen Tamil Tigers involved all died in the attack. The raid has had a devastating effect on tourism to Sri Lanka. The national airline lost or had damaged 350 million dollars-worth of aircraft; insurance costs have naturally increased enormously. It will take at least a year for the air force to replace its losses. The LTTE is known to have purchased a number of microlights for use in suicide attacks but this plan was called off after several crashed during training.

The events of 11 September could well have encouraged the Tamil Tigers to mount an airborne suicide attack. They have been designated a foreign terrorist organisation by US executive order 13224. However, the Norwegians have been successful in arranging an end to the fighting; on 22 February 2002 the Norwegian ambassador gained the agreement of both the government and the LTTE to respect a long-term cease fire. Since then the road to Jaffna has been opened for the first time in twelve years and goods are being allowed into Tamil areas. By 1 May a monitoring mission with staff from the Nordic countries had been established to investigate violations of the ceasefire. However the Tamil leader, Velupillai Prabhakaran, has said there will be no peace until an independent Tamil state has been achieved. Nevertheless peace talks are scheduled to start on 16 September. the death toll is estimated to be over 64,000.

TRAVEL ADVICE

FCO: Advise against travel in northern and eastern Sri Lanka except for Trincomalee and Nilaveli. Advised not to visit Batticaloa or Ampora districts.

State: No specific advice other than warning US citizens of Sri Lankan descent.

BIBLIOGRAPHY AND WEBSITES

Tambiah, S.J., *Sri Lanka: Ethnic Fratricide and the Dismantling of Democracy*, IB Tauris, 1986
Tremayne, Penelope, *Tamil Terrorism: Nationalist or Marxist?* Institute for the Study of Terrorism, 1986

Marga Institute, Colombo: www.lanka.net/marga
Regional Centre for Strategic Studies: www.lanka.net/rcss
Sri Lankan Ministry of Foreign Affairs: www.lanka.net/fn
Tamil Eelam: www.eelam.com

North and East Asia

This section covers the rest of Asia. In North Asia the problems concerning China, Tibet, Taiwan, the two Koreas and the South China Sea are discussed. In east or south-east Asia the civil unrest and fighting in the Philippines and across Indonesia are described, as is the gaining of independence by East Timor.

China

Population: 1,293,239,000
Han-Chinese 92%, Manchu 0.87%, Uighur 0.64%, Mongolian 0.42%, Tibetan 0.41%
Armed Forces: 2,310,000
Nuclear Capability: 20+ ICBM, 150 IRBM, 12 SLBM
Per capita GDP: $US 4,300
Currency: yuan

There are those who consider that China will soon be, if it is not already, a regional hegemon and one day may even be able to challenge the United States. The US believes it may be challenged by a regional power in about fifteen years' time; it does not name China as that power but there are no other contenders. Others, though, forecast the break-up of China as democracy and prosperity replace communism and centralisation.

China has an ancient history but has not always ruled all of its present territory. The first Chinese dynasty, the Shang, emerged shortly after the start of the Bronze Age. Since then the central core of the country has been ruled by a succession of dynasties interspersed with periods of disintegration into smaller states before the next reunification. It has been invaded and ruled by outside powers, the Mongols and the Manchus, and it has expanded its borders on a number of occasions. At its peak, under the Ch'ing Manchu dynasty, China stretched northwards as far as the Argun River and the Altai Mountains, and included Outer Mongolia. In the west it reached Lake Balkhash and the Pamirs. Tributary states included Nepal, Burma, Siam, Laos, Tongking (Vietnam) and Korea. China's modern history has been equally violent, with the revolution of 1911 when the country became a republic; fighting between the communists and Chiang Kai-shek began as early as 1926. The Japanese invaded Manchuria in 1931 and then China in 1937. The Second World War was followed by the civil war between the Kuomintang under Chiang Kai-shek and the communists that left the latter in control and the Kuomintang withdrawn to Formosa. Communist rule has not been peaceful: 'the Great Leap Forward' cost some twenty million lives in floods and famine in 1959–61, while the Cultural Revolution between 1966 and 1969 was a period of chaos.

Of the total Chinese population of 1,293 million, approximately 10 per cent are not Han Chinese; of these the most significant minorities are the Uighurs and Kazaks in Xinjiang, the Mongols of Inner Mongolia and the Tibetans (see pp. 194–7). There is little separatist talk in Inner Mongolia, though the Mongols would prefer to be independent but not necessarily as part of what used to be called Outer Mongolia. Less than 20 per cent of the regional

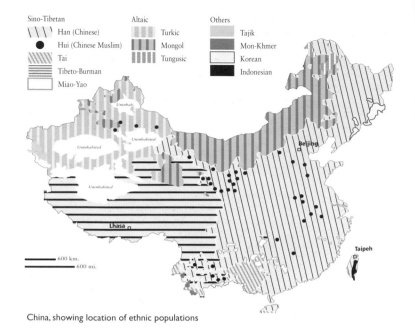

Sino-Tibetan
- \\\\ Han (Chinese)
- ● Hui (Chinese Muslim)
- Tai
- Tibeto-Burman
- Miao-Yao

Altaic
- Turkic
- Mongol
- Tungusic

Others
- Tajik
- Mon-Khmer
- Korean
- Indonesian

Uninhab.
Uninhabited
Uninhabited
Uninhabited
Beijing
Lhasa
Taipeh

600 km.
600 mi.

China, showing location of ethnic populations

population is made up of ethnic Mongolians. Both the Uighurs and Kazaks are Muslim and Xinjiang has a record of revolt.

The earliest revolt in western China occurred in the 1860s, when an East Turkestan authority ruled the region until defeated in 1878. The revolution of 1911, when Outer Mongolia gained its independence, had little impact in Xinjiang, whose turn came in 1931 after the autonomous Khanate of Kumul had been annexed. Hui (a Chinese-speaking Islamic minority) troops from Gansu supported the rebellion but Kumul was destroyed and over a hundred thousand people killed. This was followed by a revolt in southern Xinjiang in 1933 when the Turkish-Islamic Republic of East Turkestan was proclaimed. The Soviet Union supported continued revolt in the north but feared that East Turkestan could encourage Muslim dissidents in Central Asia.

Another revolt took place in 1944 when Muslims again established an East Turkestan Republic and managed to drive Chinese forces out of north-west Xinjiang. As war with Japan was still in progress, the government negotiated with the rebels. It promised them self-government, and undertakings were made in respect of religious and linguistic freedom; however, the reforms were never implemented. The Soviet Union had an interest in Xinjiang's natural assets during the Second World War and had a powerful influence there, at times backed by a military presence. Now that the Central Asian countries are independent, there are growing fears of the resurgence of an East Turkestan. There are thought to be about a million Kazakhs, twenty thousand Tajiks and a significant number of Kyrgyz living in western China. There are still unresolved border disputes with Pakistan and Tajikistan, while the solution to the Kyrgyzstan border problem has displeased many hard-liners there. The Chinese are continuing to bring in Han Chinese to the region and their proportion of the population had risen from 10 per cent in 1954 to around 40 per cent by the 1990s. In February 1997 there were large-scale demonstrations in the Xinjiang city of Yining when the authorities reportedly killed a hundred Uighurs. There are Uighur Liberation Committees in Kazakhstan, Kyrghyzstan, Tajikistan and Turkey. In April 1996 Kazakhstan, Kyrgyzstan, Tajikistan, China and Russia signed an agreement at Shanghai on confidence-building measures in their border regions. Further agreements on border region force reductions and cooperation on fighting separatism, religious extremism, terrorism and arms and drug trafficking were reached in 1997 and 1998.

For the Chinese government a more worrying factor than ethnic separatist issues, which can be controlled by military force and by increasing the Han population in minority regions, must be the growing divergence in the economic prosperity across China. People in areas such as the Special Economic Zones enjoy a far higher standard of living than those elsewhere and demonstrate the success of capitalism. Other factors that could lead to challenges to the government include civil rights issues, with the recent persecution of both Christian Chinese and cults such as the Falun Gong, and the one child per family rule (relaxed in Shanghai in 2002 to allow a second child but at a cost of about £9,000). The ratio of male to female births is riosing steadily; in 2000 it was 117 boys to 100 girls. Most Chinese want male chi.ldren and if a girl baby is discovered by ultrasound scan it is aborted. By 2020 it is forecast there may be as many as 30 million unmarried men, with potentially serious social consequences.

Chinese communism sees religion as a threat to its monopoly of power. However, five religions are officially sanctioned: Buddhism, Islam, Catholicism, Protestantism and Taoism. Tibetans and Mongols are Buddhists and Uighurs and Kazaks are Muslims. Christianity was introduced by European missionaries and has been spread by foreign churches. In 1949 there were estimated to be four million Christians in China; today the number is thought to be between thirty and forty million, most of whom worship in 'house' churches to avoid persecution. The law that outlawed the Falun Gong also declared ten Christian sects to be illegal cults. China challenged Christianity by appointing five Roman Catholic bishops without the Pope's authority. There is also a dispute over the reincarnation of the Panchen Lama: there are two, one recognised by the Dalai Lama and one chosen by the Chinese. As it is the Panchen Lama who selects the next Dalai Lama, he too may be a Chinese choice.

The Falun Gong Buddhist sect claims to have a hundred million members, though this may be an exaggeration; certainly it was able to organise peaceful demonstrations in more than thirty cities on a single day. It is a spiritual movement and claims to be apolitical. Its members are mainly middle-aged and many are women. The sect was banned in July 1999. A number of disillusioned officials and Communist Party members have been recruited by the sect and over a thousand have been sent for re-education and self-criticism classes by the government. Some commentators have compared Falun Gong with the earlier T'ai P'ing and the Boxers. The former led a rebellion in 1850 which, after gaining control of much of the Chang Jiang valley, continued until 1864; its leader was a Christian. The Boxer rebellion in 1900 was aimed at the European community, and many Christian Chinese were murdered. Falun Gong is not the only large cult to emerge in China – there are many others but little information about them is available.

Another cause for discontent will be the relocation of over a million people to make way for the Three Gorges Project (the Sanxia Dam on the Yangtze). They will join the other ten million already relocated since 1950 by other river projects. Many believe that pollution will contaminate the water collected by the scheme. A further two hundred thousand people are likely to be displaced by the plans to reroute water from the Yangtse and Yellow rivers to solve the water shortage in China's northern cities. A discontented population does not necessarily want civil war but can certainly cause political change at a national level.

To achieve a recognised hegemony, armed forces far stronger than those of any potential opposing alliance are needed, as is the economic strength both to support those forces and to challenge opponents in the economic field. China's forces are certainly being modernised but progress is slow and there are a number of key items either missing or available in very small numbers. During the Cold War China anticipated that it was most likely to be attacked over its land borders and so defence doctrine was based on making use of its vast land space and huge manpower. An invader would be allowed to penetrate deep into the country and then would be cut off from his supply lines and then eliminated. Now the fear is more of airborne and seaborne attack. Since 1987 manpower has been scaled down in

China, showing Three Gorges and water transfer schemes

the active forces by a million men and by three million in the reserves. All arms are being modernised but priority is being given to elements that will facilitate an offensive strategy – attacks on an opponent's strategic assets, his command, control and communications elements, his logistic infrastructure and even population centres – in an effort to avoid large-scale fighting between conventional forces.

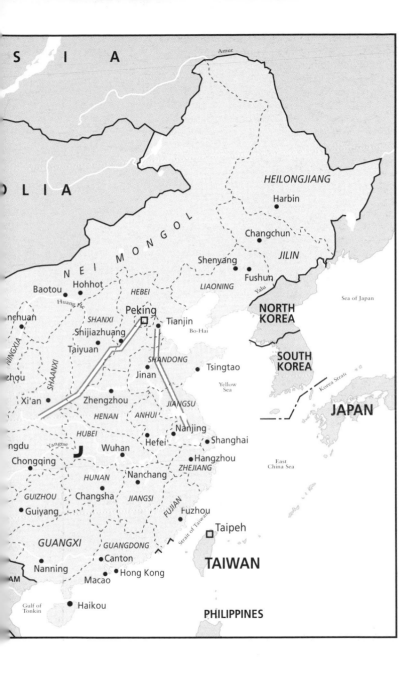

When viewed as a proportion of the total inventory, China's development and purchase of advanced equipment is so small as to make little difference to its capability. For example, 70 Russian Su-27 fighters have been purchased or produced under licence and 180 more will be. Also half of the forty ordered Su-30 fighter/ground attack aircraft have been delivered, to join a total inventory of over three thousand less capable combat aircraft.

There are as yet no airborne early warning aircraft (the US persuaded Israel not to fit out a number of planes for the Chinese) and only a few in-flight refuelling tankers. The navy is also lacking a 'blue water' capability, being mainly a coastal defence force with the exception of its submarine force which has been upgraded substantially in the last three years. There are still no aircraft carriers, though two scrapped Russian carriers have been purchased to allow feasibility studies. The two Sovremenny-class guided missile destroyers delivered by Russia are armed with the 500km-range SS-N-22 surface to surface missile; this is a step forward but only a small one. There is a possibility that more Sovremenny vessels will be ordered. Two ships under construction are likely to be of the same design. At present most other countries in the region are keeping pace, and may be ahead – in terms of quality – of Chinese equipment capability, whether in the air or at sea.

The nuclear missile arm (the second artillery) is also being modernised and longer-range and more accurate missiles are due into service. The first of the 8,000km-range DF-31s, test-fired in August 1999, may already be operational. A new submarine-launched ballistic missile is also under development, as is a nuclear-powered submarine from which to launch them; neither will be in service before 2008. The existing SSBN is purely a trials vessel and has never been operational. A new cruise missile, the YJ-63, with a 500kg warhead, is being developed which will increase short-range missile accuracy. It is not surprising that China is protesting about American plans to deploy an anti-ballistic missile system because this project could require China to deploy many more missiles than planned.

The official Chinese defence budget has been rising by over 10 per cent for the last eleven years, with a 17 per cent rise in 1999. Officially defence expenditure is put at $17 billion but many analysts believe the true figure is three times that amount; but even that is only a small percentage of the US defence budget of over $300 billion. It will take several years of greatly increased defence spending for China to achieve regional, let alone global, hegemony.

BIBLIOGRAPHY AND WEBSITES

Goodman, David and Segal, Gerald (eds), *China in the Nineties: Crisis Management and Beyond*, Clarendon, 1991
Heberer, Thomas, *China and Its National Minorities: Autonomy or Assimilation?*, ME Sharpe Inc., 1989
MacKerras, Colin, *China's Minorities: Integration and Modernization in the Twentieth Century*, Oxford University Press, 1994
Shambaugh, David (ed.), *Greater China: The Next Superpower?*, Clarendon, 1995
Stokes, Mark, *China's Strategic Modernization: Implications for the United States*, Strategic Studies Institute, 1999

China Daily: http://chinadaily.com.cn.net
Chinese Ministry of Foreign Affairs: www.fmprc.gov.cn/english/dhtml
Falun Jong (Dafa): www.FalunCanada.net
Inside China Today: www.insidechina.com
Xinhua News Agency: www.xinhua.org.eng

Tibet

Population: 13,500,000 (includes 'historic Tibet')
Tibetan: 6,000,000
Chinese: 7,500,000

The origins of Tibetan ethnicity are unclear but it is believed the people are descended from the Ch'iang tribes on the Tibetan–Chinese border, who probably over-ran the indigenous Mon. Another ethnic constituent could be Indo-Europeans who migrated to Tibet from the north. The very different environments in which they developed means that there is no cultural ecology common to the Tibetans and the Chinese. Until the seventh century AD the Tibetans were a number of nomadic tribes living on the Tibetan plateau, today referred to as 'political Tibet'. An early kingdom was Yarlung based on central Tibet, which formed a confederation of tribes eventually spread across the Tibetan plateau. After the death of Namri, the Yarlung sovereign, a number of tribes revolted but were soon subdued by Tsanpo Songsten Gampo, Namri's son. He went on to expand the Tibetan kingdom and conquered the surrounding countries; he also arranged matrimonial alliances with China and Nepal. The two new brides introduced Buddhism to Tibet in the late eighth century.

The Tibetans had expanded their empire to its greatest extent by the mid-eighth century. To the west it reached over the Pamir Mountains to Samarkand and touched the borders of the Arab and Turkic Empires. In the south it took in Nepal and extended its influence to the banks of the Ganges and the Brahmaputra. In the north it reached deep into Chinese Turkestan and in the east into Gansu and Sichuan, capturing the capital of the Tang dynasty, Changan (X'ian). Ethnic Tibetans inhabit a much wider area than the Chinese Tibetan Autonomous Region, and more ethnic Tibetans live in the Chinese provinces of Qinghai, Gansu, Sichuan and Yunnan than in Tibet. They also live in the Indian provinces of Ladakh, Sikkim, Uttar Pradesh and Arunchal Pradesh, and in Bhutan and Nepal.

The Tibetan Empire lasted for two hundred years, and it ended after the assassination of two rulers in 836 and 842 caused by the split between the adherents of Bon and Buddha and the persecution of the latter. By early in the tenth century Tibet had lost virtually all its conquests and was reduced to the Tibetan Plateau. The thirteenth century witnessed the rise and conquests of Genghis Khan and in 1240 Genghis's grandson made a treaty with a leading Tibetan Buddhist Lama in which the Lama was granted nominal authority over Tibet. So began the tradition of relationships between Mongol (and later Chinese) emperors and the Tibetan Lamas; the former protected Tibet and the latter became regent rulers on behalf of the Mongols and instructed them in religious affairs.

Though Tibet was dominated by the Mongols, it was never fully integrated into their empire and it regained its independence under a secular ruler in 1358. This development was accepted by the Yuan dynasty, established by Kublai Khan when he conquered China in 1279, and by the ethnically Chinese Ming dynasty which overthrew the Yuans. Tibet remained independent for the next three hundred years.

A tenet of the Buddhist faith is the belief that life consists of a sequence of birth, death and rebirth until one has achieved 'nirvana'. Reincarnation became the method of religious succession in Tibet as early as 1193. The tradition of the Dalai Lama began when Gyatso ('Dalai' is the Mongolian translation of 'Gyatso', the name of the second reincarnation of Gedun Trupa, a leading disciple of the Geluk Buddhist reform movement) visited the Mongol court and became the spiritual teacher of the Mongol emperor. The next reincarnation was found to be the great-grandson of the Mongol emperor; the next or fifth Dalai Lama became, after the Mongols defeated the rival Tibetan army, both the spiritual and political head of Tibet in 1633. Tibet now became permanently involved with the Mongol/Qing Manchu dynasty rivalry.

The fifth Dalai Lama built a strong and united Tibet. He passed administrative power to a 'depa', who then concealed the Dalai Lama's death for fifteen years. The depa encouraged the Dzungar Mongols to unify all the Mongols and they defeated the Qoshot Mongols in 1682. The Qoshot appealed to the Manchus, who had overthrown the Ming dynasty, for help. The Manchus, who founded the Qing dynasty, marched north and defeated the Dzungars at the Kalulun River. The Qing discovered the subterfuge of the Dalai Lama's death and therefore supported Lhabsang Khan, who staged a coup, executed the depa and exiled the sixth Dalai Lama, who died or was murdered shortly after. Lhabsang was recognised by the Manchus as the ruler of Tibet and he agreed to pay tribute in return for their protection, thus placing Tibet in a subordinate position to China.

Four times over the next hundred years the Manchus had to send an army into Tibet, each time at Tibetan request: in 1720 to evict Dzungar Mongols; after two internal revolts

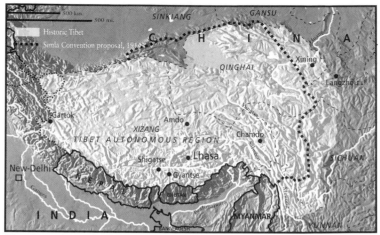
Tibet showing historic borders

in 1728 and 1780; and to defeat a Nepalese invasion in 1793. On each occasion the administration of Tibet was revised to give the Manchus more authority. Also Tibetan-populated areas outside 'political' Tibet were transferred to Chinese provinces. In 1793 the Qings drafted the 'Agreed Regulations for the Better Governing of Tibet', which included the power to confirm the reincarnation of the Dalai Lama. The following hundred years saw a reduction in Qing influence as the dynasty faced other, more pressing problems. By the time the British became interested in Tibet towards the end of the nineteenth century, Manchu authority over Tibet was purely symbolic.

British interest in Tibet began in the mid-1800s as a result of fears of Russian infiltration but the Tibetans steadfastly kept both the Russians and the British out. The main result of Sir Francis Younghusband's expedition to Lhasa in 1904 and the subsequent Anglo-Tibetan Treaty – in which the Tibetans undertook to give no foreign power concessions nor allow them to intervene in its affairs without British consent – was to give Britain a hand in Tibetan-Manchu relations. The Manchus refused to accept the treaty and negotiations began to draw up an Adhesion Treaty, which was signed by Britain and the Manchu government in 1906. This treaty, which the Tibetans were not consulted about nor asked to sign, gave away much that the Younghusband treaty had gained. It shifted the responsibility for implementing the Anglo-Tibetan Treaty from the Tibetans to the Manchus, who were excluded from the term 'Foreign Powers', and the British undertook not to interfere in Tibetan internal affairs.

In 1909 the Manchus invaded Tibet but neither Britain nor Nepal (also bound by treaty to aid Tibet) did more than complain to the Manchu authorities. The Dalai Lama was deposed and fled to India where he formally renounced all ties with the Manchus and their claim to suzerainty (not sovereignty) over Tibet. Within two years the Chinese revolution had taken place and the Republic of China had been established. In Tibet the Manchu troops mutinied, surrendered and left the country; the Dalai Lama returned and declared Tibet's independence.

In October 1912 Chinese troops entered eastern Tibet and British pressure on Peking led to the Three Power Conference, at which the Tibetan and Chinese positions on Tibet's status were far apart. The British devised a compromise dividing Tibet in two; in the eastern part (or Inner Tibet) the Chinese could establish a degree of control, in return for which they would play no part in the affairs of Outer Tibet and would allow direct Anglo-Tibetan relations. Although the Chinese envoy signed the convention, it was immediately repudiated by Peking and China lost an opportunity for its suzerainty to be internationally recognised. Britain went ahead to conclude the Anglo-Tibetan Treaty of 1914 which included the declaration that until China signed the convention it could not enjoy the advantages – including the recognition of Chinese suzerainty over Tibet.

Until October 1950, when the People's Liberation Army (PLA) entered the country, Tibet maintained its independence from China, though the new Chinese constitution held that Tibet was a province of the republic. The 40,000-strong PLA force soon defeated the 8,000 men of the Tibetan army but it did not enter Lhasa until September 1951. During this period a number of protests were made to the Chinese and the Dalai Lama was persuaded to accept the role of Tibet's supreme ruler. At the UN it was decided that the Tibetan appeal over Chinese aggression would not be debated, mainly because of the coincidental entry of China into the Korean War and because the Indians believed they could still negotiate a peaceful settlement.

Chinese troops occupied all Tibet's major cities but the Dalai Lama remained in Lhasa and the government continued to function at a local level. The Chinese embarked on a series of measures to downgrade Tibetan regional importance. The Tibetan provinces of Amdo and Kham were broken up into smaller entities and became parts of the Chinese provinces of Gansu, Qinghai, Sichuan and Yunnan. A number of Tibetan minorities such as the Jangpas, Lhopas, Monpas, Sherpas and Tengpas were reclassified as Chinese ethnic minorities. Unpalatable reforms were effected in Amdo and Kham which led to violent resistance and harsh repression; a number of religious and political figures disappeared. By 1959 there was a growing fear that the Dalai Lama might be taken to Beijing and a mass demonstration prevented him from attending a function at the Chinese barracks. In March fighting broke out, the Dalai Lama escaped to India and the Chinese dissolved the government of Tibet. Over the next eight months 87,000 Tibetan resistance fighters were killed, according to Chinese intelligence, and some 80,000 refugees managed to leave the country.

The Chinese claim to sovereignty over Tibet dates back to the marriage in AD 635 of the Tubo (Tibetan king) and a Tang princess and the Tang–Tubo alliance which agreed 'that their two territories be united as one, have signed this alliance of great peace to last to eternity' (inscription on monument in Lhasa). They claim that from the unification of China by the Yuan dynasty, Tibet has been an administrative region of China, citing the establishment of the office of the 'High Pacification Commissioner'. In November 2001 the Chinese vice-president, Hu Jintao, said that China was ready to talk to the Dalai Lama but only on condition that he accepted Chinese rule in Tibet. Hu was head of the Communist Party in Tibet in 1988–9. The Dalai Lama had described Tibet as an occupied territory to the European Parliament only a month earlier.

India is the country most affected by the Chinese occupation of Tibet for both military and environmental reasons. India sees Chinese missile deployment in Tibet as directly aimed at it. The deforestation of Tibet has led to soil erosion and flooding; desertification has begun and the Indus and Brahmaputra are much more silted. The waste products from the Amdo uranium mine and the nuclear research centre, with the possibility of nuclear waste dumping, worry not just Tibetans but all its neighbours whose rivers flow from Tibet.

TRAVEL ADVICE
FCO: Warns not to take letters or packages from Tibetans for posting in Europe.

BIBLIOGRAPHY AND WEBSITES
Anand, Kumar (ed.), *Tibet: A Source Book*, Sangam Books, 1995
Anand, R.P., *The Status of Tibet in International Law*, International Studies vol. 10, no. 4, April 1969
Smith, Warren W., *Tibetan Nation: A History of Tibetan Nationalism and Sino-Tibetan Relations*, Westview, 1996
Van Walt van Praag, Michael, *The Status of Tibet: History, Rights, and Prospects in International Law*, Westview Press, 1987

International Campaign for Tibet: www.tibet.org
Tibetan Government in Exile: www.tibet.com

Taiwan (Republic of China)

Population: 22,124,000
Taiwanese 84%, Mainland Chinese 14%
Armed Forces: 370,000
Per Capita GDP: US$ 16,800
Currency: Taiwan dollar

Taiwan – known earlier as Yizhou, Liuqiu and Formosa – has belonged to China since ancient times. The earliest recorded Chinese settlement was recorded in the Seaboard Geographic Gazetteer in the time of the Three Kingdoms over 1,700 years ago. Other settlements took place in the third and seventh centuries AD. The Chinese population was over a hundred thousand by the end of the seventeenth century and more than 2.5 million by the end of the nineteenth.

The first foreign invaders were the Dutch, who occupied southern Taiwan in 1624, and the Spanish, who seized the north of the island in 1626, only to be evicted by the Dutch in 1642. Mainland Chinese evicted the Dutch in 1662. After the Chinese defeat in the war of 1894, Taiwan was ceded to Japan under the terms of the 1895 Treaty of Shimonoseki. There were regular popular uprisings against the Japanese until war broke out between China and Japan in 1937. China, then governed by Marshal Chiang Kai-shek, recovered the island in 1945. In the Chinese civil war that followed, the nationalists, the Kuomintang, were forced out of mainland China by the communists and withdrew to Taiwan with some 600,000 troops, hoping to regain the mainland that they still claimed as theirs. The US continued to recognise the Kuomintang as

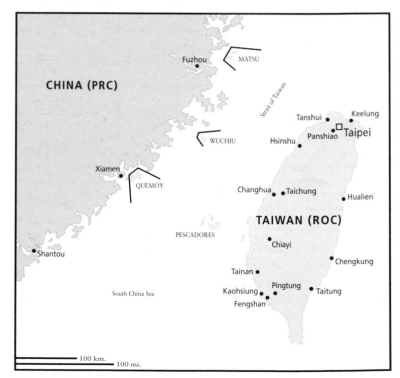

Taiwan (Republic of China) and the off-shore islands

the rightful government of China and it held the Chinese seat at the United Nations until 1971 when it was expelled and replaced by the People's Republic of China (PRC). The Kuomintang (Guomindary) also retained control of a number of offshore islands, notably Quemoy and the Matsu Islands, which became the scene of regular shelling from the mainland in 1958.

US naval forces protected Taiwan during the Korean War and the US and Taiwan signed a defence treaty in 1954. The US had to cancel the treaty and break off diplomatic relations with Taiwan in 1979 when the US and the PRC normalised their relations. Both the PRC and Taiwan agreed that there is only one China, at present under two systems, which both claim sovereignty over the whole of China. Taiwan has declared that it will not use force to regain control of the mainland but the PRC as recently as July 1998 reaffirmed 'that it will not commit itself not to resort to force'. The PRC are concerned over any Taiwanese moves towards independence and Taiwanese applications for membership of the UN have been continually blocked. The previous Taiwanese president, Lee Teng-hui, said in July 1999 that bilateral talks could only continue on a state-to-state basis; the idea of one indivisible China had to be dropped. Immediately China strongly warned Taiwan that it should not declare its independence. Independence is, of course, the goal of the Taiwanese opposition party, the Democratic Progressive Party, which won both the last two presidential elections. The US accepts that the PRC has sovereignty over Taiwan, again on the principle of one country, two systems. It can be claimed that the 1979 Congressional Taiwan Relations Act, which was deliberately ambiguously drafted in an attempt both to ensure Taiwan's security and to follow the 'one China' policy, commits the US to defending Taiwan.

After earlier military exercises, missile-firing begun in July 1995 led to a US carrier group passing through the Taiwan Strait. In March 1996 the PRC conducted missile tests in two areas not far from the Taiwanese ports of Keelung and Tsoying, to demonstrate that these could be closed. The tests were followed by large-scale ground, sea and air exercises close to the islands of Matsu. These military moves were in response to Taiwan's holding its first democratic presidential election. The US reinforced its carrier battle group deployed to the east of Taiwan with a second carrier group, and the crisis did not escalate.

In February 1999 Taiwan claimed that the PRC had increased the number of missiles facing it by over a hundred; the US Pentagon acknowledged that the missiles had been modernised but not increased in number. However, in a more recent (2002) assessment, the US estimates the numbers are increased by 50 a year. Nevertheless a missile attack is precisely what Taiwan fears most because the PRC does not yet have the amphibious capability to mount a successful invasion of Taiwan. The development of the Xiong Ying cruise missile means that targets in eastern Taiwan protected by the Chung Yang Shan Mountains could be attacked. Taiwan has purchased US Patriot missiles and is keen to acquire a missile defence system. The PRC objects to all purchases of US weaponry by Taiwan but particularly any type of anti-ballistic missile system.

Meanwhile, although the PRC is unlikely to deliberately attack Taiwan, it is always possible that the use of military manoeuvres to support political pressure could get out of hand and escalate to conflict. Taiwan is unlikely to drop its application to join the UN and its desire to gain greater international recognition (the establishment of diplomatic relations with Macedonia in early 1999 caused the PRC to veto the extension of the mandate of the UN force there). Neither side will halt their arms build-up.

BIBLIOGRAPHY AND WEBSITE

Lee, Bernice, The security Implications of the New Taiwan, International Institute for Strategic Studies, Adelphi Paper 331, 1998

Republic of China Information Office: www.gio.gov.rw
Taiwan Research Institute: www.taiwaninformation.org
Taiwan Security Institute: www.taiwanstudies.org
Taiwan Security Research: www.taiwansecurity.org

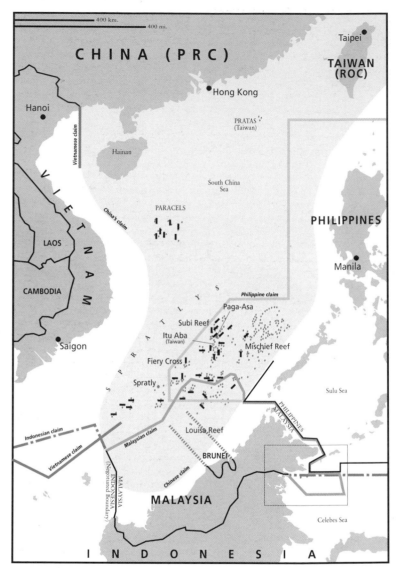

South China Sea showing rival claims

South China Sea

The Spratlys and Paracels are two groups of small islands, reefs and sandbanks spread over some 800,000 sq. km of the South China Seas. China, Taiwan and Vietnam have put forward rival claims to the Spratlys (or Nansha Islands); the Philippines and Malaysia also claim parts of the island group. Brunei claims the Louisa Reef, which lies in an extension of its maritime boundaries. The Paracels (Xisha Islands) occupied by China are also claimed by Vietnam. The distances involved are vast; the Union Reefs, roughly in the centre of the Spratlys, lie 350km

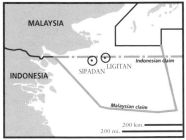

All of the Spratly Islands and Paracel Islands are claimed by China (PRC), Taiwan (ROC) and Vietnam.

Presently occupied by:

I	China (PRC)
–	Vietnam
↖	Malaysia
✔	Philippines

Extent of maritime claim by:

China (PRC)

━━━ Vietnam

━━━ Malaysia

━━━ Philippines

━ ━ Indonesia

········· Brunei

from the Philippines, 450km from East Malaysia, 650km from Vietnam and 1,200km from China (Hainan). Few of the Spratlys are inhabited and those that are, are inhabited only by the military, oil exploration staff and fishermen. There have been wildly different estimates of the oil and gas potential of the Spratlys, ranging from one to over seventeen billion tons: at present about one million tons is being extracted a year. The Spratlys are also rich in fish: 2.5 million tons were caught in 1980.

The Chinese claims, both of the People's Republic (PRC) and of the Republic of China (ROC, Taiwan), stem from ancient history, when the Chinese reputedly discovered the islands as long ago as the Han dynasty in the second century BC. The Chinese claim is for territorial waters covering the whole South China Sea and extending to within 80km of the Philippines, East Malaysia and Vietnam. The evidence for Chinese occupation is dependent on the acceptance of Chinese maps drawn in the eighteenth and nineteenth centuries. They claim that their fishermen have lived and fished there for centuries. After the surrender of Japan, which had controlled the islands after 1937 and during the Second World War, General Chiang Kai-shek's forces took over from the Japanese, carried out surveys and set up stone markers. In 1947 the PRC published its boundaries in the South China Sea. In 1992 the PRC enacted the Territorial Waters Law, which stated that Taiwan, Sekaku, the Pescadores, the Macclesfield Bank, the Paracels and the Spratlys were all Chinese.

The Vietnamese claim is also based on history. A seventeenth-century atlas reported annual visits to the Paracels to salvage the cargoes of ships wrecked there. The Paracels were shown as dependencies of Annam in a French publication in 1834 and on a Vietnamese map of 1838. However, the French recognised Chinese claims in 1887, 1921 and 1929; but in 1931, when Japan was attacking China's north-east provinces, France backed Annam's claim to the Paracels and in 1933 occupied nine islands in the Spratlys. In 1946 a French warship placed markers claiming the islands of Spratly and Itu Aba. In September 1957 the South Vietnamese government claimed both the Spratlys and Paracels in continuation of earlier French claims. After Vietnam claimed its territorial waters, contiguous zone, exclusive economic zone and continental shelf in 1977, Hanoi published *Vietnam's Sovereignty over the Hoang Sa* (Paracels) *and Truong Sa* (Spratlys) *Archipelagos* in 1979; this contained all the documentary evidence supporting the Vietnamese claim.

The Philippine claim is based on treaties signed between the US and Spain in 1898 and 1900, and between the US and the UK in 1930. It is also based on the Philippines' right to an exclusive economic zone that it claims covers the eastern part of the South China Sea. The Malaysian claim is also based on its exclusive economic zone under the UN Convention on the Law of the Sea.

The view of most impartial observers is that most of the claims of sovereignty are weak and would not be upheld at the International Court of Justice; few claims can be supported by the necessary evidence of continuous and effective control. Nor, once sovereignty is agreed, do many of the small islets qualify for an exclusive economic zone, as to do so they must be able to sustain human occupation. The area of the largest island is less than half a square kilometre and only the next six largest are more than 100 sq. metres in size. Claims based on continental shelves are more likely to succeed than those founded on other evidence.

Until 1974 the Paracels were occupied by both the PRC and South Vietnam but in that year the PRC took advantage of the collapse of South Vietnam to seize the western islands; as North Vietnam was being supported by the PRC it declined to question the take-over but in 1988 Vietnam renewed its claim to both the Paracels and the Spratlys. The ASEAN countries with claims in the South China Sea would prefer to see the whole question settled by an international conference, while the PRC is only prepared to engage in bilateral negotiations. All the claimants have occupied a number of islands over the last ten years, with the PRC occupying the remainder. In 1988 the PRC set up sign-boards on six reefs at Chigua Reef in the Spratlys claimed by Vietnam and in 1995 occupied Mischief Reef which is clearly in the Philippine exclusive economic zone; in 1998–9 it increased the construction of facilities there. Oil exploration began in 1992 when the PRC granted a concession to Crestone in the Vanguard Bank area. Soon after, Vietnam gave a Japanese/US consortium concessions in the nearby Blue Dragon field. There have been isolated clashes between rival claimants. Most recently, in May 2001, PRC sailors boarded a Taiwanese fishing boat and the Philippine navy fired at PRC boats fishing in disputed waters.

The Philippines and Vietnam drafted a Code of Conduct for discussion at the ASEAN meeting in 1999. China rejected the code as it aimed at maintaining the present position and would legitimise 'foreign' occupation of islands claimed by the PRC. China drafted its own proposed Code of Conduct which only covered the Spratlys and not, as Vietnam wants, the Paracels.

Actual conflict over the Spratlys would be hard to sustain given the distances involved and the claimants' lack of aircraft carriers and in-flight refuelling capability. Even maintaining large numbers of naval craft would prove difficult as few local navies have developed at-sea replenishment ships and tankers. Only the PRC could maintain naval forces continuously in the Spratlys and then with only very limited air cover. Malaysia is capable of defending its relatively limited claims off the East Malaysian coast. The Philippines are militarily the weakest of the claimants and could not mount an effective defence of the islands it presently occupies; the US has made it clear that it is not prepared to support Philippine claims with military action.

There are other island disputes at the north and south ends of the South China Sea. Japan, the PRC and the ROC all claim the Senaku (Diaoyus in Chinese) Islands that lie 160km north-east of Taiwan and 320km west of Okinawa. The uninhabited islands became part of Japan in 1895 and China recognised this when Taiwan (then Formosa) was ceded to Japan. The Chinese claim was renewed in 1992 when it passed its law on Territorial Seas and Contiguous Zones. The Philippines and the PRC both claim – and had a confrontation at – Scarborough Reef in 1997. In the south Malaysia and Indonesia both claim the islands of Sipedan and Ligitan that lie due east of the Malaysian–Indonesian border; both countries have agreed to refer the dispute to the International Court of Justice.

BIBLIOGRAPHY AND WEBSITES

Dzurek, Daniel J., *The Spratly Islands Dispute: Who's on First?*, International Boundaries Research Unit, Maritime Briefing, 1996

Garver, John, 'China's Push Through the South China Sea: The Interaction of Bureaucratic and National Interests', *The China Quarterly*, 1992

Kien-hong Yu, Peter, *A Study of the Prats, Macclesfield Bank, Paracels and Spratlys in the South China Sea*, Critical Issues in Asian Studies Monograph Series, 1988

'New Security Issues in the South China Sea', *Pacific Review*, January 2001

'Politics and Concepts Regarding the South China Sea', *Issues and Studies*, September 1993

Energy and Security in the South China Sea (University of Oslo): www.sum.uio.no/southchinasea
South China Sea Informal Working Group (University of British Colombia): http://faculty.law.ubc.ca/scs

North and South Korea

	Democratic People's Republic of Korea (DPRK)	Republic of Korea (ROK)
Population:	24,500,00	47,295,000
Armed Forces:	1,082,000	683,000
Foreign Forces:	nil	US 36,000
Per Capita GDP:	US$ 1,000	US$ 15,000
Currency:	won	won

Korea claims to be able to trace its history back to the Tangun dynasty in 2333 BC. For many years it was a vassal state to China, the northern two-thirds of the country being part of both the Han and Ch'in Empires. Japan invaded and devastated the Korean peninsula on three occasions in the sixteenth century AD but the Japanese always withdrew until their defeat of Russia in 1905, when the then independent Korea became a Japanese protectorate. It was annexed and Japanese settlers brought over in 1910. At the end of the Second World War the Russians declared war on Japan forty-eight hours after the first nuclear bomb had been dropped on Hiroshima. Russian forces marched into Korea and so were able to claim it as an occupied zone when the war ended. The dividing line between the Russians and the Americans was the 38th Parallel. In 1948 the US military government handed over control to the newly elected government of the Republic of Korea (ROK). In the north the Russians imposed the Executive Committee of the Korean People, led by Soviet-trained Korean communists; this became the Democratic People's Republic of Korea (DPRK) in 1948, by which time the communist way of life was well established. The last Soviet forces withdrew in 1949 but an American garrison remains in the ROK.

The DPRK launched an invasion of the ROK on 25 June 1950 and by August had occupied some 90 per cent of the country, with only a small enclave around Pusan holding out. The UN condemned the attack and, as the Soviets had walked out by that time, voted to provide forces to repel the invasion. General Douglas MacArthur, the US Commander-in-Chief in the Far East, made a large-scale landing at Inchon on the west coast just south of the 38th Parallel in September. The North Koreans were forced to withdraw, first over the parallel and then further north as the UN advanced virtually to the Yalu River on the Chinese border. The Chinese then attacked over the Yalu and the UN forces were driven back south of the 38th Parallel; the Chinese captured Seoul in January 1951. The UN managed to recover the territory south of the parallel and some way north of it on the eastern side of the peninsula; then the war reached a stalemate with both sides entrenched. Peace negotiations began in July 1951 but an armistice was not signed until two years later. A demilitarised zone was established as a buffer between the two sides and peace negotiations continued at Panmunjom without reaching a conclusion.

North and South Korea showing North Korea's nuclear facilities

A strong UN military force remained in the south but, other than the Americans, all foreign forces had been withdrawn by 1958. Initially the US kept the ROK army short of fuel and ammunition as they feared that the war might be restarted with an invasion of the north by the south. Over the years South Korea has become more and more prosperous while the North, through mismanagement and heavy military spending, has become poorer and poorer, with much of the population facing starvation, and causing perhaps over two million deaths. Following the unification of East and West Germany, and the realisation of the cost to West Germany, South Korea became rather less keen on the aim of reunification.

Balance of Forces

	South Korea	North Korea
Tanks:	2,300	3,500
Artillery:	5,000	10,400
SSM:	12 (NHK-I/-II)	54 (FROG, Scud-C)
Combat aircraft:	570	620
Warships:	39	3
Coastal:	84	310
Submarines:	19	26
Amphibious:	14	10

The DPRK announced in March 1993 that it was withdrawing from the Nuclear Non-Proliferation Treaty which it had acceded to in December 1985. The decision appears to have been provoked by the International Atomic Energy Agency's determination to inspect two undeclared waste disposal sites thought to contain nuclear waste, examination of which could show how much plutonium North Korea might have separated since 1975. On 21 April 1994 North Korea announced that it was to replace the core of its 5-megawatt reactor. After several requests North Korea eventually agreed to allow IAEA inspection of the removal of the fuel but started the work before the inspectors arrived. The IAEA was unable to verify whether plutonium had been extracted from the reactor in previous years. The 8,000 fuel rods being removed could contain about 25–30kg of plutonium: enough to make four or five nuclear weapons. The US and others felt their earlier suspicions were confirmed and that the North could have amassed sufficient fissile material to make up to five nuclear weapons. The most recent assessment, made in May 2001 by the CIA's deputy director, is that the DPRK probably has one or two bombs.

Following a visit by Jimmy Carter, the former US president, North Korea agreed to resume negotiations and committed itself to neither reprocessing nor separating plutonium, not to restart its 5-megawatt reactor, to halt construction of two gas-graphite reactors, to close and seal the laboratory suspected of being a separation plant, and to keep the spent fuel rods from the reactor in the cooling pond until their disposal was arranged. The US agreed to organise the financing and construction of lightwater reactors to replace the frozen reactors and to deliver 500,000 tons of heavy oil annually as an alternative source of energy. The Korean Energy Development Organisation (KEDO) is an international consortium, led by the US, Japan and South Korea, to implement the provision of lightwater reactors. KEDO and North Korea signed a contract for the construction of two 1,000-megawatt reactors with an aimed completion date for the first of 2003, but this date has slipped to 2008. On 13 August 2002 North Korea announced it would not allow international inspectors into suspected sites; it is likely that the US will halt the supply of equipment for the two reactors.

North Korean Nuclear Facilities

Hungnam: Uranium mine
Kusong: Uranium processing
Nanam: Uranium mine

Pakch'on: Uranium mine and reprocessing
P'yongsan: Uranium mine and reprocessing
P'yongsong: Nuclear research and training
P'yongyang: Nuclear science and engineer training, sub-critical facility
Sinp'o: Construction of nuclear power plant
Sunch'on: Uranium mine
Taechon: Construction of nuclear power plant
Unggi Uranium mine
Yongbyon: Two nuclear reactors and one under construction. Plutonium reprocessing, fuel-rod fabrication, fuel storage and suspected nuclear waste storage

The US demanded access for inspectors to an underground construction site at Kumchangri, about 40km north-west of the nuclear plants at Yongbyon, which it suspected had a nuclear weapons purpose. Access was at first refused and then offered at a price of $300 million, which the US refused to pay; the US denies that the provision of 500,000 tons of food has any direct link with the issue. The site was visited in May 1999 and was found to be an extensive, but empty, tunnel system; the US has the right to return to the site.

North Korea is also developing long-range missiles and has exported the technology for this, notably to Iran. The latest test-flight was of a multi-stage missile that the Koreans described as a satellite launch. The missile was fired over Japan in August 1998. The first stage separated and fell into the sea 300km east of North Korea, while the second stage crossed Honshu Island and fell 330km east of Japan. The test is believed to have been of the Taepo Dong-1, which could have a range of 2,000km. When preparations for another missile test – this time probably of the Taepo Dong-2, with a potential range of up to 6,000km – were spotted the US strongly warned North Korea not to hold another trial. In September 1999, following North Korea's promise not to continue testing, the US said it would lift a number of trade sanctions that have been imposed for the last forty years. Japan also said it would lift sanctions and would consider resuming food aid deliveries, halted after the 1998 missile test. The US assesses that the North has developed biological weapons.

South Korea's President Kim Dae Jung met the North's Kim Jong II for three days of talks at Pyongyang in June 2000. The summit communique included pledges to improve trade and economic relations, to achieve reconciliation and, eventually, reunification. However, it was very short of details as to how these aims might be implemented. A month later officials had agreed to holding regular ministerial talks and to opening liaison offices. South Korean conglomerates, headed by Hyundai, are keen to invest in industrial development but in locations close to the border rather than, as the North Koreans suggest, in the far north of the country.

There have always been small-scale incursions into South Korea from the North, sometimes through tunnels dug under the demilitarised zone. Agents are also delivered to the coast by submarines, one of which was caught in a South Korean fisherman's nets in June 1998. Shortly afterwards the body of a North Korean commando was washed ashore. There have also been confrontations at sea and in June 1999 a clash in the disputed sea buffer zone resulted in the sinking of a North Korean torpedo-boat; several ships of both sides were damaged. The North does not recognise the sea demarcation line that curves up to the 38th Parallel from the coastal border and runs between the North Korean coast and the South Korean-held islands of Paengnyong Do.

South Korea has been following a 'sunshine' policy aimed at improving Korean relations; it was therefore displeased by the US's inclusion of North Korea in the so-called axis of evil. Many observers, American and others, feel that Bush has been unfair to North Korea. They point to the differences between North Korea and Iran and Iraq. They say that North Korea is willing and able to abide by international agreements. Bush back-pedalled somewhat during his Asian tour in February 2002, saying he was 'troubled by a regime that tolerated starvation', and remarked that 'we have no intention of invading North Korea'.

A naval clash on 29 June when two North Korean patrol boats crossed the disputed maritime border resulted in one South Korean boat being sunk and four sailors killed. The incident caused a US delegation to cancel its planned visit and halted the South's 'Sunshine' policy. On 25 July the North issued a statement of regret regarding the incident and called for a renewal of the North-South reconciliation talks.

South Korea, although its armed forces are smaller (but better-equipped) than those of the North, fears a surprise attack employing short-range missiles, possibly with chemical and biological warheads, aimed at its capital Seoul and its one million inhabitants. Seoul lies only 50km from the border. With US support South Korea would be able to repulse any Northern attack, but not before suffering large-scale damage and many casualties.

TRAVEL ADVICE
State: Warns US citizens not carry any document that identifies them as citizens of North or South Korea.

BIBLIOGRAPHY AND WEBSITES

Grinker, Roy Richard, *Korea and Its Future: Unification and the Unfinished War*, Macmillan, 1998
Oberclonfer, Don, *The Two Koreas*, Little Brown, 1998

Democratic People's Republic of Korea News Agency: www.kcna.co.jp
South Korean Ministry of Foreign Affairs: www.mofat.go.kr
South Korean Ministry of Reunification: www.uinkorea.go.kr

The Philippines

Population: 77,318,000
Christian 90%, Muslim 5–8%, Chinese 2%
Armed Forces: 107,000
Opposition: MILF 10,000, NPA 9,500, MIRF 900, Abu Sayyaf 1,500
Per Capita GDP: US$ 3,400
Currency: peso

The Philippines are an archipelago of over seven thousand islands lying to the east of the 'Wallace' line (a biogeographical boundary to the east of which the fauna is Australasian and to the west Asian). Before the arrival of the Spanish the region had no central government, nor had it been subject to any external power. Arab traders had reached the Philippines in the thirteenth century and by 1521, when the first Spaniards arrived, Islam was well established in the southern coastal areas of Mindanao and the southern half of Palaawan. The Spanish conquest was complete by 1565 and Catholicism was the national religion; only in the Sultanates of Mindanao and Sulu did Islam remain predominant. A revolutionary movement, Katipunan, headed by Emilio Aguinaldo, was formed in 1896 and demanded independence. During the Spanish–American war the Spanish fleet was sunk in Manila Bay in 1898. The Filipinos declared independence, only to be put down by the US with some 200,000 killed. The islands were ceded to the US by Spain by the Treaty of Paris in exchange for $20 million; a form of self-government was introduced. Armed resistance to the Americans continued for some time after Aguinaldo's arrest in 1901.

The US found the Philippines an expensive burden, and US agricultural interests (because of cheap Filipino imports) and the Federation of Labor (because of cheap immigrant labour) called for Philippine independence. The Commonwealth of the Philippines was established in November 1935 as a first step towards independence, planned for 1944. During the Japanese occupation there was little active resistance and an anti-American movement, Kalibapi, was formed. In an attempt to gain Philippine support the Japanese encouraged

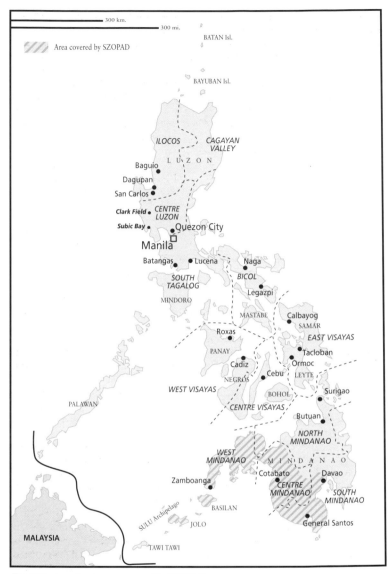

The Philippines showing area covered by SZOPAD

nationalism and the use of native languages (English was the *lingua franca*). Independence was granted in October 1943 but Japanese occupation remained until the islands were liberated in 1944/5.

The Philippines became fully independent in July 1946. The presidential election held in April 1946 was won by the strongly pro-American Manuel Roxas. He managed to assemble the 75 per cent Congressional support needed to alter the constitution to give US citizens parity rights. In 1947 the US was given a 99-year lease for the Subic Bay naval base, Clark Field air base and another twenty-one military installations. Ferdinand Marcos gained power in 1965 and ruled the country until 1986. Military law was in force from 1972 to 1981 on account of insurgency by both communists and Muslim separatists.

The New People's Army (NPA) was the military wing of the banned Communist Party; its guerrilla organisation was based on the Huk movement (a follow-on from the Hukbalahap which had been the most effective resistance movement to the Japanese). It called for land reform and social justice for the peasants, and by 1972 it had taken control of several remote areas and small islands. The Moro National Liberation Front (MNLF), formed in 1968, aimed to achieve independence or autonomy for the Muslim population. Talks between the MNLF and the government took place in Tripoli in December 1976 and led to a cease fire and the establishment of an autonomous region of thirteen provinces in Mindanao, Sulu and Palawan. The cease fire broke down but the autonomous region persisted; the MNLF continued to demand full independence. In 1982 the MNLF broke into three groups: the main MNLF, the Moslem Islamic Liberation Front (MILF) and the Bangsa Moro National Liberation Front (BMNLF). At about the same time the threat from the NPA increased and their armed strength rose from 350 in 1971 to 10,000 in 1981.

In 1981 presidential elections were held, based on popular election rather than being chosen by the National Assembly. There were widespread allegations of fraud nevertheless, as Marcos won re-election with 88 per cent of the vote. An anti-Marcos alliance was formed and Benigno Aquino returned to Manila to help lead it; he was shot as he left the airliner. By 1985 the NPA had increased its strength to 20,000 and had embarked on a campaign of assassinations. In the presidential elections of 1986 the two opposition parties agreed to unite to oppose Marcos's re-election; although Marcos was declared the winner again there had been so many irregularities and widespread election-related violence that the true result was in considerable doubt. Eventually, after strong US pressure, Marcos agreed to step down and left the country via Clark airbase.

Aquino's widow, Corazón, was elected president. She immediately set about restoring human rights, ordering the release of political prisoners, replacing the judiciary and ending press and media censorship. In her first year in office she survived three attempted coups, all involving the armed forces. During the second half of 1986 talks were held with the NPA and its political wing, the New Democratic Front; a cease fire was respected but the talks broke down at the end of January 1987. Talks were also held with the MILF and BMNLF factions of the MNLF who indicated that they would accept full autonomy rather than continue to fight for independence. Another military coup attempt failed in August 1987. NPA activity increased in the wake of the coup attempt, to counter which a growing number of vigilante groups were formed. Talks took place with the Muslim rebels, with various proposals and counter-proposals being made in respect of autonomy for a group of 23 provinces (the Bangsa Moro Autonomous Region), and for groups of ten and 13 provinces.

In 1990 the government agreed to set up the Autonomous Region of Muslim Mindanao (ARRM) as part of its efforts to achieve peace, but only four provinces voted to join the autonomous region. Elections were held in 1996. The government reached agreement with the MNLF in 1996 and proposals to establish the Special Zone of Peace and Development (SZOPAD), which covered fourteen Muslim provinces and ten cities in southern Mindanao, were announced; the MILF continued its campaign to achieve an independent Islamic state. The MILF and the MNLF reached a unity pact in August 2001 and this was followed by the MILF signing in Kuala Lumpur a cease fire agreement brokered principally through Malaysian mediation. President Gloria Arroyo has done much to improve Philippine/Malaysia relations since her election in January 2001. Her immediate policy change, from the hard-line approach of former President Joseph Estrada (who was forced from office and now stands trial for corruption), was to suspend military operations against the MILF and to institute negotiations for a cease fire. In March the government announced a month's cease fire with the NPA in the eleven provinces of Luzon Island. In May Arroyo had to contend with a large-scale violent demonstration by Estrada supporters; termed a 'rebellion' by the government, it was promptly broken up. In November a surprise attack was made by members of the MNLF, in support of their former leader Nur Misuari, on an army base on Jolo Island. Over half the attackers were killed.

The only dissident group still fighting the government is the Abu Sayyaf, which has made a habit of kidnapping non-Philippinos (usually), and demanding ransoms. The group has been designated a terrorist organisation by the US which has sent special forces troops to help train Philippine army units and coordinate their operations against Abu Sayyaf. Abu Sayyaf members operate mainly on Jolo and Basilan Islands. Following the events of 11 September the US sent more special forces troops, backed by Chinook and Pave Hawk helicopters, to assist in the training of anti-terrorist forces on Basilan Island. Abu Sayyaf still held two US hostages but one was killed, the other wounded, in a Filippino rescue operation in June. US withdrawal began in July 2002, leaving some 100 special forces men behind. In August Abu Sayyaf kidnapped eight people on the island of Jolo; two Jehovah's Witnesses were beheaded.

TRAVEL ADVICE

FCO: Strongly advises against travel to Zamboanga, Penin and islands south of Mindanao.
State: avoid Basilan, Tawi-Tawi and Jolo. Defer visits to beach resorts in sothern Philippines Abu Sayyaf has threatened us citizens..

WEBSITES

Manilla Times: www.manillatimes.net
Philippines government: www.govt.ph
Philippines Ministry of Foreign Affairs: www.dfa.gov.ph
Philippines News-Link Online: www.philnews.com

Indonesia

Population: 216,213,000
Javanese 45%, Sudanese 14%, Madurese 8%, Malay 8%, Chinese 3%, Others 22%
Religion: Muslim 87%, Christian 10%, Hindu 2%, Buddhist 1%
Armed Forces: 297,000
Paramilitary: 195,000
Per Capita GDP: $US 4,000
Currency: rupiah

Indonesia is a huge archipelago made up of more than thirteen thousand islands. It stretches over 5,120km from east to west and 1,760km from north to south. There are five main islands: Java (the most dominant throughout modern history), Sumatra, Kalimantan (which is shared with Malaysia and Brunei and was previously known as Borneo), Sulawesi (originally called the Celebes) and Irian Jaya (shared with Papua New Guinea and earlier known as New Guinea). The population of over 200 million is divided ethnically, by religion and by language. There are some three hundred different ethnic groups in the population. The majority of Indonesians are Muslim and most provinces have Muslim majorities, the exceptions being Bali, which is overwhelmingly Hindu, and Irian Jaya, Nusa Tenggara Timur and Timor Timur (East Timor), which have large Christian majorities. There are roughly 70 million Javanese speakers, 25 million Sundanese and 10 million Malay; 13 other languages, out of the total of 669, are each spoken by over one million people. The national language is Bahasa Indonesian and is spoken by about 6.7 million. In addition some 2 million speak one of the Chinese dialects.

The Indonesian peoples belong to a wider Indo-Malayan grouping that includes the Filipinos and Malays. From about 500 BC to AD 500 Indonesian contacts were primarily with south and east Asia. Only small indigenous coastal states existed at this time. Trade with India introduced both Hinduism and Mahayana Buddhism into the region and an element of Indian culture was acquired. The region became more organised and larger states were formed, such as Srivijaya, for example, which emanated from Palembang and gained suzerainty over most of Sumatra, western Java and the Malay peninsula. Although trade with Muslim Arabs started much earlier, conversion to Islam began only in the late thirteenth century and spread slowly throughout the archipelago until some 87 per cent of the population were Muslim by the late twentieth century. Pockets of earlier religions held out and in the east of the archipelago there was strong competition from Portuguese priests.

The Portuguese were the first Europeans to come to Indonesia, and in the early sixteenth century they established a chain of trading posts from Arabia to Japan, with the intention of wresting the lucrative spice trade from the Muslims and the Venetians. The Dutch arrived in 1596. In 1602 the Dutch East India Company (Vereenigde Oost-Indische Compagnie or VOC) was formed and the Dutch colonisation of the archipelago began. The VOC was terminated in 1816 and replaced by the Netherlands Indies government. The Treaty of London in 1824 agreed that the Malay peninsula should be a British sphere of influence and Sumatra a Dutch one; it also provided for the continued independence of Aceh at the western end of Sumatra. However, the Dutch occupied this area after a long and bloody war between 1873 and 1903. In 1840 the British established themselves in North Borneo. This alarmed the Dutch who began to colonise the eastern part of the archipelago but this was not completed until the early twentieth century. Gowa and Bone were only conquered in 1906, Bali in 1908 and the western half of New Guinea after the First World War. Dutch colonisation established the future borders of Indonesia.

Indonesian indigenous political movements started to form in the early twentieth century. In 1928 Achmad Sukarno and others founded the Indonesian Nationalist Party (PNI) which had independence as its goal; he was arrested in December 1929 and sent to prison. His party was dissolved in 1931 and its successor, the Indonesia Party, which Sukarno joined, was suppressed by the Dutch and also dissolved.

The Dutch Indies supplied Japan with 25 per cent of its oil requirements but in 1941 it followed the US in imposing an oil embargo, thus precipitating the Japanese invasion. The Dutch surrendered on 9 March 1942 offering no resistance, after the Allied Fleet had been defeated in the Battle of the Java Sea. With the Dutch administrators and business community imprisoned, Indonesians were given the opportunity to join the Japanese administration and a number of paramilitary forces that were formed. Sukarno cooperated with the Japanese. Towards the end of the war the Japanese realised that the archipelago would become independent and in March 1945 a committee was formed in an attempt to include East Timor, Borneo and Malaya in the new state – this was the forerunner of Sukarno's Greater Indonesia policy.

Japan surrendered on 15 August 1945 and Sukarno declared Indonesia's independence on the 17th. The Dutch were determined to regain their colony but were in no state to impose their authority. The main priorities of the Allied troops sent to Indonesia was to disarm and send home Japanese forces and to free European prisoners; they were less interested in Indonesia's future but the Indonesians, believing that the Allies would attempt to reinstate the Dutch, hastened to take control, sometimes assisted by the Japanese who handed over weapons to the paramilitary groups they had formed. These later became the basis for the Indonesian army. During 1946 and early 1947 the Dutch negotiated the future of the archipelago, planning to establish a republic in Java and Sumatra and a Netherlands–Indonesian Union elsewhere; an agreement that pleased neither side was signed in May. The Dutch then attacked and managed to regain Sumatra and all of Java bar the Yogyakarta region; the UN sponsored negotiations and both sides agreed to a referendum being held in the areas retaken by the Dutch. The Indonesian Communist Party took a hand but was defeated by the republicans, who were now seen by the US as anti-communist and not communist-inspired as the Dutch claimed. The Dutch then captured Yogyakarta but they had lost the support of the international community and were forced

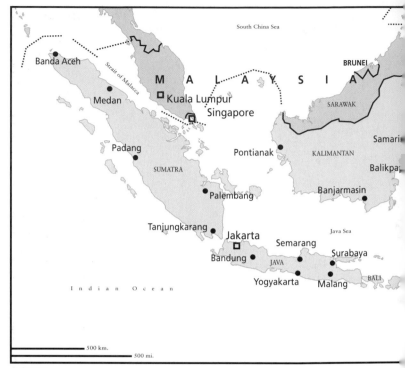

Indonesia

to give Indonesia its independence as the Republic of the United States of Indonesia (RUSI) on 27 December 1949. By May 1950 all the federal states had been incorporated into the Republic of Indonesia. Only West New Guinea remained under Dutch control with East Timor under the Portuguese.

General Suharto took charge after an abortive coup against Sukarno was put down in 1965. This was followed by a purge of suspected communists in which as many as half a million people may have died. Suharto became president in 1967 and remained in power until 21 May 1998. His downfall, only two months after he had been re-elected for a seventh term, resulted from a combination of financial crisis, large-scale unemployment and starvation in some areas. Rioting and looting broke out in Jakarta. Army troops were sent in but they were cheered by the rioters and simply stood by while the looting continued. Demonstrations by students took place across the country, the largest being in Jakarta. Much of the looting was at the expense of the Chinese community. After Suharto had been forced out of office, the vice-president, B.J. Habibie, was installed as an interim president until democratic elections could be held.

Political reform in Jakarta encouraged separatists and Indonesia faces revolt or ethnic violence in a number of provinces. The Free Papua Movement was formed in Irian Jaya in the 1970s, and it claims that since then some 42,000 have died in military operations against it. The independence movement in Aceh is the Gerakan Aceh Merdaka, and over 2,000 were killed there in army repression between 1989 and 1992. Following the publication of a report by Amnesty International and Human Rights Watch on army atrocities in Aceh the president apologised and ordered the army to withdraw. The withdrawal was halted in September 1998 when looting of Chinese shops broke out. Since then there have been further attacks against the army. In December violence broke out in widely separated centres, notably in Sumatra, Sulawesi and in Kupang in West Timor where Christians burned

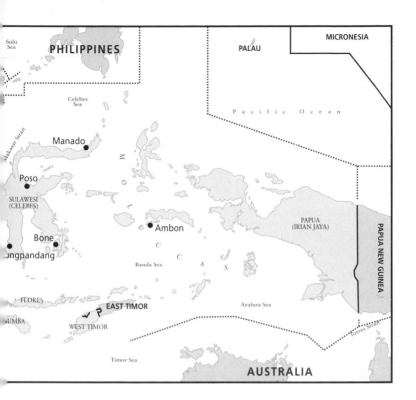

four mosques in retaliation for the burning of over twenty churches in Jakarta in November. In West Kalimantan in February and March 1999 the indigenous Dayaks and Malays attacked Madurese settlers, who have been setting up farms there since the 1970s, leaving ninety dead and several thousand refugees; however, there is no independence movement in Kalimantan. In Ambon, capital of the eastern island province of Maluku, often referred to as the Spice or Molucca Islands, there have been clashes between Christians and Muslims since January 1999. In April 1999 there were Christian/Muslim clashes in Jakarta.

An election was held on 7 June 1999. The army declared its neutrality, and the first genuine, and surprisingly peaceful, vote since 1955 took place. Counting was slow but at the end Megawati Sukarnoputri and the Indonesian Democratic Party had 34 per cent of the vote to the 21 per cent of Habibie's political alliance, Golkar. It was not at all certain that Megawati would be the next president; both elected and nominated members of the parliament choose the president. Recent events in East Timor raised the spectre of another military take-over. In the event Abdurrahman Wahid, a respected Muslim scholar, was elected president and he chose Megawati as his vice-president.

Violence continued throughout 2000 in Aceh, Irian Jaya and the Moluccas. A wave of coordinated attacks on Christian churches on Christmas Eve was seen as an attempt to provoke the Christian minority into retaliation. Ethnic violence broke out in Kalimantan when Dayaks attacked Madurese and destroyed their homes; over five hundred people died, most of them hacked to death by machetes. Several thousand had to be evacuated by sea.

A political crisis developed in 2001 as dissatisfaction with President Wahid grew. He was censured by parliament over two financial scandals. Neither the army nor the police were prepared to support Wahid as he faced impeachment; in an effort to stay in power he tried to declare a state of emergency and to suspend parliament. Finally he left Indonesia on 26

July 2001 and Megawati Sukarnoputri assumed the presidency without the violence that had been predicted.

In October Irian Jaya received greater autonomy, was granted the province to be called Papua and permitted to receive 70 per cent of the proceeds from its oil and gas production. After 11 September attention was turned to Indonesia's Islamic militia, Laskar Jihad, which was formed in January 2000 to fight Christians in the Moluccas. Since then it has sent fighters to the Poso region of Sulawesi where it claimed the security forces had failed to protect Muslims from Christian attack. Neither Laskar Jihad nor another Islamic militia, Jemaah Islamiyah, has been designated a terrorist organisation by the US.

TRAVEL ADVICE

FCO: Advises against all travel to West Timor, Ambon and Maluku, Poso in Sulewsi and Aceh.
State: Advises against all travel to Aceh, Irian Jaya, Maluku, West Timor, central and west Kalimantan, central and south Suluwesi. STOP PRESS: Post 12 October. FCO and State advise against all travel to Indonesia. The threat to British and US nationals remains high.

BIBLIOGRAPHY AND WEBSITES

Huxley, Tim, 'Disintegrating Indonesia? Implications for Regional Study', IISS Adelphi Paper 349, 2002
Indonesia: A Country Study, Federal Research Division, Library of Congress, 1993

Indonesian Department of Foreign Affairs: www.dfa-deplu.go.id
Inside Indonesia: www.insideindonesia.org
Jakarta Post: www.thejakartapost.com
Tempo: www.tempo.co.id

East Timor

Population: 800,000 + 122,000 refugees in West Timor
Armed Forces: 1,500 under training
Foreign Forces: UNTAET 8,200

The first Portuguese conquest in the Far East was of Malacca in 1511. From there they developed contacts with the sources of spices at Amboina and Ternate where they built and occupied fortresses until they were driven out in 1575. Portuguese traders first visited Timor in 1514, where they traded for sandalwood. Dominican priests came in 1561 and set up a mission that successfully introduced Christianity. In 1602 the Dutch East India Company sent an expedition to the Moluccas, which captured Tidore but made no attempt to take Timor and Solor. By 1640, when Portugal had recovered its independence, the resistance of the Timorese and their priests had driven the Dutch from the north-east of the island.. In 1859 the Dutch ceded the eastern part of the island to Portugal. By the beginning of the twentieth century Timor was prosperous, most Timorese were Christians and they spoke a different language from their neighbours in Java and Bali.

Elsewhere in what is now Indonesia the Dutch had established colonies on the main islands and had captured Malacca from the Portuguese. In 1824 under the terms of the Anglo-Dutch Treaty the British withdrew from their colonies in Sumatra and the Dutch handed over Malacca and their remaining interests in India. In 1913 Portugal and the Netherlands agreed to split the island of Timor between them. During the Second World War the Japanese occupied the whole archipelago and later, after the Japanese surrender, their troops were employed by the British to help maintain law and order. The Portuguese recovered East Timor. In 1974 the Portuguese army took over government and embarked on a programme of decolonisation. In Timor the Timorese Democratic Union (UDT) called for self-determination but federation with Portugal before independence. The other main political party, with a much younger membership, was the Timorese Social Democratic Association

(ASDT); it called for gradual independence and then only after administrative, economic, social and political reform. There was also a pro-Indonesian party, Apodeti. The Indonesians were already planning to absorb East Timor, preferably without using force, and they were encouraged by the views of Gough Whitlam, the Australian prime minister who considered that an independent East Timor would not be viable and could destabilise the region.

In September 1974 the ASDT held a conference at which, taking into account the growing demand for independence and following the examples of the independence movements in Angola and Mozambique, it changed both its name and objectives. The new Frente Revolucionara do Timor Leste Independente (FRETILIN) was prepared to fight for independence. In October an Indonesian delegation to Portugal convinced the government that the only viable future for East Timor was integration with Indonesia or self-government under Portugal; it argued that independence was not an option. The Portuguese sent a new governor to oversee the process of decolonisation. On arrival he found that his predecessor believed the colony was to be integrated with Indonesia. There also appeared to be differences of opinion over East Timor's future under the new regime in Portugal.

A coalition of FRETILIN and the UDT was formed in January 1975 and called for a government in which FRETILIN, UDT and the Portuguese government would be equally represented and which would last for three years before independence. The Indonesians increased their claims that Apodeti was being persecuted and built up their forces in West Timor; they also began a campaign to win over the UDT by stressing the leftward movement of politics in Timor. FRETILIN demonstrated its growing popularity with large majorities in local elections. The Portuguese held talks with the coalition on transforming the administration into a transitional government; Apodeti refused to attend the talks. The UDT had now become apprehensive of FRETILIN's strength and in May announced that it was leaving the coalition.

The Portuguese then held a conference in Macao intended for all parties to discuss decolonisation; FRETILIN would not attend the event, which went ahead without it. Apodeti was able to show that it was a viable political party and the UDT had its view of FRETILIN as a Marxist organisation confirmed. The Indonesians stepped up their propaganda campaign. In August, after two days of UDT demonstrations in Dili, they took over the police station and arrested FRETILIN supporters there and in other towns; there were rumours of executions. FRETILIN supporters were handed the keys of the armoury in Dili and, with the assistance of two army garrisons, attacked the UDT. By 27 August they had gained control of Dili and driven the UDT forces westwards. Some 500 soldiers and 2,500

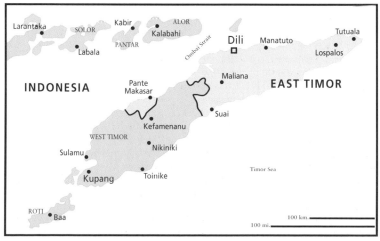

East Timor

refugees crossed into Indonesian Timor on 24 September and were forced to sign a petition calling for integration with Indonesia.

Indonesia now began a series of incursions, mainly with special forces, some disguised as UDT soldiers; these operations provoked little complaint either from the Portuguese or from the Australians and the US. Indonesia next mounted an amphibious attack on Atabae, which they captured on 27 November; FRETILIN appealed to the UN. On the 28th the FRETILIN administration proclaimed the independence of the Democratic Republic of East Timor. In early December President Gerald Ford visited Indonesia, and the invasion of East Timor was delayed until he had left. In 1976 Indonesia annexed East Timor, a move that was recognised only by Australia and not by any other country nor by the UN.

In late 1978 the FRETILIN leader Nicolau Lobato was killed by troops. He was succeeded by Xanana Gusmão, who was arrested in 1992 and sentenced to twenty years' imprisonment. He was released from jail in September 1999. East Timor's campaign for independence gained momentum with the award of the Nobel Peace Prize to Jose Ramos-Horta, an independence campaigner, and Carlos Felipe Ximenes Belo, Bishop of Dili. In June 1998 the new Indonesian government announced that it would give East Timor special status with a large degree of autonomy. Talks between Portugal and Indonesia under the auspices of the UN began in October. The Indonesian army opposed the granting of independence and helped to form and arm a pro-integration with Indonesia militia. In January 1999 Indonesia said it was prepared to grant independence if autonomy was rejected. Gusmão, who had been transferred from prison to house arrest, authorised the resumption of the insurrection on 5 April after the integrationist militia killed seventeen people. The next two weeks witnessed further atrocities. An autonomy proposal was agreed and a UN monitoring mission was sent to supervise the referendum vote. Violence broke out again in the days before the vote, which was delayed by the UN until 30 August. The election was declared as fair and free and when the result was announced on 4 September 78 per cent of East Timorese had voted for independence. Even before the results were known the militias turned against the UN staff and a number were killed. The result of the vote brought a much-increased scale of violence, supported by the Indonesian forces in East Timor. Reinforcements were dispatched but they were unable or unwilling to prevent the militias from causing several hundred thousand refugees to flee either into the hills and jungle or over the border into West Timor. Many still remain there.

On 12 September Indonesia's President Habibie agreed to accept an international peacekeeping force and the UN mandated this on the 15th. Indonesian forces began to withdraw and the first elements of the peacekeeping force, provided mainly by Australia, began to deploy on the 20th. The world's press criticised the peace plan as too little and much too late. This is somewhat unfair and, thanks to Australian planning and preparation, the force was able to move swiftly once the UN had approved the deployment. A deployment *before* the referendum result was announced might have prevented the violence, the destruction of most of Dili and the refugee crisis, but at that stage there was no willingness on Indonesia's part to accept foreign troops on what it saw as its soil.

The UN has replaced the Australian-led peacekeeping force with the UN Transitional Authority in East Timor (UNTAET), which has the task of creating new institutions – a defence force, a police force, a judiciary and all the elements of government – as well as assisting with the reconstruction of the country following the widespread destruction caused by the integrationist militia. It estimates that the task will take at least three years and that between $260 and $300 million would be needed to rebuild the country and to establish a health service and education. An election was held on 30 August 2001 and East Timor became fully independent on 20 May 2002.

TRAVEL ADVICE
FCO: Advise against all holiday and non-essential travel.
State: Take appropriate precautions and exercise caution.

Latin America

Some twenty years ago this section would have contained three times as many items as it does now. At that time it was the most dangerous continent in the world, its nations ruled by military dictators or juntas either at war with one another or struggling with a civil war. There was a nuclear arms race between Argentina and Brazil; both countries have now renounced their nuclear weapons and their missile programmes. Border disputes involved Chile and Argentina, and Peru and Ecuador. Civil wars were tearing apart Guatemala, Nicaragua and El Salvador; all are now over after the UN supervised disarmament. Honduras was threatening Belize and Argentina invaded the Falklands. In 1999 the US and eighteen other Central and South American countries signed the Inter-American Convention on Transparency in Conventional Weapon Acquisitions. The Convention requires annual reports of all arms imports and exports.

A number of civil wars still continue in Mexico, Colombia and Peru, and these are detailed below. Haiti is still a dangerous place to visit. Argentina has not given up its claim to the Falklands so that topic is still included. In April 2002 there was a military coup in Venezuela and President Hugo Chavez was arrested; the coup did not last long as paratroops loyal to Chavez restored him to power within a couple of days.

Mexico

Population: 100,564,000 (Chiapas Province 4%)
Armed Forces: 193,000
Paramilitary: 11,000
Opposition Forces: strengths not known – Zapatista National Liberation Army (ZNLA), Popular Insurgent Revolutionary Army (EPR), Mexican Peasant Workers' Front of the South-East, Popular Movement of National Liberation, Revolutionary Insurgent Army of the South-East (EPRI)
Per Capita GDP: $US 8,800
Currency: new peso

A number of problems face the Mexican government. The longest-standing one is the revolt by the Zapatistas in Chiapas Province, but several other terrorist opposition groups have also been formed. Mexico is the principal route into the US for drugs from Colombia and there is an ever-growing movement of Mexican workers into the US, in some instances encouraged by US firms.

The province of Chiapas was originally populated by Mayans, one of the pre-Spanish civilisations of Central and South America. Today about a million Mayan Indians live in Chiapas Province, the poorest in Mexico, which is separated from the rest of the country by mountains and the Lacandon Forest. It was conquered by the Spanish between 1524 and 1527 and was then part of Guatemala. The diseases brought by the Spanish decimated the indigenous population except in the cooler highlands. Dominican monks who followed the conquest were instrumental in ending slavery and gaining permission

Mexico showing Chiapas and poppy cultivation

for the Mayans to control their own community affairs. Chiapas became a province of Mexico in 1824.

Throughout the last decades of the nineteenth century the number of private estates in Chiapas steadily increased, from about 1,000 in 1880 to 6,800 in 1909, all established at the expense of the Indian community. The counter-revolution that began in 1911 was set off by the government's decision to abolish debt servitude and grant workers the right to a minimum wage; this was violently opposed by the landowners. They managed to coerce the Indians into joining their private armies but they were defeated. When Alberto Pineda reorganised these armies in 1915 the Indians did not support him and by 1917 they had joined the government forces. They retook their communal lands as the plantation owners were forced out. Unfortunately, Pineda managed to defeat the army and by 1920 Chiapas had regained its autonomy under the landowners and labour reform was halted.

In the 1960s there was widespread clearing of the rainforest to provide more land for farming and to ease the problem of overpopulation. Thousands of acres were deforested. However, the farming methods used elsewhere in Mexico proved unsuitable for this area; after only a few harvests the farms collapsed and the land fell into the hands of the old established owners of large estates. The Mayan peasants once again became impoverished labourers.

Armed rebellion in Chiapas broke out in January 1994 when Indian peasants seized four towns and six villages and kidnapped the state governor. The rebels were led by the Zapatista National Liberation Army (Ejercito Zapatista Liberacion Nacional). The name is derived from the hero of the Mexican revolution of 1911–15, Emiliano Zapata, whose aim was to recover communal land for the peasants from the rich landowners. The ZNLA was formed in 1983 after the violent eviction of three peasant communities from the Lacandon Forest; it was a self-defence force rather than a revolutionary one. By 1986 it still had only twelve members but recruiting in 1988 and 1989 brought numbers up to about 1,300 and arms began to be obtained secretly. It is still not clear to what extent the ZNLA owes its origins to other revolutionaries from northern and central Mexico, nor how much it is supported by Mexican volunteers who fought in Nicaragua's and El Salvador's civil wars, as the government claims. The ZNLA is primarily a Mayan peasant force. The rebellion that began in 1994 was prompted by a combination of human rights abuses, failure to bring in adequate land reform and the effect on the many small farmers of the 50 per cent drop in world coffee prices.

The Mexican army swiftly recovered the six captured towns. ZNLA forces melted away into the forests and their leaders intimated that they were ready for negotiations. The government initially over-reacted and committed acts of indiscriminate violence. It also violated human rights, executing suspects and employing torture during interrogation. However, it quickly showed that it too was ready to negotiate. The Zapatistas' demands included the relief of peasant poverty, an end to racism and the introduction of democracy throughout Mexico. They have promised to continue the war until their demands are met, and indeed have done so.

The August 1994 election replaced the authoritarian President Carlos Salinas with Ernesto Zedillo, who is more committed to political and economic reform. In February 1995 the army entered Chiapas in strength with the aim of capturing the ZNLA leader, known as sub-commandante Marcos. (He is now thought to be Rafael Guillén Vicente, who had taken part in the Sandanista uprising and had had military training in the Soviet Union.) The ultimate intention was the crushing of the revolution. As before, the ZNLA did not stay to fight an obviously superior force but retired into the mountains. Marcos's main aim, to gain worldwide publicity and sympathy for the cause, was achieved. A military zone was established. Talks between the ZNLA and the government were held between April and July 1995 without agreement being reached. However, some progress was made: extra funds were allocated to the region and a food distribution programme for children was to be set up. In February 1996, after a further six months of negotiation, an agreement covering the rights of indigenous natives was signed, although other issues concerning land, democracy and justice remained unresolved.

In September 1996 the Zapatistas, claiming that the government had not followed the agreed agenda, refused to attend further talks. In fact it was the emergence of another revolutionary party, the Ejercito Popular Revolucionario (EPR) that led to the change of tactics. The EPR was formed in Guerrero Province. It has similar aims to those of the ZNLA but is considered to be a more terrorist-oriented organisation. Its first round of attacks in August 1996 took place against army and police posts in four provinces. The EPRI also operates in Guerrero and Oaxaca. A further problem for the Mexican government was the discovery that General Gutiérrez, the officer in charge of anti-drug enforcement, had been collaborating with drug traffickers responsible for the transit of 70 per cent of the cocaine that reaches the US through Mexico. Two other senior army generals were also imprisoned in September 2000 for drug trafficking offences.

During his election campaign Vincente Fox, who replaced Ernesto Zedillo as president in December 2000, claimed he could solve the Zapatista problem in fifteen minutes. Zapatista leader Marcos took him at his word and announced that he would march to Mexico City to hold peace talks. When the Zapatistas reached Mexico City and addressed the Congress on 28 March Marcos did not take part; Fox's National Action Party had voted not to allow the address to take place while the opposition Institutional Revolutionary Party voted in favour. Congress approved a constitutional change to give Indian peoples special rights but the change had been watered down and did not give the Indian communities autonomy or 'the collective use and enjoyment' of the land that they had sought.

TRAVEL ADVICE

FCO: Risk of robbery in Guerrero, Oaxaca and Chiapas. There is still tension in north and central Chiapas.

State: Exercise caution in Chiapas. The EPR and EPRI operate in Guerrero and Oaxaca. There is tension and violence in San Cristobel de Las Casas, Ocosingo Muni and the jungle part of the province east of Comitan. Violent crime levels are high.

BIBLIOGRAPHY AND WEBSITE

Harvey, Neil, *The Chiapas Rebellion: The Struggle for Land and Democracy*, Duke University Press, 1998

Mexican Presidency: www.presidencia.gob.mx/welcome

Colombia

Population: 42,400,00
Armed Forces: 153,000
National Police: 95,000
Non-Government, right-wing Paramilitary: AUC ±5,000
Opposition: Revolutionary Armed Forces of Colombia (FARC) 17,000, National Liberation Army 5,000 (ELN), People's Liberation Army (EPL) 500.
Per Capita GDP: US$ 5,800
Currency: Colombian peso

For many years Colombia has been one of the most dangerous countries in the world. The Spanish conquered the Chibcha Indians in the sixteenth century and Colombia formed part of the colony of New Granada, which also contained Panama and most of Venezuela. The problems caused by its large area and the distance between centres of population meant that central government was hard to exercise and vast estates had a high degree of independence. Government was corrupt, inefficient and abusive, just as it was in most of the world at that time. These conditions led to a tradition of violence caused not by the government, as elsewhere in Latin America, but by a lack of it. In 1819 Ecuador was added to the colony and its name was changed to Gran Colombia; it became independent under Simón Bolivar. Ecuador and Colombia split in 1830. Little was done to create a strong administration: Colombia's leaders had witnessed other new states losing their democracy to powerful institutions such as the army, nor did they want to pay the high taxes needed to develop a national army and police force. They preferred to provide their own security. Leadership was divided between anti-church radicals and defenders of the faith who became Liberals and Conservatives respectively.

After independence from Spain in 1819, the country suffered seven civil wars between the Liberal and Conservative factions; the last took place between 1899 and 1902 which the Conservatives won. The next forty-five years were peaceful. The Liberals gained power in the 1930 elections when the Conservatives were split. Violence re-emerged in 1946 when the reunited Conservatives regained power. There followed ten years of near civil war between Liberal/left-wing guerrilla groups, infiltrated to some extent by communists, and Conservative militias formed to protect themselves and to retaliate. Some 250,000 people are thought to have died during 'La Violencia'.

In 1958 the political parties joined to share government through the National Front constitution which required the presidency to alternate between Liberals and Conservatives and for the two parties to share posts in the bureaucracy and legislature. The military assumed the leading role in ending La Violencia; it received US aid and training and trebled in size in twenty years. The power of the army grew and it was authorised to try suspected guerrillas. The military was involved in anti-drug operations but that led to corruption. Officers were bribed and the US funds given to aid the campaign against drugs were spent instead on the war with the guerrillas.

The formation of the four guerrilla groups stems from the final years of La Violencia. The first to be formed, in 1962, was the pro-Castro Army of National Liberation (Ejército Liberación Nacional, ELN), composed mainly of university students. Next, in 1966, the Communist Armed Forces of the Colombian Revolution (Fuerzas Armadas de la Revolución Colombiana, FARC) was formed. A pro-Chinese group, the People's Liberation Army (Ejército Popular de Liberación, EPL) was founded in 1974. The best-known guerrilla movement was M-19 (Movimiento 19 de Abril), which first appeared in 1974; it was formed from factions of both the FARC and the political National Popular Alliance of which it claimed to be the military wing. The Liberal president ended the National Front arrangements in 1986.

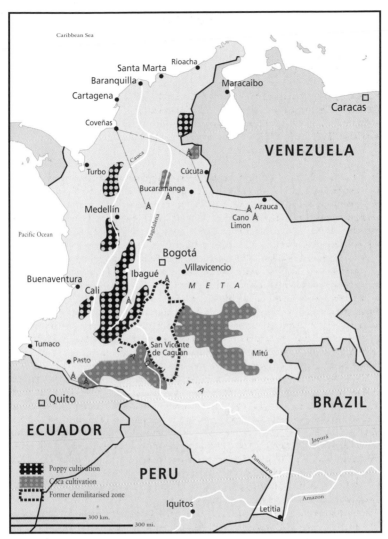

Colombia showing poppy and coca cultivation

In addition to the guerrilla problem Colombia has had to contend with a large-scale drug industry. The production of marijuana escalated following the major campaign launched against drug trafficking in Mexico in 1975. In addition to processing its own coca crop, Colombia also refines and exports most of the coca grown in Peru and Bolivia. The Colombian drug-barons accumulated massive wealth and power and were seemingly above the law. They even formed their own paramilitary groups. The attorney-general, who favoured extradition for trial in the US, was assassinated in 1988, as were more than fifty judges over a three-year period. Two cartels, the Cali and the Medelin, whose rivalry has added to the Colombian death rate, dominated the drug trade. The cartels have subsidised guerrilla groups but the tendency of the FARC to kidnap leading drug-traffickers and hold them for ransom led to fighting between the two organisations.

Threatened by both guerrillas and drug cartels, it is not surprising that a number of self-defence paramilitary groups were formed to provide some protection for business concerns and peasant communities. The army created a number of special units to combat the guerrillas, employing the same vicious tactics, and this led inevitably to human rights abuses, torture and illegal killing.

In 2000 a form of peace process evolved. It was driven by the increasing strength and capability of FARC and the ELN, which specialises in harassing the activities of foreign oil companies, and by the general weariness of the people after so many years of civil conflict. President Pastrana agreed to the establishment of a zone from which all army and police were withdrawn, leaving FARC in complete control. FARC also wants the disbandment of the paramilitary groups who are now more centrally organised. They oppose negotiations with the guerrillas and intend to continue to fight them. The government appears unable, or unwilling, to counter the activities of the paramilitary groups, now known as the United Self-Defence Forces of Colombia (AUC).

In June 2001 the FARC released over 300 prisoners, some of whom had been held for over three years; in return 15 FARC guerrillas were released. However, this exchange did not lead to a cease fire. Only two weeks earlier the FARC had killed 30 soldiers and the next week released all the prisoners from a Bogota jail. While peace talks have continued so has FARC's campaign of kidnap and extortion. At the end of 2001 and in early 2002 the peace process was off, then on, then off again until FARC dropped its demand for an end to the increased army surveillance around its haven and agreed to the resumption of peace talks. However, in February FARC killed over 40 people, set-off a number of car-bombs and destroyed more than 50 electricity pylons. Peace was finally off the agenda when President Andres Pastrana's patience ran out and he ordered the army to attack FARC's safe haven area. The air force flew some 200 sorties against FARC camps. FARC withdrew from the haven's five towns as the army began its advance.

A separate war and attempts to hold peace talks has been going on with the ELN. Its supporters were offered their own safe haven but this was never implemented. The ELN announced a unilateral truce in December 2001 after holding talks with the government in Cuba. The US has designated FARC, ELN and AUC as foreign terrorist organisations.

A third war involving the US is that against drugs under the Plan Colombia programme launched in 1999. The US provided $1.3 billion, mostly in military aid but also in cash to compensate farmers who stop growing coca and to improve human rights. The US is attempting to keep its aid separate from the cost of the civil war and is restricting its training and re-equipping programmes to anti-drug units. Of course, restricting drug-related activity automatically reduces the funds available to the rebel guerrillas.

A more worrying factor is the possibility of the insurgency spreading to Colombia's neighbours. Panama, Ecuador and Venezuela have been used as both safe havens and training grounds for FARC and as refuges for Colombians attempting to escape the fighting. Colombia processes most of Peru's coca crop, while Panama is an essential link in the smuggling out of cocaine and the smuggling in of arms for FARC. The worst-case scenario is a return to a New Granada or Gran Colombia run by drug-barons.

The May 2002 presidential election was won by Alvaro Uribe with 53 per cent of the vote. Uribe is giving priority to restoring law and order and has invited the UN to investigate the possibility of new peace talks once rebel hostilities are ended. FARC have also offered new talks but only if they are given control of a much larger area (the provinces of Caqueta and Putumayo, where 40 per cent of the drug crop is produced). In July 2002 the AUC announced it was being disbanded as the organisation had been infiltrated by both drug traffickers and anarchists and had lost control of some elements. Some see the move as an attempt by AUC leaders to become the government. Uribe was sworn-in on 7 August as FARC launched a mortar attack on his palace, killing 21 people; he declared a state of emergency on the 12th.

FCO: Advise against all travel to Choco, Putamayo, Meta and Caqueta provinces and to rural areas of Antiquia, Cauca, Narino and Nove de Santader..

State : Warns against travel. US citizens are targeted in response to the drug eradication programme. People were kidnapped in 2001.

BIBLIOGRAPHY AND WEBSITES

Kline, Harvey F., *State Building and Conflict Resolution in Colombia, 1986–1994*, University of Alabama Press, 1999

Maullin, Richard, *Soldiers, Guerrillas and Politics in Colombia*, Lexington, 1973

Safford, Frank and Palacios, Marco, *Colombia: Fragmented Land*, Divided Society, Oxford University Press, 2002

Amnesty International: www.amnesty.org/ailib/countries
Colombian Ministry of Foreign Affairs: www.minrelext.gov.co.english
US Drug Enforcement Agency: www.usdoj.gov/dea

Peru

Population: 26,058,000
Armed Forces: 1,000,000
Opposition: Sendero Luminoso (Shining Path) ±1,000
MRTA ±600
Per Capita GDP: $US 4,700
Currency: new sol

The first act of violence committed by the 'Sendero Luminoso', or 'Shining Path' (officially the Communist Party of Peru) was the burning of the registry and ballot boxes at the electoral registration office in Chuschi on 17 May 1980. The Shining Path was formed in 1969 in the Ayacucho Department; its founder leader was a philosophy professor, Manuel Ruben Abimael Guzman. It was a rural organisation whose aim was to restore the traditions of the Quechua Indians using Maoist and Marxist principles; it employed assassination and mutilation of victims to increase the terror effect of its operations. Although the Shining Path advocates a rural, peasant revolution it is led by middle class intellectuals who employ indoctrination, particularly of the young (12–15-year-olds), in their recruiting and motivation practices.

The Shining Path originated in Huamanga University as an elitist group but it soon spread throughout the educational system to both urban secondary and village single-class schools. Its strategy is based on the uniqueness of the Andean environment, with its three ecological floors at different altitudes. The Andes have always been a refuge for the underprivileged and half of Peru's population lives there, existing on labour-intensive farming. The region is of little importance to the government, which has not made the investment needed to maintain effective control. It is an ideal area for a patient communist organisation with very long-term aims. The Shining Path exploits the disparities between the lives of the urban and rural populations, exemplified by the difference in prices with as much as a 200 per cent mark-up in some Andean markets. Land ownership has long been a source of peasant anger. First the best land was in the hands of the hacienda owners. They were then replaced by the cooperatives which, in their turn, were broken up. Subsequent land redistribution was both arbitrary and chaotic: it favoured neither local communities nor the landless peasants.

The Shining Path has made widespread use of violence both to intimidate the peasant population and to undermine government efforts. It aims to disorganise politics and create

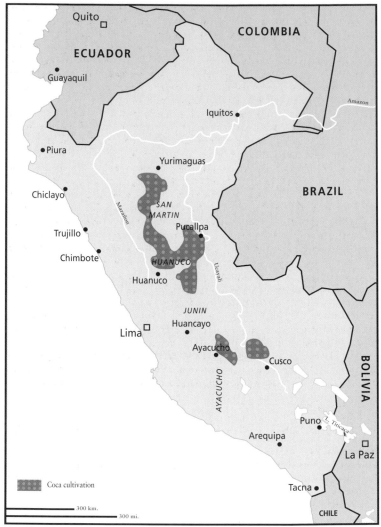

Peru showing coca cultivation

a vacuum by murdering the most unpopular and persuading the most respected to leave. The Shining Path has both an authoritarian and a cell structure, making it hard to infiltrate.

The Andes and the Amazon jungle form the base for Shining Path operations. It is a large area, some 1,200 by 320km, over which the government cannot maintain law and order. From it the Shining Path can strike west to the Pacific coast. The organisation has survived as a terrorist/guerrilla organisation because of its ideology, and through its use of violence both to ensure loyalty and to disrupt any form of authority. Its alliance with the drug cartels has provided much of its finance. It has never been strong enough to win the war against the government but has been content to wait until corruption in authority destroys itself.

In September 1993, from his prison cell, Guzman called on his followers to abandon the armed struggle and turn to political activity. There followed a period of reduced terrorist attack and several thousand guerrillas surrendered in response to President Fujimori's

'Repentance Law'. Estimates vary between 25,000 and 30,000 for the number who died during the fifteen-year-long civil war. The tactics adopted by the army to counter the guerrillas were as brutal as those of the rebels and many of the casualties were the innocent caught between the two. Fujimori's suspension of the Congress and the introduction of 'faceless judges' to try terrorists removed most of the restraints on army activity. The US found it hard to support anti-drug operations while condemning the human rights abuses of the counter-guerrilla war. At roughly the same time, US and Peruvian government efforts to eliminate the drug trade – from which the Shining Path acquired much of its finance – had a high degree of success. The rate of production dropped dramatically – some 65,000 hectares, about 56 per cent of the total, being eradicated – while the air force shot down any aircraft suspected of drug-trafficking. But the Shining Path, though much reduced in size, did not give up completely and in 1996 there was a resurgence of terrorist attacks against government targets. The movement's current leader, Oscar Ramirez Durand, was arrested on 14 July 1999. Though this was a major blow to the organisation, the Shining Path is not expected to collapse. However, its strength, probably about a thousand fighters, is much reduced from the ten thousand it had in the early 1990s.

The Shining Path is not the only rebel movement the government has to contend with. The Tupac Amaru Revolutionary Movement (MRTA) is a smaller and less vicious organisation than the Shining Path. It began its campaign of terrorism in 1984 by attacking targets that would gain them maximum publicity, such as the US Embassy and American business interests. They probably numbered some three thousand guerrillas in the mid-1980s. They inevitably clashed with the Shining Path over the sharing of drug-trafficking profits. MRTAs boldest moment came on 17 December 1996 when it managed to take control of the Japanese ambassador's compound while a diplomatic cocktail party was in progress. The seventy-two remaining hostages were freed in an assault made on 21 April 1997 in which all fourteen terrorists were killed, along with one hostage. MRTA has gained no publicity since then.

The Shining Path has become more active since the end of Alberto Fujimori's regime in late 2000. It is not clear that it was responsible for the bomb attack that killed nine people just before President George Bush's visit in March 2002, but it is certainly the prime suspect.

TRAVEL ADVICE
FCO: Following serious sexual attacks in Cusco be extra vigilant and not alone there.
State: Shining Path violence in 2000–1 occurred in Junin, Huanuco, San Martin and Ayacutho.

BIBLIOGRAPHY
Clawson, Patrick and Lee, Rensselaer, *The Andean Cocaine Industry*, Macmillan, 1996
McClintock, Cynthia, *Revolutionary Movements in Latin America: El Salvador's FMLN and Peru's Shining Path*
Palmer, David Scott (ed.), *Shining Path of Peru*, Hurst, 1992
Stern, Steve J., (ed.), *Shining and Other Paths: War and Society in Peru 1980–95*, Duke University Press, 1998

Haiti

Population: 8,448,000
Armed Forces: nil
Per Capita GDP: $US 1,100
Currency: gourde

Haiti forms the western part of the island of Hispaniola; the eastern part is the Dominican Republic. The island was originally inhabited by Arawak Indians who died out in the sixteenth century, mainly because of diseases brought in by Europeans. At first the island was a Spanish colony, with the western part colonised by France; it was ceded to France by Spain in 1697. The colony suffered a number of rebellions by slaves at the turn of the eighteenth century; in 1791 the slaves took over and slavery was abolished, only to be restarted when the French recovered control. Haiti became independent in 1804 but has been unstable ever since.

The US ruled the country from 1915 to 1934, following violence between those of African descent and mulattos (half-castes of African and European birth). After the US left a number of coups occurred; François Duvalier, who led one of the coups, became president in 1956. His rule became a dictatorship, and he was kept in power by the Tonton Macoutes, his private army. It employed terror to subdue the population and caused some forty thousand deaths. In 1964 'Papa Doc', as Duvalier became known, made himself life-president and decreed that he would be succeeded by his son Jean-Claude. François Duvalier died in 1971 but there was no change to the manner of governance under his son. Although political parties were allowed in 1985, only one, Duvalier's National Progressive Party (PNP), ever registered. A military coup ousted Duvalier in 1986. Elections in 1987 were disrupted by pro-Duvalier gangs which destroyed the electoral process and killed many voters. A number of military regimes held power briefly until elections were held in December 1990. The first fully democratic election, supervised by the Organisation of American States (OAS) and the UN, was won, by a landslide, by Jean-Bertrand Aristide.

Aristide began a programme to restore human rights. He dismissed most of the senior military officers and replaced the system of rural control by section chiefs (who had had unchecked power backed by Tontons Macoutes). He was overthrown in September 1991 in a violent military coup that killed thousands, released all those imprisoned for human rights crimes and reinstated the section chiefs. The international community was outraged and the OAS condemned the coup and demanded Aristide's reinstatement. A delegation was sent to Haiti but was forced to leave by soldiers. A series of meetings were held by the OAS and UN with the new authorities in Haiti and the exiled Aristide. At a meeting in January 1993 the Haiti leadership agreed to the deployment of a civilian mission to help resolve the political crisis.

The International Civilian Mission in Haiti (MICIVIH) was a joint UN and OAS mission; by March 1993 it had deployed observers to Port-au-Prince and had teams in all nine departments of the country. In June the UN Security Council, acting under Chapter VII of the Charter, imposed an oil and arms embargo and required a freeze on all funds whether in the name of the Haiti government or the de facto regime. In June/July 1993 Aristide and General Raoul Cédras, the leader of the coup, met at talks held in New York and agreed that Aristide would return to Haiti in October and that the UN would assist in the creation and training of a new army and police force. In August the Haitian parliament ratified the appointment of Mr Robert Malval as prime-minister designate and the UN lifted all sanctions.

The UN Mission in Haiti (UNMIH) was established and an advance party deployed to Haiti. However, when the ship transporting the UN military group reached Port-au-Prince in October, Tonton Macoutes, now known as attachés, prevented the ship from docking. The UNMIH advance party and the staff of MICIVIH left Haiti. Some members of MICIVIH remained in Haiti and they were joined by several observers who reported a serious outbreak of violence; many of those killed were Aristide supporters. Aristide did not return to Haiti and UN sanctions were reimposed. An international naval blockade was established. During the summer of 1994 the human rights situation deteriorated sharply. In July the de facto government in Haiti ordered the staff of MICIVIH to leave the country.

Also in July the UN Security Council authorised the formation of a multinational force to use all necessary means to restore the legitimate government. It also expanded the mandate and strength of UNMIH, which would take over from the multinational force 'when a secure and stable environment had been established'. The multinational force, derived from twenty-eight nations and led by the US, deployed in September and was able to report substantial progress in restoring democracy; by then 21,000 troops had landed in Haiti. The first UNMIH observers arrived in late September. On 15 October, after the

Haiti

military leadership had left for Panama, which had agreed to give them asylum, Aristide returned and UN sanctions were lifted. The Haitian armed forces, which included the police force, disintegrated on the arrival of the international force; the section chiefs were dissolved again. While human rights abuses decreased the incidence of crime increased throughout the country. The transition from the multinational force and UNMIH took place on 31 March 1995; its military strength was 6,000 with eight hundred civil police.

A 3,000-strong Interim Public Security Force was formed from screened and retrained former army personnel and a new national police force was established. A presidential election was held in December 1995 in which the candidate of the governing Lavalas (meaning 'avalanche' in Creole) Party, René Préval, was elected. UNMIH's mandate came to an end in February 1996 but the new president asked the UN to stay on in Haiti and this was agreed to. The UN Support Mission in Haiti (UNSMIH) comprised 600 troops and 300 civil police, and its mandate was to run until 30 November 1997. In July the mandate was extended by four months. Of the military force, only 50 were UN-funded; the other 1,000 from Canada and Pakistan, were paid for by Canada and the US. There were also some five hundred US military engineers building roads and schools. The UN military force finally left in December 1997 but the police component remained and was renamed the UN Civilian Police Mission in Haiti (MIPONUH).

Throughout 1998 there was political stalemate as differences between the president and parliament blocked most legislation. In March 1999 President Préval appointed a new government by decree, which was immediately welcomed by the local business sector and by the international community. Préval's rule by decree continued until May 2000 when the Lavalas Party won 16 of 17 Senate seats in an election preceded by a wave of murders of the opposition candidates. In the presidential election held on 26 November 2000 Aristide was returned to power. A coup was attempted in December 2001 and was followed by attacks by Aristide supporters on opposition-owned property across the country. It is claimed that the coup had been staged to give the Aristide supporters an excuse to attack their opponents.

At the end of 1999 the UN General Assembly decided to replace MIPONUH and MICIVIH with a new mission, to be called the International Civilian Support Mission (MICAH). However, no funds were received to support the mission and the Secretary General recommended that it should be closed; in the event it continued to operate until the end of its mandate in February 2001.

The government has not passed a budget for the last six years and it is suspected that it survives on pay-offs made by the drug-traffickers who have used Haiti as a transit route to the US. Foreign aid has been withheld since 1999. Haitians survive on funds repatriated by the overseas community. The future remains bleak for Haitians and no doubt drug-trafficking and the numbers of refugees leaving the island will both increase.

TRAVEL ADVICE

FCO: Advises against all holiday and non-essential travel.
State: Take common-sense precautions, avoid all crowds. Do not expect assistance from the police. Several US citizens have been victims of kidnapping recently.

BIBLIOGRAPHY AND WEBSITES

Stotzky, Irwin P., *Silencing the Guns in Haiti: The Promise of Deliberative Democracy*, University of Chicago Press, 1997
The Blue Helmets: A Review of United Nations Peacekeeping, UN, 1996

Embassy of Haiti, Washington: www.haiti.org
Human Rights Watch, Haiti: www.hrw.org/americas/haiti
UN Support Mission in Haiti: www.un.org/Depts/DPKO/Missions/unhmih

The Falklands or Islas Malvinas

Population: 2,913 (excluding armed forces)
Armed Forces: 1,500
Per Capita GDP:

Captain John Strong of the British navy made the first landing on these uninhabited islands in 1690 and he named them The Falklands after the then First Lord of the Admiralty, Viscount Falkland. The islands were visited during the eighteenth century by French seal hunters, who named them Les Iles Malouines; in 1764 a small French colony was established on East Falkland, which was sold to the Spanish in 1767. The settlement became known as Puerto de la Soledad and 'Malouines' was translated to 'Malvinas'.

A British expedition took possession of West Falkland in the name of George III in 1765 and a settlement was established in 1766; the settlers were driven out by the Spaniards in 1770, nearly bringing Spain and Britain to war. The settlement was returned to the British in 1771 but the presence had to be withdrawn for financial reasons in 1774. However, the British claim they never gave up their sovereignty. In 1811 the Spanish settlement was also withdrawn and the islands were uninhabited until 1820 when an American, Colonel Daniel Jewitt, claimed possession of the islands for the government of Buenos Aires (which had become independent from Spain in 1816 but was not yet recognised by other powers). He only remained there for a few days and the islands remained uninhabited until a settlement was established in 1826 under an Argentinian governor, despite the protests of the British government.

In 1825 a US warship destroyed the Argentinian fort in reprisal for the arrest of three US ships and its captain declared the islands free from all government. The Argentinians appointed a new governor in 1832 but mutinous soldiers murdered him shortly after he arrived. The British sent a warship to the islands in 1833. Its captain claimed the right of sovereignty and required the Argentinian commander with his troops and most of the settlers to withdraw. There has been a British population on the islands since then.

Argentina renewed its interest in the Falkland Islands, and in South Georgia and the South Sandwich Islands which it also claims, in 1963. In 1964 it raised its claim to them with the United Nations Special Committee for Implementing the Declaration of the Granting of Independence to Colonial Countries and Peoples. The UN General Assembly invited Argentina and the UK to negotiate and talks were held during 1966. The UK's initial position was that the question of sovereignty should be 'frozen' for thirty years, after which the islanders themselves could decide on their future; this was rejected by Argentina. In

March 1967 the UK said for the first time that it would give up sovereignty under certain conditions and subject to the wishes of the islanders and the UK parliament. The islanders saw and objected to a draft memorandum of understanding in February 1968. In 1971 an agreement on communications between the islands and Argentina was agreed, without sovereignty being mentioned, and air and sea services from Argentina were instituted.

The situation became more intense after the military coup in Argentina in March 1976. That the UK's interest in protecting the islands had diminished was seen in the withdrawal of the Royal Navy frigate, the ending of the Simonstown Agreement, and the decision not to lengthen the airstrip. In the Defence Review of 1981 it had been decided to sell the aircraft carrier *Invincible* and to withdraw the ice patrol ship *Endurance* from service. Talks continued in 1976 and 1977, and in 1978 a number of working groups were established. After the Argentinian elections Argentina called for a more dynamic pace to the negotiations.

The Argentinians invaded the islands on 2 April 1982. Within two months the UK had assembled a naval task force to sail to the Falklands and British troops landed on 21 May 1982. The Argentinians surrendered on 14 June; they had lost about 650 men and their cruiser *Belgrano* had been sunk. The British suffered 256 killed; naval losses were substantial. After the war the British constructed an airfield and deployed aircraft and a military

South Atlantic and the Falkland Islands

garrison. In Argentina the military junta was disgraced and replaced by a democratically elected government.

In 1987 Britain established the Falklands Islands Interim Conservation and Management Zone, with a radius of up to 240km from the centre of the islands, and the Falkland Islands government began issuing fishing licences. Following a meeting with the Argentinians the British–Argentinian South Atlantic Fisheries Commission was set up to ensure the preservation of fish stocks. The Falklands Outer Conservation Zone extends conservation control up to a further 80km beyond the interim zone. Between 250,000 and 300,000 tonnes of fish are caught each year, generating £22 million annually in licence fees. Gross National Product was £5 million in 1980, today it is £55 million.

Argentina amended its constitution in 1994 to allow the pursuit of its claim to the Falklands in accordance with International Law. Earlier, during talks in Madrid, the two sides had agreed a formula protecting their respective positions on sovereignty; this has allowed substantial progress to be made in a number of fields.

Argentina and the UK signed a Joint Declaration on cooperation on hydrocarbon development in September 1995 and set up the South West Atlantic Hydrocarbons Commission – neither development affects either side's position over sovereignty. So far seven licences to explore areas to the north of the islands have been awarded. Six wells, in four of the blocks, were drilled during 1998 and although there were traces of oil and gas none was found in commercial quantities. Drilling data revealed that there was a rich organic source rock which could have formed up to sixty billion barrels of oil; this is more likely to lie under the source rock rather than above, where the first wells were targeted.

Despite the cooperation achieved between Argentina, the United Kingdom and the Falklands, the Argentinians have not dropped their claim to the islands. In January 2002 the Argentinian foreign minister, Carlos Ruckauf, called on Britain to reopen talks over the islands. Argentina repeats its claim to the islands annually on 3 January and goes to the UN De-colonisation Committee with its claim. In April 2002 the Argentinian President Eduardo Duhalde repeated the claim, saying 'the Malvinas are ours, we will get them back'. The islanders are determined to remain British.

BIBLIOGRAPHY AND WEBSITES

Argentine Embassy London: www.argentine0embassy.uk.org
Falkland Islands government: www.falklands.gov.fk
Falklands-Malvinas Forum (Inter-Mediación): www.falklands-malvinas.com
UK Foreign Office: www.fco.gov.uk

United States

Population: 281,404,000
Armed Forces: 1,368,000
Forces Overseas: 290,000
(excludes navy at sea)
Per Capita GDP: $34,300

This section is devoted to the affairs of the United States and three topics will be addressed. The first, entitled 'The World Policeman', examines how the US employs its military and looks at its approach to the United Nations, its more recent attitude to arms control and its views on European defence. Secondly the topic of attempting to keep drugs out of the US is discussed. Lastly the new topic 'The War on Terrorism and The Axis of Evil' is explored.

The World Policeman

After the end of the Cold War and the collapse of the Soviet Union, the US became the only superpower. The US armed forces may not be the largest in numbers but they are more powerful in every other aspect than any others in the world. The American economy is the strongest in the world and expects to remain so until 2015, when a regional power may come to rival it. It is therefore not just a regional hegemony but a global one, although until 11 September 2001 it was reluctant to use its power and influence for the good of humanity. Of course, the exception to this was the Gulf War of 1991 and the continued air operations flown over most of Iraq since then. The terrorist attacks on New York and Washington have led to a complete reversal of much US policy.

The US military has a global reach. US strategic nuclear forces have long had that capability, as has its network of satellites providing electronic and photographic intelligence, global positioning information and worldwide communications. US bombers in the conventional role have shown they can attack targets anywhere in the world from bases in the continental USA. The deployment of aircraft carriers, and other surface ships and submarines with cruise missile capability, gives credence to any threat of the use of force, as does the permanent embarkation of US Marines in the Mediterranean, the Indian Ocean and the Pacific. The US also has a number of prepositioned stockpiles for ground forces both afloat and ashore. US forces are permanently stationed in over twenty countries, not counting peacekeeping and training deployments. The largest overseas garrisons are in Germany, Japan and South Korea.

One reason sometimes put forward to explain the US reluctance to use its military power other than to suit its own policies is that US forces have to be ready to fight two major theatre wars simultaneously, Iraq and North Korea being given as possible examples. This policy has now been dropped. There is also the 'body bag' syndrome, whereby virtually any US casualties are seen as unacceptable to the public; this fear is qualified by some as only having effect when there is no national interest at stake. Certainly US casualties in the interventions in Lebanon in 1983 and Somalia in 1993, where there was no US national

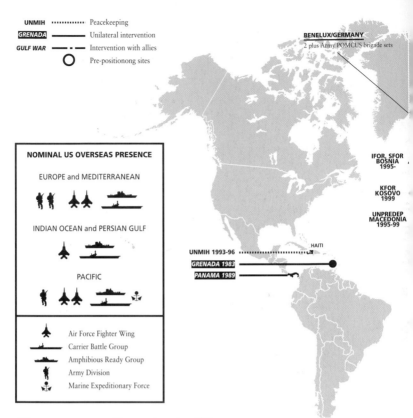

US overseas presence and interventions since 1981

interest, caused a relatively swift withdrawal from the operations. The lawlessness in Somalia that led to the intervention continues nine years later; however, a new intervention is now being contemplated in the war against terrorism. The risk of casualties led to a reliance on air power to solve problems, as in the bombing of Serbia over Kosovo. Restrictions were placed on the air forces taking part in order to avoid casualties, but this meant mistakes were made, unintended collateral damage and casualties were caused, and few Yugoslav troops operating in Kosovo were destroyed. Operations against Taliban and al Qaida in Afghanistan have been air-power led but were much more successful because of the deployment of special forces to direct the air attacks and to coordinate the troops of the anti-Taliban Northern Alliance.

There were other reasons for the US's apparent reluctance to commit forces. One is the built-in 'check and balance' of the constitution that can mean that the president may not command a majority in the Congress. An opposing majority can deny him the financial backing needed to commit troops or can invoke the 'war powers' act. (The American system is not well understood in countries where a parliamentary majority allows a prime minister to implement foreign policy virtually unquestioned.) In the case of the invasion of Kuwait it was essential to get UN authority before risking a vote in Congress. But there are advantages as well as disadvantages to the American way; when the Executive and Congress agree then long-term policies can be sustained. Congress approval also helps to gain the support of the general public. Members of the Congress are particularly vulnerable to

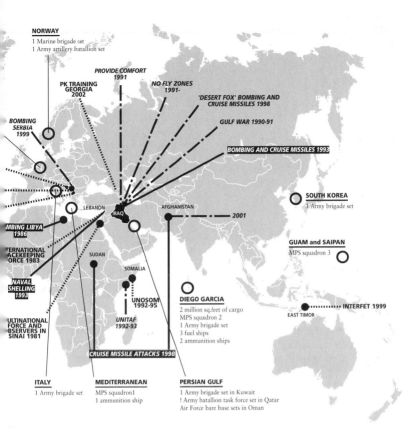

special interest groups lobbying for their cause, whether it is a domestic or a foreign policy issue. This can lead to policy decisions being held hostage to action on quite separate issues.

Another reason for this hesitance is the US's refusal to place its troops under the command of a non-American officer. In Bosnia this was avoided by the chain of command leading from the force commander (not always an American) up to NATO's SACEUR, an American officer. US forces are not designed, nor equipped, for peacekeeping and peace support operations. The Powell (Coln Powell, chairman of the Joint Chiefs of Staff, 1990–2) doctrine of using overwhelming force for the shortest possible time suits US forces. One of their criteria for taking part in operations is to have an exit strategy so that they are not trapped there, as in Bosnia, indefinitely. On occasion there have been three different foreign policies on the same issue, depending on the views of the White House, the State Department and the Department of Defense.

Of course there are those who do not see the US as reluctant to use its military power, which has been used unilaterally on a number of occasions – notably the bombing of Tripoli in 1986, the invasions of Grenada and Panama, and the cruise missile attacks on targets suspected of being connected to Usama Bin Laden in Afghanistan and Sudan. The war on terrorism will inevitably see an increase in the use of military forces; already there has been some deployment of special forces to assist the Philippine authorities in their operations against the Abu Sayyaf group, to train Yemeni forces and to carry out reconnaissance missions in Somalia, presumably in preparation for military intervention there.

The US has been described in many contradictory ways (arrogant, bully, paper tiger, satanic conspirator, interventionist, irrational, revisionist, quick on the trigger), none of them complimentary, and examples can be quoted to confirm them all. US foreign policy seemed to be inconsistent, though others might have described it as pragmatic. The bully in the US was exemplified by its readiness to impose unilateral sanctions on numerous countries for relatively minor reasons; worse, it passed legislation that allows it to take action against foreign firms that trade where the US opposes it (major investment in the Iranian energy industry, for example). Iran and Iraq called the US a satanic conspirator on account of its long-held policy of dual containment; their grievance is understandable. Other Muslim countries are dismayed by the all-too-evident lack of evenhandedness when the US invariably opposes any criticism of Israel at the UN Security Council. Certainly the US was quick on the trigger over the cruise missile attacks on a Sudanese chemical plant suspected of making chemical weapons for Usama bin Laden: a suspicion which was, it is now alleged, not strongly held by the CIA before the attack.

At times the US sets a bad example. Fortunately the long-standing saga of US non-payment of dues to the UN appears to be over, but only after the US came dangerously close to losing its vote at the General Assembly under Article 19 of the UN Charter. It mounted a campaign and used its veto to ensure that Boutros Boutros Ghali was not re-elected to serve a second term as Secretary General. Ghali, in his recently published book, has written: 'the United States sees little need for diplomacy; power is enough . . .'. There were concerns that the new administration would apply conditions to its payment of arrears but President Bush said there would be no withholding of funds, which members of the House of Representatives had threatened when the US was voted off the UN Human Rights Commission.

In the arms control field the US sends out, on occasion, the wrong signal. The Senate's recent refusal to ratify the Comprehensive Nuclear Test Ban Treaty (CTBT) has horrified the non-nuclear armed nations, especially as the Senate had the option of not voting on the issue. At least the Senate cannot order the reintroduction of nuclear testing. The US stand against the Ottawa Convention on anti-personnel mines is not understood by many. One reason for its decision not to sign the treaty until 2006, and then only if other alternatives are not available, is that it believes anti-personnel mines are essential for the defence of South Korea. The US has also blocked the Biological Weapons Convention on the grounds that the inspection regime proposed would be too intrusive and might reveal commercial secrets. On the other hand the US has played a major part in successfully negotiating bilateral treaties such as START I and II (though the latter has now been abandoned) and multilateral treaties like the Conventional Forces in Europe Treaty. It cannot be accused of being anti-arms control. Away from arms control, the US will not ratify the Kyoto Accord on environmental issues, saying that it is unfair and would harm the US economy. The most recent example of US uncooperativeness is its stand over the International Criminal Court, when it vetoed the extension of the UN mandate in Bosnia unless the UN agrees to immunity from prosecution to US peacekeepers.

Many Europeans cannot understand the US position on European defence [see pp. 1–5]. For some time the US has criticised the Europeans for not doing enough for their own defence; however, when Europe began announcing plans for the future (albeit without, as yet, promises to spend more and invest in 'high tech' weaponry, which is the US's main complaint) the Americans quickly criticised these as undermining NATO. President Chirac of France has attacked this criticism; the French foreign minister put it slightly differently: 'The US has to make a choice. They have always been for sharing the burden. They've never been much for sharing the decision-making.' A genuine US complaint concerns the difficulty – or was it reluctance? – that the European states encountered in raising the 50,000 men needed for the Kosovo peacekeeping force from the total of nearly two million in the armies of the European NATO members.

The legal position on military action is clearly defined by the UN Charter, but the permanent members of the Security Council often vote contrary to the Charter's terms and adopt the most humane course of action. Use of force may not be authorised because of the possible implications for actions being taken in permanent members' own countries. Russia, for example, opposed action against Serbia as the Russians were behaving in a similar manner in Chechnya (and are now using a version of NATO's tactics there to destroy the Chechens). Likewise, China opposes the use of force in case it is itself threatened over its treatment of Tibet, however unlikely this might be. The US, and on occasion its allies, finds it necessary to take military action without specific UN authorisation, normally finding enough suitable wording in the Charter to justify their actions.

It is easy to criticise the US, either for doing too much or for not doing enough. Quite often it is accused of both in respect of the same incident. Without US hegemony the world might well be a far more unstable place; certainly its leadership of NATO has at last brought peace to the Balkans. Consider the implications of any other global hegemon – Russia or China, for instance.

BIBLIOGRAPHY AND WEBSITES

Boutros Ghali, Boutros, *Unvanquished: A US-UN Saga*, IB Tauris, 1999
Kagan, Robert and Maynes, Charles William, *US Dominance: Is It Good for the World?*, Foreign Policy, Summer 1998
Kagan, Robert and Kristol, William (eds), *Present Dangers: Crisis and Opportunity in American Foreign and Defense Policy*, Encounter Books, 2000
Nye, Joseph S., *The Paradox of American Power: Why the World's Only Superpower Can't Go It Alone*, Oxford University Press, 2002
Survival Winter 1999–2000, International Institute for Strategic Studies, 1999

Armed Services Committee (House of Representatives): www.house.gov/hasc
US Joint Chiefs of Staff: www.dtic.mil/jcs
US Secretary of Defense: www.defenselink.mil/osd
US State Department: www.state.gov

Keeping Drugs Out of the US

Many tons of cocaine and opium are smuggled into the US, where some $110 billion is spent on drugs each year. The Drug Enforcement Agency, assisted by a number of other agencies, attempts to reduce drug imports by crop eradication, destruction of laboratories, interception en route by land, sea and air, and seizures at the border and ports. The search,

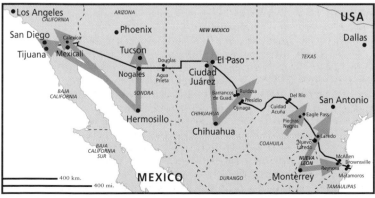

Drug smuggling routes from Mexico

of course, continues within the US. The number of drug users in the US has dropped from 25 million in 1979 to 14 million. At the same time street prices have also dropped: heroin from $5,000 per gram in 1981 to $1,000 and cocaine from $500 to $150. Marijuana rose from $6 in 1981 to a peak of $15 before dropping to $9 (source: ABT Associates).

Colombia now produces the world's largest drug crops and manufactures the most cocaine and opium from the raw products, coca leaves and poppies. The US therefore supports Plan Colombia, the Colombian government's programme to reduce drug production and to promote the peace process, but is careful to focus its support on anti-drug operations rather than on anti-terrorist action. President Clinton signed into law in July 2000 an assistance package of $1.3 billion.

The action against crops is two-pronged: aerial eradication, using glyphosate, of large-scale farming, and persuading small-scale farmers (3 hectares or less) to grow other crops. The US helps these farmers with advice, training, high-class seeds and marketing the alternative crop. The US also funds local infrastructure projects to improve social and economic conditions, without which farmers would return to coca crop cultivation. Support for alternative development is costing $106 million.

A major US objective in Plan Colombia is to protect human rights, improve the government and reform the judicial system. US training schemes cover a wide range of Colombian institutions, including the police, prosecutors, judiciary, prisons, customs, banking supervision, countering financial crime and money-laundering, military human rights, military judge advocates and maritime and port security. Some $119 million is budgeted for these activities.

Drugs costs US$ per kilo

Heroin	Cocaine
Farmgate 90	Coca leaves 610
Domestic retail 2870	Cocaine base 860
US wholesale 80,000	Cocaine hydrochloride
US retail 290,000	Export 1,500
	US wholesale 25,250
	US retail 50, 000 (crack)
	US retail 110,000 (powder)

Source: UNODCP World Drug Report 1997

The US has funded, equipped and trained the Colombian army's counter-narcotic brigade and two counter-narcotic aviation battalions, one equipped with UH-60 Blackhawk and one with UH-1N Huey helicopters. The cost is $416.9 million. Congress has capped the number of US military personnel in Colombia at five hundred and civil support staff at three hundred; US military personnel are prohibited from taking part in combat operations. The Colombian police are also supported to the tune of $115.6 million, spent mainly on helicopters and spray aircraft. As success in Colombia will automatically drive drug operations over the country's borders, the US also supports anti-drug programmes in Bolivia, Ecuador and Peru. Bolivian coca planting has been reduced from 38,000 hectares in 1997 to only 6,000 in 2001; however, in Peru coca cultivation has remained at about 34,000 hectares (US estimate) despite the eradication of 6,000 hectares during 2001.

The US Coast Guard carries out joint interdiction missions with the authorities of most Central American and Caribbean states and also in the Caribbean with the UK, Netherlands and France. The attacks of 11 September have meant that the Coast Guard has had to pull back to concentrate on patrolling US coasts. The US has provided fast patrol boats to twenty-two countries in 2000 and 2001. The US Air Force has established an air-base for surveillance aircraft at Manta in Ecuador to replace the former base in Panama.

The South West Border Initiative is a joint operation by the DEA, the FBI and the Customs Service to collect intelligence on drug-trafficking, mainly by wire-tapping. The DEA has an aviation wing with ninety-five aircraft for surveillance purposes. Aircraft are stationed in the Bahamas, Bolivia, Colombia, Mexico, Peru and Puerto Rica.

The US has the most comprehensive system for tackling drugs. Each year the president reports to Congress those he considers to be major illicit drug-producing or drug-transit countries. The December 1998 list contained twenty-eight countries, two fewer than a year earlier. Five other countries were considered to be major producers but were not listed as their production was consumed locally or not exported to the US. The president then certifies which of these countries has cooperated fully with the US or has taken sufficient steps to comply with the UN Convention. The definition of a major drug-producing country is one that has 1,000 hectares or more of either opium or coca or 5,000 hectares of cannabis cultivated or harvested during a year. In 1998 the US identified forty-five major money-laundering countries, that is countries whose financial institutions engaged in transactions involving the proceeds of serious crime. The list includes the US itself and others such as Canada, France, Germany and the UK. Each year the US State Department publishes an International Narcotics Control Strategy Report; the 1999 report was over 700 pages long and gives, in addition to data on cultivation and production, details of each country's actions taken against drugs during the year and the extent of cooperation with and assistance given by the US.

BIBLIOGRAPHY AND WEBSITES

US Drug Enforcement Administration Briefing Book, 2001

Inter-American Drug Abuse Control Commission: www.cicad.oas
US Drug Enforcement Administration: www.usdoj.gov/dea

The War on Terrorism and the 'Axis of Evil'

President George W. Bush described the terrorist attacks of 11 September 2001, which destroyed the twin towers of the World Trade Centre in New York and severely damaged part of the Pentagon in Washington, 'as more than acts of terrorism, they were acts of war'. President Clinton had also used the phrase 'war on terrorism' after the bombing of the US embassies in Kenya and Tanzania in 1998. On 16 September Bush said to the American people that 'this crusade, this war on terrorism, is going to take a while'. The Muslim world immediately took offence as it links the word crusade with a Christian holy war against Islam; the term has been quietly dropped. In his speech to Congress on 20 September Bush promised 'the war on terrorism will not end until every terrorist group of global reach has been found, stopped and defeated'. To the rest of the world he said: 'Either you are with us or against us. From this day forward, any nation that continues to harbor or support terrorism will be regarded by the United States as a hostile regime': a promise which has had positive effects.

In his State of the Union address to Congress on 29 January 2002 President Bush widened his horizon, saying: 'Our second goal is to prevent those that sponsor terror from threatening America or our friends with weapons of mass destruction.' He then listed the threats posed by Iran, Iraq and North Korea, remarking: 'States like these constitute an axis of evil, aiming to threaten the peace of the world.' There has been concern that the war on terrorism and the axis of evil may degenerate into a war on Islam but the US has taken pains to stress this is not its intention. However, the fact remains that all the 11 September hijackers were Muslim; that all eleven organisations listed by Executive Order 13224 are Islamic; and that of the original twenty-two organisations designated foreign terrorist organisations half are Islamic. Virtually all the individuals and the banks and business companies similarly designated are Muslim.

The 'war on terrorism' should perhaps be kept separate from that against the axis of evil (which could contain others than the three named states). In the war on terrorism top

The War on Terrorism: US deployments since 11 September 2001

priority has been given to destroying al Qaida and its supporters, the Taliban, in Afghanistan. Some thirty-four countries are believed to harbour al Qaida cells but it is assumed that the three countries most likely to be supporting al Qaida and other terrorist organisations are Somalia, Sudan and Yemen; all three are known to have strong links with al Qaida. Unsurprisingly all three quickly demonstrated cooperation with the US.

In Somalia, which is known to have allowed al Qaida and al-Ittihad camps to be established, seven locations have been cited: three in the south, one in Puntland, two in Somaliland and one on the Somaliland/Puntland border. Somalia has its own indigenous terrorist organisation, Al-Ittihad Al Islamiya, designated by the US as a terrorist organisation for the first time in September 2001 when US Executive Order 13224 blocked their assets; it is known to be allied to al Qaida. Intervention in Somalia, considered to be a 'failed' state, would not raise much international opposition. Already there have been reports of US Central Intelligence Agency agents and US special forces carrying out reconnaissance missions in Somalia and of maritime and aerial surveillance carried out by US, British, French and German ships and aircraft.

Sudan has been engaged in a civil war since 1983 (see pp. 116–18). It has been listed by the US as a country sponsoring terrorism, mainly on account of its giving safe haven and training facilities to a number of organisations including al Qaida, al-Gama'a al-Islamiyya, Egyptian Islamic Jihad, Palestine Islamic Jihad and HAMAS. However, Sudan was cooperating with the US over terrorism well before 11 September, with talks beginning in mid-2000. Since then Sudan has signed a number of international conventions on terrorism but has still not fully complied with the UN resolutions passed in 1996 which required it to end all support for terrorists. Sudan has no indigenous terrorist group, nor has the Sudanese People's Revolutionary Army (SPLA) resorted to terrorist tactics in its quest for independence. There have been no reports of increased US involvement since 11 September. The Sudanese government has handed over the names of suspected allies of Usama bin Laden and has given permission for US military aircraft to overfly its airspace. Tracking down terrorists should be relatively simple given the all-out support of the Sudanese government, and Islamic terrorists are unlikely to be found in the southern part of the country.

The US has long suspected that Yemen was, after Afghanistan, a country it resembles in many ways (mountainous countryside, dissident tribes and poor government control), the second largest supporter of al Qaida. Large numbers of Yemenis have joined al Qaida's ranks and have been found fighting in Afghanistan. (Similarly many Yemenis supported the Afghan mujahedin against the Soviet army.) One of the 11 September hijackers was a Yemeni. Al Qaida is strongly suspected of being responsible for the suicide attack on the USS *Cole* in Aden Harbour in October 2000. The Yemeni government did not provide any support to the terrorists but was less than fully cooperative with the US investigators. The Yemeni army has attempted to arrest al Qaida men but has, so far, been unsuccessful and has sustained casualties. The US is to send a training team to Yemen; there are said to be several hundred deployed there already.

The US has also been active elsewhere, in addition to these three countries. The first US deployment was to the Philippines, where six hundred soldiers including special forces were sent in January to train Philippino forces operating against Abu Sayyaf. This relatively small Islamic group is based on the southern islands of Basilan and Sulu and is guilty of kidnapping foreign tourists, including those holidaying on a Malaysian island. Some US troops will accompany Philippine units on operations but will not, it is said, be involved in fighting (though this may become unavoidable). However, there have been reports of US special forces joining the hunt for the two American hostages held by Abu Sayyaf. It has been suggested, somewhat unkindly, that the real aim is to secure a quick victory in the war against terrorism and so boost morale generally. The best assistance the US could give would be to use its intelligence assets in order to pinpoint Abu Sayyaf locations.

The US is also sending troops to Georgia, again to train the local army, and has already given the government ten helicopters. The aim is to create a force capable of clearing out those terrorists hiding in the Pankisi Gorge – mainly Chechens regrouping after fighting the Russians, although numbers of Afghans and Arabs have also sought refuge there. While some Russian army generals oppose the US deployment, President Putin has welcomed it as it will remove a safe haven for the Chechen rebels. The US will also provide weapons, transport and communications systems for the four Georgian battalions that it will train.

Another country of concern is Algeria; a number of Algerians have been found fighting with al Qaida. There are two Algerian Islamist terrorist groups, both designated by the US – Groupe Islamic Armée (GIA) and Groupe Salafiste Pour la Prédication et le Combat (GSPC). Since 11 September Algeria has found the West more sympathetic to its claims that these are terrorist organisations and not human rights activists. On the other hand the head of Algeria's Human Rights League, Ali Yahya Abdennour, has said that 'the internal terrorism is caused by the country's dictatorship'.

The war on terrorism is not being fought only by the military and other security forces; it is also being waged on the economic, political and diplomatic fronts. A long list of individuals, commercial and financial concerns has been compiled and their funds are liable to be frozen by the US. Much of the legislation enacted by the US since 11 September was already the object of UN conventions, most of which concerned specific acts of terrorism against, for example, aircraft and ships. Since then the UNSC has adopted Resolution 1373 which mandates all nations to impose financial sanctions against terrorists and their supporters. Exchange of intelligence is a major requirement in defeating terrorism.

The war against the axis of evil is more concerned with countering, or rather forestalling, the terrorist use of weapons of mass destruction (WMD). All three countries named have such weapons; these are described on p. 104 for Iran, p. 96 for Iraq and p. 203 for North Korea. Their terrorist connections, apart from Iran which sponsors Hizbollah in Lebanon and HAMAS in the Palestinian territories, are not significant. Iraq is mainly involved in terrorising its own population and Iraqis living abroad. North Korea does not sponsor foreign organisations but has used terrorism itself on several occasions. How these countries should be tackled is a matter of concern.

At present Iraq appears to be the US's number one target. Internal rebellion will not be as easy to set off as it was in 1991, and the rebels of that time will doubtless remember how they were left unsupported by the US and its coalition allies. The Kurds appear relatively content with their situation, which in many respects is preferable to that in the rest of Iraq; they may not be too eager to take on the role played by the United Front in Afghanistan. US efforts against Iraq will not garner as much support as the operations in Afghanistan. Most European countries and all Muslim countries oppose the bombing of Iraq. While long-range bombing is practical, mounting a ground force invasion of the size needed to defeat Iraqi forces, even if a sizeable number of them defect, will not be easy. Not all the countries neighbouring Iraq will necessarily allow US deployment on their territory.

Listing Iran as part of the axis of evil is affecting Iranian policies towards Afghanistan. So far Iran has acted positively, refusing to allow al Qaida to cross its borders and being a major contributor to the international efforts to rebuild Afghanistan. Its actions to assist the Shi'a community in Hazara are unwelcome to some but are perfectly natural in the circumstances. South Korea sees the naming of North Korea as hurtful to its 'sunshine' campaign for reconciliation with the North.

BIBLIOGRAPHY AND WEBSITE

Hoge, F. James and Rose, Gideon (eds), *How Did This Happen? Terrorism and the New War*, Public Affairs, 2002

Talbot, Strobe and Chanda, Nayan (eds), *The Age of Terror: America and the World After September 11*, Basic Books, 2002

US government: www.firstgov.gov/Topics/Usgresponse

Causes of Trouble

Security Concerns

This section covers a wide variety of topics having a common factor: all are concerned with weapons and their use.

The term 'weapons of mass destruction' has come to mean nuclear, biological and chemical weapons (BCW) and the long-range missiles that can deliver them. Nuclear weapons give rise to the greatest concern, possibly because they have been used less often than the others and possibly because the effects of a massive nuclear exchange, while unpredictable, are known to be catastrophic. In some ways nuclear weapons have been a benefit in that they surely contributed, though this cannot be proved, to the fact that there was never a war between democracy and communism – an event that many thought likely fifty years ago.

Three topics are as old as the hills and have been a matter of concern throughout history. They are: terrorism, now the top priority for the US and its friends and allies; piracy, which is becoming a growing threat to shipping, particularly in the Far East; and anti-personnel land-mines, which, – though useful in war – have become the scourge of countries attempting to recover from civil war.

The final three topics are relatively new. Missile defence was controlled by treaty during the Cold War when a massive nuclear-armed missile attack was the likely outcome of any East–West conflict. Now the threat is from a handful of missiles held by 'rogue' states, which are thought more likely to use them than the superpowers, which were deterred by the threat of 'Mutual Assured Destruction'. Until the US unilaterally withdrew from the Anti-Ballistic Treaty in 2002, missile defence and its implications had been at the top of the international agenda. Linked to this is the whole question of war in space. So far weapons have been kept out of space although the use of space has become more and more essential to military operations. The newest addition to the array of war fighting options is cyber warfare – attacking one's opponent's use of information technology.

Nuclear Weapons

Nuclear weapons are the most powerful in the world but have only been used twice in anger, against Japan in the Second World War. Their political importance was the cause of the nuclear arms race between the US and the Soviet Union and led to other states acquiring or attempting to acquire them. The US and Soviet Union realised that the use of nuclear weapons was self-defeating and would inevitably lead to Mutual Assured Destruction or MAD. The US and Soviet Union embarked on a series of arms control measures to reduce the risks of nuclear war but without eliminating the threat of their use. The Strategic Arms Limitation Treaty (SALT) was agreed in 1972 and purely limited their numbers. The Intermediate Nuclear Forces Treaty (INF) was the first treaty to require reductions and the two states eliminated all their land-based ballistic and cruise missiles

Recognised nuclear powers
"De facto" nuclear powers
States developing nuclear weapons
States that have abandoned nuclear programmes

Countries that have nuclear weapons or
have had nuclear weapon programmes

with ranges between 500 and 5,500km. By June 1991 the US had destroyed 608 weapons and the Soviet Union 899. The Strategic Arms Reduction Treaty (START) signed in July 1991 committed the two sides to deploying no more than 1,600 delivery vehicles – intercontinental ballistic missiles (ICBMs), submarine-launched ballistic missiles (SLBMs) and heavy bombers – with no more than 6,000 'attributable' warheads. Before the treaty could be ratified the Soviet Union broke up and four of the new republics (Belarus, Kazakhstan, Russia and Ukraine) had strategic weapons deployed on their territory. At a conference in Lisbon the four republics and the US signed a protocol to START in which the four, as successor states, assumed the obligations of the USSR under the treaty. Further, and most importantly, Belarus, Kazakhstan and Ukraine committed themselves to joining the Nuclear Non-Proliferation Treaty (NPT) as non-nuclear armed states in the shortest possible time and so would give up all of their nuclear weapons (tactical as well as strategic). START 2, which was signed on 3 January 1993 but was only ratified by the Russian Duma with conditions attached to it, would have further reduced strategic nuclear holdings to between 3,500 and 3,000 warheads each. There are no treaties controlling tactical nuclear weapons but both the US and the Soviet Union have made a number of pledges regarding their disposal. However, there are no verification measures to ensure these have been implemented.

The main weapon in the battle to prevent nuclear weapon proliferation is the Nuclear Non-Proliferation Treaty (NPT) which came into force on 5 March 1970. The background to the treaty was the adoption by the UN General Assembly (UNGA) in 1959 and 1961 of

resolutions calling for nuclear-weapon states (China, France, Russia, UK and US) to refrain from providing weapons to non-nuclear states, and insisting that nuclear weapons should be subject to inspection and control. The UN Committee on Disarmament was tasked by the UNGA in 1965 to negotiate an international treaty to prevent the proliferation of nuclear weapons; the committee was co-chaired by the US and the USSR who after intense negotiations produced identical revised drafts. The treaty was adopted by the UNGA in June 1968 and then opened for signature on 1 July 1968, when sixty-two nations agreed to it. Now only Cuba, Israel, India and Pakistan have not signed it. The main elements of the treaty are:

I.   Nuclear Weapon States agree neither to transfer nuclear weapons nor to assist non-nuclear states in acquiring nuclear weapons.
II. Non-Nuclear States undertake not to receive or manufacture nuclear weapons.
III. Non-Nuclear States undertake to accept safeguards and verification of their nuclear facilities by the International Atomic Energy Agency (IAEA).
IV. NPT parties have the right to develop nuclear energy.
V.   Nuclear Weapon States are obligated to pursue agreement on a treaty on complete disarmament under international control.

India and Pakistan both tested nuclear weapons in May 1998, demonstrating that they were nuclear powers; in his State of the Union address to Congress in January 2002 President

Bush clearly accused Iran, Iraq and North Korea of developing nuclear weapons. If proliferation continues, some commentators believe that all Middle East countries will be nuclear-armed within twenty or thirty years. On the other hand four of the five recognised nuclear-armed states have reduced their holdings of deployed nuclear weapons; only China has not. Israel has long been considered a nuclear-armed state although it has always claimed that it will not be the first to introduce nuclear weapons into the region.

A large number of countries have the technical capability and the financial resources to develop nuclear weapons should they decide to do so. Programmes were initiated in South Korea and Taiwan but both countries were persuaded by the US to terminate the projects. In June 1975 the then South Korean president stated that 'Korea had the capacity to produce nuclear weapons' but had no plans to do so unless the US withdrew its nuclear umbrella. Taiwan's president said in 1996 that it had the means to develop nuclear weapons and that, following Chinese naval and missile exercises, it would have to study whether it needed them to defend itself.

Argentina and Brazil undertook weapons development programmes. Both countries had safeguarded agreements with the IAEA but these only covered part of their nuclear activities. Unsafeguarded plants included a uranium enrichment plant and a plutonium separation plant in Argentina; Brazil also had uranium enrichment and plutonium separation facilities. However, in 1990 a 320m-deep bore hole on a test-site in the Cachimbo Mountains was symbolically filled in by the Brazilian president, who then declared that Brazil would not develop nuclear weapons. Later it was revealed that the Brazilian military had begun to design two nuclear weapons in 1977. Argentina and Brazil made commitments to the exclusively peaceful use of nuclear energy in a number of joint declarations between 1985 and 1990. In 1991 they signed the Bilateral Agreement for the Exclusively Peaceful Use of Nuclear Energy, which was ratified by both Congresses in December 1991. This led to the establishment of the Brazilian–Argentine Agency for the Accounting and Control of Nuclear Materials (ABACC). Argentina acceded to the NPT in October 1995 and Brazil joined in July 1998.

South Africa surprised the world in March 1993 when the then president, Frederick de Klerk, informed parliament that South Africa had manufactured six nuclear fission devices, that these had been dismantled before the country had joined the NPT in July 1991 and that all other nuclear materials and facilities had been placed under international safeguards. The fact that South Africa had had a nuclear weapons programme was no surprise – a nuclear test site in the Kalahari Desert had been identified in August 1977, and US and Soviet pressure had caused the test to be cancelled – but the news that the weapons had been completed was totally unexpected. De Klerk also stated that 'at no time did South Africa acquire nuclear weapons technology or materials from another country' and 'South Africa has never conducted a clandestine nuclear test'. The true nature of the double flash noted in the South Atlantic in September 1979 remains unconfirmed but no other evidence of a nuclear explosion has been found. In addition to the two shafts at the Vastrap test site South Africa had both uranium enrichment and plutonium extraction plants, with research and assembly facilities at Pelindaba, the dismantling of which has been verified by the IAEA.

Details of India and Pakistan's nuclear programmes and tests are set out on pp. 165–6 & 177. The details of Iraq's programme, its progress towards achieving a bomb before the Gulf War, and the measures taken to try to prevent any future development, and the suspicions regarding Iran's nuclear ambitions are both given at pp. 98, 73. North Korea has also come under suspicion of having developed nuclear weapons, although it was subject to IAEA inspection. Failure to allow access to a suspected waste site led to a confrontation. The details of events and the measures being taken to halt the Korean programme are described on pp. 204–6.

The NPT was extended indefinitely at the Review Conference held in May 1995 although there was some opposition to the form of words used. At the same time agreement was reached on 'Principles and Objectives for Nuclear Non-Proliferation and Disarmament'; in all, the agreement included twenty principles aimed at ensuring wider cooperation and greater transparency in nuclear matters. The nuclear weapon states 'affirmed their commitment to pursue in good faith negotiations on effective measures relating to nuclear disarmament'. Disarmament, or the lack of it, is given a far higher priority by the non-nuclear states than those with nuclear weapons, which seem loath to consider the total nuclear disarmament required by the NPT.

Five nuclear-weapon-free zones (NWFZ) have been established across the world. The first was established by the Antarctic Treaty in December 1969. The treaty prohibits nuclear explosions and the dumping of radio-active waste in the region south of 60° South latitude. The Treaty of Rarotonga covers a large part of the South Pacific and came into force on 11 December 1986. It became a blueprint for the subsequent NWFZs. The parties to the Treaty undertook not to manufacture or otherwise acquire, possess or control any nuclear explosive device; not to provide fissionable material or equipment for processing or producing fissionable material for peaceful purposes to any state unless it was subject to the safeguards required by the Nuclear Non-Proliferation Treaty or, in the case of nuclear weapon states, International Atomic Energy Agency safeguards; to prevent the stationing of nuclear weapons on their territory (but each could decide its own policy regarding the

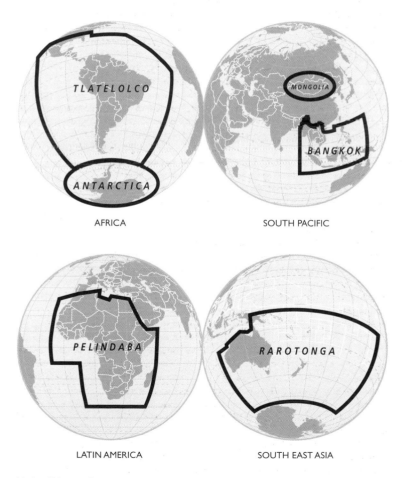

AFRICA   SOUTH PACIFIC

LATIN AMERICA   SOUTH EAST ASIA

Nuclear Weapons-Free zones

245

transit of foreign ships and aircraft); to prevent the testing of nuclear weapons in its territory; and not to dump and to prevent the dumping of radioactive matter in its territorial waters. France, the UK and the US became parties of all three protocols to the treaty and the USSR and China to protocols 2 and 3. Protocol I concerned dependent territories in the NWFZ and the parties undertook to abide by the prohibitions of the treaty covering manufacture, stationing and testing. Protocol 2 required the parties to it not to use or threaten to use nuclear weapons against parties of the treaty and not to contribute to any violation of the treaty. Parties to Protocol 3 committed themselves not to test nuclear weapons within the NWFZ. France signed only after it had carried out its final nuclear test at Moruroa.

The Treaty of Tlatelolco created the Latin American and Caribbean NWFZ. Opened for signature in 1965, it was not signed by Argentina, Brazil and Chile until 1994 and only came into force in March 1995 after Cuba signed the treaty. On 11 April 1996 all fifty-three states in Africa signed the Treaty of Pelidaba to establish the African NWFZ. The Organisation of African Unity recognises Diego Garcia as part of Africa though no African state controls it; the US may be storing nuclear weapons there. The South-East Asian NWFZ was created by the Bangkok Treaty which came into force in March 1997; the treaty does not prohibit attacks on civil nuclear facilities, as do the other NWFZ treaties. So far only one state, Mongolia, has achieved NWFZ status, which was endorsed by the UNGA in 1998. The countries of Central Asia are negotiating a NWFZ treaty at Geneva but progress is slow.

In November 2001 President George Bush announced a unilateral US reduction of strategic nuclear weapons to between 1,700 and 2,200 operationally deployed warheads over the next ten years. The impact of the decision was marred by the later revelation that many of the warheads, bombs and missiles were to be kept in 'inactive' stores but would be available for redeployment if necessary. The Russians reacted strongly and demanded that all withdrawn weapons should be destroyed; however, it is worth noting that neither START I nor II required warhead destruction. The Russians are ready to reduce their nuclear forces too, but insist on a legally binding and verifiable and irreversible arrangement; they provided treaty drafts in early 2002. However, on 24 May 2002 Presidents Bush and Putin signed the Strategic Offensive Reductions Treaty (SORT) requiring both sides to reduce their deployed nuclear warheads to no more than 1,700 – 2,200 by 31 December 2012. Each side will decide the composition and structure of its own offensive weapons. In February 2002 the US released some details of its Nuclear Posture Review, which for the first time named countries which might possibly be targeted by the US. It suggests that the US could use nuclear weapons against those that threaten it with CBW, even if they are not nuclear-armed. This contradicts a US pledge. In March the UK's defence minister, Geoff Hoon, intimated in a House of Commons committee briefing that the UK was also prepared to use nuclear weapons under certain conditions.

As can be seen in the table, a good deal of progress has been made in eliminating nuclear weapons. START I limits have been achieved by both sides and there are no longer any nuclear warheads, missiles, missile silos or bombers in Belarus, Kazakhstan and Ukraine. Weapons have not only been destroyed, however. Since September 1990 Russia has added one more train set of three missiles to complete the deployment of its rail-mobile SS-24 ICBM; production of the mobile SS-25 ICBM has continued and a further 126, including those originally in Belarus, have been deployed. A new single warhead ICBM, the RS-12M, has been developed and the first 30 deployed in former SS-19 silos.

Strategic Nuclear Weapons Holdings

	United States			USSR/Russia	
	1991	2002		1991	2002
			ICBM		
Minuteman II	450	0	SS-11, SS-13, SS-17	413	0
Minuteman III	500	500	SS-18	308	150

MX Peacemaker	50	50	SS-19	300	150
			SS-24	89	36
			SS-25	288	360
			RS-12M	0	30
			SLBM		
Poseidon C-3	160	0	SS-N-6, SS-N-17	204	0
Trident C-4	384	168	SS-N-8	280	24
Trident D-5	96	264	SS-N-18	224	112
			SS-N-20	120	100
			SS-N-23	112	96
			Bombers		
B-52 (ALCM)	172	97	Tu-95 Bear B/G	64 0	
B-52	38	47	Tu-95 H6	0	32
B-1B	97	90	Tu-95 H16	62	34
B-2A	0	20	Tu-160 Blackjack	15	15

(Treaty countable weapons: some may be non-operational)

France and the United Kingdom, but not yet China, have also reduced their nuclear forces. The French have eliminated their intermediate range S-3 missiles, of which eighteen were deployed on the Plateau D'Albion, and forty short-range Pluton missile launchers and the Pluton's replacement, the Hadés missile, of which only fifteen were produced but never deployed. Only in the ballistic missile submarine field have there been any new deployments: the submarine force previously consisted of five boats each armed with sixteen M-4 SLBMs, but now there are two M-4 armed submarines which are being replaced by the Le Triomphant class which has sixteen M-45 SLBMs. Four Le Triomphant submarines are planned; two have already been commissioned. It has been estimated that the French still have about eighty Air-Sol-Moyenne Porté (ASMP) missiles for delivery by its Air Force Mirage 2000N and carrier-borne Super Etendard aircraft.

The United Kingdom has ended the Royal Air Force's nuclear role; in 1990 there were eight nuclear-capable squadrons equipped with some 120 Tornado GR-1 and Buccaneer aircraft. The Polaris SLBM fleet of four submarines each armed with sixteen SLBMs has been replaced by four Vanguard class submarines each with the capability of carrying sixteen Trident D-5 SLBMs. Polaris SLBMs carried three warheads while Trident can be armed with as many as twelve; originally the UK announced it would only arm each submarine with no more than 128 warheads (an average of eight per SLBM) but that figure was reduced to 96 in 1993 and in the 1998 Strategic Defence Review was further reduced to 48.

Several sound reasons can be advanced in favour of retaining some nuclear weapons. These include the argument that nuclear weapons cannot be disinvented so there will always be a risk, in a nuclear-free world, of combatants racing to re-acquire them. Nuclear deterrence can be said to have worked in the case of NATO and the Warsaw Pact in that there was no war between these two major military alliances. Finally, it has been argued that there is no guarantee of preventing cheating and it would be possible for states to hide a number of nuclear weapons while professing to have disarmed; verifying total nuclear disarmament would require unacceptably intrusive and expensive measures.

It is likely to be a good many years before all the nuclear powers agree to total disarmament, and many more before it is fully implemented. The best that can be hoped for is continued reductions in nuclear-weapon holdings and an increase in the measures to ensure that those weapons which remain are subject to transparency regarding their deployment and alert status, and to agreed measures restricting their operational readiness. The main reason for naming Iran, Iraq and North Korea as the 'axis of evil' was on account of their ambitions to acquire nuclear, chemical and biological weapons and the long-range missiles to deliver them. Meanwhile there are some who believe the US will resume nuclear testing and that plans are being considered to develop nuclear-armed missile defence

Declared CW states

Suspect CW states

LIBYA Non-signatories of CWC
(plus 10 small island states)

Chemical weapons armed and suspect states

weapons which would be in violation of the Partial Test Ban Treaty which bans nuclear tests in the atmosphere and outer space.

BIBLIOGRAPHY AND WEBSITES

Alves, Péricles Gasparini and Cipollone, Dariana Belinda (eds), *Nuclear Weapons-Free Zones in the 21st Century*, UNIDIR, 1997

Cochrane, Thomas B.C., Arkin, William M.A. and Hoenig, Milton M.H., *Nuclear Weapons Databook*, Ballinger, 1984

Charpak, George and Garwin, Richard, *Will-o'-the-Wisp and Nuclear Mushrooms*, Macmillan, 1998

Kokoski, Henry (ed.), *Fighting Proliferation: New Concerns for the Nineties*, Air University Press, 1996

Kokoski, Richard, *Technology and the Proliferation of Nuclear Weapons*, SIPRI, 1996.

Quinlan, Michael, *Thinking About Nuclear Weapons*, RUSI Whitehall Papers Series, 1997

Report of the Canberra Commission on the Elimination of Nuclear Weapons, Australian Ministry of Foreign Affairs, 1996

Arms Control Association. www.armscontrol.org

Bulletin of Atomic The Scientists. www.bullatomsci.org

Centre for Non-Proliferation Studies (Monterey Institute of International Studies): www.cns.miis.edu

Non-Governmental Committee on Disarmament: www.igc.apc.org/disarm
US State Department: www.acda.gov

Chemical and Biological Weapons (CBW)

Chemical weapons (CW) are man-made poisons. They can be disseminated by explosive charges (rockets, aircraft bombs, artillery shells) or by dispersal from aircraft spray tanks (similar to crop spraying). There are four basic types, classified by the effects they have on the human body. Choking agents cause damage to the lungs; they include chlorine and phosgene. Vesicants burn the body both externally and internally; mustard gas is the best known example. Blood agents, such as hydrogen cyanide, block the passage of blood. The most modern and potentially most dangerous type is nerve agent, which can be absorbed through the skin and disables the nervous system; they include Sarin, Tabun and VX.

Biological weapons (BW) are living organisms which cause death or illness in man and animals and can destroy plants. They are disseminated in the same ways as CW but, because they multiply once they have infected a host body, much less agent is needed than in a CW attack to cause the same level of casualties. BW agents must normally be inhaled but can also attack via contaminated food and water, open wounds or insect vectors. BW agents

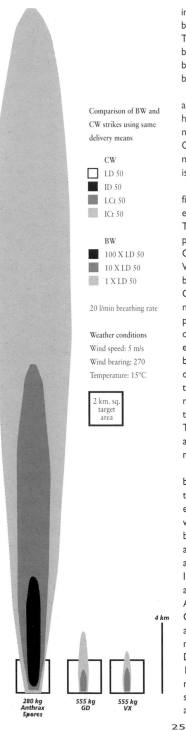

Comparison of BW and CW strikes using same delivery means

CW
☐ LD 50
■ ID 50
▨ LCt 50
▨ ICt 50

BW
■ 100 X LD 50
▨ 10 X LD 50
▨ 1 X LD 50

20 l/min breathing rate

Weather conditions
Wind speed: 5 m/s
Wind bearing: 270
Temperature: 15°C

2 km. sq.
target
area

4 km

**280 kg
Anthrax
Spores**

**555 kg
GD**

**555 kg
VX**

include bacteria (such as anthrax, plague and brucellosis), and viruses, rickettsia and fungi. Toxins such as botulinum and ricin lie between BW and CW as they are of biological origin and can also be manufactured, but they are not living organisms.

BW attack is far more effective than CW as it spreads much further and has a far higher lethality; CW potency is measured in milligrams, BW in micrograms and picograms. Given the right conditions BW can kill far more people than a nuclear attack but there is no material destruction.

Neither CW nor BW are new. CW were first employed by the Greeks in 600 BC and an early use of BW occurred in 1347 when the Tartars catapulted the bodies of bubonic plague victims into the besieged city of Caffa. Gas was used extensively in the First World War but not in the Second, despite both sides being well supplied with CW. While BW and CW are not given such a high profile as nuclear weapons in the battle against proliferation they can cause as many casualties, are much simpler and less expensive to produce, and do not require ballistic missiles or modern bombers to deliver them. The release of Sarin nerve gas in the Tokyo subway by the Aum Shinrikyo religious cult on 20 March 1995 demonstrated that BW and CW can be terrorist weapons. They can be disseminated from crop-spraying aircraft and car exhausts, and BW through municipal water supply systems.

While nuclear weapons have only ever been used operationally twice, at the end of the Second World War, CW have been employed several times in recent years. They were used by Egypt in the Yemen in the 1960s; by Iraq against Iran in 1984 against exposed and unprotected troops making human wave attacks – and later in the war this provoked Iranian retaliation but on a much lesser scale; and by Iraq against the Kurds at Halabjah in April 1988. CW were not used in the 1991 Gulf War although it was discovered afterwards that Iraq had stocks of 800 tons of mustard gas, Tabun and Sarin nerve agents. Delivery could have been by aircraft (over 1,300 bombs were found), artillery shells and rockets (9,000 were found), and by surface-to-surface missiles (30 warheads for Al-Hussein and Scud missiles). Shortly after 11 September a number of anthrax-contaminated letters were posted, some to Congressmen, in the US. Although al Qaida was immediately suspected, it is now thought that a lone, probably American, citizen was responsible. As yet the culprit has not been found.

The lethality of CBW is expressed as the dosage needed to kill 50 per cent of the exposed, unprotected population. For example, an agent with a LCt 50 rating of 150 will be lethal to 50 per cent of those (assuming they breathe 10 litres of air per minute) who are exposed to a concentration of 15mg/cu. m for ten minutes, or experience a thirty-second exposure to a concentration of 300mg/cu. m. Another measure is expressed in milligrams of agent per kg of body weight; a man weighing 100kg would be killed by a 10,000mg dose of an agent with a LD 50 rating of 100. In both forms of measurement the lower the rating the more lethal the agent.

Just as weapons of this type have been around for centuries, so arms control in the CBW field is not new either; in 1675 the French and Germans agreed to prohibit the use of poisoned bullets. The first major treaty was the 1925 Geneva Protocol 'for the Prohibition of the Use in War of Asphyxiating, Poisonous or Other Gases and of Bacteriological Methods of Warfare', which was signed and ratified by the majority of the leading powers. It did not ban development or manufacture, nor was there any provision for verification. In 1972 a 'Convention on the Prohibition of the Development, Production and Stockpiling of Bacteriological (Biological) and Toxin Weapons and on their Destruction' was signed and has since been ratified or acceded to by 144 countries; ratification is awaited from sixteen other signatory countries. The 1972 Convention came into force after ratification by the depository states – the US, the UK and the USSR – on 26 March 1975. However, there are no measures to ensure compliance. Verification and compliance were the subject of negotiations for a legally binding protocol begun in 1994 and being conducted by the Ad Hoc Group in Geneva. It was hoped to reach agreement on a compromise text at the Group's meeting in July 2001 but the US rejected the current draft protocol and refused to take part in further negotiations to reach agreement.

The US stated that it was firmly committed to combating BW threats but it had concluded that the protocol would not strengthen confidence in compliance, would not achieve verification and would do little to deter countries intent on producing BW. It also declared that transparency visits envisaged by the protocol would put national security and commercial information at risk. At the BW Convention review conference held in November the US Under-Secretary for Arms Control claimed that a number of countries had told the US privately that they agreed with its opinion of the draft protocol. He revealed that some of the 11 September hijackers had made inquiries about renting crop-spraying aircraft. He went on to name Iran, Iraq and North Korea as three countries that the US believed had BW development programmes; the BW Convention had not prevented this nor would the protocol have done so. The US proposed the strengthening of the BW Convention, first by requiring states to enact legislation that would make it a criminal offence to violate BW Convention prohibitions. Secondly, it advocated international investigation of suspicious outbreaks of disease or other suspected BW incidents. The next review conference is to take place in November 2002.

In 1968 the Conference for Disarmament in Geneva began negotiating a 'Convention on the Prohibition of the Development, Production, Stockpiling and Use of Chemical Weapons and their Destruction' (CWC) but real progress towards a treaty only started in June 1990 after the US–USSR CW agreement was reached. The treaty text was adopted in September 1992, unanimously endorsed by the United Nations General Assembly in November and opened for signature in Paris on 13 January 1993, when 130 countries signed it. The convention came into force on 29 April 1997, 180 days after sixty-five countries had ratified it; all CW stocks and production facilities must be destroyed by 2007. The UN has established the Organisation for the Prohibition of Chemical Weapons (OPCW), which includes an Executive Council with a quota of members from each region of the world and a Technical Secretariat whose Verification Division has 140 inspectors and 100 other staff.

Routine verification includes a comprehensive data exchange, including details of national production of forty-three specific chemicals listed in the CWC, on-site inspections of chemical industries, and analysis of samples collected. Challenge inspections can be called for by parties to the treaty but are carried out by the Technical Secretariat.

Prior to CWC only two nations – the USSR and the US – had declared a CW capability, both holding enormous stocks of CW agent. First, the two states signed a Memorandum of Understanding regarding a bilateral verification experiment and an exchange of data; then in June 1990 they signed an agreement on the destruction and non-production of CW which required the destruction of all CW agent bar 5,000 tons each by the end of 2002. Within eight years of the CWC coming into force their stocks would be reduced to 500 tons. Destruction of the large quantities involved has not been easy both for financial reasons and on account of local opposition to destruction facilities being operated in their region for fear of environmental pollution. The Russians admitted in June 2001 that its destruction programme had fallen years behind schedule and asked that the 2007 deadline be extended to 2012. The cost of Russian CW destruction will be over $8 billion; so far the US, which has pledged $888 million, has only provided $30 million in assistance. In August 2002, the first CW destruction facility, paid for by Germany, was formally opened. Construction of two further facilities is well behind schedule as US funds are being withheld by Congress. India and South Korea both declared CW stocks and both had met their commitment to have destroyed one per cent of their stockpiles by the end of 1999.

In addition to stockpiles of current CW there are also 'old chemical weapons' (OPW) and 'abandoned chemical weapons' (ACW). Every year amounts of OPW are discovered, mainly buried in First World War battle sites. ACW are abandoned on the territory of a third party. The Japanese left large quantities of CW in China and the two countries have been jointly working to solve the problem.

Another effort to halt the proliferation of CBW agents takes the form of controls agreed to by members of the Australia Group, formed in 1985, regarding the export of dual-use materials and technology. The Group has twenty-eight members and has published detailed lists of chemicals, biological agents and equipment the export of which should be controlled.

There are a number of disadvantages to both BW and CW as battlefield weapons. Modern armies now equip their soldiers with protective clothing and so unless total surprise can be achieved casualties may not be high and conventional artillery fire would have to accompany any CBW attack. BW needs time to take effect, perhaps even several days, and so will not produce the instant casualties required to guarantee the success of a battlefield attack. CBW is also affected by weather conditions. Although there is no wind speed that precludes the use of CBW, clouds of agent will be blown away from target areas more quickly by stronger winds and the rate of evaporation of liquid agent increases as wind speeds rise. Winds rarely maintain a constant speed or direction, and the more unstable the atmospheric conditions, the less effective the CBW attack will be. Turbulence, which depends mainly on changing air temperatures at different heights, will mix vapour clouds with clean air and reduce the concentration of agent. On the other hand, rain has little cleansing effect on CBW; if it falls on contaminated ground then the evaporation rate of the agent will increase and the concentration of agent in the atmosphere will rise. The effectiveness of CW is not governed by temperature, although high temperature and humidity makes the wearing of protective clothing even more uncomfortable. The wearing of protective clothing degrades troops' capability, particularly where tactile skills are needed.

The US Director of Central Intelligence reported to Congress on the 'Acquisition of Technology Relating to Weapons of Mass Destruction', and the unclassified version of his report: can be summarised as follows: Iran: has a CW capability and a limited BW capability; Iraq: may have hidden CW weapons and may still be producing BW agents; North Korea: is capable of delivering CW and some BW agents; Libya: still has the goal of establishing an offensive CW capability; Sudan: has been developing a CW production capability for many years.

BIBLIOGRAPHY AND WEBSITES
Krutzsch, Walter and Trapp, Ralf, *A Commentary on the Chemical Weapons Convention*, Martinus Nijhoff, 1994
Lederberg, Joshua (ed.), *Biological Weapons: Limiting the Threat*, MIT Press, 1999
Leeuwen van, Marianne, *Crying Wolf: Assessing Unconventional Terrorism*, Clingendael, 2000
Roberts, Brad (ed.), *Terrorism with Chemical and Biological Weapons: Calibrating Risks and Responses*, Chemical and Biological Arms Control Institute, 1997
Stern, Jessica, *The Ultimate Terrorists*, Harvard University Press, 1999

Centre for Civil Biodefense Studies: www.hopkins-biodefense.org
Chemical and Biological Institute (Washington): www.chaci.org
Harvard Sussex Program: fas-www.harvard.edu/~hsp
Joint University of Bradford and SIPRI CBW Project: www.brad.ac.uk/acad/sbtwc

Missiles

Weapons of mass destruction (nuclear, biological and chemical (NBC)) can be delivered by a variety of means, depending on the weight of warhead, the range and accuracy needed, and the favoured option of the deliverer. Delivery means include ground- and submarine-launched intercontinental ballistic missiles (ICBMs and SLBMs); intermediate and short-range missiles (IRBMs, SSMs); cruise missiles launched from the ground, ships, submarines or aircraft; aircraft bombs; artillery and rocket launchers; and by covert action by terrorists.

This analysis concentrates on missiles as they are regarded as the main danger from proliferating countries; most modern combat aircraft can be adapted to carry nuclear and CBW weapons. There are advantages and disadvantages in employing both aircraft and missiles. Missiles are less expensive than aircraft and there is no danger to a pilot, but they can only be used once. In first and second generation missiles accuracy is poor and so they are only suitable for delivering nuclear warheads unless a large number can be fired. Range is of less importance if the target area is a small country not far away; for example, Syria only needs missiles with a range of some 400km to be able to strike the whole of Israel; its SS-21 SSM can reach as far south as Tel Aviv. Aircraft can carry far heavier payloads than any missile, and with in-flight refuelling can reach targets anywhere in the world. They can be recalled (as the bombers sent to attack Iraq in December 1998 were when Saddam Hussein agreed to US demands), while missiles, once launched, have to be destroyed to prevent them reaching their targets. Aircraft involve the human factor that can lead to the misidentification of targets, but missiles can and do go astray. Aircraft are more vulnerable to air defences, though they can to some extent be protected by electronic means. A further disadvantage of missile attack is that the launch site can be readily detected whereas it could be possible to mount either an aircraft or a terrorist attack without the attacker being identified. Anti-missile weapons are being developed and may soon be operational but this may only accelerate the production of missiles in an attempt to swamp the defences.

The most worrying missile developments are in those countries known or thought to be developing nuclear weapons or CBW and in countries eager to export their missiles or missile technology. Among the former are India, Iran, Iraq, Israel, Libya, North Korea, Pakistan and Syria; in the latter are China, North Korea and Russia. India, Iran, Israel, North Korea and Pakistan are developing their own missiles but, except for Israel, with substantial outside help. In September 1999 the US made a deal with North Korea and agreed to lift a number of sanctions imposed some forty years ago in return for the North Koreans promising not to carry out any more test-flights of their long-range missile, the Taepo Dong 2. Also in September Israel accused Syria of upgrading its SCUD missiles so that they could reach all of Israel. The US has agreed to assist South Korea in improving its missile capability in terms of

Missile-armed countries

▮ —— Over 5000 km. range
▮ — 500-5000 km.
▮ — 100-500 km.

▒ MTCR members

USA

Countries armed with missiles with over 100 kilometre range

quantity and range. Since 1979 and until now the US had restricted South Korea to missiles with a range no greater than 180km. Indian and Pakistani missile capability is described on pp. 166–7, that of Iran, Israel and other Middle East states on pp. 74–5.

In an attempt to halt the spread of missile technology the Missile Technology Control Regime (MTCR) was formed by seven founding members in 1987. It consists of a set of guidelines to govern members' export of missiles and unmanned aerial vehicles, their components and technology. Originally the regime only covered delivery vehicles for nuclear weapons; after the Gulf War it was agreed to include delivery systems for CBW in the regime. In practical terms the regime seeks to ban the transfer of missiles with a range of 300km carrying a 500kg payload. The new guidelines included the 'strong presumption' to deny the export of components for missiles with ranges and payloads below the MCTR limits if they are intended for the delivery of weapons of mass destruction. The MCTR now has twenty-nine members and a further eight countries have said they will abide by its provisions. By signing the Intermediate Nuclear Forces Treaty which came into force on 1 June 1988 the USSR and the US agreed to eliminate and not replace their ground-launched ballistic and cruise missiles with ranges between 500km and 5,500km; other nations can and have deployed missiles of this type.

Developing long-range missiles is as much a demonstration of power projection as a requirement for the delivery of NBC weapons. Once countries have acquired the capability to produce BW or CW they would find it far cheaper to deliver them by covert means.

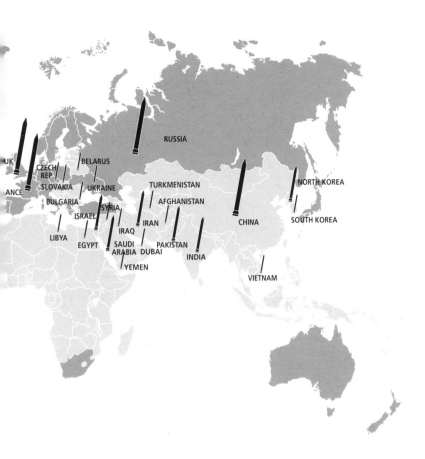

What might potentially be achieved was shown by the inefficient use of CW by the Aum Shinriko cult on the Tokyo subway in March 1995: a more professional attack could have killed thousands.

Sophisticated cruise missiles that can 'jink' and follow contours will be harder to shoot down than ICBMs. Cruise missiles do not need to be that sophisticated and very simple ones employing the same characteristics as unmanned aircraft (UAV) or remotely piloted vehicles (RPV), if fired in sufficient quantity, could penetrate defences just as the German V1 did in the Second World War.

There is a growing realisation that major cities may face CBW attack by a variety of means and that passive defence by way of protective masks and clothing and antidote serums should be readily available, in addition to active measures such as ballistic missile defence, as described on pp. 256–259.

BIBLIOGRAPHY AND WEBSITES

International Perspectives on Missile Proliferation and Defenses, Monterey Institute of International Studies, 2001

Arms Control Association: www.armscontrol.org
Ballistic Missile Defence Organisation: www.acq.osd.mil/bmdo
Center for Defense Information: www.cdi.org

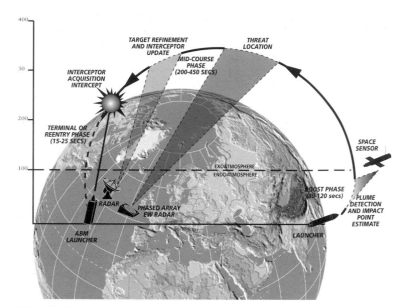

Ballistic Missile Defence

Ballistic Missile Defence

The announcement that the US would withdraw from the Anti-Ballistic Missile Treaty in June 2002 has completely changed the possibilities for ballistic missile defence. One of the paradoxes of the post-Cold War world is the new-found emphasis on ballistic missile defence. During the Cold War, when both sides faced large numbers of strategic nuclear missiles, the deployment of US and Soviet anti-ballistic missiles (ABMs) was controlled by treaty. In the tactical field, where the Warsaw Pact was plentifully equipped with surface-to-surface missiles (SSMs) such as Scaleboard, Scud and Frog, and NATO rather less plentifully with Pershing and Lance SSMs, there were no anti-SSM weapons at all. Now, when the threat comes from, or rather may come from, a handful of strategic missiles and from improved SSMs in the hands of 'rogue' states, much effort and money is being expended by the US, and to a lesser extent by Israel (but with faster results), on the development of both national and theatre missile defence (NMD and TMD).

The development of ABMs was seen to lead to a race to procure even more strategic missiles so that any defence system would be overwhelmed. To avoid an accelerated arms race in ballistic missiles the ABM Treaty signed by the US and USSR in 1972 prohibited the deployment of a nationwide defence against strategic ballistic missiles. Originally each side could deploy two systems, later amended to only one, to defend either the national capital or one ICBM launch area. The Soviet Union established a system around Moscow and the US deployed the Safeguard system to protect the ICBM complex at Grand Forks, North Dakota. The Moscow system is thought to be still operational although a number of the essential early warning radars have been shut down as they no longer stand on Russian soil. The US ABM system ceased to be operational in 1976.

A number of the new ABM systems proposed by the US would violate the ABM Treaty and Russia was adamant that it should not be amended, even though the US claimed that its ABM would be limited to defend against rogue states' missiles and not Russian ICBM and

SLBM. The Russians reaffirmed their opposition to altering the treaty as recently as November 2001 at the Putin/Bush summit. China is also opposed to any ABM defences as the deployment of a theatre system in defence of Taiwan 'would only undermine security and stimulate the proliferation of missiles'. Taiwan, however, is determined to deploy TMD. America's allies were concerned too; radar facilities located in the UK and Greenland would have to be upgraded to allow them to contribute to missile defence and both countries might have been unwilling to assist the breaking of the ABM Treaty on their territory. Many Europeans believe that abrogating ABM will lead to the end of nuclear arms control and disarmament and could lead to China and Russia improving their offensive capability so as to be able to swamp US missile defences. Russia and the US have agreed various parameters that demarcate between TMD and strategic missile defence. One parameter would only allow the deployment of TMD with an interceptor velocity of no more than 3km/second; short-range missiles can achieve this speed and more.

In March 1983 President Reagan embarked on the Strategic Defence Initiative (SDI), and had spent over $30 billion before the concept was radically altered in 1993. After SDI the US turned to developing TMD and returned to the concept of NMD in January 1999. Among the concepts evolved for SDI were space- and ground-based surveillance and tracking systems, kinetic energy, laser and particle beam weapons, and space-based mirrors to reflect laser beams from a ground station to a target. One of the technically most ambitious parts of the project was 'Brilliant Pebbles', which was to consist of an array of autonomous space-based kinetic energy weapons, each with its own sensor, guidance, control and battle management capability. The weapons would be light (about 45kg), low-cost, and powered by solar rechargeable batteries. While SDI was expensive and did not come to fruition, it had the effect of convincing the Soviet Union that it could not match US defence spending and so helped to lead to Mikhail Gorbachev's policies that ended the Cold War.

Of course, ICBMs are not the only way to deliver weapons of mass destruction and rather different defence systems would be needed to cope with long-range cruise missiles and with low trajectory missiles fired from submarines lying close to the target shore. Simple cruise missiles based on remotely piloted vehicles would be easier to intercept than a ballistic missile but sophisticated cruise missiles that can 'jink' and contour-hug will be difficult to acquire by ground-based radar and the US is experimenting with airborne radar to solve this problem. Many consider that BW and CW could be delivered more successfully and far more cheaply by terrorists than by missiles. It is possible that other airliners may be hijacked for this purpose.

Before any country deployed an ABM system it would need to take into account the views of the countries over whose territories the incoming missiles would be destroyed. The missiles might be armed with chemical or biological agents (though BW germs may not survive the low temperature and aridity of the upper atmosphere) and their destruction could result in fall-out of the agent over a friendly country.

The diagram illustrates a typical flight-path of an ICBM. The flight is divided into three phases: boost phase, midcourse phase and terminal phase. Different weapon systems are being developed to engage missiles in each phase. The best moment to attack an incoming missile is during the boost phase when the burning fuel presents a target easily recognised by infra-red sensors. Before separation the missile presents a much larger target and also moves more slowly. Importantly, the missile is still over the launcher's territory and so the risk of fall-out is avoided, and multiple, independently targeted re-entry vehicles and decoys will not have been released. A boost phase kill has to be achieved in less than two minutes: interceptors will need to be close, within 200km of the launch sites, and fast. They would probably need to be airborne or space-based, but in some areas a sea-based system would be possible.

Work on the Boost Defense Segment (originally called the 'boost phase') is split between the development of kinetic and directed energy weapons. Kinetic energy weapons could be both sea- and space-based. There could be two directed energy systems: an

Airborne Laser (ABL) and a Space-Based Laser (SBL). Initially development of SBL will be based on establishing components and technologies using ground-based facilities.

Successful tests of the Ground-Based Interceptor, which is a candidate for NMD, took place in October 1999 when the ABM hit a Minuteman ICBM 140 miles over the Pacific. The next test in July 2001 involved discriminating between a warhead and a single decoy, and in December another successful test was held with the 'kill' vehicle being launched from Kwajalein Atoll in the Marshall Islands against a missile warhead fired from Vandenberg, California. Each test cost $100 million. The US government has given the go-ahead for a study by the Defense Science Board that would include the use of nuclear-armed interceptors. Employing a nuclear warhead would make it possible to destroy not just the incoming warhead but also the accompanying decoys. There are, however, disadvantages to the use of nuclear weapons in space (banned by the Partial Test Ban Treaty), particularly the effect of electromagnetic-pulse on satellites.

Terminal defences are designed to destroy missiles once they have re-entered the atmosphere; they are either lower-tier weapons (such as the US Patriot) intercepting at up to 30km altitude, or higher-tier weapons that can engage at an altitude between 30 and several hundred km. The area that can be protected by either tier depends on the speed of the incoming missile, and that in turn depends largely on its range. The terminal phase for incoming missiles lasts between fifteen and twenty-five seconds only. Terminal defences can be based on land or on warships, the latter giving greater flexibility in deployment.

The Terminal Defense Segment had an ambitious programme of both lower- and higher-tier weapons. Lower-tier weapons are the Patriot Advanced Capability-3 (PAC-3) and the Navy Area Program (originally called the Navy Theater Wide System), which would have employed a phased-array radar and an upgraded Standard Missile mounted on Aegis-equipped ships. Testing at sea was expected to begin in late 2002. However, the cancellation of the programme was announced in December 2001, mainly because of poor performance and cost overrun; the programme had already cost $2.8 billion. The Medium Extended Air Defense System (MEADS) is being developed in cooperation with Germany and Italy; it will employ PAC-3, Confirmation tests of PAC-3 held between February and May 2002 were not successful, with a number of misfires, and only half of those launched hit their target.. Upper-tier TMD weapons – the Theater High Altitude Area Defense (THAAD) and the Navy Theater Wide System – are designed to intercept medium- and intermediate-range missiles at high altitude and so will be able to defend larger areas than lower-tier weapons. A successful THAAD intercept was carried out in June 1999 after six earlier test failures; the system development has cost $3 billion since 1992. The Navy Theater Wide development is behind that of THAAD but a decision on which of the two systems will be procured is to be taken in 2002 with the aim of a system entering service in 2007. THAAD could also be mounted on a warship. The Tactical High Energy Laser is designed to shoot down medium- to short-range missiles within a range of 5km. The chemical laser, which employs deuterium fluoride, is being developed in cooperation with Israel, and was successfully tested against a target in June 2000. An airborne laser (ABL) is also being developed that can intercept ballistic missiles early in their flight: the first in-flight lethality test is planned for 2003. All these weapons can also be deployed as TMD.

The development of Israel's Arrow anti-tactical ballistic missile (ATBM) began in 1986 and is being jointly funded by the US. The system comprises three elements: the ATBM, the Green Pine radar which can track fourteen incoming missiles from a distance of 500km and the Citron Tree fire control system that guides Arrow to its target. Arrow employs a blast fragmentation warhead that does not require a direct hit to destroy or injure the incoming missile. It was successfully tested against another missile in November 1999 and again in September 2000. Arrow is now considered operational and one out of three batteries has been deployed.

The academic argument is now over, and the US withdrew from the ABM Treaty in June 2002. Work began on the construction of missile silos at Fort Greely, Alaska, on 15 June.

The BMDO has been renamed the Missile Defense Agency (MDA); upgrading it to agency status recognises the national priority and the emphasis given to missile defence. The MDA is responsible for developing the systems while the military departments will be responsible for procurement and provision of missile defence operations and support. The Congressional Budget Office, on the assumption that all systems under development will become operational, estimates that the cost of BMD could be as much as $238 billion by 2025.

Have the events of 11 September altered the US requirement for ABM? Opinion is divided. Perhaps the answer lies with what the US does to counter the 'axis of evil', whose members are all known to be keen to acquire nuclear, chemical and biological weapons and the missiles to deliver them where they do not already possess these. Should the US succeed in totally eliminating not just these states' actual weaponry but also the possibility that they will ever be able to produce them, then the stated requirement for deploying ABM will have gone. However, whatever else happens deployment of ABM is likely to take place.

BIBLIOGRAPHY AND WEBSITES

Brown, Neville, *The Fundamental Issue Studies: Within the British BMD Review*, Mansfield College, Oxford, 1998

Denoon, D.B.H., *Ballistic Missile Defense in the Cold War Era*, Westview Press, 1995

Disarmament Forum Volume 1 (includes a full bibliography and Website list), UN Institute for Disarmament Research, 2001

Wilkening, D.A., *Ballistic-Missile Defence and Strategic Stability*, Adelphi Paper 334, International Institute for Strategic Studies, ????

Arms Control Association: www.armscontrol.com
Ballistic Missile Defense Organisation: www.acq.osd.mil/bmdo/
Disarmament Diplomacy: www.acronym.org.uk
Federation of American Scientists: www.fas.org/spp/starwars/
Henry L. Stimson Center: www.stimson.org

War in Space

The military use space far more than any other element of society; indeed, space has become an essential area for them. It offers several advantages. First, it belongs to no one so there is no problem regarding entry into another country's air space, as the US U-2 spy planes had to do during the 1950s. Secondly, to be able to communicate between any two points anywhere on Earth requires only three geostationary satellites on a circular orbit over the equator at an altitude of 35,680km. The main disadvantages are the difficulty of hiding in space, and probably more serious the growing reliance of the military on space-based aids, the loss of which could seriously impede operations on earth. Space is nevertheless the best place for military eyes and ears to operate from.

The US, naturally, has the widest space-based inventory and it cannot be matched, for reasons of cost, by any other country or alliance. Originally satellite-derived imagery, known as Imint, was only available to the US and the Soviet Union but now there are an increasing number of commercial satellites that can be tasked by anyone to obtain the imagery they require. Commercial satellites obviously cannot react to new requirements as quickly as military ones and so far the resolution of their imagery is far inferior to that obtainable by US military satellites. At present the US has two satellite systems providing imagery: the Improved Crystal, or advanced KH-11/12, can provide both optical and infra-red imagery with a resolution of as little as 15cm; the Lacrosse radar-imaging satellite that has a resolution of 1–2m. An example of the commercial satellite imagery available is that provided by Space Imaging, which has launched two IKONOS satellites, orbiting at 680km altitude and delivering imagery with a resolution of 1m.

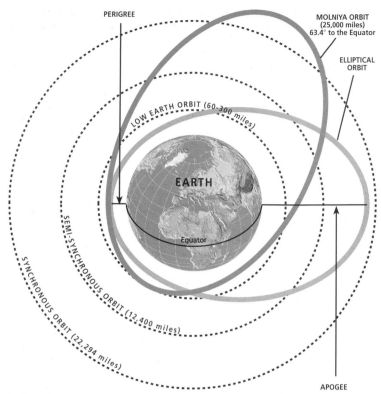

Satellite orbits

In addition to imagery, satellites also provide valuable intelligence by intercepting communications (Sigint) and other electronic transmissions (Elint) such as radar emissions. The US is believed to have at least seven such satellites. While both Sigint and Elint can be collected by ground and seaborne intercept stations and by specially equipped aircraft, satellites are ideally suited for this. Satellites in low to mid-earth orbit (800–1,120km altitude) are used to intercept air defence and early warning radar signals, and can track ships from their radar signatures. Satellites in geostationary orbit at 35,680km altitude travel at the same speed as the Earth revolves and so remain over the same area continuously; they are ideal for picking up UHF and VHF signals whose interception requires line of sight. Satellites in elliptical orbit can, depending on their inclination, spend most of their orbit over their target area as they move towards and from their apogee. The US Trump system has an elliptical orbit, as do several of the Russian satellites. One of the problems of employing both Imint and Sigint satellites is that the volume of material intercepted is vast and has to be filtered by computers programmed to identify messages containing certain keywords; these can then be analysed further. There may be no shortage of raw data but, and this was brought out during the Gulf War, there is a shortage of analysts.

Satellites also produce valuable early warning. The US Defense Support Program (DSP) employs infra-red sensors to detect missile launches (in their boost phase), nuclear detonations and other infra-red events. After spotting a missile plume or aircraft after-burner the satellites alert the appropriate ground-based early warning and missile-tracking radar. The US is currently developing its next generation Space-Based Infra-red System

(SBIRS) satellites, the first of which will be launched in 2005. The system will employ both geosynchronous high-altitude satellites and twenty-four more in low earth orbit tasked to track missiles for both National and Theatre Missile Defence.

France, Italy and Spain cooperated in the production of two Helios 1 satellites. The first was launched in 1995 to provide imagery with a 1m resolution. France, Germany and Italy have agreed to jointly fund the French-designed Helios 2 satellite, which will also have an infra-red capability, and the Horus radar satellite; the former was launched in 2001 and the latter will be sometime between 2002 and 2004. The Western European Union (WEU) established a Satellite Centre at Torrejon in Spain which was transferred to the European Union in 2002; satellite imagery interpretation takes place here. At present it relies on Helios and commercial imagery as there is no multinational European satellite.

Communications are vital to any military operation and the introduction of satellites has greatly eased the problems of long-range communications. There are a great number of both military and civil systems operated by a number of countries; this was well demonstrated in the Gulf War when both special forces patrols and television camera crews were equipped with satellite ground stations. During the Gulf War the US Indian Ocean satellite of the Defence Satellite Communications System (DSCS) was soon overloaded. The Eastern Atlantic satellite had to have its antennae realigned and a reserve satellite over the West Pacific was repositioned (an operation that took a month to complete) so that the system could cope with the massive communications load. The Americans have ambitious plans for upgrading their satellite communications capability over the next ten years.

Finally the military are becoming reliant – as also are yachtsmen, among others – on the Global Positioning System (GPS) for pinpointing their position and for guiding a number of airborne weapons including cruise missiles. The US Navigational Satellite Timing and Ranging (NAVSTAR) system comprises twenty-one satellites plus three in-orbit reserves placed in six orbital planes at 20,000km altitude. They transmit two signals. One is encrypted so that only military users can receive and decrypt them to give a positional accuracy to within 15m. Civilian users access an uncrypted signal that gives their position to within 30m. However, this facility can be degraded to allow only a 100m accuracy so as not to aid one's enemy. NAVSTAR allows a minimum of four satellites to be accessed simultaneously from any point on Earth. The European Union is planning to develop its own GPS system, known as Galileo, in the face of strong US opposition. The US sees the system as unnecessary duplication and a commercial rival to their GPS system. Galileo should be operational in 2008 and will generate 100,000 jobs.

Space-based systems are well suited to verify arms control and environmental treaties. When the first treaties were negotiated some countries were reluctant to admit that they were using space to spy on their enemies and so the anodyne phrase 'national technical means' (NTM) was crafted to cover Imint and Sigint. Most treaties include a clause forbidding interference with NTM.

Anti-Satellite (ASAT) weapons have been and are being developed. Three main types are envisaged: steerable killer satellites that would be manoeuvred alongside the target and then exploded; rocket-propelled missiles that would destroy the satellite by smashing into it; and laser or high-energy beams. The US first tested an ASAT weapon in 1959 with a nuclear-armed rocket; the test was successful but the radioactive fall-out and electromagnetic-pulse side effects were so serious that the project was abandoned. The Partial Test Ban Treaty prohibits nuclear explosions in the atmosphere and outer space. Since then the US Air Force has developed a Miniature Homing Vehicle that would be launched from an airborne platform and would destroy the satellite by the force of impact. A successful test (and the only one conducted) was carried out in September 1985 using an F-15 fighter as the launch vehicle. The US army was developing a similar weapon that would initially be launched by a Pershing II missile, which would double the range of the aircraft-launched ASAT. This programme was terminated in 1993. One problem with developing

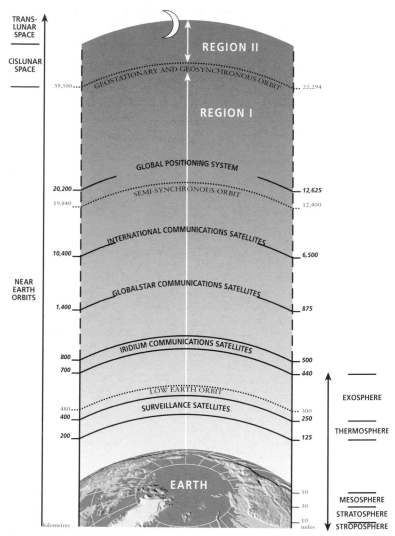

Divisions of space

ASAT was that they could also be Anti-Ballistic Missile weapons that were banned by the ABM Treaty, from which the US has withdrawn. Now the concern must be that ABM weapons could also be used to destroy satellites.

The Soviet Union developed its own ASAT, a co-orbital weapon, between 1968 and 1982: it was tested at least twenty times. In 1983 the Russians announced a unilateral moratorium on developing ASAT but failed to get the US Administration to join as the latter was already embarking on the Strategic Defence Initiative (SDI). However, the US Congress restricted ASAT testing for five years, a move that led to the cancellation of the associated F-15 programme. In 1992 a display of aircraft for the Minsk summit meeting of the Commonwealth of Independent States included a MiG-31 armed with what was claimed to be an ASAT weapon.

In December 1994 a senior research fellow at Stanford University claimed that the space-based laser known as Alpha was virtually ready for deployment. The Alpha project was part of SDI. It was also claimed that a force of twelve laser-armed satellites could engage five ballistic missiles per minute when they were still over the launching country's territory. The Soviet Union had also been conducting laser weapon development at a site in the mountains of Tajikistan.

On 17 October 1997 the US tested its ground-based Mid-Infra-red Advanced Chemical Laser (MIRACL). The chemical laser is produced by the combustion of hydrogen and fluorine. The aim of the tests was to examine the effects of 1- and 10-second bursts of the laser beam on the target satellite's imaging sensors. The trial raised a number of objections and criticisms. The Russians said, correctly, that 'laser programmes may become a step towards creating an anti-satellite potential' – something that the Soviet Union has opposed since they attempted to negotiate an ASAT Treaty with the USA in the 1970s. Democrat senators had tried to get the test postponed on the grounds that no test should take place before the whole question of ASAT had been properly debated, and that demonstrating such a capability could encourage others to embark on ASAT development. Other critics claimed the tests could just as well have been conducted on the ground. The ABM Treaty banned all space-based missile interceptors, including lasers.

If ASAT is a feasible military operation then the next development must be protection and counter-measures for satellites and an anti-ASAT weapon. Given the numerous difficulties in negotiating an ASAT treaty war in space looks a more likely option. Both President Bush and Secretary of Defense Donald Rumsfeld have shown an interest in developing space-based weapons for both ABM and to attack an enemy's ASAT weapons. In January 2001 the US Air Force held its first space war-game. Certainly the loss of intelligence-collection and communications satellites would be a major setback in any conflict situation and will eventually have to be guarded against.

BIBLIOGRAPHY AND WEBSITES
Levine, Alan J., *The Missile and Space Race*, Praeger, 1994

Space Imaging: www.spaceimaging.com
US Space Command: www.spacecom.af.mil/usspace

Anti-Personnel Mines

The initiative to complete a treaty against anti-personnel mines was taken by Canada in October 1996, as UN efforts to achieve one appeared to be making no progress. Until 1999 international law on the issue was set out in the 1980 UN Weapons Convention, the full title of which is 'Convention on Prohibitions or Restrictions on the Use of Certain Conventional Weapons which May be Deemed to be Excessively Injurious or to have Indiscriminate Effects'. The convention covered not only mines and booby-traps but also weapons such as dumdum bullets, weapons that fragment into pieces undetectable by X-rays, and incendiaries. It was a follow-on to the 1949 Geneva Convention on the Protection of War Victims. Forty-one states became parties to the convention, which only covered clashes between states and not internal armed conflict, despite the fact that the latter most frequently generates the indiscriminate laying of mines. A protocol to the convention has been opened for signature and has been approved by the US Senate. The protocol bans the use of non-detectable anti-personnel mines (some were used by the Argentinians in the Falklands) and of mines equipped with anti-handling devices. Non-self-destructing and non-self-deactivating mines may be laid only in marked areas, and signatories are committed to not exporting anti-personnel mines.

The Ottawa Convention, or the Convention on the Prohibition of the Use, Stockpiling, Production and Transfer of Anti-Personnel Mines and on Their Destruction (the Land Mine

Non-signatories of Ottawa Convention
(also PALAU, TONGA, TUVALU and MICRONESIA)

Serious landmine problems

Landmines: affected countries and the Ottawa Convention

Treaty for short) came into force on 1 March 1999, six months after the fortieth ratification. By November 2001 a total of 142 countries had signed the treaty and 122 had ratified or acceded to it. However, a number of significant states have not yet become signatories, including the US, China and Russia; the first two have ratified the 1980 convention and Russia has signed but not ratified it. It is more understandable that countries which have been involved in war in recent years have not signed; these include Egypt, India, Iran, Iraq, Israel, Pakistan, Saudi Arabia, Turkey, Vietnam and Yugoslavia. North and South Korea have not signed as both rely heavily on the use of anti-personnel mines to protect their borders from infiltration. The US cites the defence of South Korea as a reason why it has not signed; it is prepared to sign by 2006 if an effective replacement weapon can be developed. However, in December 2001 it was reported that the US was reviewing its landmine policy and it was thought likely that it would not join the Ottawa Convention. In April 2001 the foreign ministers of Greece and Turkey announced that their countries would simultaneously join the Ottawa Convention; this had not happened by February 2002.

There are sound military arguments for the use of anti-personnel mines in war by responsible states that record where and in what pattern mines have been laid, mark the perimeters of the minefields and then lift the mines once there is no longer any need for them. For example, during the Korean War (1950–3) the Chinese and North Korean tactics involved attack by massed infantry, and anti-personnel mines were essential to prevent the

total over-running of defensive Allied positions. Small forward observation posts which could be easily surprised also gained a degree of protection from the weapon, while anti-personnel mines laid among anti-tank mines made the task of clearing paths through the field slower and more dangerous. However, modern methods of laying minefields now include delivery from the air and from rocket- and artillery-delivered canisters; minefield maps of these cannot be drawn accurately. The British 'airfield runway attack' bomb not only craters the runway but also scatters anti-personnel mines to hamper repair work; the US Gator system, also delivered by aircraft, consists of seventy-four anti-tank and twenty-two anti-personnel mines, all inter-linked by wire, which cover an area some 100m long. There are also 'smart' mines, which are deactivated after a set time; the new treaty bans these too, although there had been efforts to have them excluded from its terms.

The overwhelming proportion of mine casualties come from mines laid without records or warning markers in a number of civil wars and in operations such as the Soviet Union's intervention in Afghanistan. There is now some controversy over the number of mines actually scattered in these wars and the organisations involved in mine clearance have drastically reduced the estimates made earlier. The UN worldwide estimate is of 110 million mines; the mine-clearing organisations say 2.2 million. There is no doubt about the number of casualties caused by anti-personnel mines. These are predominantly civilians and include a large number of children.

Mine clearance is now taking place in virtually all the countries that have suffered from the widespread use of these weapons. There is a thriving de-mining industry with non-governmental organisations and commercial companies supervising the de-mining activities and training local people to clear the explosives safely. However, it was estimated that in 2000 there were between 15,000 and 20,000 mine casualties in seventy countries, not all of which were at war.

The effectiveness of the new treaty still has to be proven. There are large stocks of anti-personnel mines in many countries but more than 27 million have been destroyed by over fifty countries and treaty signatories have agreed to destroy them all by March 2003. No doubt attempts will be made to acquire stocks, hide them and create a black market. There is no provision for imposing sanctions on countries which have not signed the convention and continue to export mines.

A number of countries, including Australia, South Africa, the UK and the US, are actively developing alternatives to anti-personnel mines; an outline of some of the technologies being tested follows. An area denial system is being developed in Australia that consists of unattended weapons with up to one hundred barrels that can fire, directly or indirectly, lethal or non-lethal projectiles when activated by sensors. Non-lethal alternatives to mines are also being developed and they include: calmatives or tranquillising chemicals (but their use could be classified as chemical warfare and so be banned); obscurants in the form of foam that is hard to penetrate and could form a barrier; area denial weapons such as 'sticky foam', slippery substances and entangling nets. However, these all seem more suited to riot control than to large-scale warfare.

There are still areas of the world, however, where anti-personnel mines are being laid indiscriminately – by government forces in the Democratic Republic of Congo, Israel, Kyrgyzstan and Nepal and by militant groups in Kashmir, Nepal, the Philippines, Senegal, Somalia and Uganda. It is claimed that the Russians have air-dropped them both in Chechnya and in Georgia; the Georgians too have used them in raids on Abkhazia. Both the Serbs and the Kosovo Liberation Army employed anti-personnel mines in Kosovo where over two hundred civilians have been killed by them and by unexploded NATO bombs.

Naturally there has been a recent interest in mines and unexploded ordnance in Afghanistan and its neighbours. On 9 October 2001 four employees of Afghan Technical Consultants were killed in a US air raid on Kabul. The firm has about 1,300 staff who had cleared over four million square metres of mine-contaminated land and twenty million square metres of land that could have contained unexploded ordnance in 2000. Some 2,800 mines and over 66,000 pieces of ammunition were cleared and destroyed. There are seven other mine-clearing organisations in Afghanistan; the total number of anti-personnel mines cleared in 2000 was over 13,500. The Taliban supported the ban on landmine use and accused their opponents of using mines supplied by Russia and Iran. A number of Central Asian countries have been laying mines on their borders.

BIBLIOGRAPHY AND WEBSITES

Cornish, Paul, *Anti-Personnel Mines: Controlling the Plague of 'Butterflies'*, Royal Institute for International Affairs, 1994

Doucet, Ian and Lloyd, Richard, *Alternative Anti-Personnel Mines: The Next Generation*, Landmine Action, 2001

Smith, Chris (ed.), *The Military Utility of Landmines?*, Centre for Defence Studies, King's College, 1996

Disarmament Forum, UN Institute for Disarmament Research, 1999

Hidden Killers, US Department of State, Office of Humanitarian Demining Programs, 1998

Landmine Monitor Report 1999: Towards a Mine-Free World, Landmine Monitor Core Group, Human Rights Watch, 1999

Report for the Review Conference on the 1980 UN Convention, International Committee of the Red Cross, 1994

Cambodian Mine Action Centre: www.camnet.com.kh/cmac
Canadian Mine Action Centre: http://eagle.ucb.ns.ca/demine
Geneva International Centre for Humanitarian De-mining: www.gichd.ch
International Campaign to Ban Landmines: www.icbl.org
Landmine Survivors Network: www.landminesurvivors.org
Mines Advisory Group: www.mag.org/mines
Norwegian People's Aid: www.npaid.org/mines
People Against Landmines: www.mgm.org
UN Institute for Disarmament Research: www.unog.ch/UNIDIR

Cyberwarfare

Cybernetics is described as 'the branch of science concerned with control systems in electronic devices'; cyber comes from the Greek *kubernan* – to steer or control. This piece considers a number of cyber activities – cyberwar, cyberterrorism, cybercrime – all of which employ the same methods of attack but with different ends. No definitions of cyber-activities have yet been agreed.

As the military becomes more and more dependent on computers it increases its vulnerability to cyberwarfare, although of course, military computers can also be put out of action by conventional attack and by electromagnetic pulse (here only digital attack is discussed). A definition of cyberwarfare could be a serious attack on a nation's computers by another nation. Cyberterrorism would be the same attack but carried out by non-state terrorist actors. Cybercrime is self-explanatory; at the upper end of the spectrum is large-scale fraud, at the lower end web defacement and malicious damage. (A UK Department of Trade and Industry survey reports that Cybercrime (fraud, hacking, virus insertion) is costing the UK £10 billion a year; £300 million was lost in credit card fraud in 2000.) Cyberwarfare includes not just attacks on the computers of an adversary but the defence of those computers and the ability to counter-attack – a point that must give pause for concern before launching a cyber attack. There is also the possibility of using the internet and e-mails to disseminate propaganda.

Attacks on computer systems give rise to two main types of result: 'crashing' and becoming inoperable, and the possibility of the information the computer transmits or stores being extracted or altered. The first outcome is the result of a common form of attack known as 'denial of service' and can be achieved by inundating a site with so many messages so that the computer cannot cope. Some recent trends in denial of service attacks include: distributed denial of service by attacking systems with large address blocks; incorporating a denial of service function into a worm (see below); attacking domain servers such as those using '.com' or '.net' and country domain servers '.uk' or '.fr' etc; attacking routers that are designed to pass traffic on but whose operation can be virtually halted by addressing traffic to the router itself.

A common means of cyber attack is the use of software codes known as 'malicious software' that has the aim of making a computer work in ways that were not intended or to gain unauthorised access. Some forms of malicious software are known as viruses, worms and trojans. A virus is a small computer programme which, when inserted into a computer, carries out an unauthorised task such as destroying and altering data or displaying a message on the computer screen. Viruses can be programmed to carry out a wide range of tasks. A computer feature designed to save time in entering items such as address blocks or distribution lists is known as a 'macro'. A macro virus can cause the task to be carried out in such a way as to degrade computer performance. There are two other weapons, worms and trojans. A worm is an independent programme that can self-replicate and so travel across networks from computer to computer without attaching itself to the host computer's programme. While viruses require the computer user to do something that causes the propagation to continue, a worm propagates itself. Worms occupy processing capability and can slow down communications. Trojans, like the Trojan horse, have a hidden adverse capability behind an apparent normal function. This allows them to take control of an infected computer. Malicious software can also be used to attack the Domain Name System and routers in ways other than denial of service.

Defence against computer attack relies on a multilayered approach that includes anti-virus scanning, 'firewalls', anti-intrusion devices and properly applied software upgrades. An anti-virus programme runs in the background whenever your computer is switched on and will check for viruses from e-mails, web-sites or inserted floppy discs. It will have a parent website that will carry updates on how to recognise new viruses; keeping up to date is important. A firewall is like a filter that examines all incoming material and only admits what has been authorised by the system's security policy. Its main task is to exclude unauthorised people, often known as hackers, from accessing the computer network files either to steal information or to alter it. A hacker or a virus can enter a computer network through a server, which is the system's access to the internet or e-mail; a 'stand-alone' systems that has no outside connections should be safe from intrusion except where someone with authorised access to the system decides to insert a virus. Survey reports from the US Computer Security Institute showed that 'insider' attack was the most common form; more recently 'outsider' attack has risen greatly while 'insider' attack has not reduced. Intrusion detection devices monitor unauthorised access and other abnormal activity.

In cyberwarfare national infrastructure targets are more likely to be attacked than military operational systems as the latter may be better defended and are more likely to be 'stand-alone' networks. Nevertheless some military systems will be vulnerable, particularly those like logistic systems which have been electronically connected. Of course the capture of a field computer and its associated communications could allow access to that operational network. Given some countries' military dependence on satellites protection of ground stations and uplinks is essential. Critical infrastructure targets such as emergency services (ambulance, police and fire-fighting) public utilities (gas and electricity providers, telecommunications, broadcasting, water and sewage services, transport and health services), commercial operations (banking and financial services, food and fuel suppliers) and the government agencies that control them could all be targets. The successful destruction, denial, delay and deception of these caused by digital attack will seriously damage a nation's war effort and its population's morale. The list of potential targets seems endless. It is not clear whether cyber attack would be more effective and less expensive in effort than conventional attack.

Given the seamless nature of cyberspace, defence from digital attack will be hard to guarantee. Attackers can work from any country, not just from their own, to attack targets in any other. International cooperation may offer possibilities to reduce the effects of cyberterrorism and cybercrime but is unlikely to be effective in conflict involving cyberwarfare. The defensive mechanisms mentioned so far – firewalls and anti-virus scanning – are passive measures and will not stop an attacker from developing other modes of attack. Active defence is not easy as initially the identity of the attacker will not be known until he has been tracked down. The perpetrator of the 'I love you' virus was eventually traced to the home-computer of the sister of a Filipino computer-school drop-out – but only after the virus had affected some 45 million computers worldwide. The killers of the US journalist Daniel Pearl were traced through their use of Hotmail (e-mail service), which attaches the Internet Protocol (IP) address of the sending computer to e-mails. Of course hackers and other cyberterrorists or cybercriminals do not need to use a home-based computer but can move from internet café to internet café to avoid identification, and it is possible to disguise an IP. The main threat remains from an 'inside sleeper' waiting for the time to cause the most disruption.

Active defence naturally includes identifying the attacker and taking appropriate action; gaining evidence and prosecuting in the case of cybercrime and conducting digital, electronic or conventional force counter-attack in the cases of cyberwar and cyberterrorism. Having an active defence policy could act as a deterrent to some attackers. Since 11 September the US has established the Office of Homeland Defence to coordinate the activities of all federal and state authorities engaged in the protection of the US and its population against terrorist attack. But well before 11 September the Federal Bureau of Investigation had established a National Infrastructure Protection Center and the Department of Defense a Joint Task Force – Computer Network Operations. A think-tank, the ANSER Institute for Homeland Security, has as its main priorities for research cyberwarfare and BW.

A number of countries, including the US, Russia, China and India, and the NATO alliance are taking the potential for cyberwarfare seriously and are developing strategies to attack an enemy's systems and to protect their own. It is believed that cyberwarfare was used to a limited extent in both the Gulf War of 1991 and the Kosovo air campaign, and that the US obtained information from Haitian government networks in support of Operation 'Restore Hope'. Cyberwarfare, also known as 'netwar' and by NATO as Computer Network Operations, forms part of Information Operations (IO) which also includes the ability to collect and distribute information and to prevent the enemy from doing this by a number of means (including conventional and electronic attack), not only digital. The Israeli removal of all the Palestine Authority's computer discs during their operations in the West Bank is an example of non-digital IO. IO is also being used by a number of countries to restrict access to the internet and to try to control what is considered unsuitable and undesirable material. Such access to the internet might be limited by government-controlled servers or by legally compelling commercial servers to censor their traffic and report those attempting to breach the rules.

The first international treaty dealing with cyberspace issues is the Convention on Cybercrime drafted by experts from the Council of Europe, the US, Canada and Japan. It deals mainly with infringements of copyright, computer related fraud, child pornography and violations of network security. Treaty signatories have to adopt appropriate national legislation including powers and procedures for interception and searches of computer networks. The convention has come in for some criticism as some of its provisions may be unacceptable to some potential signatories but it reflects the growing awareness of the need to take into account the international dimensions of cyber activity. There is evidence that hackers using communications switches in Saudi Arabia, Indonesia and Pakistan have been studying a number of infrastructure systems; possibly with a view to disrupting these after a terrorist attack, adding to the chaos and casualties. As examination of computers found in Afgfhanistan has detected similar research, al Quaida is suspected of planning cyber attacks.

BIBLIOGRAPHY AND WEBSITES
Campen, Alan D., Dearth, Douglas H. and Goodden, R. Thomas, *Cyberwar: Security, Strategy and Conflict in the Info Age*, 1996
Cronkite, Cathy and McCullough, Jack, *Access Denied: The Complete Guide to Protecting Your Business Online*, McGraw-Hill, 2001
Denning, Dorothy E., *Information Warfare and Security*, Addison Wesley Longman, 1999
Rattray, Gregory J., *Strategic Warfare in Cyberspace*, MIT Press, 2001

ANSER Institute for Homeland Security: www.homelandsecurity.org
Computer Emergency Response Team (Carnegie Mellon University): www.cert.org
Computer Security Institute: www.gocsi.com
Convention on Cybercrime: http://conventions.coe.int/Treaty/en
National Infrastructure Protection Centre: www.nipc.gov/warnings
Security Focus Online: http://online.securityfocus.com/library

Terrorism

Even before the events of 11 September 2001 the world was becoming increasingly concerned about terrorism as it became more likely that terrorists could acquire and use nuclear, chemical and biological weapons. However, terrorism is not new. There are many instances throughout history of terrorist tactics being employed for a variety of reasons; the Assassins Sect in the Middle East in the twelfth and thirteenth centuries and the Thugs in India were two early examples. The statistics of international terrorism have been relatively consistent for the last decade bar one or two horrific incidents, such as the attacks on the US embassies in East Africa, which distort the figures. The casualty count for 2001 will be the highest ever. Statistics on domestic terrorist operations are more difficult to quantify and obviously vary more significantly as terrorist campaigns are defeated or initiated. In December 1999 the UN General Assembly voted to establish the 'International Convention for the Suppression of the Financing of Terrorism', which aims to deny terrorist groups funds held in other countries. This measure has not had the support nor the success expected, as witnessed by the US's decision to freeze some $24 million belonging to al Qaida within four weeks of the events of 11 September when it could have done so earlier. By April 2001 only fifty-three states had signed and ratified the convention, with another eight having signed but not yet ratified it. Of course, no moneys had been frozen.

There is no globally accepted definition of terrorism. The United States offers the following descriptions: 'the term terrorism means premeditated, politically motivated violence perpetrated against non-combatant targets by subnational groups or clandestine agents, usually intended to influence an audience'; 'the term international terrorism means terrorism involving the citizens or territory of more than one country'; and 'the term terrorist group means any group practising, or that has significant subgroups that practise, international terrorism'. A British definition is more succinct: 'Terrorism means the use of violence for political ends, and includes any use of violence for the purpose of putting the public or any section of the public in fear.' Once, the main aim of terrorism was to gain publicity for whatever cause was espoused; terrorists realised that causing too horrendous a scale of casualties was usually counter-productive in that it revolted public opinion and provoked the authorities into taking more effective action against them (of course, this counter-action sometimes actually helped the terrorist cause). Modern terrorism is less easy to define but there is certainly now no restraint on the scale of its atrocities. It is conducted far more by ideological extremists, often with a strong if misguided religious belief. Where 'old' terrorists had a political or national cause that they cited as the motivation for resorting to action, today's terrorists have a more fanatical desire to punish rather than to influence and they often do not claim their successes. Groups are to penetrate and tend to be much more professional in their operations; al Qaida group is the best and most recent example to demonstrate this. Their attacks on New York and Washington, employing hijacked airliners, took over three years to plan and execute. The hijackers were typically middle-class and university-educated – not the types usually associated with terrorists.

Before examining the subject further, it is necessary to distinguish between the phenomenon of terrorism and the legitimate use of force. The use of force by a state is legitimate if it is used as the law permits. It should strengthen the public's confidence in the rule of law, and aim to improve both personal safety and the security of possessions. It should also prevent the formation of vigilante groups and the carrying of weapons for personal protection. The statement 'one man's terrorist is another man's freedom fighter' is often true. However, 'freedom fighters' who employ terrorism must expect to be labelled terrorists; there is a fine line between the two. For example, Hizbollah rocket attacks on Israeli towns and settlements were clearly terrorism, while Hizbollah ambushes of Israeli troops in South Lebanon could be considered legitimate military operations. One of the main problems regarding Kashmir is that the Indians view the militants there as terrorists while the Pakistanis see them as freedom fighters. But it is what they do that counts.

Most democratic governments apply the following policy principles in combating terrorism: there must be no concessions to hostage-takers or other terrorists; the fight against terrorism needs close international cooperation and the highest standards of human rights behaviour; and the rule of law must apply equally to suspected terrorists and the security forces. These principles are not always followed, often with unfortunate results for the authorities concerned. The US announced a new policy in respect of kidnapping in February 2002; all cases of kidnapping of US citizens would be reviewed by an inter-agency committee which would decide what action, if any, would be taken by the authorities. Certainly negotiating for the release of hostages only encourages further hostage-taking. The temptation to fight terrorism with terrorism is great but it usually leads to the discredit of the government authorising such tactics – for example, the Israeli policy of targeting known terrorist organisers for assassination. Now the US government has authorised assassination.

Countering terrorism is not easy; over reaction is what the terrorist wants. The Israeli policy of inevitably responding to a terrorist attack by bombing suspected terrorist camps usually leads to civilian casualties and in the storm of adverse publicity this provokes, the original terrorist attack, which may also have killed women and children, is forgotten. Israel's policy of retaliation has not yet succeeded in halting terrorist attacks on Israeli targets. In fact, aerial bombing in retaliation for terrorist attack is usually internationally condemned, as the US found out when it attacked Colonel Ghadaffi's Libya in 1986 after an attack on US servicemen in Berlin. On the other hand, on only one occasion have sanctions imposed after a terrorist attack proved successful, if slow: the sanctions imposed on Libya over the involvement of Libyan nationals in the bombing of the Pan Am aircraft over Lockerbie in December 1988 took nearly ten years to have an effect.

The only proven method of defeating a terrorist group is by infiltration of the group and by patient intelligence and police work; a long and often painful process. However, other measures that can aid the international fight against terrorism include: preventing fund-raising for terrorist causes; freezing assets; sharing intelligence; allowing extradition; and offering assistance with counter-terrorist training. The US is now urging all those who condemned the 11 September attacks (only Iraq did not express sympathy to the US) to adopt all these measures. Before 11 September there were 12 United Nations conventions on counter-terrorism.

The US takes terrorism seriously, and well before September 2001 had taken the lead in countering international terrorism. Each year it publishes a list of those states it considers sponsor terrorism; in April 2001 seven states were named: Cuba, Iran, Iraq, Libya, North Korea, Sudan and Syria. Three of these, Iran, Iraq and North Korea, form the 'axis of evil'. The US also publishes descriptions of some 43 terrorist groups. The budget for the financial year 2000 provided $11 billion for counter-terrorism. Plans are in hand to establish civil defence groups in 120 US cities to react to the effects of terrorist use of chemical or biological weapons.

The number of international terrorist attacks each year does not vary much, ranging between 666 which took place in 1986 and 274 in 1998; the number of attacks in each region does not vary much either, other than in western Europe where 272 attacks were recorded in 1995 and only 48 in 1998. There were 423 international terrorist attacks in 2000; the majority, 193, took place in Latin America, with 98 in Asia and 55 in Africa. Only 30 attacks were recorded in western Europe and none in North America. Between 1995 and 2000 only 15 international terrorist attacks had been made in North America. Palestinian attacks in Israel are not classified as international by the US.

The most difficult type of terrorist to defeat is the suicide bomber, who often achieves the most dramatic results. Three car bombs in Lebanon in 1983 killed 241 US Marines, 58 French and 60 Israeli soldiers, and in February and March 1996 four suicide bombers killed 56 Israelis in Tel Aviv and Jerusalem, influencing the May 1996 election, which ended Labour Party rule. So far, only Islam and the Sri Lankan Tamil Tigers have produced volunteers to carry out such attacks. The most recent suicide attacks have been the bombs exploded in

1 Abu Nidal Organisation (ANO)
2 Abu Sayyaf Group
3 Afghan Support Committee (ASC)
4 Al-Jihad (Egyptian Islamic Jihad)
5 Al-Itihaad al-Islamiya (AIAI)
6 Al-Qaida/Islamic Army
7 Armed Islamic Group (GIA)
8 Aum Shinrikyo
9 Basque Fatherland and Liberty (ETA)
10 Continuity Irish Republican Army (CIRA)
11 First of October Antifascist Resistance Group (GRAPO)
12 Gama'a al-Islamiya (Islamic Group)
13 Hamas (Islamic Resistant Movement)
14 Harakat ul-mujahidin (HUM)
15 Hizballah (Party of God)
16 Islamic Army of Aden
17 Islamic Movement of Uzbekistan (IMU)
18 Kahane Chai (KACH)
19 Kurdistan Workers `Party (PKK)
20 Lashkar e-Tayyiba (LET)
21 Liberation Tigers of Tamil Eelam (LTTE)
22 Libyan Islamic Fighting Group
23 Loyalist Volunteer Force (LVF)
24 Mujahidin el-Halk Organisation (MEK)
25 National Liberation Army(ELN)
26 Orange Volunteers (OV)
27 Palestinian Islamic Jihad (PIJ)
28 Palestinian Liberation Front (PLF)
29 Popular Front for the Liberation of Palestine (PFLP)
30 PFLP-General Command (PFLP-GC)
31 Real IRA
32 Red Hand Defenders (RHD)
33 Revival of Islamic Heritage Society (RIHS)
34 Revolutionary Armed Forces of Columbia (FARC)
35 Revolutionary Nuclei (formerly ELA)
36 Revolutionary Organisation 17 November
37 Revolutionary People's Liberation Army/Front (DHKP/C)
38 Salafist Group for Call and Combat (GSPC)
39 Shining Path (Sendero Luminoso, SL)
40 Ulster Defense Association/Ulster Freedom Fighters (UDA/UFF)
41 Umma Tameer e-Nau (UTN)
42 United Self-Defense Forces of Columbia (AUC)
43 El-Aqsah Martyrs Brigade

Source: U.S. Department of State

States sponsoring terrorism

Israel from June 2001 onwards and the Tamil Tiger attacks on the international airport and air force base outside Colombo in July 2001. In a recent development Palestinian women have become suicide bombers. Most suicide bombers make their attacks alone, so the teams of terrorists who hijacked the four US airliners on 11 September added a new dimension to international terrorism in more ways than one. Another development is the appearance of lone fanatics, often suffering from some feeling of injustice, who have carried

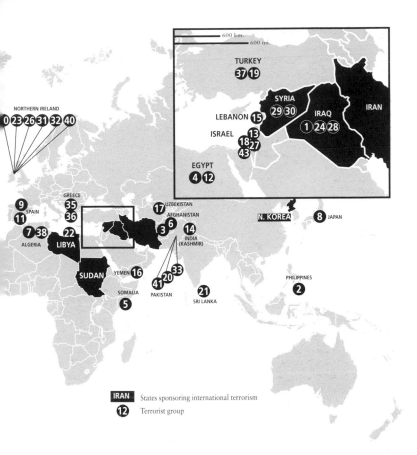

NORTHERN IRELAND
0 23 26 31 32 40

IRAN States sponsoring international terrorism
12 Terrorist group

out terrorist acts including the Oklahoma City bomb, that at the Atlanta Olympics, and most recently the bombs in London aimed at the Black, Indian and homosexual communities. At the bottom end of the terrorist scale are the anti-abortionists, who have bombed clinics in the US, and animal rightists who release mink, attack experimental stations that use animals for medical research and disrupt hunts. Globalisation has become the target of violent demonstration that has not yet reached the level of terrorism.

A new form of terrorism, whose target is information technology systems, is known as cyberterrorism. It can take three forms: website defacement; insertion of viruses that can destroy databases and computer files; and denial of service attacks that overload a system and cause it to close down. The 'I love you' bug that infected millions of computers in May 2000 is claimed to have cost an estimated $10 billion. Cyberterrorism is being aimed at both Israeli and Palestinian targets.

So far the use of weapons of mass destruction by terrorists has been limited, the best known example being the release of nerve gas into the Tokyo subway system by the Aum Shinrikyo cult. The attack killed ten and injured as many as five thousand people in March 1995; a more professional attack could have caused thousands of deaths. Chemical and biological weapons are easier to manufacture and to smuggle into a target country than nuclear or radioactive weapons. Known as 'catastrophic terrorism', the scale of casualties that could be caused by chemical and biological weapons requires their use to be forestalled and this means a much-increased covert intelligence effort. On the other hand, manufacturing and disseminating these weapons is not as simple as is often assumed. A crude nuclear weapon would require over 50kg of highly enriched uranium, and engineering a plutonium bomb would be beyond the capability of a terrorist organisation. More likely would be the construction of a radiological bomb possibly using cobalt-60 or caesium-137 and detonated by explosive plus incendiary material; such a bomb could be constructed from material more easily available than HEU or plutonium. There have been a number of cases of nuclear material smuggling but none involved large quantities; there have always been fears of the theft of a nuclear weapon from Russia since the break up of the Soviet Union.

However, of the many terrorist campaigns, there are few that can claim success. The lengthy campaigns waged and in some cases still being waged are witness to this. The Irish Republican Army (IRA), Euzkadi Ta Askatasuna (ETA), the Kurdistan Workers' Party (PKK), the Liberation Tigers of Tamil Eelam (LTTE) and the Revolutionary Armed Forces of Colombia (FARC) have all been engaged in violence for over twenty years. None has achieved its political aims – but none has yet totally given up the struggle either.

BIBLIOGRAPHY AND WEBSITES

Patterns of Global Terrorism, United States Department of State, annually

Cameron, Gavin, *Nuclear Terrorism: A Threat Assessment of the 21st Century*, Macmillan, 1999

Falkenrath, R., Newman, R. and Theyer, B., *America's Achilles Heel; NBC Terrorism and Covert Attack*, MIT Press, 1998

Higgins, Rosalyn and Flory, Maurice (eds), *Terrorism and International Law*, Routledge, 1996

Kegleey Jr, Charles W., *International Terrorism: Characteristics, Causes and Controls*, St Martins Press, 1990

Leeuvre, Marianne van, *Crying Wolf: Assessing Unconventional Terrorism*, Cligendael, 2000

Roberts, Brad (ed.), *Terrorism with Chemical and Biological Weapons: Calibrating Risks and Responses*, Chemical and Biological Arms Control Institute, 1997

Tucker, Jonathan B. (ed.), *Toxic Terror: Assessing the Use of Chemical and Biological Weapons*, MIT Press, 2000

Wilkinson, Paul, *Terrorism versus Democracy*, Cass, 2001

Jane's Intel Watch: http://intelweb.janes

Terrorist Incidents, 1945–98 (CDISS Lancaster University): www.cdiss.org/terror

Terrorism Research Center: www.terrorism.com

US State Department Counter-Terrorism: www.state.gov/www/global/terrorism

Piracy

Freedom of the High Seas is a cardinal principle of international law. However, it is not an unrestrained freedom as measures are necessary to ensure navigational safety, the protection of the marine environment, and the orderly exploitation of the seas' resources. There are a number of maritime arms control agreements, notably the nuclear-weapon-free zones, described on p. 245, and the Russian/US agreements on limiting the numbers of nuclear ballistic missiles deployed on submarines (now abandoned). The Partial Test Ban Treaty that banned nuclear test explosions in outer space and under water was signed by 121 states in 1963; it will be replaced by the Comprehensive Test Ban Treaty when this eventually comes into force.

In 1958 the UN agreed a number of conventions and in 1982 completed the Comprehensive Convention on the Law of the Sea that defines the jurisdiction of coastal states and the 'Freedom of the Seas'. The convention came into force in 1994 after sixty states had ratified the treaty; today 132 states have joined the regime but the US has still not ratified its signature.

The baseline between internal waters and the sea is normally the low-water mark along the shore. Coastal states may claim a territorial sea zone up to 12 miles offshore through which all ships have the right of innocent passage (any passage not prejudicial to the peace, good order and security of the coastal state). Shipping is afforded the unimpeded right of transit (this applies in straits) where territorial waters extend across an international strait (one that connects two areas of high seas). Coastal states may also enforce their customs, fiscal, immigration and sanitary laws over a further 12-mile zone, known as a contiguous zone, where the same freedoms apply as to the high seas. States have the right to exploit resources of the sea and the seabed in a 200-mile Exclusive Economic Zone (EEZ). Military activity is not forbidden in EEZs. The convention has ruled that the continental shelf shall also be 200 miles wide and that where it is wider then the International Sea-Bed Authority (ISBA) will delineate it in accordance with agreed guidelines. The waters of an EEZ or above a continental shelf are governed by the same rules as the high seas.

The convention also grants archipelagic states the right to establish perimeter baselines and they have sovereignty over the waters within them. To maintain the freedoms of navigation and overflight in archipelagos, archipelagic sea lanes, where there is a right to transit, are created. Outside the lanes, ships have the right of innocent passage through archipelagic waters. The seabed beyond national jurisdiction is known as 'the area' and the ISBA is responsible for regulating the exploitation of resources there.

Problems over maritime borders naturally arise when the waters between two states have to be divided – the case of the Greek-Turkish dispute is covered on pp. 18–20. Normally the division is based on the median line.

Although there are still maritime 'choke points' which if blocked would cause considerable inconvenience, most countries can be reached by other sea-routes, overland or by pipeline, by air or by a combination of these. The blocking of 'choke points' by naval forces employing submarines or mines is possible but the level of retaliation that can be mounted today could make this counter-productive and the threat of shore-based missiles against shipping would swiftly be countered by air power. The sea is still a vital component in the enforcement of sanctions, the utility of which is discussed on p. 19.

Today, the old threat has returned. Piracy became increasingly common in the 1990s, reaching a peak in 2000 of 471 incidents. This fell by 21 per cent in 2001 with decreases, in all areas bar the waters off West Africa. The South China Sea, the Malacca Strait and the Indian Ocean are among the worst-affected areas, with 120, 58 and 86 incidents respectively (some 600 ships a day pass through the Malacca Strait and the South China Sea). In the first six months of 2002, 197 incidents were reported to the International Maritime Organisation. The scale of acts of piracy varies considerably, from the hijacking of ships and the theft of their complete cargo, down to armed robbery from private yachts often at anchor. Many more acts of piracy against ships at berth or anchor have been reported in the South China Sea, Indian Ocean, West African and South American waters and the Caribbean since 1999, but one report suggests that only about half the total number are actually reported. Reasons for not reporting include: avoiding delay while making the report; avoiding accusations that negligence allowed the attack to be successful; avoiding giving offence to host countries; and incurring higher insurance premiums. Smugglers are unlikely to make a report when they are the victims of piracy. Roughly $200m goods are seized by pirates each year.

In territorial waters the responsibility for countering piracy lies with the government concerned and on the high seas each government is responsible for the safety of its own ships. Little, therefore, is done to prevent piracy on the high seas, and unless coastal states cooperate and allow 'hot-pursuit' into their territorial waters pirates can escape relatively easily. The best example of anti-pirate operations is in the Malacca Strait where the International Maritime Bureau has established a Regional Piracy Centre giving a 24-hour service both in receiving reports and providing warnings. Indonesia, Malaysia and Singapore have established coordinated patrols. At first these measures proved effective, the number of incidents dropping from 32 in 1991 to 6 in 1998, but since then the total has increased to 37 in 1999 and to 112 in 2000 falling back to 58 in 2001. The rise in piracy in the Far

Santa Rosalia 2

Rio Haina 5

Gulf of Paria 1
Punta Toleda 1

Cartagena

Georgetown

Belem

Gayaquil Bay 9

Macapa

Recif

Incidents of Piracy in 2001

East is mainly the result of the region's economic problems and the lack of adequate laws in some countries to deal with the problem. The Comité Maritime International is drafting a model national piracy law that states can adopt.

The International Maritime Organisation now issues reports each month of the previous month's incidents of piracy. A relatively new phenomenon is 'phantom ships'; these actually exist but are irregularly or falsely registered and sail under flags of convenience offering low transportation rates. Cargo owners are often defrauded as the ship simply changes its name. There is now a satellite system that will allow ship-owners to track their vessels.

BIBLIOGRAPHY AND WEBSITES

Churchill, R.R. and Lowe, A.V., *The Law of the Sea*, 3rd edn, Juris Publications, 1999
Goldbla, Jozef (ed.), *Maritime Security: The Building of Confidence*, UN Institute for Disarmament Research, 1992
Pennell, C.R., *Bandits at Sea: A Pirate's Reader*, New York University Press, 2001
Report on Acts of Piracy and Armed Robbery at Sea, 2000, International Maritime Organisation, annually

International Chamber of Commerce Commercial Crime Service:
www.iccwbo.org/oos/imb_piracy
International Maritime Organisation: www.imo.org
Ocean and Law of the Sea home page: www.un.org/depts/los

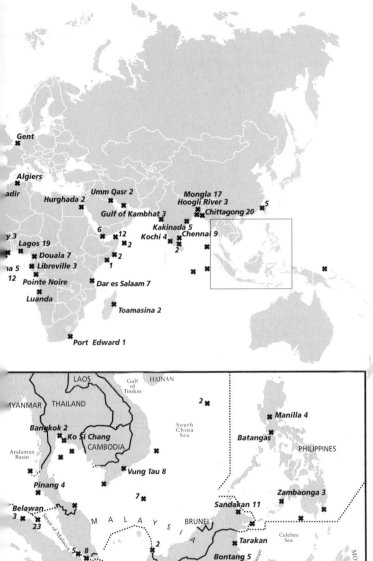

Gent

Algiers

adir

Hurghada 2

Umm Qasr 2

Gulf of Kambhat 3

6

12

y 3

Lagos 19

Douala 7

Libreville 3

a 5

12

Pointe Noire

Luanda

2

2

1

Dar es Salaam 7

Toamasina 2

Port Edward 1

Mongla 17

Hoogli River 3

Chittagong 20

5

Kakinada 5

Kochi 4

Chennai 9

2

LAOS

Gulf of Tonkin

HAINAN

MYANMAR

THAILAND

2

Manilla 4

Bangkok 2

Ko Si Chang

CAMBODIA

South China Sea

Batangas

PHILIPPINES

Andaman Basin

Vung Tau 8

Pinang 4

7

Zambaonga 3

Belawan

3

23

M A L A Y S I A

BRUNEI

Sandakan 11

Tarakan

Celebes Sea

MOLUCCAS

5

8

2

Bontang 5

17

Kepulauan 10

BORNEO

CELEBES

Balikpapan 8

2

Sebuku 2

Makassar Strait

Merak 2

Panjang 4

Cigading 1

Anyar 1

Labuhan 1

Semangka 1

Tg Priok 12

3

Jakarta 7

JAVA

Semarang

BALI

Java Sea

Banda Sea

FLORES

SUMBA

TIMOR

Arafura Sea

500 km.

500 mi.

SUMATRA

Strait of Malacca

Countries under sanctions

'Countries under UN general sanctions and US arms and economic sanctions

Social and Economic Concerns

In this section a pot-pourri of topics is addressed. All are of concern to some states and some are of concern to all states. Sanctions and their likely effectiveness are included here, as it is often the only way 'something can be done' short of military action. Global concerns are covered in pieces on the environment, AIDS, refugees and drugs: all topics that may one day be solved but at present represent growing threats to social and economic stability. Economic topics have focused on scarce resources, the quest for which could, ultimately lead to conflict. The subject of diamonds has been included as the illegal, and in some cases legal, marketing of them in Africa is responsible for paying for and keeping going a number of civil wars. After water, oil is probably the most sought-after substance and so the question of when it will run out is also included.

Water is essential to life. Of the world's many water problem areas, three of the most vexatious – the Nile, the Euphrates and Tigris, and the sources of Israel's water – have been chosen for detailed examination but they are not the only water situations that give cause for alarm. The UN has estimated that some three hundred potential conflicts around the world might be caused by differences over water. China has severe water supply and

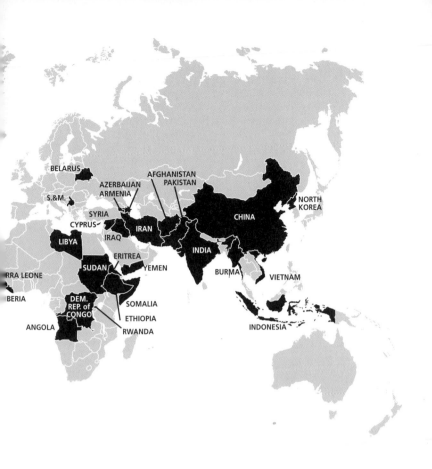

distribution problems. Its 21 per cent of the world's population has to survive on 7 per cent of its water. Massive river divergence schemes and the Three Gorges reservoir will result in the displacement of thousands of people. A system of dams being planned for the Mekong is likely to affect the water supply of downstream Cambodia, Laos, Thailand and Vietnam. Several parts of the US face water difficulties: Texas, Oregon and southern California, to name a few. Confrontation between the US and Mexico is growing over the latter's inability to meet the requirements of an agreement to share the waters of the Rio Grande and the Colorado river. The causes being drought on both sides of the border, the vastly increased Mexican population just south of the border, and Mexican farmers changing outputs to more profitable but water-intensive crops.

There is also the perennial problem with Canada, which has ample water but is keen to hold on to it. Central Asia's water situation is covered on [pp. 158–9]. The Nile is not the only African river to be a potential cause of trouble; the Chobe, a tributary of the Zambezi, is causing friction between Botswana, Mozambique, Zambia and Zimbabwe, while Senegal and Mauritania argue over the River Senegal. In northern Spain there have been large-scale demonstrations against plans to divert water to the much drier south of the country. Virtually all cases of water shortage are made worse by the ever-increasing size of the dependent population.

Sanctions

Sanctions of any kind are a halfway house between diplomatic protest and military action. They can be imposed by the UN, by regional or ad hoc organisations or by individual countries. The most usual form of sanction is either a ban on arms exports to the state in question or the banning of trade between the sanctioner and sanctioned. Other forms involve prohibitions on travel and the transfer of technology and restrictions on sporting activities. Just how successful sanctions are in altering the policies of the sanctioned party is open to question. They have had the desired effect on some occasions but more usually they only contribute to the outcome. The great advantage of imposing sanctions is that something is 'seen to be done' when public opinion demands this, but no military action has to be taken.

Arms embargoes and other trade restrictions imposed by the UN, for example, are not always upheld by all states. Therefore, sanctions may have to be backed by physical measures, normally naval, to enforce a blockade. However, even these are often not totally successful. If a state is unable to obtain a commodity because of sanctions then the value of that commodity to the state is raised and this can encourage sanction-'busting' by the unscrupulous. Sanctions can also be counter-productive because of the injurious effects on the sanctioning parties, through loss of trade for example. They can also cause the sanctioned state to take action that makes the ban relatively pointless – the best example of this is South Africa's creation of a thriving arms industry after the imposition of an arms embargo. Examples of the effects or failures of sanctions are often used to support or to denigrate their efficacy according to the policy inclination of the commentator; there is no clear agreement on what constitutes success but history provides more examples of failures than successes. The threat of sanctions can sometimes be effective.

Before 1990 the UN had only imposed sanctions twice – on Rhodesia and South Africa – whereas the US had initiated sanctions on forty occasions. Since 1990 the UN has imposed arms embargoes on Angola, Haiti, Liberia, Libya, Rwanda, Sierra Leone and Yugoslavia; oil embargoes were also imposed on Angola, Haiti and Sierra Leone. The UN freeze on funds and an embargo on aircraft landing in Libya is the most recent example of the successful use of sanctions: the two Libyan men suspected of causing the Lockerbie air disaster have now been tried in Holland under Scottish law. Libya's earlier refusal to hand over the suspects prompted sanctions that were at the lower end of the severity scale, but despite their relatively mild character the measures worked. On the other hand, the US sanctions imposed on Cuba in 1960 have still not had any effect on the Cuban leader, Fidel Castro, and little progress has been made towards isolating Cuba, which now has a growing tourist market. Most recently the UN, at US insistence, placed a ban on international flights to Afghanistan and froze its overseas assets. The reason for the sanctions was Afghanistan's continued protection of the terrorist sponsor Usama bin Laden, and its refusal to expel him. Many new multilateral and unilateral sanctions have been imposed since 11 September.

UN Sanctions Resolutions

661/90 Iraq and Kuwait	985/95 Liberia
748/92 Libya	1132/97 Sierra Leone
781/92 Somalia	1267/99 Afghanistan
864/93 Angola (UNITA)	1298/00 Ethiopia and Eritrea
918/94 Rwanda	1343/01 Liberia

The sanctions imposed on Iraq after the Gulf War in 1991 continue to generate considerable controversy. Here, as in other cases of trade embargoes, the sanctions have had more effect on the population than the leadership or elite, its prime target. To complicate the argument, Iraq was allowed to sell up to four billion dollars-worth of oil annually, the proceeds from which had to be used to buy food and medical supplies. There should be no starvation or malnutrition in Iraq, and that there is could be blamed on Saddam Hussein's failure to distribute the imports fairly and to his misuse of the funds generated. However, many attribute any suffering directly to the sanctions and argue that they should be lifted. This argument is put forward particularly strongly by those who are owed large sums of money by Iraq and those eager to renew trading. The US has said it will veto the lifting of sanctions until Saddam Hussein has been removed from power. Meanwhile the ban is bypassed on a regular basis.

The US resorts most often to imposing unilateral sanctions. In some cases sanctions are imposed on individual companies that have offended against US trade regulations or other sanctions. Seventy-five countries or organisations within them are currently under US sanctions. For example, in 1999 the US placed sanctions on two of the leading Russian research centres for assisting Iran's nuclear programme. A measure that affronts many is the US law preventing foreign companies from investing more than $40 million in Iranian or Libyan energy projects or occupying any premises in Cuba formerly owned by US companies. Companies caught violating the law are banned from trading in the US. The US argument is that companies would prefer to trade with it than with Iran. Economic sanctions are the responsibility of the Office of Foreign Assets Controls in the US Treasury, and arms embargoes that of the Office of Defence Trade Controls in the State Department.

While the US is happy to impose sanctions on others it is not prepared to accept the decisions of other countries to restrict US exports. This has been made clear in the recent 'banana' dispute with the European Union and the confrontation over US hormone-fed beef and genetically modified crops.

Sanctions may not be guaranteed to work, but they must be tried before the drastic decision to employ military force is taken.

BIBLIOGRAPHY AND WEBSITES

Doxey, Margaret P., *International Sanctions in Contemporary Politics*, Macmillan, 1996
Freedman, Lawrence (ed.), *Strategic Coercion*, Oxford University Press, 1998
Hufbauer, G., Schott, J. and Elliot, K., *Economic Sanctions Reconsidered*, 1990
Simons, Geoff, *Imposing Economic Sanctions: Legal Remedy or Genocidal Tool*, Pluto Press, 1999

United Nations: www.un.org
US Treasury, Office of Foreign Assets Control: www.treas.gov/ofac
US State Department, Office of Defense Controls: www.pmdtc.org

Refugees

Every war, every civil war and every natural disaster, whether flood, earthquake or volcano, brings about a new wave of refugees and displaced persons. They are always homeless, often starving and soon sick. The United Nations High Commissioner for Refugees (UNHCR) is probably the busiest of the UN's agencies with 244 offices in 120 countries and a budget of over $1 billion a year; it is responsible for over 22 million 'people of concern'. The UNHCR was preceded by the League of Nations High Commission for Refugees established in 1920 to cope with the aftermath of the First World War. The High Commissioner's first tasks were the repatriation of 500,000 prisoners of war, the famine in the USSR where 30 million were starving, the return or settlement of 1.5 million refugees and in 1922 the population exchange between Greece and Turkey. When the United Nations was established in 1945 it set up the International Refugee Organisation (IRO) to help the repatriation of the 21 million refugees caused by the Second World War. The IRO was replaced by the Office of the UN High Commissioner for Refugees in 1951.

The UNHCR is concerned with a number of different categories of people who need help. A refugee, as defined by international law, is a person who has left and cannot return to his

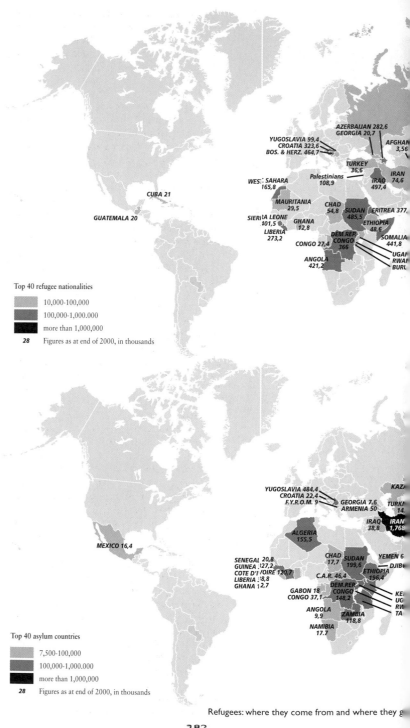

Top 40 refugee nationalities

- 10,000-100,000
- 100,000-1,000.000
- more than 1,000,000

28   Figures as at end of 2000, in thousands

AZERBAIJAN 282,6
GEORGIA 20,7
AFGHAN
3,56
YUGOSLAVIA 99,4
CROATIA 323,6
BOS. & HERZ. 464,7
TURKEY
36,6
IRAN
74,6
WEST SAHARA
165,8
Palestinians
108,9
IRAQ
497,4
CUBA 21
MAURITANIA
29,5
CHAD
54,8
SUDAN
485,5
ERITREA 377,
GUATEMALA 20
SIERRA LEONE
101,5
GHANA
12,8
ETHIOPIA
48,6
LIBERIA
273,2
DEM.REP.
CONGO
366
SOMALIA
441,8
CONGO 27,4
UGAN
RWA
BUR
ANGOLA
421,2

Top 40 asylum countries

- 7,500-100,000
- 100,000-1,000.000
- more than 1,000,000

28   Figures as at end of 2000, in thousands

YUGOSLAVIA 484,4
CROATIA 22,4
F.Y.R.O.M. 9
KAZ
GEORGIA 7,6
ARMENIA 50
TURK
14,
IRAQ
38,8
IRAN
1,768
MEXICO 16,4
ALGERIA
155,5
SENEGAL 20,8
GUINEA 27,2
COTE D'IVOIRE 120,7
LIBERIA 8,8
GHANA 2,7
CHAD
17,7
SUDAN
199,6
YEMEN 6
DJIB
C.A.R. 46,4
ETHIOPIA
196,4
GABON 18
CONGO 37,1
DEM.REP.
CONGO
148,2
KE
UG
RW
TA
ANGOLA
9,9
ZAMBIA
118,8
NAMIBIA
17,7

Refugees: where they come from and where they g

282

country for fear of persecution or who has escaped from conflict. Today there are nearly twelve million refugees. However, the UNHCR warns that collecting precise figures for refugees in any particular circumstance is difficult and so such estimates should be treated with caution. 'Returnees' are refugees who have returned to their home country but who are still in need of assistance. The UNHCR monitors their well-being on return, but normally for no more than two years. Currently the UNHCR monitors over 3.45 million returnees. Asylum-seekers are those who leave their countries and then apply for refugee status elsewhere; while the UNHCR is concerned about asylum-seekers, it is the prerogative of the receiving country to grant refugee status. Finally there are 'internally displaced persons' (IDP) to whom the UNHCR extends protection or assistance when requested to do so by the UN Secretary General or the UN General Assembly, as this category was not included in the UNHCR's original mandate. The latest figure for IDP and others of concern is 5.97 million, of which the largest number are in Afghanistan (759,000), Sri Lanka (706,000) and Sierra Leone (670,000); one source claims there are as many as 20–22 million IDP in fifty-five countries. Not all IDP are caused by war or civil conflict; large numbers are displaced by natural disasters including famine, and by development projects such as the Chinese Yangtze River 'Three Gorges' project and Turkey's Ilisu hydroelectric scheme on the Tigris.

The 1951 Convention on the Status of Refuges and the 1967 Protocol define who is considered a refugee and lay down the commitments that the contracting parties make in respect of the treatment of refugees. There are 141 parties to the convention and 44 states have yet to join. The statute of the UNHCR, adopted by the UN General Assembly in December 1950, lays out the responsibilities of the Office: its main duty is to provide international protection for refugees and to 'seek permanent solutions to the problems of refugees by assisting governments . . . to facilitate voluntary repatriation of such refugees or their assimilation within new national communities'. Originally, refugee relief was seen as the responsibility of the state granting asylum but the UNHCR has found in many cases that it must provide the food and shelter needed by large-scale refugee movements. It normally takes the lead role in coordinating the work of other UN agencies and of non-governmental organisations (NGO) that also play a significant role in refugee relief.

The UNHCR is not responsible for the 3.8 million Palestinian-registered refugees in the Near East – these are the responsibility of the UN Relief and Works Agency for Palestine Refugees (UNRWA). The refugee status of these people originated in the 1948 Israeli War of Independence when the Palestinians fled from Israeli-occupied land to the West Bank and Gaza Strip, in some cases being encouraged to do so – revisionist historians claim the figure is much higher than previously admitted. When Israel overran the West Bank in 1967, some fled from the area, first to Jordan and then to Lebanon. Their Arab hosts kept most refugees in camps; today, more than thirty years later, over a million Palestinian refugees still live in camps. The question of the right to return has already been raised in the Israeli-Palestinian peace talks but without resolution. Israel is most unlikely to accept many of the refugees into Israel other than in token numbers and then spread over a number of years. The West Bank and Gaza are most unlikely to be able to house the total number. Many may not wish to return but host countries may well want to shed the burden of their presence. UNRWA defines the term refugee differently from the UNHCR, and those in the West Bank and Gaza would be classified as IDP by the UNHCR. About 1.6 million Palestinians in Jordan have been granted Jordanian citizenship. Many believe the UNRWA numbers are inflated by the under-reporting of deaths. By UNHCR criteria the number of Palestinian refugees is less than one million.

Despite the work of the UNHCR mass refugees place a heavy burden on the receiving countries which are often ill-equipped to cope with the influx. Refugee communities can be destabilising; they may alter the political or ethnic balance in the host country, are a breeding ground for crime and may be used as cover by guerrillas or terrorists fighting the government from which they fled and so can cause security problems for the host country. Large-scale refugee populations cause environmental problems, particularly the destruction of trees as wood is sought for fuel. Many remain in the host country for a good many years; others are unwilling to return home and must be assimilated by their hosts. On some occasions countries agree to accept populations before they become refugees, one example being the Kenyan Indians expelled by Idi Amin and taken in by the UK.

BIBLIOGRAPHY AND WEBSITES

Blavo, Ebenezer Q., *The Problems of Refugees in Africa: Boundaries and Borders*, Ashgate Publishing, 1999

Cohen, Roberta and Deng, Francis, *Masses in Flight: The Global Crisis of Internal Displacement*, Brookings Institute, 1998

Hampton, Janie (ed), *Internally Displaced People: A Global Survey*, Earthscan, 1998

Korn, David A., *Exodus Within Borders: An Introduction to the Crisis of Internal Displacement*, Brookings Institute, 1999

Loescher, Gil, *The UNHCR and World Politics: A Perilous Path*, Oxford University Press, 2001

Nicholson, Frances, *Refugee Rights and Realities: Evolving International Concepts and Regimes*, Cambridge University Press, 1999

Refugee Council: www.refugeecouncil.org.uk
Refugee Study Centre (Oxford): www.geh.ox.ac/rsc
UNHCR: www.unhcr.ch
UNRWA: www.unwra.org
US Committee for Refugees: www.refugees.org

Environmental Change

Everyone agrees that the world's environment is changing but as yet there is little agreement about how much and what the long-term implications of that change will be. There are several reasons for the changes and mankind can do something to halt or reduce a number of them, but all too often the likely costs of reform act as a brake on action.

The element of environmental change that is most worrying, but about which something can be done to reduce its rate, is generally known as global warming, an effect brought about by the build-up of 'greenhouse' gases in the atmosphere. The principal greenhouse gas is carbon dioxide. Emissions increase with expanding populations and industrialisation since both lead to increased fossil fuel use and continued deforestation. Other greenhouse gases include methane, nitrous oxide, chlorofluorocarbons (CFCs) and carbon tetrachloride; their emissions are also increasing because of human activity. Carbon dioxide and other gases in the atmosphere act like the glass in a greenhouse: they let most of the rays of the sun through but then trap some of the resultant heat that would normally be radiated back into space.

The increase in global temperature over the last century is put at between 0.3° and 0.6°C. This could be just natural variation or it could be the result of greenhouse gas emissions. Whatever the cause, scientists are certain that global warming will take place. It is forecast that if greenhouse emissions can be reduced by some 60 per cent the temperature will rise another 0.2°C per decade, but if emissions are not reduced then the temperature rise is likely to be 1.0° by 2015 and about 3.0°C before the year 3000. The reason for the continued rise in temperature even if emissions are significantly reduced is that most greenhouse gases have a long atmospheric lifetime – over fifty years for carbon dioxide.

One consequence of global warming is a rise in sea level, caused mainly by the thermal expansion of the sea and melting mountain glaciers, Greenland sheet ice and the West Antarctic Sheet. (Antarctica contains 90 per cent of the world's ice: most of this is land ice which is less likely to melt than sea ice.) Over the past hundred years the rise in sea level has been estimated as being between 1 and 2cm per decade. One prediction has it that without a reduction in greenhouse gases the sea level could rise some 18cm by 2030 and 44cm by 2070; even with a reduction of emissions the sea will continue to rise at a rate about 30 per cent below these estimates. The warmer sea water becomes, the greater is its expansion due to temperature rise: a 1° rise at 5° will expand water by one part per 10,000; at 25° after a 1° rise the expansion will be by three parts per 10,000 and that could cause a 3cm rise in sea level. The first areas to be affected by rising sea levels will be populated river deltas and Pacific and Indian Ocean atolls and islands. Over three hundred atolls could disappear but they will become uninhabitable earlier as they suffer more frequent storms and freshwater sources become saline. Already some islets off Kiribati have been submerged and the government of Tuvalu is making plans for the relocation of its population; the first group will be evacuated to New Zealand in 2002. The problem for deltas is accentuated by the fact that land there is often sinking owing to either excessive extraction of drinking water or loss of soil as upstream dams trap the silt that formerly replenished the delta land. Most coastal cities at risk can probably afford to build sea defences to protect themselves and to adapt their ports to the changed conditions, but the work will be expensive. One estimate of the cost of protecting North America from inundation by a 1m rise in sea level is $106 billion; for the Northern Mediterranean coast it is $21 billion. Other consequences of a higher sea level are increased shoreline erosion, more coastal flooding, inundation of coastal wetlands and increased salinity in estuaries and aquifers. Bangladesh is the country most at risk: some six million of its people live less than a metre above sea level.

The effect of global warming inland will be more mixed: some areas will gain from it and others will lose. There will be little change at the equator, more to its north and south. Winters will become shorter and summers longer. In high northern latitudes it will be wetter in the winter but drier in the summer. There will be more rain in the tropics but less in the sub-tropics. There will be drier soil over wide areas. One estimate predicts that the harvest from Midwest America could be cut by a third, causing a reduction of grain exports of 70 per cent. New land for crops will appear in Canada and Siberia. Arid areas in North Africa and the Horn of Africa are likely to become drier still. No conclusive opinion has yet been published on whether global warming will assist or

Possible effects of global warming

hinder world food production overall. Agriculture contributes some 14 per cent of greenhouse gases; methane is produced by rice cultivation and by cattle and sheep, while nitrogen fertilisers contribute to nitrous oxide emissions. With the fast-growing world population agriculture will have to expand dramatically and this could lead to increased global warming. However, increased levels of carbon dioxide will stimulate extra growth in crops such as wheat, rice and soya bean.

Another factor contributing to global warming is the loss of rain forests as these are cut down to make way for agriculture or to provide timber and fuel. This has a number of malign effects, one of the most serious being the total extinction of large numbers of plant, animal, bird and insect species. In relation to global warming, deforestation generates an increase in carbon dioxide emissions from the burning of cleared vegetation and timber waste. It also reduces the environment's ability to absorb carbon dioxide through photosynthesis. In addition, deforestation inevitably causes erosion, particularly where rainfall is heavy and tons of soil are washed away. The loss of forest also causes a loss of evapotranspiration which results in less cloud cover and therefore less rain. Finally, without forest wood people turn to burning animal dung and crop residues, thus depriving the soil of nutrients.

In addition to global warming the ozone layer is being damaged. Ozone is found in the atmosphere in varying concentrations between sea level and 60km altitude. Ozone at

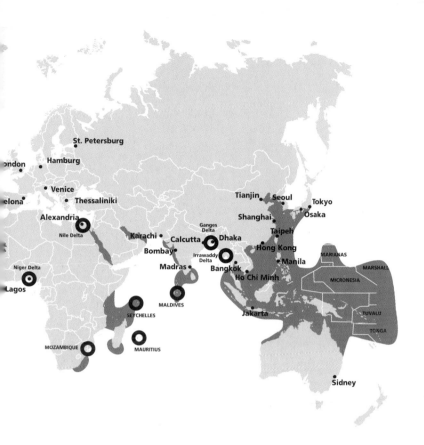

around 25km altitude critically filters out ultra-violet C radiation that causes sunburn, eye-damage and skin cancer. But the gas is being depleted by the action of chlorofluorocarbons (CFCs). The main effect of CFCs has been the creation of an ozone 'hole' over the Antarctic each spring, a hole that is increasing in size each year. There has also been a general reduction of about 5 per cent in the ozone over the mid-latitudes of both hemispheres. CFCs are produced by solvents such as methyl chloroform, carbontetrachloride and CFC 113 (25 per cent) and by aerosols, foams, refrigeration and air conditioning which employ CFC 11 and 12 (71 per cent). Halon 1301 in fire extinguishers (4 per cent) has the same effect. CFCs release chlorine that combines with ozone, and remains in the atmosphere for some hundred years.

Action is being taken in three areas to redress the harm being done to the environment. The Montreal Protocol agreed in 1987, which came into force in 1989, required that the manufacture of CFCs be ended by 1996 in industrialised countries and by 2006 in developing countries. The protocol has resulted in a new crime: the smuggling of CFCs. The main exporting countries are China, India and Russia; the main importing country is the US where it is cheaper to top up your car air-conditioner with blackmarket CFC than have the system replaced by an environmentally friendly model (thirty million US cars have air-conditioning). The market for CFCs could involve 30,000 tonnes costing over £500 million.

Halting the destruction of the rain forests is more difficult as the rain forest countries are among the poorest in the world and much of the logging is carried out despite governmental disapproval.

Establishing the parameters of global warming is the task of the Intergovernmental Panel on Climate Change set up by the World Meteorological Organisation and the United Nations Environment Programme. In 1990 it published reports on 'Climate Change: IPCC Scientific Assessment', 'IPCC Impact Assessment' and 'IPCC Response Strategies'. From these the Framework Convention on Climate Change (FCCC) was negotiated at Rio de Janeiro in 1992 and came into force in 1994. The convention was reinforced by a protocol agreed at Kyoto in 1997 and is the subject of annual follow-up meetings. The aim of FCCC is to achieve a 5 per cent improvement on 1990 levels of greenhouse gas emissions, and the best way to achieve this aim has been the subject of many debates which have resulted in the introduction of a number of mechanisms. Full agreement as to what should be done and how was expected to be decided at the year 2000 meeting at the Hague. One area to be decided was the question of allowing OECD countries to buy reduction quotas from developing countries; another is the giving of credits for strengthening carbon sinks. These are areas where vegetation absorbs carbon dioxide from the atmosphere; it is argued that ending deforestation and reforestation should be rewarded. The Hague conference was suspended without reaching agreement, but negotiations have continued in other fora.

A major factor in achieving reductions in global warming is the attitude of the US which is by far the largest emitter of greenhouse gases (25 per cent of all emissions from only 4 per cent of the world's population). At Kyoto the US agreed to reduce its greenhouse gas emissions by 7 per cent below 1990 levels but in March 2001 President Bush said the US would not ratify the treaty. He claimed the treaty was unfair as it only affected 20 per cent of the world and countries such as China and India, with very large populations, were exempted. In the US the treaty would lead to higher energy charges and would damage the economy. The Marrakesh Accords of November 2001 have settled some issues and produced a legal text which is likely to have been ratified by sufficient countries for it to come into force at the Johannesburg summit on sustainable development in September 2002. Despite President Bush's refusal to ratify the Kyoto Protocol, the US is showing considerable interest in climate change. Bush has come up with a proposal that appears more significant than it is. The US aim is to reduce the intensity of emissions (the level of emissions per unit of economic output), not the actual level of them, by 18 per cent over the next ten years. It is claimed that this will allow an overall higher level of emissions.

The situation is improving gradually. Nevertheless, global warming and its associated rise in sea levels will continue, land will be lost and populations will have to be relocated but the numbers involved will be small compared with the forecasts of the rise in the world's population. This reached six billion on 12 October 2000 and is forecast to rise to eight billion by 2028. Populations in the developed world are expected to decline and the largest increases will occur in the least developed countries. Refugee problems, accusations of failing to meet environmental targets and the cost of feeding, providing fresh water and educating the extra millions will cause local discontent and international disagreement but should not lead to war. But there is a noticeable growth in eco-terrorist activity, such as that of the US Earth Liberation Front, which uses intimidation, destruction of equipment and arson to draw attention to their cause.

It must be stressed that really accurate information on which to base exact predictions is not available. However, at the two ends of the spectrum there are those who claim that the ecological crisis is a myth and those who are so committed to the cause of environmentalism that they pursue policies that may also damage the eco-system. Overreaction is normally counter-productive and can lead to unforeseen consequences. Examples of this include the release by animal activists of farmed mink that devastated neighbouring wildlife and the Greenpeace action that stopped an oil-rig from being sunk at sea, leading to more pollution when it was dismantled on shore.

BIBLIOGRAPHY AND WEBSITES

Grainger, Alan, *Controlling Tropical Forest*, Earthscan Publications, 1993

Houghton, J.T.H., Jenkins, G.J.J. and Ephraums, J.J.E. (eds), *Climate Change: The IPCC Scientific Assessment*, Cambridge, 1990

Houghton, John, *Global Warming: The Complete Briefing*, Lion Publishing, 1994

Lomborg, Bjorn, *The Sceptical Environmentalist*, Cambridge University Press, 2001

Rootes, Christopher (ed.), *Environmental Movements*, Frank Cass, 1999

Sorrel, Steve and Skea, Jim (eds), *Pollution for Sale: emissions trading and joint implementation*, Edward Elgar, 1999

Greenhouse Gases, UNEP/GEMS no. 1, 1987

The Ozone Layer, UNEP/GEMS no. 2, 1987

The Impact of Ozone Layer Depletion, UNEP/GEMS no. 7, 1992

Global warming and climate change: www.cru.uea.ac.uk/tiempo

Greenpeace: www.gn.apc.org

Oxford Centre for the Environment, Ethics and Society: http//users.ox.ac.uk/~ocees

The UN Framework Convention on Climate Change: www.unfccc.de

United Nations Environmental Programme: www.unep.org

AIDS

The Acquired Immune Deficiency Syndrome (AIDS) first came to western attention in the late 1970s as an immune system deficiency that spread through the homosexual community in west-coast USA. In July 1982 it was named AIDS. It has been described as the new 'Black Death' but that epidemic of bubonic plague only affected Europe, killing over one-third of the population, while AIDS is a worldwide disease and is on course to infect over a hundred million people by 2005. In 1983 an AIDS epidemic occurred in the Central African Republic where a French virologist reported finding a retro-virus that may cause AIDS.

AIDS begins through infection from the Human Immunodeficiency Virus (HIV) which was first isolated in 1983. The virus enters the body through the sexual organs, the bloodstream and the mouth and overcomes the body's immune system. Without treatment of any sort at least half of those infected with HIV will develop AIDS within ten years; however, AIDS can kill far more quickly and between 5 and 10 per cent may die within a year. When HIV infects a body it replicates itself until some disease is caught which an unimpaired immune system would cope with. The process of developing into AIDS is a battle between the virus and the immune system. Virologists and immunologists cannot agree on whether treating the virus or the immune system is the best answer; a combination of the two is likely to be best for those whose immune system has been substantially impaired. HIV can also spread other diseases such as tuberculosis; this is known as opportunistic infection.

HIV infection is mainly caused by unprotected sexual intercourse; other causes include exposure to HIV-tainted hypodermic needles, whether used for drug-taking or medical injections, and transfusions of tainted blood. Infected women can pass the virus to their unborn babies. Basic causes are poverty and lack of education. The first precludes the use of protection and the second permits ignorance of the need for protection. These and other factors must account for the exceptionally high figures for African HIV/AIDS deaths and HIV infection both in overall numbers and in proportion to the region's population (see map). The absence of these factors resulted in the numbers of infected Los Angeles homosexuals being reduced from eight thousand in 1982 to less than five hundred today. But education does not automatically ensure safety from the disease as there are reports of over 250 teachers dying of AIDS in the Central African Republic in 1999 and an estimated 860,000 children have lost their teachers to AIDS in sub-Saharan Africa. AIDS is

NORTH AMERICA
20.000
940.000
0.6%

CARIBBEAN
30.000
420.000
2.2%

GLOBAL TOTALS
3 millions
40 millions
1.2%

Source UNAIDS Organisation, December 2001

LATIN AMERICA
80.000
1.4 million
0.5%

AIDS Statistics

also claiming large numbers of African doctors, teachers, health workers, civil servants and army officers. However, Africa's reaction to the pandemic has varied from the efforts of Uganda's President Yoweri Museveni, which by May 2001 had reduced the infection rate from 14 per cent in the early 1990s to 8 per cent (though doubts have been cast on the validity of this claim), to South Africa's Prime Minister Thabo Mbeki's policy of denying the link between HIV and AIDS.

Africa may be the worst affected area at present but other continents are now experiencing increasing rates of infection. In Russia the number infected has risen from 523 in 1991 to 56,000 new cases in 2000 and 75,000 in 2001. China for some years denied it had an AIDS problem but now admits to 600,000 cases – a figure that is set to escalate on account of China's one hundred million itinerant workers and a growing sexual freedom. In China the disease is also spread by the custom of selling blood often collected by insanitary methods.

Once the AIDS stage has been reached the number of illnesses that can be suffered is too long to detail here, but various cancers, hepatitis and wasting syndrome (caused by reduced food intake and diarrhoea) are among the most serious.

The implications of an AIDS epidemic in any country are primarily economic and social. Economies are saddled with extra medical costs at the same time as the workforce is shrinking. The UN Food and Agricultural Organisation (FAO) reports that seven million farmworkers have died from AIDS since 1985 and predicts that a further sixteen million will

WESTERN EUROPE
6.800
560.000
0.3%

EASTERN EUROPE AND CENTRAL ASIA
23.000
1 million
0.5%

NORTH AFRICA AND MIDDLE EAST
30.000
440.000
0.2%

SUB SAHARIAN AFRICA
2.3 million
28.1 million
8.4%

EAST ASIA AND PACIFIC
35.000
1 million
0.1%

AUSTRALIA AND NEW ZEALAND
120
15,000
0.1%

die over the next twenty years. The World Bank estimates that a country that has a 10 per cent rate of infection may suffer from a 33.3 per cent reduction in its rate of income growth. Businesses and industry incur extra costs in training, insurance, sickness and absenteeism. Foreign investment is less likely to be made in countries with a high level of AIDS.

As with all illnesses, the sooner the treatment begins the greater the chance of recovery. The cost of HIV treatment is high and most developing countries cannot afford the cost of the necessary drugs. Until recently only large international pharmaceutical companies had developed and patented anti-retroviral drugs; the cost of treatment with highly active anti-retroviral therapy (HAART), for example, is $15,000 a year. The supply and payment for these drugs is a constant source of friction and the meanness of the drug-producing companies is resulting in patents being broken. Brazil, India and Thailand are all manufacturing generic versions of HIV drugs at a greatly reduced cost. A single tablet of imported fluconazole costs $9.30 in Malawi while locally made tablets in India cost $0.72. The social costs are equally high. Large numbers of children are going without education as they have no teacher or because they have to nurse sick parents or work to keep their siblings fed. There is a growing number of orphans.

There are security concerns too. A finger of accusation is pointed at the military and particularly peacekeeping forces as one of the main spreaders of the disease. Soldiers have long been the customers of prostitutes as they spend much time away from their homes and families, predominantly in an all-male environment. It is also pointed out that they frequently have a disposable income (usually higher when on peacekeeping duties than when serving at home). There is no consistent policy of testing troops before they are sent on peacekeeping missions. But if it became universally mandatory what would the outcome be for those tested HIV-positive? Human-rights activists would claim this to be unfair if they were then debarred from peacekeeping missions. The most recently established UN peacekeeping force, the mission to Ethiopia and Eritrea (UNMEE), has received a request from the Eritrean government, which tests all its own troops, for UNMEE members to be tested before arrival. Soldiers who do become infected will spread the disease in their home communities on their return home and demobilisation. The US National Intelligence Council has estimated that 40–60 per cent of the armed forces of Angola and the Democratic Republic of Congo are HIV-infected; Congo, Côte d'Ivoire, Nigeria and Tanzania all have more than 10 per cent infected. Any form of sickness affects combat-readiness and losing men through HIV/AIDS adds to the training requirement and cost. A further worry for the military is the possibility of medical staff becoming infected from the blood of wounded AIDS sufferers. Many African armies have an infection rate as much as five times higher than the civilian rate. It has been predicted that advantage might be taken of states with armed forces weakened by AIDS and so lead to conflict; there has been no example of this yet.

BIBLIOGRAPHY AND WEBSITES

Forman, Johanna Mendelson and Carballo, Manuel, 'A Policy Critique of HIV/AIDS and Demobilisation', *Journal of Conflict, Security and Development*, 2000
Smith, R. (ed.), *Encyclopedia of AIDS: A Social, Political, Cultural and Scientific Record of the Epidemic*, Fitzroy Dearborn, 1998
Whiteside, Alan and Fitzsimons, David, *The AIDS Epidemic: Economic, Political and Security Implications*, Research Institute for the Study of Conflict and Terrorism, 1992

Aidsmap (NAM Publications): www.aidsmap.com
International Crisis Group: www.intl-crisis-group.org
Joint UN Programme on HIV/AIDS: www.unaids.org
Kaiser Family Foundation: www.kff.org

Drugs

Drugs, and the fight against their use and distribution probably cause more problems than anything else in the world today. The list is endless: mental and physical health and its human and financial cost, the spread of AIDS, crime to pay for drugs, turf wars between pushers at the street level, outright war between producers at the national level, terrorism to deter governments in producing countries from cracking down on trafficking, money laundering, bribery and corruption. The battle against drugs is fought on a number of levels. The eradication of crops, efforts to eliminate processing, interception during transit, seizure at ports of entry, action to stop street sales and education to deter use all play a part, but as yet without much success. The riches that can be gained by all those involved in the production and supply chain are too tempting, despite the undoubted successes some authorities achieve in interrupting production and intercepting consignments. It is hard to calculate accurate statistics for illegal activity but it has been estimated that over 160 million users spend some $400 billion on drugs each year.

There are five main types of drugs: narcotics, stimulants, depressants, hallucinogens and cannabis. Narcotics produce a general sense of well-being and euphoria. The narcotic heroin is synthesised from the opium poppy. Opium poppies are cultivated in the 'golden triangle' of the Shan states of Myanmar, Laos and north-west Thailand; in central Afghanistan; astride the

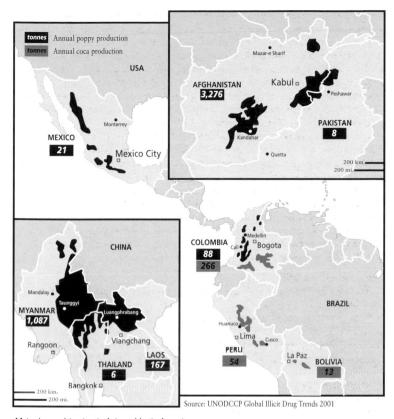

tonnes   Annual poppy production

tonnes   Annual coca production

USA

MEXICO
21

Monterrey

Mexico City

AFGHANISTAN
3,276

Mazar-e Sharif

Kabul □

Peshawar

PAKISTAN
8

Kandahar

Quetta

200 km.
200 mi.

CHINA

Mandalay ●

MYANMAR
1,087

Taunggyi

Luangphrabang

Viangchang

Rangoon □

LAOS
167

THAILAND
6

Bangkok □

200 km.
200 mi.

COLOMBIA
88
266

Medellin

Cali

Bogota

BRAZIL

Huanuco

Lima □

Cusco

PERU
54

La Paz
□ ●

BOLIVIA
13

Source: UNODCCP Global Illicit Drug Trends 2001

Main drug cultivation in Asia and Latin America

Afghan/Pakistan border; and in Mexico and Colombia. In 1999 over 217,000 hectares of poppies were under cultivation with the potential to produce 578 tonnes of heroin – sufficient for nearly sixty billion 'bags' or single doses. The trade in heroin attracts drug dealers because addicts can take the drug for far longer than, for example, cocaine, which can kill a constant user within five years. High-purity heroin can be sniffed, thus avoiding the use of needles. Most heroin reaches Europe through Iran, Turkey and the Balkans. From there, mainly controlled by the Turkish Mafia, it is transported either on the northern route via Romania, Hungary and Slovakia or the Czech Republic, or the southern route through Greece, Albania, the Former Yugoslav Republic of Macedonia (FYROM), Croatia and Slovenia. Another route is northwards through Central Asia and Russia and thence into western Europe. South-east Asian heroin is mostly sent to North America, usually through China, by air or sea. Colombian heroin reaches the eastern US via couriers using commercial air flights.

The second group of drugs, stimulants, produce exhilaration; they also reduce appetite and help to keep the user awake. Cocaine is the most potent stimulant. It is extracted from the leaf of the coca plant that is indigenous to the Andean highlands and is now cultivated in Bolivia, Peru and Colombia, where the size of the crop has dropped considerably over the last five years. The peak year for cultivation was 1993, when close to 216,000 hectares were under cultivation, producing a potential 941 tons of cocaine. In 1999 some 183,000 hectares were cultivated producing a potential 765 tons of cocaine. However, Colombian cultivation tripled and production quadrupled from a potential of 119 tons in 1993 to 520 tons in 1999. The US has cooperative programmes with producer countries to reduce the size of the annual crop; the programmes have been successful in Bolivia and Peru and the compensatory scheme in Bolivia has been ended. The reduced production in these two countries has encouraged Colombian syndicates to increase cultivation, despite spraying operations over the last five years. Cocaine reaches the US either through Central America or the Caribbean with the former being the current preferred route. Large-scale seizures have been achieved: in 1998 nearly 50 tons in all was seized by the Central American authorities and 9 tons in the Caribbean. 'Crack' cocaine is cocaine that has been processed from cocaine hydrochloride to make a ready-to-use free base for smoking. Smoking 'Crack' delivers large quantities of cocaine to the lungs.

Other types of drugs are abused on a far smaller scale. They are: depressants – mainly barbiturates and benzodiazepines; hallucinogens – mescaline produced from the peyote cactus and LSD (lysergic acid diethylamide); and cannabis – derived from the hemp plant and containing tetrahydrocannabinol (THC) which induces a sense of well-being and dreamy relaxation. Marijuana and hashish are both derived from cannabis. Marijuana is the most commonly used drug in the US: in a 1996 national survey it was estimated that one-third of the population had used marijuana at least once, and over eighteen million at least once in the previous twelve months. Although most marijuana is smuggled into the US, it can be grown outdoors there either as a crop or in a domestic garden. Indoor growing allows production all year round. One outdoor operation in the US produced sixteen thousand plants estimated to be worth $27 million when seized; in 1997 some four million plants worldwide were eradicated that could have been processed into 1,820 tons of marijuana.

In addition to the drugs derived from plant crops there are chemically manufactured drugs. Methamphetamine or 'speed' is a euphoric drug which increases heart rate, blood pressure, body temperature and rate of breathing. It produces hyperactivity and a sense of increased energy, and can result in violent behaviour in users. The effect of smoking 'ice' (crystal methamphetamine) lasts longer than that produced by smoking 'crack'. Large quantities of 'speed' are manufactured in eastern Myanmar. 'Ecstasy' is methyllenedioxymethamphetamine (MDMA) which has the properties of the stimulant methamphetamine and the hallucinogen mescaline. It is not addictive like heroin or cocaine. Often taken at all-night 'rave' parties it can result in serious dehydration and exhaustion. Other chemically produced drugs include: lysergic acid diethylamide (LSD), a strong hallucinogen; phencyclidine, which was originally manufactured as veterinary anaesthetic and has varied effects, the worst being paranoia and violent behaviour; and ketamine hydrochloride, another veterinary anaesthetic, which has hallucinatory effects.

Estimating the international value of drug-trafficking is problematical because of the many variables involved. For example, there is a wide range of street prices in the US dependent on the city in which the purchase is made – the per gram price for cocaine in 1997 in Miami was half that in New York. 'Farmgate' prices naturally vary from crop to crop and country to country. Opium prices in Asia varied from $50 per kilo in Afghanistan to $627 in Vietnam, with the Colombian price at $580. Some 200,000 families in Afghanistan were estimated to be involved in drug cultivation, earning $560 per annum; in Columbia there were 80,000 families earning $1,680. Both wholesale and retail prices of heroin and cocaine have been going down for the last twelve years. Heroin is about three times as expensive in the US than in Europe, while cocaine is twice as expensive in Europe as in the US. European retail prices for both cocaine and heroin are at least double the wholesale price. An estimate made in 1992 put the cost of 1kg of cocaine paste as between $200 and $775 depending on the source; 1kg of cocaine hydrochloride (HCl) was $800–$8,500. In Miami the wholesale price varied from $14,500 to $25,000 for 80 per cent purity and the street price for 1gm of 55 per cent purity was $40 to $175 (or $80,000 to $350,000 per kg after dilution).

The two most important international measures to halt drug-trafficking are the UN Convention Against Illicit Traffic in Narcotic Drugs and Psychotropic Substances and the Basel and Vienna Declarations regarding money laundering. The UN Convention requires parties, of which there were 150 by 1999, to institute legal measures to ban and punish all aspects of illegal drug production or trafficking, including drug-money laundering. Parties also answer annual report questionnaires (ARQ) so that the UN International Drug Control Programme can publish an analysis of trends in the illicit drug trade. In addition to governmental reports the UN receives reports from the International Criminal Police Organisation, the International Narcotics Control Board, the World Customs Organisation and their own Field Offices. A hundred countries completed ARQs in 1998. The Basel Declaration concerns the G7 countries and commits their central banks to attempt to identify customers and the source of their funds and to refuse all dubious transactions. The Vienna Declaration commits ratifying states to introducing the crime of money laundering and to taking steps to identify, trace and confiscate the proceeds of drug-trafficking.

BIBLIOGRAPHY AND WEBSITES

Drugs Enforcement Agency Briefing Book, US Department of Justice, DEA, 2001
Drugs of Abuse, US Department of Justice, DEA, 2001
International Narcotics Control Strategy Report, US State Department, 1999

Drug Watch International: www.drugwatch.org
UN International Drug Control Programme: www.undcp.org
US Drug Enforcement Administration: www.usdoj.gov/dea

The Nile

The Nile is critical to both Egypt and Sudan. The Egyptian population is growing at the rate of about one million a year and it has been predicted that Egypt will be suffering a 16–30 per cent water deficit by 2000. There are two main sources of the Nile: the Blue Nile rises in Ethiopia and joins the White Nile at Khartoum. The White Nile flows out of Lake Victoria through Uganda, which shares the coastline of the lake with Kenya and Tanzania. Lake Victoria is fed by the River Kagera, which crosses Rwanda and Burundi. The Albert, Edward and George Lakes also contribute to the White Nile and their western shores lie in the Democratic Republic of Congo (formerly Zaire). Thus there are seven riparian states, all of which, except possibly Kenya, enjoy ample precipitation, have a relative surplus of water and do not use as much Nile water as they are entitled to by virtue of their share of and contribution to the river.

The Nile waters were first controlled in 3400 BC by the ancient Egyptians who aimed to improve irrigation, flood control and navigation. In more modern times Mohammed Ali in 1834 created a system of canals in the Nile Delta to enlarge the irrigated area. In 1861 British engineers constructed the first successful barrage. The first Aswan Dam was built in 1902 and after its height had been raised in 1934 it could store six million cubic metres. The first attempt to extend control of the Nile came in the early 1900s; the plan envisaged storing water in Sudan and further south for use in times of drought by building dams on both the Blue and White Niles and on the River Atbara, and constructing storage reservoirs on the lakes further south. British officials in Egypt and Sudan supported schemes that favoured the country in which they worked. Sudanese officials opposed the building of a canal through the Sudd swamps, which Egyptian officials saw as increasing the water flow northwards, because of the implications for the local population. With no agreed overall plan for the control of the Nile the riparian states, especially Egypt, developed their own projects.

Egyptian plans for constructing the Aswan High Dam began in the early 1950s. Its potential effect on Sudan was not taken into account, however, agreement was reached in 1959 on sharing the then available water reaching Aswan: Egypt was allocated 55.5 billion cubic metres and Sudan 18.5 billion. The agreement was based on the average Nile flow at Aswan being 84 bn m^3 and the evaporation loss 10 bn. Construction began in 1960 and was

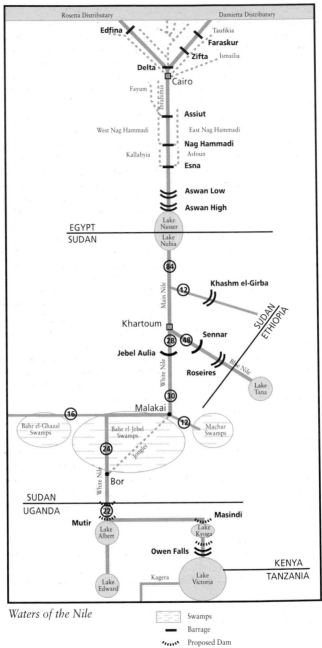

Rosetta Distributary   Damietta Distributary

Edfina   Taufikia

Faraskur

Zifta   Ismailia

Delta

Cairo

Fayum   Ibrahimia

Assiut

West Nag Hammadi   East Nag Hammadi

Nag Hammadi

Kallabyia   Asfoun

Esna

Aswan Low

Aswan High

Lake Nasser

EGYPT

SUDAN

Lake Nubia

84

Main Nile

12   **Khashm el-Girba**

SUDAN

ETHIOPIA

Khartoum

28   48   **Sennar**

Jebel Aulia

White Nile

Roseires   Blue Nile

Lake Tana

30

Malakai

16   12   Machar Swamps

Bahr el-Ghazal Swamps

Bahr el-Jebel Swamps

24   Jonglei

White Nile

Bor

SUDAN

UGANDA

22

Mutir   **Masindi**

Lake Albert   Lake Kyoga

Owen Falls

KENYA

TANZANIA

Lake Edward   Kagera   Lake Victoria

Waters of the Nile

Swamps

Barrage

Proposed Dam

Dam

Dam and Power Station

Irrigation Canal

22   Discharge (billion m3)

Source: Water Resources and Conflict in the Middle East

296

completed in 1971. The aim was to store some 162 bn m³ of water and to generate 10 bn kWh of electricity per year. It was expected that water supply would be guaranteed, including for irrigation, throughout the year without seasonal fluctuations; 1.3 m hectares of extra cultivation would be provided. The dam has had some negative effects, the main one being the loss of the silt that used to be washed down the Nile, enriching the farming soil and providing the material for brick-making. Now large quantities of expensive fertilisers and pesticides must be used and they reduce the quality of the water significantly. Bricks now have to be made from productive soil.

The Sudd swamps cover between 20,000 and 30,000 sq. km depending on the season. Some 30 bn m³ of water a year – over 50 per cent of the inflow into the swamp – are lost from the area through evaporation and seepage. The Jonglei Canal scheme was planned to save and deliver to Aswan an additional 3.8 bn m³. There have been several plans for the canal. The construction work begun in 1978 was for a 360km-long canal carrying 25 bn m³ a day or 1.6 billion a year. A second canal was then to be built doubling the capacity. Work was halted by the civil war in 1984 after 267km had been completed. The canal was not a cause of the war but it has become a symbol for the Nilotic population of the Sudd and southerners generally of the government's exploitation of their resources. The extra water the canal would provide is essential for Egypt but not for Sudan, which currently does not use all its quota.

Egypt's population is increasing by around 2.5 per cent per year; it reached over 70 million in 2001. There will be a need for an increase in the area irrigated if the population is to be fed (already Egypt imports some two-thirds of its food). One estimate is that water requirement will grow to 70–75 bn m³ by 2005. Another suggests that an additional 12.7 bn m³ will be needed to irrigate all the land that has been earmarked for reclamation. A number of measures are under way to better employ the available water. They include the use of waste-water, improving the efficiency of irrigation schemes (traditional methods waste about 60 per cent) and reducing the amount of water-intensive crops. At best Egypt could recover up to 12 bn m³ by these measures. In the long term Egypt's water requirements can only be met by gaining more from Nile improvement schemes but these might only achieve an additional 18 bn m³ and then only if all the proposed schemes can be funded and implemented, and if Egypt is given priority in water allocation.

As yet other riparian states have made no plans that would jeopardise the water supply of Egypt and Sudan. The East African riparians have other water sources and use relatively little of the Nile's waters. At present Ethiopia has a poor system of water distribution and no funds to improve matters. Irrigated land could be increased by some 50 per cent. The Blue Nile has a high potential for generating electric power but massive funding would be needed. Egypt views any Ethiopian increase in the use of Blue Nile water as a hostile act but any large-scale additional use is unlikely in the short term. In the longer term any shortfall for Egypt could be more than compensated for by creating a water storage capability in Ethiopia where the evaporation rate would be three times less than that at Aswan.

BIBLIOGRAPHY AND WEBSITE

Erschoner, Natasha, *Water and Instability in the Middle East*, IISS Adelphi Paper no. 273, 1992
Kliot, Nurit, *Water Resources and Conflict in the Middle East*, Routledge, 1994
Soffer, Arnon, *Rivers of Fire: The Conflict over Water in the Middle East*, Rowman & Littlefield, 1999

School of Oriental and African Studies, Water Issues Study Group: www2.soas.ac.uk/Geography/WaterIssues

The Tigris and Euphrates

There is as yet no international law covering the non-navigational use of transboundary surface or ground water resources. Legally binding commitments on water allocation and quotas can only be reached by treaty and so each applies only to a specific situation. The International Law Commission has been asked to develop international legislation on the non-navigational use of international watercourses and it has submitted a framework convention that is being negotiated at the UN. Articles of the convention include the following principles: transboundary rivers should be used in an equitable, reasonable and optimum manner; equity does not mean equal distribution, as many factors have to be taken into consideration; watercourse states must not harm others significantly; and riparian states must cooperate and regularly exchange information. Legal experts reject the notion that any state can have absolute sovereignty over an international water system and support the concept of a community of riparian interests.

Syria depends on the River Euphrates for much of its water and Iraq on both the Euphrates and Tigris; both rivers originate in Turkey where the south-east Anatolian or Güneydogu Anadolu Projesi (GAP) project is claimed by Syria and Iraq to threaten their water supply. The GAP project, begun in the early 1970s, is ambitious; it aims to double the irrigated area of Turkey, provide nearly half its electricity and create 3.3 million jobs,. Iraq (originally Mesopotamia, that introduced integrated water planning) has depended on Tigris–Euphrates waters for some 6,000 years.

There is no agreed data for the annual flow of the Euphrates, Tigris and their tributaries; for example, two experts have respectively calculated the Euphrates average annual flow at Hit, in Iraq, as 26.4 and 32.7 bn m³. Turkey has provided the following data: of the average annual flow of the Euphrates of 35 bn m³ (it has been as high as 55 bn and as low as 15 billion) Turkey contributes 89 per cent, Syria 11 per cent and Iraq nil; of the Tigris flow of 49 bn m³ 52 per cent comes from Turkey, 48 per cent from Iraq and none from Syria. These flows represent some 28.5 per cent of Turkey's total surface water. Iran contributes to the Tigris through the Lesser Zab and Diyalah. The three countries' claims for shares of the

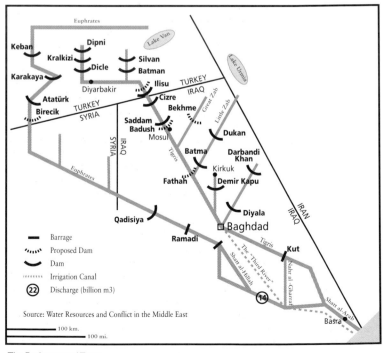

The Euphrates and Tigris

298

water amount to far more than what is available. Turkey plans to use 52 per cent of the Euphrates water, leaving 37 per cent, which it contributes for the riparian states; similarly it plans to use 14 per cent of the Tigris, leaving 38 per cent for the others. However, Syria is claiming 32 per cent of the Euphrates, of which it contributes 11 per cent, and 5.4 per cent of the Tigris, to which it does not contribute at all (the river constitutes the border between Syria and Turkey for about 32km and so allows Syria to claim to be a riparian state). Iraq wants 65 per cent of the Euphrates, to which it does not contribute, and 92.5 per cent of the Tigris, to which it contributes 48 per cent. The combined demands of Iraq and Syria, if met, would mean that Turkey could use none of the two rivers' waters.

All riparian states have constructed, or are constructing, a number of dams and barrages on both rivers to provide very large water storage capacities. Upstream storage can seriously reduce the flow downstream, but in times of drought the stored water could be allowed to flow downstream. In the droughts of 1974 and 1988–9 Turkey and Syria preferred to keep their reservoirs filled and so reduced the amount of water available for Iraq. In 1988–9 the discharge at the Turkish–Syrian border was reduced from 500 to 150 cubic metres per second. All reservoirs suffer large-scale loss through evaporation; it has been estimated that when completed the Turkish reservoirs could lose up to 2 billion cubic metres a year.

In 1982 Turkey and Iraq set up a Joint Technical Committee; Syria joined the next year. The committee meets regularly to exchange data but has been unable to reach any agreement on the long-term sharing of the Euphrates–Tigris waters. As part of a wider economic cooperative agreement with Syria, Turkey committed itself to releasing an annual average of more than 500 cubic metres per second at the Turkish–Syrian border until a final agreement is reached. Syria and Iraq are calling for a larger release, in the order of 700 cubic metres per second. Syria and Iraq have agreed an allocation of Euphrates waters that gives Iraq 58 per cent and Syria 42 per cent of annual flows regardless of quantity.

The GAP project may not be completed until 2010. It comprises the development of 22 dams, 25 irrigation schemes and 19 hydroelectric power stations generating some 7,500 million watts. It is estimated that GAP will add 70 per cent to Turkey's energy output and an additional 1.7 million hectares of land will be irrigated. The reduction of flow caused by the additional irrigation and evaporation loss could be as high as 50 per cent. To compensate for the loss Turkey has proposed a 'Peace Pipeline' plan that would bring water, estimated at about 16 million cubic metres a day, from the Seyhan and Ceyhan rivers that now flow into the sea, not just to Syria and Iraq but also to Jordan, Saudi Arabia and the Gulf States. The cost of this water would be substantially less than that produced by the only other alternative, desalination.

Accurate figures are not available but it has been estimated that Iraq is likely to face water shortages by 2005 and Syria fifteen to twenty-five years later. This estimate does not take into account the possibility of serious drought and unless Turkey increases the annual commitment to release 16 bn m³ shortages will occur earlier. The latest development – Turkey's plan for a dam at Ilisu – could threaten Iraq's Tigris water supply and at the same time make thousands of Turkish Kurds homeless. The dam's reservoir will hold over a million cubic hectares of water and will cover 300 sq. km.

Two other cross-border factors – support of Turkey's Kurdish rebels and the Hatay province controversy – heighten the disagreement between Turkey, Iraq and Syria. Turkey accuses both Syria and Iraq of giving support and safe havens to PKK guerrillas. The two countries nearly came to blows in June 1996 when Syria massed forces on its northern border following a spate of bomb attacks blamed on Syrian Turks. Hatay became a Syrian province after the break-up of the Ottoman Empire but was ceded to Turkey in 1939 by France, then the mandatory power, following a unanimous vote by the Hatay Assembly. Syria still considers Hatay to be its rightful territory. Turkey's increasing cooperation and alliance with Israel does not help matters. Given Turkey's military strength a water war is unlikely but shortages are bound to increase tension between the states.

BIBLIOGRAPHY AND WEBSITES

Berschorner, Natasha, *Water and Instability in the Middle East*, IISS Adelphi Paper no. 273, 1992

Kliot, Nurit, *Water Resources and Conflicts in the Middle East*, Routledge, 1994

Silber, Laura and Little, Alan, *The Death of Yugoslavia*, Harmondsworth, 1995

Soffer, Arnon, *Rivers of Fire: The Conflict Over Water in the Middle East*, Rowman & Littlefield, 1999

Facts About The Euphrates–Tigris Basin, Turkish Government

GAP Southeastern Anatolian Project, Turkish Ministry of Public Works, 1994

Water Development in South-East Anatolia: Essays on the Ilisu Dam, Turkish Embassy, 2000

Turkish Ministry of Foreign Affairs: www.mfa.gov.tr

GAP: www.gap.gov.tr

Israel's Water Sources

Throughout the Middle East water is one of the scarcest resources. It is, therefore, a constant factor influencing every country's security and none more so than Israel where most sources of water originate beyond its pre-1967 borders. The problem is exacerbated by Israel's very high rate of consumption, which is far greater per capita than that of its Arab neighbours. Israelis use, for all purposes, 344 cubic metres per head per annum compared to 94 for West Bank Palestinians and 205 for Jordanians. The problem can only get worse as the population rises. Israel's current supply is some 2 billion cubic metres a year, including brackish water and re-treated sewage, both used for agriculture. Israeli water consumption has increased by 30 million cubic metres a year for the last ten years.

There have been a number of plans to utilise the waters of the Jordan and Yarmouk rivers. Chaim Weizman realised that water would be essential to any Zionist state and he called on the Paris peace conference of 1919 to include the Litani and the southern and western slopes of Mount Hermon in Palestine. David Ben Gurion, prime minister from 1955 to 1963, wanted the Litani to be in Israel; there have been suspicions of Israeli ambitions ever since. In 1926 the British granted the Jewish Palestine Electricity Corporation the use of the Jordan and Yarmouk rivers at the expense of Arab farmers. In 1936 a hydrologist, Ionides, recommended the diversion of the Yarmouk and the Jordan into the Ghor Canal which runs parallel to and east of the Jordan and is used to irrigate the Jordan Valley. His plan was frustrated by the electricity concession. Other plans were proposed: that of Walter Clay Loudermilk included the first suggestion for a canal from the Mediterranean to the Dead Sea, which has been reconsidered more recently but has not progressed further.

In the 1950s President Eisenhower sent Eric Johnston as a special envoy to solve the water conflict. He proposed a plan prepared by Charles Main but this was rejected by both Arabs and Israelis, who then proceeded to prepare their own proposals. Their two plans naturally favoured themselves and Johnston negotiated hard to take both into account. This resulted in the Main plan being altered in Israel's favour. While the Arab Technical Committee accepted the revised plan it was rejected by the Arab League for political reasons.

Israel has two main sources of water – the River Jordan and the West Bank aquifers. The Jordan is fed in the north by four sources: the Hasbani and Iyon which rise in Lebanon and discharge 150 and 8 million cubic metres a year respectively; the Dan, which rises in the northern tip of Israel and discharges 250 million cubic metres; and the Banias, which rises in Israeli-occupied Syria and discharges 110 million cubic metres. The Upper Jordan feeds the Sea of Galilee which is Israel's main reservoir and which is also fed by its own springs, some of which are saline – water from the latter is capped and led away. The Sea of Galilee loses between 160 and 270 million cubic metres a year through evaporation. Just south of the sea the Yarmouk flows into the Jordan down the Syrian–Jordanian border. The Yarmouk discharges between 450 and 475 million cubic metres annually. Syrian plans to build a dam

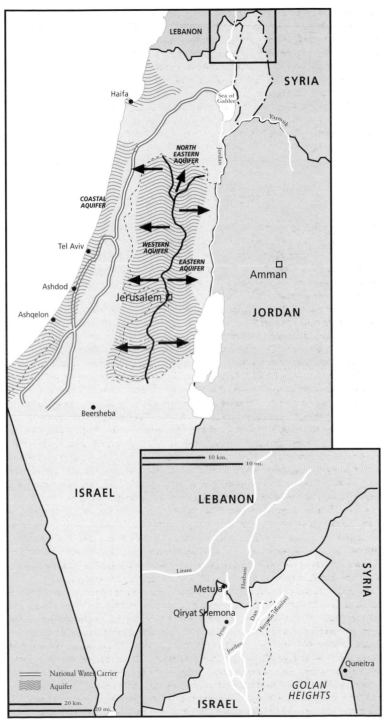

on the Yarmouk were frustrated by Israeli military action in the mid-1960s, and because the scheme included the diversion of water from the Banias. The Israelis attacked the Banias project sites in March and May 1965 and in July 1966. In May 2000 the Jordanian authorities informed the Israelis that they were reconsidering the construction of a dam at Makrain (Al Wahada) on the Yarmouk but no action has yet been taken.

Israel takes between 350 and 500 million cubic metres annually from the Upper Jordan as it reaches the Sea of Galilee, from where it is piped down as far as the Negev desert by the National Water Carrier, the construction of which was completed in 1964.

The importance of agreement on water resources was demonstrated by the inclusion of the Israeli commitment to concede a greater share of the Yarmouk to Jordan in the peace treaty signed in 1994. The agreement was for a finite quantity (40 million cubic metres annually) rather than a percentage and Israel was accused of violating the peace treaty when it found it was unable to provide the full amount owing to the severe drought experienced during the winter of 1998/9 when allocations to Israeli farmers had to be cut by 25 per cent. No doubt water resources will also feature in any Israeli/Syrian and Israeli/Lebanese peace treaties. The commitment to cooperation in the field of water management is included in an annex to the Declaration of Principles on Interim Self-Government Arrangements signed by Israel and the PLO in Washington on 13 September 1993.

However, reaching agreement over control of the West Bank aquifers, on which both Israel and the Palestinian Authority depend, will be difficult. At present Israel gets about one-quarter of its water from the West Bank aquifers. The present arrangements are hardly fair to the Palestinian population but allowing uncontrolled drawing of water from the aquifers would lead to the salination of Israel's coastal aquifer. The latest estimates show that some 1.48 billion cubic metres are being taken from the aquifers each year but that replenishment provides only 1.25 billion cubic metres. Israel will want to continue to control the West Bank aquifers and this will affect the amount of land they will be prepared to hand back to the Palestine Authority; hard bargaining lies ahead. One report claims that Israel must retain control of a western strip of the West Bank, at places up to 15km east of the Green Line. However, Israel has already withdrawn from some territory over the aquifers.

A further anxiety has been realised only recently. When the Palestine Authority becomes a Palestinian state, and if that state has the Jordan as its eastern border, then as a riparian state it will be entitled to a share of the river's sources, including the Sea of Galilee. Presumably, if Syria succeeds in its claim that the Israeli–Syrian border should be the line of Syrian control pre-1967, then it too would claim a share of Galilee. The line of control reached the shore for some 20km along the north-eastern corner of the Sea of Galilee even though the negotiated cease fire line followed the mandatory border which lies 10m above the lake's high water-mark.

A number of ambitious schemes for solving the water shortage, not just for Israel but for the Palestinians and Jordan too, have been suggested. The simplest, but one that would be vulnerable to interference by Syria, is a 'peace pipeline' bringing water from Turkey. Water could also be brought from Turkey by large plastic dracones. Turkey has already invested some $150 million in a project to export water from the River Manavgat in Anatolia. Israel and Turkey have signed contracts for the supply of water. Costs have risen during the negotiating process; transport costs could be as high as $0.90 per cubic metre as opposed to $0.425 two years ago; the cost of purchasing and converting an old oil tanker has trebled. Work has not yet started on the unloading and storage facility that will be needed at Ashdod and this will take two years to complete. Two canals to the Dead Sea, one from Elat on the Red Sea and one from the Mediterranean, have been proposed. The electricity generated by the drop of roughly 400m would be used to desalinate the water going through the system. Desalination employing a nuclear-powered reactor could be employed but suspicions over any nuclear activity could preclude this option. It would certainly be a prime strategic target should war break out again. After years of avoiding the issues, the current drought, which is in its third year, has concentrated minds and at long last a decision has been made. A desalination plant, costing $200 million and producing 50 million cubic metres a year, is to be constructed at

Ashkelon and a slightly smaller one (45 million cubic metres) at Ashdod, both on the Mediterranean coast. The plants are likely to be in operation in late 2004 and 2003 respectively. It has been estimated that the total annual production of 95 million cubic metres will be needed just to cover the anticipated increase in consumption by then.

The water requirement for both Israel and the territory of the Palestine Authority are both rising yearly, mainly because of population increase; the most critical area is the Gaza Strip which has one of the highest population growth rates in the world. For peace to be sustained between Israel and the Palestinians water must be shared equitably and this will certainly mean finding new sources whether by desalination or by large-scale imports. It is also clear that any attempts to reduce Israel's water supply from Lebanon or Syria could start a water-war.

BIBLIOGRAPHY AND WEBSITES

Berschorner, Natasha, *Water and Instability in the Middle East*, IISS Adelphi Paper no. 273, 1992
de Villiers, Marq, *Water Wars: Is the World's Water Running Out?* Weidenfeld & Nicolson, 1999
Elmusa, Sharif, 'The Jordan–Israeli Water Agreement: A Model or an Exception', *Journal of Palestine Studies* XXIV, no. 3, 1995
Kliot, Nurit, *Water Resources and Conflict in the Middle East*, Routledge, 1994
Low, Miriam, *West Bank Water Resources and the Resolution of Conflict in the Middle East*, Princetown University, 1992

Transboundary Freshwater Dispute Database: http://terra.geo.oust.edu/users/tfdd
Water and conflict: http://allserv.rug.ac.be/~sdconic/waternet

Diamonds

'Diamonds are a girl's best friend' is the traditional saying but today it would be more accurate to say that 'diamonds are a rebel's best friend' as they have sustained rebellion and civil war in Angola, the Democratic Republic of Congo, Liberia and Sierra Leone for quite a few years. During the Cold War industrial diamonds were classified as a strategic mineral because of their hardness and use in cutting, grinding and drilling.

However, not all diamonds are mined in these countries; the major diamond deposits are in Russia and southern Africa. The statistics of the world diamond business show that each year something like 114 million carats (a carat weighs 0.2g) in several billion individual rough stones, weighing about 24 tons, are mined at a cost to the mining companies of $2 billion. They sell the stones for about $7 billion. By the time the diamonds have been cut, polished and mounted in jewellery they are worth $50 billion. It is surprising that the demand still remains but it has been estimated that by 2005 world production will have risen to 120 million carats a year.

The Angolan civil war ended temporarily in 1994 and re-erupted in 1998. During this time UNITA mined an estimated 2.5 billion dollars-worth of diamonds which it used to fund rearming. It captured a large amount of territory and was able to threaten international interests in the Angolan oil industry. As a result an international effort was made to curb UNITA's ability to export diamonds and so fund its campaign. UN Security Council Resolutions 1173 and 1176 passed in 1998 prohibited the import of Angolan diamonds not supported by a certificate of origin issued by the Angolan government; they also imposed financial sanctions on UNITA. Much of the research into the Angolan diamond industry was carried out by the NGO Global Witness, which reported in 1998 that de Beers was trading with UNITA, as were diamond companies in Belgium, Israel, the UK and the US.

In Sierra Leone a similar link was established between diamond sales and arms purchases by rebels. The UN Security Council passed Resolution 1306 in July 2000, imposing a ban on the import of diamonds from Sierra Leone without a government certificate of origin. A panel of experts was established to collect information on violations of the resolution. The

Estimated diamond production, 1999 (US $ millions)

more than 1,000
more than 100
more than 10
less than 10

Source: De Beers

Source of Diamonds

panel reported that illegal diamonds could not be exported without the assistance of the Liberian government. UNSC Resolution 1343 of March 2001 reimposed an arms ban on Liberia and after two months the UN banned the import of all rough diamonds from Liberia regardless of origin. In 1999 Liberia, which has a domestic diamond mining capacity of 150,000 carats a year, exported 6 million carats to Belgium.

The UN has appointed a committee of experts to consider the question of conflict and natural resources in the Democratic Republic of Congo; while it condemned the illegal exploitation of such resources it has not passed a resolution on the export of diamonds mined there. Virtually all the armed forces supporting either the government or the rebels are as much concerned with acquiring wealth as with ending the civil war.

As a result of Global Witness's campaign to increase public awareness of the link between the exploitation of natural resources, particularly diamonds, and conflict, the diamond industry (although 'conflict' or 'blood' diamonds were only a very small proportion of the overall diamond trade), began to put its house in order. De Beers announced in February 2000 that it would no longer deal in African diamonds originating from areas controlled by rebel forces and later that it would only trade in diamonds from mines which it owned. In September representatives of twenty countries and from the diamond industry agreed a scheme of certification for all diamonds entering the industry.

'Conflict' diamonds are not the only problem area. There are also 'illicit' diamonds which are mined and traded outside official channels but which have not been proscribed

RUSSIA 1,625

CHINA 14

INDIA 8

JINEA 40
SIERRA LEONE 70
LIBERIA 10
COTE D'IVOIRE 20
GHANA 12

CENT. AF. REP. 67

DEM. REP. CONGO 396

INDONESIA 2

TANZANIA 24

ANGOLA 618

NAMIBIA 430   BOTSWANA 1,782

AUSTRALIA 367

LESOTHO 3

SOUTH AFRICA 776

by UN resolution. It is also considered possible that 'conflict' or 'illicit' diamonds could be smuggled across borders and mixed with indigenous diamonds at the mines and so acquire certification.

The Kimberley Process is a series of inter-governmental meetings aimed at dealing with 'conflict' diamonds. Its first meeting was held at Kimberley in May 2000, followed by three further meetings. The UN General Assembly mandated an expanded process with Resolution 55/56 of December 2000. The aim of drafting an agreement on diamond certification was reached at a meeting at Gaborone in November 2001 attended by thirty-four governments; the proposal must now go to the UNGA before implementation by member states. The US Congress, on the same day, passed the Clean Diamonds Act which prohibits the import into the US of rough diamonds from countries without control regimes. As the US imports roughly 50 per cent of the diamond market, this is an important step.

BIBLIOGRAPHY AND WEBSITES

National Geographic, March 2002, National Geographic Society
Diamond High Council (HRD): www.diamond.be
Diamond Trade Network: www.diamond.net
Global Witness: www.oneworld.org/globalwitness
United Nations, Conflict Diamonds: www.un.org/peace/africa/Diamonds
World Diamond Council: www.worlddiamondcouncil.com

CANADA
1,907
4.9
8.28
63.9

USA
5,881
21.8
18.82
167.4

MEXICO
2,906
28.4
1.29
30.4

VENEZUELA
2,826
72.6
1.09
142.5

ARGENTINA
802
2.6
1.22
24.2

1,907 Oil production, 1,000 barrels per day
4.9 Oil reserves, billion barrels
8.28 Gas production, trillion cubic feet
63.9 Gas reserves, trillion cubic feet

Source: US Department of Energy/Oil and Gas Journal

Oil and gas production and reserves

Oil: The World Scene

Oil, or rather the need for it, has been the cause of war, of economic blackmail and of political confrontation. In the First World War the German-backed Turkish plan was to invade the Russian Caucasus to seize the Anglo-Persian oilfields and deny its oil to the Royal Navy. The British forestalled this by mounting the Mesopotamian campaign. In the Second World War the safety of oil supplies was a concern not just for the British but also for the Germans and the Japanese. The Dutch embargo of oil from Indonesia to Japan precipitated the region's invasion. Britain was particularly susceptible to shortage as all supplies had to come by sea. The invasion of Kuwait by Iraq in 1990 took place because the Iraqis claimed that Kuwait was extracting oil from under its territory; more probably it was because Saddam Hussein wanted to increase his power by acquiring more oil and, had the US and its allies not intervened, he might even have gone on to invade Saudi Arabia. When the world's oil supplies begin to run out there will be an increased danger of military intervention to secure supplies.

After the Arab–Israeli war of 1973 Middle East oil prices were roughly doubled, causing economic problems for Europe. In April 2002 Saddam Hussein suspended Iraq's exports for

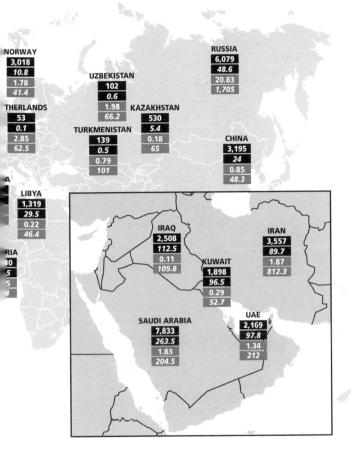

NORWAY
3,018
10.8
1.78
41.4

THERLANDS
53
0.1
2.85
62.5

A

LIBYA
1,319
29.5
0.22
46.4

RIA
0
5
5

UZBEKISTAN
102
0.6
1.98
66.2

TURKMENISTAN
139
0.5
0.79
101

KAZAKHSTAN
530
5.4
0.18
65

RUSSIA
6,079
48.6
20.83
1,705

CHINA
3,195
24
0.85
48.3

IRAQ
2,508
112.5
0.11
109.8

KUWAIT
1,898
96.5
0.29
52.7

IRAN
3,557
89.7
1.87
812.3

SAUDI ARABIA
7,833
263.5
1.83
204.5

UAE
2,169
97.8
1.34
212

a month as a protest against the Israeli operations in the West Bank; he also urged Iran and other Middle East oil producers to follow suit but the OPEC cartel did not support him. Nevertheless oil prices hit a six-month high of $27.63 a barrel (after 11 September they rose to over $30 a barrel for two days). Political antagonism is caused by the US's low petrol price and high consumption and its implications for global warming. Oil prices are affected by political events as much as by supply and demand.

There is no doubt that demand is going to continue to rise both on account of the growth in the world's population but also because of the increasing industrialisation of the developing world. Two frightening estimates have been made. The first is that sometime between 2005 and 2010 production will be outstripped by demand, and the second is that oil supplies could run out in about forty years' time. But not all analysts agree with these estimates and some believe oil production will not peak until 2050. Several imponderables will influence how long the oil supplies last. These include: improved technology, which aids the discovery of new reserves and improves the ability to recover more oil from existing wells; policies on allowing oil production in environmentally sensitive areas; the production of unconventional oil from materials such as oil sands and shale; government action over taxation and global warming; and the costs the market will bear to recover oil from inaccessible sources.

A reduction in the amount of oil available will have the greatest effect on transportation. Currently 18 per cent of the world's energy is used by transport, an increase of 7 per cent in the last twenty years; about 50 per cent of oil production provides 95 per cent of the world's transport fuel. Transport's demands for fuel will increase as the developing world acquires more motor cars and if air travel continues to grow. Action is already under way to develop new types of vehicles that are less dependent on oil for fuel. Global warming is influencing developments as much as the expected shortage of oil. All branches of the military are particularly dependent on fuel for both strategic and tactical mobility.

Most of the world's oil reserves are located in the Gulf States, one of the most volatile areas in the world. Gulf countries are already threatening to cut supplies to the rest of the world. Iraq has suspended exports for one month in protest at Israel's treatment of the Palestinians; so far it has not persuaded any other oil producer to join its boycott; although Iran has urged the region to suspend exports to the West it has not yet done so itself. Saudi Arabia has told the US that oil is not a weapon; however, oil prices rose amid fears of a Saudi boycott until the denial was made. Oil undoubtedly *is* a weapon and one that could well be used should the US attack Iraq as part of its war against the 'axis of evil'. In such an eventuality there would be a strong temptation for the US to take control of some of the region's oil supply – Iraq's for instance.

General Bibliography

BOOKS

Dictionary of World History, Hutchinson, 1998

Dupuy, Trevor (ed.), *International Military and Defense Encyclopedia*, Brassey's (US), 1993

Roberts, Adam and Kingsbury, Benedict (eds), *United Nations, Divided World: The UN's Roles in International Relations*, Clarendon, 1993

Stack, John and Hebron, Lui, *The Ethnic Entanglement: Conflict and Intervention in World Politics*, Praeger, 1999

Wiberg, Hakan and Scherrer, Christian, *Ethnicity and Intra-State Conflict: Types, Causes and Peace Strategies*, Ashgate, 1999

JOURNALS

Arms Control Reporter, Institute for Defence and Disarmament Studies

Arms Control Today, US Arms Control Association

Disarmament Diplomacy, The Acronym Institute

Foreign Affairs

Foreign Policy, Carnegie Endowment for International Peace

International Affairs, Royal Institute of International Affairs

Report to The President and The Congress, US Department of Defense

SIPRI Yearbook, Stockholm International Peace Research Institute

Strategic Assessment, US National Defense University

Strategic Comment, International Institute for Strategic Studies

Strategic Survey, International Institute for Strategic Studies

Survival, International Institute for Strategic Studies

The International Security Review, Royal United Services Institute

The Military Balance, International Institute for Strategic Studies

Today, Royal Institute for International Affairs

WEBSITES

Amnesty International: www.amnesty.org/ailib/countries

Arms Control Association: www.armscontrol.org/

Automated Historical Archives System: http://leav-www.army.mil/aknahas

British American Security Council: www.basicint.org/

Central Intelligence Agency: www.cia.gov

Country Studies/Area Handbook Program: http://lcweb2.loc.gov/frd/country

Economist Country Briefings: www.economist.com/countries

Foreign Affairs Online: www.people.virginia.edu

International Boundaries Research Unit: www.ibru.dur.ac.uk/links

International Institute for Strategic Studies: www.iiss.org

International Security Information Service: www.isisuk.demon.co.uk

Jane's Defence Discovery: www.defence-discovery.com

Library of Congress Studies: http://catalog.loc.gov

Royal Institute for International Affairs: www.riia.org

Royal United Services Institute: www.rusi.org
Scientific and Technical Information Network: http://stinet.ddtic.mil
United Nations Website Locator: www.unsystem.org
War, Peace and Security Guide, Information Research Centre: www.cfcsc.dnd.ca/links

CARTOGRAPHY

Atlas of World History, The Times, 1999
National Geographic Atlas of the World, 7th edn, 1999
Grosser Historischer Weltatlas, Bayerischer Schulbuch-Verlag, 1995
Ade, Ajayi and Crowder, Michael, *Historical Atlas of Africa*, Longman, 1985
Bahat, Dan, *Carta's Great Historical Atlas of Jerusalem*, Carta, 1989
Crampton, Richard and Ben, *Atlas of Eastern Europe in the Twentieth Century*, Routledge, 1996
Duby, Georges, *Atlas Historique*, Larousse-Bordas, 1998
Vidal-Naquet, Pierre and Bertin, Jacques, *Histoire de l'Humanité*, Hachette, 1987

CARTOGRAPHIC WEBSITES

Australian Defence Forces Academy: www.adfa.oz.au
Central Intelligence Agency: www.odci.gov/cia
Chechen Republic Online: www.amina.com
Foundation for Middle East Peace: www.fmep.org
Rainforest Action Network: www.ran.org
Slavic Research Centre, Hokkaido University: www.src.home.slav.hokudai.ac.jp
Swedish Armed Forces: www.swedint.mil.se
The Latin American Alliance: www.latinsynergy.org
United Nations: www.un.org
University of Texas at Austin: www.lib.utexas.edu
University of Virginia: www.lib.virginia.edu
World Resources Institute: www.wri.org

Index

Departure Lounge

Travel warnings for countries that are not covered elsewhere

AFRICA

Central African Republic FCO: Avoid border with Chad. Do not travel at night. State: Avoid all unnecessary travel.

Chad FCO: Do not visit Bourkoou, Ennedi, Tibesti provinces and border with CAR. State: Travel in Tibesti is risky. Beware landmines in border area with Libya.

Comoros FCO and State: Avoid demonstrations and political rallies.

Cote d'Ivoire FCO: Advises against all travel except for essential business in Abidjan only. State: Defer all travel.

Ghana FCO: Keep in touch if visiting the north. State: Avoid Northern Region.

Guinea FCO and State: Avoid area south of Kissidougou. Main road between Conakry and N'Zerekore safe but avoid area between road and Sierra Leone and Liberian borders.

Guinea-Bissau FCO: Avoid north-west border with Casamence province of Senegal. State: Warns against all travel.

Madagascar FCO and State: Advise essential travel only.

Mali FCO and State: Avoid all non-essential travel to Timbouktou and beyond. Exercise extreme caution in northern Mali.

Mozambique FCO: Armed robbery prevalent in Maputo. State: Don't travel out of Maputo after dark. Danger of landmines off roads remains.

Namibia FCO: Travel on Trans-Caprivi Highway between Rundu and Katina Mulilo by day only and keep to the road. State: Avoid night travel. Danger of mines in border region.

Senegal FCO: Avoid all travel to western part of Casamence. State: Defer travel to Casamence region.

Uganda FCO: Avoid northern Uganda including Murchison Falls National Park, Karamoja and Katawaki Province in the east and in the west Bundibugyo including Semliki National Park but Game Reserve safe to visit. State: Avoid northern border with Sudan and western border with DRC. US citizens have been specifically targeted.

LATIN AMERICA Ecuador FCO: Advises against travel to Sucumbios and Orellana provinces. Warns of danger of piracy. State: Advises against travelling to the north-east provinces of Sucumbios, Orellana and Carchi. Dramatic increase in number of kidnappings in Guayaquil.

Venezuela FCO: Warns against travel in border area with Colombia and of piracy. State: Colombian dissidents have targeted US citizens. Keep out of the area within 50 miles of the Colombian border.

PACIFIC

Solomon Islands FCO and State: Avoid Malaita, Honiara and rural Guadalcanal.